KAPLAN

TEST PREP AND ADMISSIONS

SAT®*

Purple Book of Practice SATs

*SAT is a registered trademark of the College Entrance Examination Board, which was not involved in the production of, and does not endorse, this product.

CONTENTS

Preface iv

Practice Test 1

Answer Sheet 2
Test 9
Scoring Your Test 59

Practice Test 2

Answer Sheet 68
Test 75
Scoring Your Test 125

Practice Test 3

Answer Sheet 134
Test 141
Scoring Your Test 191

Practice Test 4

Answer Sheet 200
Test 207
Scoring Your Test 257

PREFACE

Practice SAT Tests

One of the most proven methods of raising your SAT score is to take practice tests, and then carefully read the explanations to the questions that you got wrong. The *Purple Book of Practice SATs* gives you four practice SATs to work through.

Taking these practice SATs under test-like conditions will increase your familiarity with the instructions, timing, types of questions, and types of answers on the SAT. Remember to login to Smart Track to access the answers and explanations for each test. This is critical to understand why you got a problem wrong so that the next time you see a similar question, you will get it right.

Remember, this book will supplement the work you are doing in class and the four in-class practice tests you will take. The more work you do, the more you will be able to raise your score.

In addition to these tests, you can find additional practice in your My Skills tab on Smart Track.

Practice makes perfect and in this case, practice raises scores.

Remember, by working through practice tests, you will feel prepared and confident on Test Day.

How the SAT is Timed

The SAT is 3 hours and 45 minutes long, not including the two short breaks you are given. The exam is mostly Multiple Choice, and it is divided into three Math, three Critical Reading, and three Writing sections. Section 1 will always be the 25-minute Essay Writing section. Sections 2–7 are 25 minutes each: one Writing Multiple Choice, two Math, two Critical Reading, and one experimental[1] section (Math, Critical Reading, or Writing Multiple Choice). Sections 8 and 9 are 20 minutes each: one Math and one Critical Reading. Section 10 is a 10-minute Writing Multiple Choice section.

How the SAT is Scored

The Critical Reading, Writing, and Math scores equal the number you got right minus a fraction of the number you got wrong. Your Essay score and your Multiple Choice Writing score are used together to calculate your overall Writing score.

---

[1] Every SAT has a 25-minute experimental section. The experimental section is used by the test developers to try out new questions before including them in upcoming SATs. The experimental section DOES NOT COUNT in your score. It can show up anywhere in Sections 2–7 on the exam and will look just like a normal section. You shouldn't try to figure out which SAT section is experimental—you will be unable to do so. Just treat all the sections as if they count toward your score.

For all Multiple Choice sections on the SAT, you gain one point for each correct answer and lose 1/4 point for each wrong answer. With Grid-ins, you lose nothing for a wrong answer. You do not lose any points for questions you leave blank.

This is important, so we'll repeat it:

You do not lose *any* points for questions you leave blank.

These raw scores are converted into scaled scores, with 200 as the lowest score and 800 as the highest.

The three scaled scores are added together to produce your final score of 600–2400.

Ground Rules

These are the SAT rules you can use to your advantage. Knowing these rules will keep you from asking questions and wasting precious time, and from committing minor errors that may result in serious penalties. Follow these rules while you are taking these Practice Tests, and you will be well prepared on Test Day.

- You are NOT allowed to jump back and forth among sections.
- You are NOT allowed to return to earlier sections to change answers.
- You are NOT allowed to spend more than the allotted time on any section.
- You CAN move around within a section.
- You CAN flip through a section at the beginning to see what types of questions are coming up.

These are the basics you need to know about the structure of the SAT before you take the test. You'll become more familiar with the format and setup of the SAT question types and components as you work your way through the four tests in this book.

Gridding Instructions for the Purple Book Tests

You can self-score the Practice Tests in this book by following the directions in the Scoring Your Test section that follows each test.

If you would like Kaplan to score your test for you and give you a print-out of your results, you will need to:

1. Obtain an SAT Answer Grid (item number SP5083C) from your teacher or Kaplan Center.

2. Fill in your name, your enrollment ID, and the Scan Code (see table below) on the Answer Grid Booklet.

Purple Book Practice Test #	Scan Code
1	1101
2	1102
3	1103
4	1104

3. Take a test from this book under test-like conditions. Begin with Section 1, the Essay. Give yourself 25 minutes. Do not score your essay yet.

4. Continue on to the multiple-choice sections, bubbling in your answers on the Answer Grid. Work on only one section at a time. Time yourself carefully. If you finish before the allotted time is up, you may check your work on that section only. Do not allow yourself extra time on self-proctored tests. Time management is very much a tested skill on the SAT. Give yourself a 5-minute break after Section 2, a 1-minute stretch after Section 4 and a 5-minute break after Section 6.

5. When you're done, follow the directions in Step 1: Score Your Essay, found in the Scoring Your Test section of this Purple Book, to assign a score of 1–6 to your essay. Bubble in your essay score on page 8 of your Answer Grid.

6. Bring your answer grid to your Kaplan Center and the Center staff will scan it for you and produce print-out of your scores.

7. The answers and explanations to all the test questions appear after each test in your Purple Book. Take some time to review questions that you missed, guessed on, or were unsure of. Read the explanations thoroughly to learn from these questions as you continue to study.

PRACTICE TEST 1

For additional practice before Test Day, take this Practice Test under test-like conditions at home or at a Kaplan Center, bubble in your answers on a Kaplan SAT Answer Grid, and have the grid scanned at a Kaplan Center to receive your results.

Scan Code: 1101

Practice Test 1
Answer Sheet

Remove (or photocopy) the following answer sheet and use it to complete the practice test. See the answer key following the test when finished.

Start with number 1 for each bubble-in section. If a section has fewer questions than bubbles, leave the extra bubbles blank.

Use this page to *plan* your essay.

SECTION 2

1. (A) (B) (C) (D) (E)	11. (A) (B) (C) (D) (E)	21. (A) (B) (C) (D) (E)	31. (A) (B) (C) (D) (E)
2. (A) (B) (C) (D) (E)	12. (A) (B) (C) (D) (E)	22. (A) (B) (C) (D) (E)	32. (A) (B) (C) (D) (E)
3. (A) (B) (C) (D) (E)	13. (A) (B) (C) (D) (E)	23. (A) (B) (C) (D) (E)	33. (A) (B) (C) (D) (E)
4. (A) (B) (C) (D) (E)	14. (A) (B) (C) (D) (E)	24. (A) (B) (C) (D) (E)	34. (A) (B) (C) (D) (E)
5. (A) (B) (C) (D) (E)	15. (A) (B) (C) (D) (E)	25. (A) (B) (C) (D) (E)	35. (A) (B) (C) (D) (E)
6. (A) (B) (C) (D) (E)	16. (A) (B) (C) (D) (E)	26. (A) (B) (C) (D) (E)	36. (A) (B) (C) (D) (E)
7. (A) (B) (C) (D) (E)	17. (A) (B) (C) (D) (E)	27. (A) (B) (C) (D) (E)	37. (A) (B) (C) (D) (E)
8. (A) (B) (C) (D) (E)	18. (A) (B) (C) (D) (E)	28. (A) (B) (C) (D) (E)	38. (A) (B) (C) (D) (E)
9. (A) (B) (C) (D) (E)	19. (A) (B) (C) (D) (E)	29. (A) (B) (C) (D) (E)	39. (A) (B) (C) (D) (E)
10. (A) (B) (C) (D) (E)	20. (A) (B) (C) (D) (E)	30. (A) (B) (C) (D) (E)	40. (A) (B) (C) (D) (E)

right in Section 2

wrong in Section 2

SECTION 3

1. (A) (B) (C) (D) (E)	11. (A) (B) (C) (D) (E)	21. (A) (B) (C) (D) (E)	31. (A) (B) (C) (D) (E)
2. (A) (B) (C) (D) (E)	12. (A) (B) (C) (D) (E)	22. (A) (B) (C) (D) (E)	32. (A) (B) (C) (D) (E)
3. (A) (B) (C) (D) (E)	13. (A) (B) (C) (D) (E)	23. (A) (B) (C) (D) (E)	33. (A) (B) (C) (D) (E)
4. (A) (B) (C) (D) (E)	14. (A) (B) (C) (D) (E)	24. (A) (B) (C) (D) (E)	34. (A) (B) (C) (D) (E)
5. (A) (B) (C) (D) (E)	15. (A) (B) (C) (D) (E)	25. (A) (B) (C) (D) (E)	35. (A) (B) (C) (D) (E)
6. (A) (B) (C) (D) (E)	16. (A) (B) (C) (D) (E)	26. (A) (B) (C) (D) (E)	36. (A) (B) (C) (D) (E)
7. (A) (B) (C) (D) (E)	17. (A) (B) (C) (D) (E)	27. (A) (B) (C) (D) (E)	37. (A) (B) (C) (D) (E)
8. (A) (B) (C) (D) (E)	18. (A) (B) (C) (D) (E)	28. (A) (B) (C) (D) (E)	38. (A) (B) (C) (D) (E)
9. (A) (B) (C) (D) (E)	19. (A) (B) (C) (D) (E)	29. (A) (B) (C) (D) (E)	39. (A) (B) (C) (D) (E)
10. (A) (B) (C) (D) (E)	20. (A) (B) (C) (D) (E)	30. (A) (B) (C) (D) (E)	40. (A) (B) (C) (D) (E)

right in Section 3

wrong in Section 3

If sections 2 or 3 of this practice test contain math questions that are not multiple choice, continue to item 9 below. Otherwise, continue to item 9 above.

9.   10.   11.   12.   13.

14.   15.   16.   17.   18.

- 6 -

SECTION 6

1. Ⓐ Ⓑ Ⓒ Ⓓ Ⓔ	11. Ⓐ Ⓑ Ⓒ Ⓓ Ⓔ	21. Ⓐ Ⓑ Ⓒ Ⓓ Ⓔ	31. Ⓐ Ⓑ Ⓒ Ⓓ Ⓔ
2. Ⓐ Ⓑ Ⓒ Ⓓ Ⓔ	12. Ⓐ Ⓑ Ⓒ Ⓓ Ⓔ	22. Ⓐ Ⓑ Ⓒ Ⓓ Ⓔ	32. Ⓐ Ⓑ Ⓒ Ⓓ Ⓔ
3. Ⓐ Ⓑ Ⓒ Ⓓ Ⓔ	13. Ⓐ Ⓑ Ⓒ Ⓓ Ⓔ	23. Ⓐ Ⓑ Ⓒ Ⓓ Ⓔ	33. Ⓐ Ⓑ Ⓒ Ⓓ Ⓔ
4. Ⓐ Ⓑ Ⓒ Ⓓ Ⓔ	14. Ⓐ Ⓑ Ⓒ Ⓓ Ⓔ	24. Ⓐ Ⓑ Ⓒ Ⓓ Ⓔ	34. Ⓐ Ⓑ Ⓒ Ⓓ Ⓔ
5. Ⓐ Ⓑ Ⓒ Ⓓ Ⓔ	15. Ⓐ Ⓑ Ⓒ Ⓓ Ⓔ	25. Ⓐ Ⓑ Ⓒ Ⓓ Ⓔ	35. Ⓐ Ⓑ Ⓒ Ⓓ Ⓔ
6. Ⓐ Ⓑ Ⓒ Ⓓ Ⓔ	16. Ⓐ Ⓑ Ⓒ Ⓓ Ⓔ	26. Ⓐ Ⓑ Ⓒ Ⓓ Ⓔ	36. Ⓐ Ⓑ Ⓒ Ⓓ Ⓔ
7. Ⓐ Ⓑ Ⓒ Ⓓ Ⓔ	17. Ⓐ Ⓑ Ⓒ Ⓓ Ⓔ	27. Ⓐ Ⓑ Ⓒ Ⓓ Ⓔ	37. Ⓐ Ⓑ Ⓒ Ⓓ Ⓔ
8. Ⓐ Ⓑ Ⓒ Ⓓ Ⓔ	18. Ⓐ Ⓑ Ⓒ Ⓓ Ⓔ	28. Ⓐ Ⓑ Ⓒ Ⓓ Ⓔ	38. Ⓐ Ⓑ Ⓒ Ⓓ Ⓔ
9. Ⓐ Ⓑ Ⓒ Ⓓ Ⓔ	19. Ⓐ Ⓑ Ⓒ Ⓓ Ⓔ	29. Ⓐ Ⓑ Ⓒ Ⓓ Ⓔ	39. Ⓐ Ⓑ Ⓒ Ⓓ Ⓔ
10. Ⓐ Ⓑ Ⓒ Ⓓ Ⓔ	20. Ⓐ Ⓑ Ⓒ Ⓓ Ⓔ	30. Ⓐ Ⓑ Ⓒ Ⓓ Ⓔ	40. Ⓐ Ⓑ Ⓒ Ⓓ Ⓔ

right in Section 6

wrong in Section 6

SECTION 7

1. Ⓐ Ⓑ Ⓒ Ⓓ Ⓔ	11. Ⓐ Ⓑ Ⓒ Ⓓ Ⓔ	21. Ⓐ Ⓑ Ⓒ Ⓓ Ⓔ	31. Ⓐ Ⓑ Ⓒ Ⓓ Ⓔ
2. Ⓐ Ⓑ Ⓒ Ⓓ Ⓔ	12. Ⓐ Ⓑ Ⓒ Ⓓ Ⓔ	22. Ⓐ Ⓑ Ⓒ Ⓓ Ⓔ	32. Ⓐ Ⓑ Ⓒ Ⓓ Ⓔ
3. Ⓐ Ⓑ Ⓒ Ⓓ Ⓔ	13. Ⓐ Ⓑ Ⓒ Ⓓ Ⓔ	23. Ⓐ Ⓑ Ⓒ Ⓓ Ⓔ	33. Ⓐ Ⓑ Ⓒ Ⓓ Ⓔ
4. Ⓐ Ⓑ Ⓒ Ⓓ Ⓔ	14. Ⓐ Ⓑ Ⓒ Ⓓ Ⓔ	24. Ⓐ Ⓑ Ⓒ Ⓓ Ⓔ	34. Ⓐ Ⓑ Ⓒ Ⓓ Ⓔ
5. Ⓐ Ⓑ Ⓒ Ⓓ Ⓔ	15. Ⓐ Ⓑ Ⓒ Ⓓ Ⓔ	25. Ⓐ Ⓑ Ⓒ Ⓓ Ⓔ	35. Ⓐ Ⓑ Ⓒ Ⓓ Ⓔ
6. Ⓐ Ⓑ Ⓒ Ⓓ Ⓔ	16. Ⓐ Ⓑ Ⓒ Ⓓ Ⓔ	26. Ⓐ Ⓑ Ⓒ Ⓓ Ⓔ	36. Ⓐ Ⓑ Ⓒ Ⓓ Ⓔ
7. Ⓐ Ⓑ Ⓒ Ⓓ Ⓔ	17. Ⓐ Ⓑ Ⓒ Ⓓ Ⓔ	27. Ⓐ Ⓑ Ⓒ Ⓓ Ⓔ	37. Ⓐ Ⓑ Ⓒ Ⓓ Ⓔ
8. Ⓐ Ⓑ Ⓒ Ⓓ Ⓔ	18. Ⓐ Ⓑ Ⓒ Ⓓ Ⓔ	28. Ⓐ Ⓑ Ⓒ Ⓓ Ⓔ	38. Ⓐ Ⓑ Ⓒ Ⓓ Ⓔ
9. Ⓐ Ⓑ Ⓒ Ⓓ Ⓔ	19. Ⓐ Ⓑ Ⓒ Ⓓ Ⓔ	29. Ⓐ Ⓑ Ⓒ Ⓓ Ⓔ	39. Ⓐ Ⓑ Ⓒ Ⓓ Ⓔ
10. Ⓐ Ⓑ Ⓒ Ⓓ Ⓔ	20. Ⓐ Ⓑ Ⓒ Ⓓ Ⓔ	30. Ⓐ Ⓑ Ⓒ Ⓓ Ⓔ	40. Ⓐ Ⓑ Ⓒ Ⓓ Ⓔ

right in Section 7

wrong in Section 7

If sections 6 or 7 of this practice test contain math questions that are not multiple choice, continue to item 9 below. Otherwise, continue to item 9 above.

9. 10. 11. 12. 13.

14. 15. 16. 17. 18.

SECTION 8

1. Ⓐ Ⓑ Ⓒ Ⓓ Ⓔ	11. Ⓐ Ⓑ Ⓒ Ⓓ Ⓔ	21. Ⓐ Ⓑ Ⓒ Ⓓ Ⓔ	31. Ⓐ Ⓑ Ⓒ Ⓓ Ⓔ
2. Ⓐ Ⓑ Ⓒ Ⓓ Ⓔ	12. Ⓐ Ⓑ Ⓒ Ⓓ Ⓔ	22. Ⓐ Ⓑ Ⓒ Ⓓ Ⓔ	32. Ⓐ Ⓑ Ⓒ Ⓓ Ⓔ
3. Ⓐ Ⓑ Ⓒ Ⓓ Ⓔ	13. Ⓐ Ⓑ Ⓒ Ⓓ Ⓔ	23. Ⓐ Ⓑ Ⓒ Ⓓ Ⓔ	33. Ⓐ Ⓑ Ⓒ Ⓓ Ⓔ
4. Ⓐ Ⓑ Ⓒ Ⓓ Ⓔ	14. Ⓐ Ⓑ Ⓒ Ⓓ Ⓔ	24. Ⓐ Ⓑ Ⓒ Ⓓ Ⓔ	34. Ⓐ Ⓑ Ⓒ Ⓓ Ⓔ
5. Ⓐ Ⓑ Ⓒ Ⓓ Ⓔ	15. Ⓐ Ⓑ Ⓒ Ⓓ Ⓔ	25. Ⓐ Ⓑ Ⓒ Ⓓ Ⓔ	35. Ⓐ Ⓑ Ⓒ Ⓓ Ⓔ
6. Ⓐ Ⓑ Ⓒ Ⓓ Ⓔ	16. Ⓐ Ⓑ Ⓒ Ⓓ Ⓔ	26. Ⓐ Ⓑ Ⓒ Ⓓ Ⓔ	36. Ⓐ Ⓑ Ⓒ Ⓓ Ⓔ
7. Ⓐ Ⓑ Ⓒ Ⓓ Ⓔ	17. Ⓐ Ⓑ Ⓒ Ⓓ Ⓔ	27. Ⓐ Ⓑ Ⓒ Ⓓ Ⓔ	37. Ⓐ Ⓑ Ⓒ Ⓓ Ⓔ
8. Ⓐ Ⓑ Ⓒ Ⓓ Ⓔ	18. Ⓐ Ⓑ Ⓒ Ⓓ Ⓔ	28. Ⓐ Ⓑ Ⓒ Ⓓ Ⓔ	38. Ⓐ Ⓑ Ⓒ Ⓓ Ⓔ
9. Ⓐ Ⓑ Ⓒ Ⓓ Ⓔ	19. Ⓐ Ⓑ Ⓒ Ⓓ Ⓔ	29. Ⓐ Ⓑ Ⓒ Ⓓ Ⓔ	39. Ⓐ Ⓑ Ⓒ Ⓓ Ⓔ
10. Ⓐ Ⓑ Ⓒ Ⓓ Ⓔ	20. Ⓐ Ⓑ Ⓒ Ⓓ Ⓔ	30. Ⓐ Ⓑ Ⓒ Ⓓ Ⓔ	40. Ⓐ Ⓑ Ⓒ Ⓓ Ⓔ

☐ # right in Section 8

☐ # wrong in Section 8

SECTION 9

1. Ⓐ Ⓑ Ⓒ Ⓓ Ⓔ	11. Ⓐ Ⓑ Ⓒ Ⓓ Ⓔ	21. Ⓐ Ⓑ Ⓒ Ⓓ Ⓔ	31. Ⓐ Ⓑ Ⓒ Ⓓ Ⓔ
2. Ⓐ Ⓑ Ⓒ Ⓓ Ⓔ	12. Ⓐ Ⓑ Ⓒ Ⓓ Ⓔ	22. Ⓐ Ⓑ Ⓒ Ⓓ Ⓔ	32. Ⓐ Ⓑ Ⓒ Ⓓ Ⓔ
3. Ⓐ Ⓑ Ⓒ Ⓓ Ⓔ	13. Ⓐ Ⓑ Ⓒ Ⓓ Ⓔ	23. Ⓐ Ⓑ Ⓒ Ⓓ Ⓔ	33. Ⓐ Ⓑ Ⓒ Ⓓ Ⓔ
4. Ⓐ Ⓑ Ⓒ Ⓓ Ⓔ	14. Ⓐ Ⓑ Ⓒ Ⓓ Ⓔ	24. Ⓐ Ⓑ Ⓒ Ⓓ Ⓔ	34. Ⓐ Ⓑ Ⓒ Ⓓ Ⓔ
5. Ⓐ Ⓑ Ⓒ Ⓓ Ⓔ	15. Ⓐ Ⓑ Ⓒ Ⓓ Ⓔ	25. Ⓐ Ⓑ Ⓒ Ⓓ Ⓔ	35. Ⓐ Ⓑ Ⓒ Ⓓ Ⓔ
6. Ⓐ Ⓑ Ⓒ Ⓓ Ⓔ	16. Ⓐ Ⓑ Ⓒ Ⓓ Ⓔ	26. Ⓐ Ⓑ Ⓒ Ⓓ Ⓔ	36. Ⓐ Ⓑ Ⓒ Ⓓ Ⓔ
7. Ⓐ Ⓑ Ⓒ Ⓓ Ⓔ	17. Ⓐ Ⓑ Ⓒ Ⓓ Ⓔ	27. Ⓐ Ⓑ Ⓒ Ⓓ Ⓔ	37. Ⓐ Ⓑ Ⓒ Ⓓ Ⓔ
8. Ⓐ Ⓑ Ⓒ Ⓓ Ⓔ	18. Ⓐ Ⓑ Ⓒ Ⓓ Ⓔ	28. Ⓐ Ⓑ Ⓒ Ⓓ Ⓔ	38. Ⓐ Ⓑ Ⓒ Ⓓ Ⓔ
9. Ⓐ Ⓑ Ⓒ Ⓓ Ⓔ	19. Ⓐ Ⓑ Ⓒ Ⓓ Ⓔ	29. Ⓐ Ⓑ Ⓒ Ⓓ Ⓔ	39. Ⓐ Ⓑ Ⓒ Ⓓ Ⓔ
10. Ⓐ Ⓑ Ⓒ Ⓓ Ⓔ	20. Ⓐ Ⓑ Ⓒ Ⓓ Ⓔ	30. Ⓐ Ⓑ Ⓒ Ⓓ Ⓔ	40. Ⓐ Ⓑ Ⓒ Ⓓ Ⓔ

☐ # right in Section 9

☐ # wrong in Section 9

SECTION 10

1. Ⓐ Ⓑ Ⓒ Ⓓ Ⓔ	11. Ⓐ Ⓑ Ⓒ Ⓓ Ⓔ	21. Ⓐ Ⓑ Ⓒ Ⓓ Ⓔ	31. Ⓐ Ⓑ Ⓒ Ⓓ Ⓔ
2. Ⓐ Ⓑ Ⓒ Ⓓ Ⓔ	12. Ⓐ Ⓑ Ⓒ Ⓓ Ⓔ	22. Ⓐ Ⓑ Ⓒ Ⓓ Ⓔ	32. Ⓐ Ⓑ Ⓒ Ⓓ Ⓔ
3. Ⓐ Ⓑ Ⓒ Ⓓ Ⓔ	13. Ⓐ Ⓑ Ⓒ Ⓓ Ⓔ	23. Ⓐ Ⓑ Ⓒ Ⓓ Ⓔ	33. Ⓐ Ⓑ Ⓒ Ⓓ Ⓔ
4. Ⓐ Ⓑ Ⓒ Ⓓ Ⓔ	14. Ⓐ Ⓑ Ⓒ Ⓓ Ⓔ	24. Ⓐ Ⓑ Ⓒ Ⓓ Ⓔ	34. Ⓐ Ⓑ Ⓒ Ⓓ Ⓔ
5. Ⓐ Ⓑ Ⓒ Ⓓ Ⓔ	15. Ⓐ Ⓑ Ⓒ Ⓓ Ⓔ	25. Ⓐ Ⓑ Ⓒ Ⓓ Ⓔ	35. Ⓐ Ⓑ Ⓒ Ⓓ Ⓔ
6. Ⓐ Ⓑ Ⓒ Ⓓ Ⓔ	16. Ⓐ Ⓑ Ⓒ Ⓓ Ⓔ	26. Ⓐ Ⓑ Ⓒ Ⓓ Ⓔ	36. Ⓐ Ⓑ Ⓒ Ⓓ Ⓔ
7. Ⓐ Ⓑ Ⓒ Ⓓ Ⓔ	17. Ⓐ Ⓑ Ⓒ Ⓓ Ⓔ	27. Ⓐ Ⓑ Ⓒ Ⓓ Ⓔ	37. Ⓐ Ⓑ Ⓒ Ⓓ Ⓔ
8. Ⓐ Ⓑ Ⓒ Ⓓ Ⓔ	18. Ⓐ Ⓑ Ⓒ Ⓓ Ⓔ	28. Ⓐ Ⓑ Ⓒ Ⓓ Ⓔ	38. Ⓐ Ⓑ Ⓒ Ⓓ Ⓔ
9. Ⓐ Ⓑ Ⓒ Ⓓ Ⓔ	19. Ⓐ Ⓑ Ⓒ Ⓓ Ⓔ	29. Ⓐ Ⓑ Ⓒ Ⓓ Ⓔ	39. Ⓐ Ⓑ Ⓒ Ⓓ Ⓔ
10. Ⓐ Ⓑ Ⓒ Ⓓ Ⓔ	20. Ⓐ Ⓑ Ⓒ Ⓓ Ⓔ	30. Ⓐ Ⓑ Ⓒ Ⓓ Ⓔ	40. Ⓐ Ⓑ Ⓒ Ⓓ Ⓔ

☐ # right in Section 10

☐ # wrong in Section 10

ESSAY
Time—25 minutes

The essay gives you an opportunity to show how effectively you can develop and express ideas. You should, therefore, take care to develop your point of view, present your ideas logically and clearly, and use language precisely.

Your essay must be written on the lines provided on the following pages—you will receive no other paper on which to write. You will have enough space if you write on every line, avoid wide margins, and keep your handwriting to a reasonable size. Remember that people who are not familiar with your handwriting will read what you write. Try to write or print so that what you are writing is legible to those readers.

You have twenty-five minutes to write an essay on the topic assigned below. DO NOT WRITE ON ANOTHER TOPIC. AN OFF-TOPIC ESSAY WILL RECEIVE A SCORE OF ZERO.

Think carefully about the issue presented in the following quotation and the assignment below.

> When you reach an obstacle, turn it into an opportunity. You have the choice. You can overcome and be a winner, or you can allow it to overcome you, and be a loser. The choice is yours and yours alone. Refuse to throw in the towel. Go that extra mile that failures refuse to travel. It is far better to be exhausted from success than to be rested from failure.
>
> Mary Kay Ash

Assignment: What is your view of the idea that every obstacle can be turned into an opportunity? Plan and write an essay in which you develop your point of view on this issue. Support your position with reasoning and examples taken from your reading, studies, experience, or observations.

DO NOT WRITE YOUR ESSAY IN YOUR TEST BOOK.
You will receive credit only for what you write in your Answer Grid Booklet.

BEGIN WRITING YOUR ESSAY ON PAGE 3 OF THIS BOOK
OR ON PAGE 3 OF YOUR KAPLAN SAT ANSWER GRID.

IF YOU FINISH BEFORE TIME IS CALLED, YOU MAY CHECK YOUR WORK ON THIS SECTION ONLY. DO NOT TURN TO ANY OTHER SECTION IN THE TEST.

- 9 -

Time—25 Minutes
20 Questions

Directions: For this section, solve each problem and decide which is the best of the choices given. Fill in the corresponding oval on the answer sheet. You may use any available space for scratchwork.

1. Calculator use is permitted.

2. All numbers used are real numbers.

3. Figures are provided for some problems. All figures are drawn to scale and lie in a plane UNLESS otherwise indicated.

4. Unless otherwise specified, the domain of any function f is assumed to be the set of all real numbers x for which $f(x)$ is a real number.

  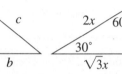

$A = \dfrac{1}{2}bh$ $c^2 = a^2 + b^2$ Special Right Triangles $A = \pi r^2$ $V = \pi r^2 h$ $A = lw$ $V = lwh$
$C = 2\pi r$

The sum of the measures in degrees of the angles of a triangle is 180.
The number of degrees of arc in a circle is 360.
A straight angle has a degree measure of 180.

---

1 If $b \neq 0$ and $ab = \dfrac{b}{4}$, then what is the value of a ?

(A) $\dfrac{1}{8}$

(B) $\dfrac{1}{4}$

(C) $\dfrac{1}{2}$

(D) 1

(E) 4

2 It takes a bus anywhere from 7 minutes to 10 minutes to travel from Town A to Town B. It takes the bus anywhere from 16 minutes to 24 minutes to travel from Town B to Town C. What are the least and greatest total travel times for a bus that travels from Town A to Town B and then from Town B to Town C ? (Disregard the time the bus could be standing still in Town B.)

(A)   7 minutes and 24 minutes
(B) 10 minutes and 24 minutes
(C) 23 minutes and 26 minutes
(D) 23 minutes and 34 minutes
(E) 26 minutes and 40 minutes

GO ON TO THE NEXT PAGE

3 By what number must the number 3.475817 be multiplied in order to obtain the number 34,758.17 ?

(A)   100
(B)   1,000
(C)   10,000
(D) 100,000
(E) 1,000,000

Number of students	Grade
18	97
13	78
18	67
7	54
5	46

4 For a university class of 61 students, the table above shows the number of students receiving each grade on the mid-term exam. What is the median of those 61 scores?

(A) 97
(B) 78
(C) 67
(D) 54
(E) 46

5 If the manager of a store adds 50 lamps to its current inventory, the resulting total number of lamps will be the same as three-halves of the current inventory. If the manager wanted to increase the current inventory by 40%, what would his new inventory of lamps be?

(A) 150
(B) 140
(C) 100
(D) 75
(E) 40

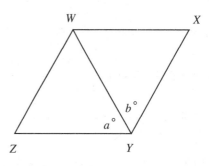

6 In the figure above, $WX = XY = YZ = ZW = WY$. What is the value of $a + b$?

(A)   60
(B) 100
(C) 105
(D) 120
(E) 135

GO ON TO THE NEXT PAGE

7 How much greater than the value of $3x - 7$ is the value of $3x + 5$?

(A) 12
(B) 10
(C) 7
(D) 5
(E) 2

8 The Environment Club receives a certain amount of money from the school to host a teach-in. They budget 40% for a guest speaker, 25% for books, 20% for use of the auditorium, and the remainder for lunch. If the club plans to spend $90 on lunch for the participants, how much do they plan to spend on the guest speaker?

(A) $40
(B) $90
(C) $120
(D) $240
(E) $600

9 Which of the following statements expresses the statement "When z is decreased by 3, the result is twice the square of the sum of y and 4"?

(A) $z - 3 = 2(y + 4)^2$
(B) $z - 3 = 2(y^2 + 4^2)$
(C) $z = 2(y + 4)^2 - 3$
(D) $z - 3 = 2(y^2 + 4)$
(E) $z + 3 = 2(y + 4)^2$

10 Line ℓ passes through the point $(-1, 2)$. Which of the following CANNOT be the equation of line ℓ ?

(A) $y = 1 - x$
(B) $y = x + 1$
(C) $x = -1$
(D) $y = x + 3$
(E) $y = 2$

GO ON TO THE NEXT PAGE

11 For all numbers c and d, the symbol # is defined by $c \# d = (c + 1)(d - 1)$. What is the value of $(5 \# 2) \# (6 \# 4)$?

(A) 35
(B) 72
(C) 108
(D) 110
(E) 140

13 If the length of one side of a triangle is 5, which of the following could be the perimeter of the triangle?

(A) 11
(B) 10
(C) 9
(D) 8
(E) 7

12 If p is an integer greater than 1, such that p divided by 4 yields a remainder of 0, which of the following could be a prime number?

(A) $\dfrac{p}{4}$

(B) $2\sqrt{p}$

(C) $\dfrac{p}{3}$

(D) p

(E) $2p$

14 The ratio of the areas of three circles is $1 : 4 : 8$, and the radius of the smallest circle is a positive integer. If the sum of the lengths of the diameters of the three circles is x, which of the following is a possible value of x ?

(A) 12
(B) $8 + 4\sqrt{3}$
(C) 15
(D) $12 + 4\sqrt{2}$
(E) $18 + 12\sqrt{2}$

GO ON TO THE NEXT PAGE

15 For any odd integer x, where $x < 0$, how many negative, even integers are greater than x ?

(A) $-x - 2$

(B) $\dfrac{-x}{2}$

(C) $\dfrac{-x - 1}{2}$

(D) $x + 4$

(E) $\dfrac{-x - 2}{2}$

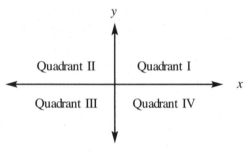

17 If the product of the x-coordinate and y-coordinate of a point is 20, in which quadrant must that point lie?

(A) I
(B) II
(C) III
(D) IV
(E) It cannot be determined from the information given.

16 A particular slot machine has three rotating wheels, called wheels A, B, and C. Each wheel displays the following pictures: a rose, a pen, a waterfall, an apple, a candle, a dollar sign, and an emerald. The machine awards a cash prize to a player whenever wheels A and B land on the same picture and wheel C lands on a candle. Assuming that for each wheel there is an equal probability of landing on each picture, what is the probability that the player will win a cash prize?

(A) $\dfrac{1}{343}$

(B) $\dfrac{1}{49}$

(C) $\dfrac{1}{21}$

(D) $\dfrac{1}{7}$

(E) $\dfrac{3}{7}$

18 If $z > 0$, $x = z^2 + 3y$, and $y - 1 = z^2$, what is z in terms of x ?

(A) $\sqrt{\dfrac{x}{2}}$

(B) $\sqrt{\dfrac{3 + x}{2}}$

(C) $\sqrt{\dfrac{3 - x}{2}}$

(D) $\sqrt{\dfrac{x + 3}{4}}$

(E) $\sqrt{\dfrac{x - 3}{4}}$

GO ON TO THE NEXT PAGE

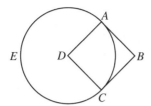

19 In the figure above, *D* is the center of the circle, and the perimeter of square *ABCD* is 24. What is the area of the entire figure?

(A) $36 + 18\pi$
(B) $18 + 27\pi$
(C) $36 + 27\pi$
(D) $27 + 36\pi$
(E) $36 + 54\pi$

20 Brand *A* drink contains 30 percent orange juice by volume. Brand *B* drink contains 40 percent orange juice by volume. Which of the following expressions gives the percent of orange juice in a mixture of *x* gallons of brand *A* drink, *y* gallons of brand *B* drink, and *z* gallons of water?

(A) $\dfrac{x + y}{x + y + z}\%$

(B) $\dfrac{40y}{x + y + z}\%$

(C) $\dfrac{30x + 40y}{x + y}\%$

(D) $\dfrac{30x + 40y}{x + y + z}\%$

(E) $\dfrac{30x + 40y + z}{x + y + z}\%$

IF YOU FINISH BEFORE TIME IS CALLED, YOU MAY CHECK YOUR WORK ON THIS SECTION ONLY. DO NOT TURN TO ANY OTHER SECTION IN THE TEST.

STOP

**Time—25 Minutes
24 Questions**

Directions: For each question in this section, select the best answer from among the choices given and fill in the corresponding oval on the answer sheet.

Each sentence below has one or two blanks, each blank indicating that something has been omitted. Beneath the sentence are five words or sets of words labeled A through E. Choose the word or set of words that, when inserted in the sentence, best fits the meaning of the sentence as a whole.

EXAMPLE:

Today's small, portable computers contrast markedly with the earliest electronic computers, which were -------.

(A) effective (B) invented
  (C) useful (D) destructive
    (E) enormous

ANSWER:
Ⓐ Ⓑ Ⓒ Ⓓ ●

1 University professors are frequently ------- to utilize multimedia materials in their class presentations; however, many ------- the expertise in new educational technology to be able to use such materials effectively.

(A) encouraged . . lack
(B) inspired . . enjoy
(C) determined . . require
(D) forced . . elect
(E) trusted . . embrace

2 Despite the poet's best efforts to ------- the symbolism in her latest work, it nonetheless remained -------.

(A) corrupt . . obscure
(B) simplify . . lustrous
(C) illuminate . . explicit
(D) clarify . . opaque
(E) cleanse . . enigmatic

3 However ------- the speech may have sounded to the audience, it was in fact the product of a great deal of rehearsal.

(A) imprecise (B) relentless
  (C) premeditated (D) practiced
    (E) impromptu

4 Acknowledging the ------- of their recent consensus, the partners struggled to uphold their ------- agreement.

(A) fragility . . tenuous
(B) persistence . . paltry
(C) durability . . stalwart
(D) estimation . . delicate
(E) omission . . tractable

5 The ------- nature of the security guard is evidenced by his ill temper and penchant for quarreling with entrants to the building.

(A) cantankerous (B) engaging
  (C) urbane (D) perspicacious
    (E) cautious

GO ON TO THE NEXT PAGE

Each passage below is followed by questions based on its content. Answer the questions on the basis of what is <u>stated</u> or <u>implied</u> in each passage and in any introductory material that may be provided.

Questions 6–7 are based on the following passage.

Ever since the movie *Jaws*, sharks have been feared and reviled as menaces of the sea. Can you picture, then, a shark swimming close to the
Line surface of the ocean, its mouth wide open, looking
(5) for all the world like it's "catching rays"? The basking shark, named for its propensity to bask (or laze about) in the sun, does just that. Don't be fooled, though; like all sharks, the basking shark can be dangerous to human beings. In fact, there
(10) are reports of harpooned basking sharks attacking the boat in which the harpooner is riding. In addition, the basking shark's skin contains dermal denticles that have seriously wounded divers and scientists who have come in contact with the
(15) sharks.

6 The second sentence ("Can...rays") is meant to convey

(A) a comical picture of an animal that is usually regarded as menacing
(B) that sharks are not dangerous, despite their portrayal in *Jaws*
(C) an in-depth look at the habits of the basking shark
(D) the reason why basking sharks have attacked boats
(E) why sharks are menaces of the sea

A dermal denticle (lines 12–13) is most likely

(A) one of the basking shark's teeth
(B) a dangerous part of the basking shark's skin
7 (C) something that protects the basking shark from the sun
(D) a conduit for the basking shark's food
(E) the only way a basking shark can defend itself

Questions 8–9 are based on the following passage.

While some playwrights are known for writing essays defending their own work or criticizing the work of competing writers,
Line Arthur Miller's essays are simply about theater.
(5) While we may discover politics and favoritism when we comb through Miller's essays looking for such things, in doing so, we may risk missing the point of the works—Miller wants only for us to benefit from his years of
(10) experience. Even his earliest essays read as virtual how-to manuals for new playwrights and directors. These works ring with clarity and forthrightness, and are filled with thoughtful and often provocative opinions. These essays
(15) teach us what the theater is, what it might be, and how to make it so.

8 In line 11, "virtual" most nearly means

(A) organic
(B) electronic
(C) moral
(D) near
(E) cybernetic

9 The author of the passage suggests that Miller's essays differ from other playwrights' essays in that

(A) Miller's essays are more recent than those of other playwrights
(B) Miller wrote more essays than most other playwrights did
(C) Miller's essays have had more influence than have anyone else's
(D) Miller's essays are not self-serving
(E) Miller wrote essays about American theater

GO ON TO THE NEXT PAGE

Questions 10–18 are based on the following passage.

The passage below is written by an Australian conservation scientist and activist.

The koala, or *Phascolarctos cinereus*, has, for decades, been Australia's most recognizable symbol and a global emblem of endangered species and conservation efforts. The unsuccessful fight to keep koalas from the endangered list—the animal was added to the U.S. list in May 2000—has in the last few years become more complex: while koala populations are on the brink of extinction in Australia's north, they are undergoing a population boom in the south where the animals are killing trees by over-browsing in their habitats. Habitat destruction and the degradation that has resulted from over-browsing have aggravated a number of factors that have placed susceptible koala populations at risk of extinction. At the same time, conservationists point out that the population boom in the south is vital to preserve the species as a whole in Australia.

The greatest current threat to koala populations in the north is the destruction of approximately 80 percent of their habitat. Degradation of eucalyptus habitats decreases the abundance of eucalyptus trees, forcing koalas to travel great distances in search of food. Koalas, known for their slothfulness caused by a low metabolic rate, do not obtain sufficient nutrients from eucalyptus leaves to enable this long-distance foraging. Degradation is further aggravated by habitat fragmentation, whereby suitable patches of eucalyptus are separated by great distances. Fragmentation increases the amount of open space koalas are forced to cross in search of foraging opportunities. This is a particular problem in urban areas, where dog attacks and accidents with cars are major causes of koala mortality.

Conservationists also point to the danger mistletoe presents to healthy eucalyptus habitats for koalas. Mistletoe is a parasite that uses eucalyptus for water and mineral nutrients. Prior to European settlement, wildfires kept mistletoe in check by burning the parasitic plant without dramatically affecting its eucalyptus host. Fire suppression by humans, however, has caused an increase in the abundance of mistletoe, enabling this parasite to destroy numerous eucalyptus trees. Many ecologists note that the danger to koala populations posed by unchecked mistletoe, while real, is far less grave than that caused by outright habitat destruction.

Genetic variance has also become a notable concern for koala populations in southern Australia. Unlike populations in the north, the southern population was established by a single genetic strain that came from French Island in the Australian state of Victoria. Genetic studies among this population have revealed a low genetic variance, which has negative implications for the fitness, and even survival, of the species. Widespread habitat fragmentation separates populations of koalas already low in genetic variance. Mating among small numbers of koalas with low genetic variance leads to inbreeding, leading to offspring that are incapable of reproducing, causing further population decline.

Conservationists propose two methods of alleviating the problem of low genetic variance. First, both the public and private spheres should be encouraged to create land corridors—long strips of eucalyptus habitat between fragmented populations to reduce the chances of genetic inbreeding. As habitats become increasingly fragmented due to urban development, these corridors will be important means of gene flow among isolated populations. Additionally, moving koalas from over- to under-populated areas would not only help to save the forests that are currently over-browsed but also introduce new genes into a population whose genetic variety has been decimated.

Conservation scientists are also concerned with identifying those habitats that can best sustain koala populations. They note that further study should be conducted to explain why koalas prefer certain forests to others that are seemingly identical, since this question is particularly important in determining which regions of Australia should be preserved for the koala. While it was once believed that the koala's preference for certain trees was based on the tree's species, new studies have found that the preference is based more on the quantity of nutrients available in a forest. Leaves of eucalyptus trees with access to abundant nutrients can better afford to lose leaves than can trees whose environments provide them with meager resources. Also, eucalyptus trees in nutrient-rich environments produce leaves with lower toxin levels, which koalas prefer. Many scientists now believe that further studies should be done to identify the forests with the highest nutrient availability so that these forests can be strongly considered for koala habitats.

Sadly, the greatest threat koalas face is the destruction of their habitats by human beings. Logging and development practices that result in forest clearing should be prevented whenever possible. Conservation efforts should focus on saving the koala habitats that remain in Australia to sustain existing populations. When commercial interests are in conflict with those of the koala, planners can implement simple but effective measures such as reducing speed limits and building roads that bypass the animals' habitat.

GO ON TO THE NEXT PAGE

10 The primary purpose of this passage is to

(A) examine the dietary habits of koalas
(B) prove the importance of koalas to the Australian ecosystem
(C) refute the argument that habitat fragmentation does not harm koala populations
(D) analyze the importance of eucalyptus trees for koala populations
(E) discuss threats facing koala populations and possible solutions

11 The author notes that the efforts to fight the extinction of the koala have recently "become more complex" (line 7) because

(A) the animals' habitats are increasingly fragmented
(B) the koalas in the northern portion of the country have a very low genetic variance
(C) it is difficult to determine which groups of eucalyptus trees will produce the lowest levels of toxins
(D) humans pose an increasing threat through land development
(E) some areas of the country now have large populations of the animal, posing a new set of problems

12 All of the following are discussed as threats to koala populations EXCEPT

(A) dogs
(B) habitat fragmentation
(C) decreasing numbers of eucalyptus trees
(D) urban development
(E) disease

13 The author would most likely support all of the following EXCEPT

(A) restricting urban development in conservation areas
(B) researching eucalyptus habitats to determine which have the richest nutrients
(C) banning the movement of the southern koala population to the north
(D) encouraging individuals near koala habitats to keep dogs on leashes or behind fences
(E) allotting public land to build corridors between habitats

14 Which of the following, if true, would undermine the author's claim that koala populations are under threat of extinction?

(A) Degradation of eucalyptus will only accelerate in the coming years.
(B) Habitats in the southern region of Australia are more fragmented and degraded than those in the northern region.
(C) Koalas only feed on eucalyptus leaves.
(D) Australian citizens oppose the use of public lands for conservation efforts.
(E) There is greater genetic variance in the south than in the north.

15 In line 77, the word "sustain" most likely means

(A) defend
(B) suffer
(C) encounter
(D) maintain
(E) endure

16 In lines 90–92, the author implies that a eucalyptus leaf with high toxin levels is

(A) made by trees living in environments without enough nutrients
(B) of high nutrient value
(C) preferred by koalas for food
(D) an insufficient source of nutrients for a koala
(E) the cause of the koala's endangered species status

17 In the sixth paragraph, the author argues that research should be designed to

(A) analyze the means by which to increase nutrient availability
(B) discover the reason that koalas prefer only eucalyptus leaves
(C) decide how much land should be allotted toward conservation efforts
(D) discover alternate habitats for koalas
(E) determine which areas of eucalyptus are richest in nutrients

18 It can be inferred from the passage that the author believes that koalas are

(A) the most vital species to Australian ecosystems
(B) doomed to become extinct
(C) in need of greater conservation efforts to preserve the species
(D) not under a grave risk of extinction
(E) not worthy of being Australia's symbol for conservation efforts

GO ON TO THE NEXT PAGE

Questions 19–24 are based on the following passage.

This passage is from a book about neurobiology and linguistics written in the 1990s. It examines theories about whether all human languages share a common underlying structure.

Noam Chomsky's influential theory of Universal Grammar postulates that all humans have an innate, genetic understanding of certain grammatical
Line "rules," which are universal across all languages and
(5) absolutely not affected by environment. We are all born, Chomsky says, with a knowledge of "deep structure," basic linguistic constructions that allow us, if not to understand all languages, at least to understand how they are put together. From there,
(10) we have only to learn how the options are set in our particular language in order to create an unlimited number of "correct" utterances.

For example, he suggests that structure dependency—a rule that says that sentences are
(15) defined by phrase structure, not linear structure—is inherent to all languages, with minor variations. (Thus, the meaning of a sentence is really dependent on the meaning of its phrases, rather than each individual word.) In addition, the head parameter
(20) rule stipulates that each phrase contains a "head" (main) word, and all languages have it in essentially the same position within the phrase. Chomsky's famous sentence "Colorless green ideas sleep furiously" exemplifies this theory of Universal
(25) Grammar—while the sentence itself is meaningless, it is easily recognizable as a grammatical sentence that fits a basic, but higher level of organization. "Furiously sleep ideas green colorless," on the other hand, is obviously not grammatical, and it is difficult
(30) to discern any kind of meaning in it. For other evidence to support this theory, Chomsky points to our relative ease in translating one language to another; again, while we may not necessarily recognize individual words in an unfamiliar
(35) language, we can certainly recognize and engage with sentences that are grammatical.

This evidence is still fairly theoretical, receiving play mostly in the linguistic sphere. Most researchers seem more concerned with attempting to draw
(40) universal parallels across languages than with searching for biological evidence of such phenomena. We might ask: Where exactly are these Universal Grammar constraints located? How and when are they altered by natural evolutionary processes—or do
(45) they remain relatively unaltered and nonmutated from generation to generation? As language evolves over time, does Universal Grammar also evolve or stay relatively stable? Other scientists say that Universal Grammar is not nearly as ordered and absolute as
(50) Chomsky and other linguists make it out to be and suggest that the Universal Grammar theory is the result of our flawed human tendency to impose order where there is none. Still others suggest that by completely ignoring the role of environment in
(55) language development, Chomsky completely discredits the possible important effect our surroundings could have on language development.

A few researchers are beginning to suggest that, rather than focusing on explaining linguistic
(60) similarities among various languages, we instead acknowledge the evolutionary roots of language, and look specifically for neurobiological explanations. Claiming that the humanistic exploration of Universal Grammar is too abstract,
(65) they recommend that we instead view language (and grammar) as a function of the brain. Because language is so unbelievably complex, offering several definitions and associations contained within a single word, any single connection
(70) between, say, two languages causes those myriad associations to become oversimplified and sterile. For example, simply pointing out the position of a sentence's subject in Turkish versus that same subject position in English as an illustration of the
(75) existence of Universal Grammar merely acknowledges that single linguistic association without taking into account any social circumstances that may cause the mind to modify that grammar. In short, say these scientists, not until
(80) we create a better marriage between biology and linguistics—and a better understanding of the human brain—can we even begin to address the complexities of human language development.

19 Structure dependency and the head parameter rule (lines 13–22) are provided as examples of observable facts that

(A) linguists cannot find a complete explanation for
(B) suggest the existence of Universal Grammar across all human languages
(C) refute the theory of Universal Grammar
(D) biologists believe are exceptions to the rule of Universal Grammar
(E) scientists think are part of typical nongrammatical sentences

GO ON TO THE NEXT PAGE

20 The primary function of the information provided in the second paragraph is to

(A) provide evidence for the theory of Universal Grammar
(B) dispute the theory of Universal Grammar
(C) explain why the theory of Universal Grammar is accepted by most linguists
(D) explain the role of head parameters in language
(E) suggest that Universal Grammar oversimplifies the mechanics of language

21 The word "play" in line 38 most nearly means

(A) fun
(B) performance
(C) imitation
(D) gambling
(E) exposure

22 In the last paragraph, the author suggests that some biologists believe an emphasis on linguistics as an explanation for language development

(A) ignores possibly useful neurobiological evidence
(B) overemphasizes biological evidence
(C) eliminates any need for study of social circumstances affecting language development
(D) requires linguists to ignore existing biological evidence completely
(E) oversimplifies the evolutionary role of language

23 The statement in lines 66–71 ("Because language… oversimplified and sterile") suggests that

(A) biological evidence for the existence of Universal Grammar does not exist
(B) biologists have begun gathering genetic evidence to refute the existence of Universal Grammar
(C) simple linguistic connections are enough to prove the existence of Universal Grammar
(D) linguistic methods for proving the existence of Universal Grammar work for some languages, but not others
(E) linguistic explanations cannot account for the complexity of all human languages

24 The author uses the term "marriage" (line 80) to refer to

(A) a flawless combination of linguistics and biology
(B) a romantic relationship between biologists and linguists
(C) a legal union between neurobiologists and Universal Grammar linguists
(D) an intellectual union between biology and linguistics
(E) a long-term unification of science and social science

IF YOU FINISH BEFORE TIME IS CALLED, YOU MAY CHECK YOUR WORK ON THIS SECTION ONLY. DO NOT TURN TO ANY OTHER SECTION IN THE TEST.

STOP

Directions: This section contains two types of questions. You have 25 minutes to complete both types. For questions 1–8, solve each problem and decide which is the best of the choices given. Fill in the corresponding oval on the answer sheet. You may use any available space for scratchwork.

Time—25 Minutes
18 Questions

1. Calculator use is permitted.

2. All numbers used are real numbers.

3. Figures are provided for some problems. All figures are drawn to scale and lie in a plane UNLESS otherwise indicated.

4. Unless otherwise specified, the domain of any function f is assumed to be the set of all real numbers x for which $f(x)$ is a real number.

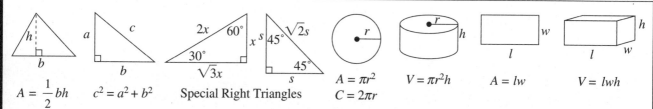

$$A = \frac{1}{2}bh \qquad c^2 = a^2 + b^2 \qquad \text{Special Right Triangles} \qquad A = \pi r^2 \qquad V = \pi r^2 h \qquad A = lw \qquad V = lwh \qquad C = 2\pi r$$

The sum of the measures in degrees of the angles of a triangle is 180.
The number of degrees of arc in a circle is 360.
A straight angle has a degree measure of 180.

---

1 If $\sqrt{ab} = 3$, $b = c^3$, and $c = 3$, what is the value of $\dfrac{1}{a}$?

(A) $\dfrac{1}{3}$

(B) 1

(C) 3

(D) 9

(E) 27

Note: Figure not drawn to scale.

2 In the figure above, if $h = 20$, $g = 4h$, and $f = 2g$, what is the value of j ?

(A) 60
(B) 80
(C) 90
(D) 100
(E) 260

3 If $x < 0 < y < 1$, which of the following CANNOT be true?

I. $xy = -\dfrac{1}{4}$

II. $\dfrac{x}{y} = -1$

III. $x + y > 1$

(A) I only
(B) II only
(C) III only
(D) I and II only
(E) I, II, and III

Note: Figure not drawn to scale.

5 In the figure above, the length of CB is t percent less than the length of DB, and the length of EC is t percent less than the length of AC. If the area of triangle EBC is 16 percent of the area of triangle ABD, then what is the value of t ?

(A)   4
(B) 16
(C) 25
(D) 51
(E) 60

4 If a and b are positive integers and the ratio of $a + 1$ to $a + 2$ is the same as the ratio of $b + 3$ to $b + 4$, which of the following must be true?

I. $a = 4$
II. $b = 2$
III. $a - b = 2$

(A) I only
(B) II only
(C) III only
(D) I and II only
(E) I, II, and III

Questions 6–8 refer to the following sequence of steps.

1. Select a number that is greater than 40 and less than 200.

2. Divide the number arrived at in the previous step by 20.

3. Find the smallest integer that is greater than or equal to the number arrived at in the previous step.

4. Subtract 5 from the number arrived at in the previous step.

5. Print the number that results.

6 Which of the following numbers could be printed in step 5 ?

(A) 17
(B) 12
(C) 1.7
(D) –1
(E) –7

GO ON TO THE NEXT PAGE

- 23 -

7 If 150 is the number chosen in step 1, then what number will be printed in step 5 ?

(A) 2.5
(B) 3
(C) 7.5
(D) 8
(E) 70

8 When the number 112 is selected in step 1, the number printed in step 5 is b. When the number a is selected in step 1, the number b is printed in step 5. What is the greatest possible value of a ?

(A) 112
(B) 114
(C) 120
(D) 123
(E) 134

GO ON TO THE NEXT PAGE

Directions: For Student-Produced Response questions 9–18, use the grids at the bottom of the answer sheet page on which you have answered questions 1–8.

Each of the remaining 10 questions requires you to solve the problem and enter your answer by marking the ovals in the special grid, as shown in the examples below. You may use any available space for scratchwork.

Answer: 1.25 or $\frac{5}{4}$ or 5/4

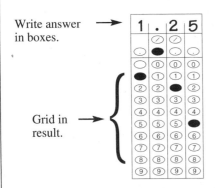

Write answer → in boxes.

Grid in → result.

Fraction line

Decimal point

Either position is correct.

You may start your answers in any column, space permitting. Columns not needed should be left blank.

- It is recommended, though not required, that you write your answer in the boxes at the top of the columns. However, **you will receive credit only for darkening the ovals correctly.**

- Grid only one answer to a question, even though some problems have more than one correct answer.

- Darken no more than one oval in a column.

- No answers are negative.

- **Mixed numbers** cannot be gridded. For example: the number $1\frac{1}{4}$ must be gridded as 1.25 or 5/4.

(If ⬚ is gridded, it will be interpreted as $\frac{11}{4}$, not $1\frac{1}{4}$.)

- Decimal Accuracy: Decimal answers must be entered as accurately as possible. For example, if you obtain an answer such as 0.1666. . ., you should record the result as .166 or .167. **Less accurate values such as .16 or .17 are not acceptable.**

Acceptable ways to grid $\frac{1}{6}$ = .1666. . .

---

9 If $a - b = 12$ and $\frac{a}{3} = 10$, then what is the value of b ?

10 A telephone call cost $0.35 for the first 3 minutes and $0.07 for each additional minute. How many minutes long was a telephone call that cost $1.75 ?

GO ON TO THE NEXT PAGE

11 The points V, W, X, Y, and Z are located on a number line in that order. The length of VW is twice the length of WX, the length of WX is twice the length of XY, and the length of XY is twice the length of YZ. If the length of VZ is 30, what is the length of WY ?

```
  BB
  BB
  BB
  BB
 +BB
 ▭
```

12 In the correctly worked addition problem above, the number covered by the shaded rectangle is a 3-digit number that is at least 250 and no greater than 400. What is one possible value of the number covered by the shaded rectangle?

13 A store sells 12 different types of radios, 10 different types of television sets, and 5 different types of vacuum cleaners. How many different combinations of one radio, one television set, and one vacuum cleaner can a customer buy?

14 If day 6 of a 30-day month lies on a Wednesday, and the last Sunday of the month occurs on day n, what is the value of n ?

GO ON TO THE NEXT PAGE

15 For all negative integers x other than -1, let $\Diamond x \Diamond$ be defined as the product of all the negative odd integers greater than x. For example, $\Diamond -7 \Diamond = (-5) \times (-3) \times (-1) = -15$.

What is the value of $\dfrac{\Diamond -75 \Diamond}{\Diamond -74 \Diamond}$?

17 If the median of $7x$, $5x$, $13x$, $11x$, and $8x$ is divisible by 20, what is the smallest possible value for x if x is a positive integer?

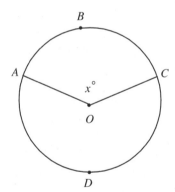

16 In the figure above, O is the center of the circle, and the ratio of the area of region $OABC$ to the area of region $OCDA$ is 3 to 5. What is the value of x ?

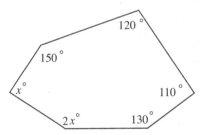

Note: Figure not drawn to scale.

18 What is the value of x in the figure above?

IF YOU FINISH BEFORE TIME IS CALLED, YOU MAY CHECK YOUR WORK ON THIS SECTION ONLY. DO NOT TURN TO ANY OTHER SECTION IN THE TEST.

STOP

Time—25 Minutes
20 Questions

Directions: For this section, solve each problem and decide which is the best of the choices given. Fill in the corresponding oval on the answer sheet. You may use any available space for scratchwork.

Reference Information

$A = \dfrac{1}{2}bh \qquad c^2 = a^2 + b^2 \qquad$ Special Right Triangles $\qquad A = \pi r^2 \qquad V = \pi r^2 h \qquad A = lw \qquad V = lwh$

$C = 2\pi r$

The sum of the measures in degrees of the angles of a triangle is 180.
The number of degrees of arc in a circle is 360.
A straight angle has a degree measure of 180.

---

1 Which of the following is NOT a factor of 90 ?

(A)   5
(B)   6
(C) 12
(D) 15
(E) 30

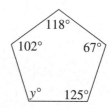

Note: Figure not drawn to scale.

2 In the pentagon above, which of the following is the value of y ?

(A) 125
(B) 126
(C) 127
(D) 128
(E) 129

GO ON TO THE NEXT PAGE

3 If $4^7 = \dfrac{4^p}{16}$, which of the following could be the value of p?

(A) 3
(B) 9
(C) 11
(D) 14
(E) 28

PRICES

	Pants	Jackets
A	$25	$115
B	$30	$120
C	$35	$125

QUANTITY

	Small	Medium	Large
Pants	60	75	65
Jackets	80	85	75

5 A department store sells pants and jackets of three different sizes at three different outlets. Each outlet has in stock the same number of pants and jackets of each size. The first chart above shows the prices of these pants and jackets at each of the outlets A, B, and C. The second chart shows the number of pants and jackets of each size in stock at each outlet. What is the total cost of the large pants and large jackets that outlet C has in stock?

(A) $8,500
(B) $9,750
(C) $10,700
(D) $11,650
(E) $12,400

4 40% of 200 people surveyed claimed their favorite fruit was the apple, while another 30% claimed their favorite fruit was the banana. If 35 people claimed their favorite fruit was the orange, how many more people claimed the apple was their favorite fruit than claimed the orange was their favorite fruit?

(A) 5
(B) 10
(C) 25
(D) 35
(E) 45

6 Abel, Carlos, and John are going to sing at a school assembly. If they stand in a single row on the stage, how many possible arrangements of the three students are there?

(A) Three
(B) Four
(C) Five
(D) Six
(E) Nine

GO ON TO THE NEXT PAGE

7 If $-5 < x < 5$, which of the following MUST be true?

(A) $x^2 > 5$
(B) $x^3 < 5$
(C) $|x - 10| > 5$
(D) $|x - 5| < 5$
(E) $x^3 > x^2$

h	-1	0	1	2	3
$g(h)$	-7	-4	-1	2	5

9 The table above gives values of the function $g(h)$ for selected values of h. If $g(h)$ is a linear function, which of the following defines $g(h)$?

(A) $g(h) = 3h - 4$
(B) $g(h) = 3h - 3$
(C) $g(h) = 2h - 4$
(D) $g(h) = \dfrac{1}{3}h - 4$
(E) $g(h) = \dfrac{1}{3}h - 3$

8 Each of the following equations is true for all integers x EXCEPT

(A) $x - 1 = -(1 - x)$
(B) $x^4 = (x^2)^2$
(C) $0x^2 = x - x$
(D) $2x = x^2$
(E) $(-x)^2 = x^2$

10 If v is a positive integer, $\dfrac{v}{t} = \dfrac{y}{x}$, and $\dfrac{v}{y} = 3$, then which of the following must equal $\dfrac{x}{t}$?

(A) $\dfrac{1}{3}$

(B) 3

(C) $\dfrac{y}{x}$

(D) $\dfrac{v}{t}$

(E) $\dfrac{v}{y}$

GO ON TO THE NEXT PAGE

11 The function $f(x) = 3x + 1$ is represented by which of the following graphs?

(A)

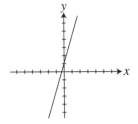

(B)

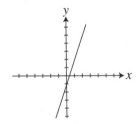

(C)

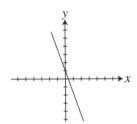

(D)

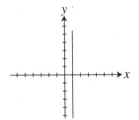

(E)

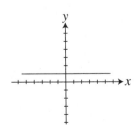

12 If a is a positive even integer, then which of the following could be a value of $(a + 2)(a - 3)$?

(A) -6
(B) 7
(C) 10
(D) 15
(E) 24

GO ON TO THE NEXT PAGE

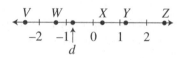

13 The number line above shows a point with coordinate *d*. Which of the lettered points is closest to −3*d* ?

(A) *V*
(B) *W*
(C) *X*
(D) *Y*
(E) *Z*

15 Jean and Miguel have taken the same number of photos on their school trip. Jean has taken 3 times as many photos as Yuki and Miguel has taken 12 more photos than Yuki. How many photos has Yuki taken?

(A) 3
(B) 6
(C) 9
(D) 12
(E) 18

14 Roberto is constructing a cubical box with a volume of 343 cubic inches. He has painted four sides of the box. What is the total painted area?

(A) 49
(B) 196
(C) 212
(D) 245
(E) 294

16 Which of the following sets of numbers has the property that if x^3 is in a set, then x is also in the set?

(A) {−3, −1, 0}
(B) {−2, −1, 0, 1, 2}
(C) {−1, 0, 1}
(D) {−1, 0, 2}
(E) {1, 2, 3}

GO ON TO THE NEXT PAGE

17 If p is an integer, $p > -1$, and $r = p^2 - p$, then which of the following can be true?

      I. $r = 0$
      II. $r = p$
      III. r is an integer

(A) I only
(B) II only
(C) III only
(D) II and III only
(E) I, II, and III

19 An Internet provider charges k dollars for the first hour of use in a month and m dollars per hour for every additional hour used that month. If June paid \$65.50 for her Internet use in one month, which of the following expressions represents the number of hours she used the Internet that month?

(A) $\dfrac{65.50 - k}{m}$

(B) $\dfrac{65.50 + k + m}{m}$

(C) $\dfrac{65.50 - k + m}{m}$

(D) $\dfrac{65.50 - k - m}{m}$

(E) $\dfrac{65.50}{k + m}$

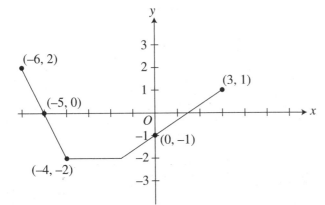

18 The figure above shows the function f, which is defined for $-6 \leq x \leq 3$. For which of the following values of x is $\left| f(x) \right| < x$?

(A) -6
(B) -5
(C) -4
(D) 0
(E) 3

20 In the figure above, $\triangle ABC$ is a right triangle. The coordinates of A are $(8 - m, m)$ and the coordinates of C are $(8, 0)$. A point that lies within square $EFGH$ is chosen at random. The probability that this point lies in

the shaded triangle is $\dfrac{1}{3}$. What is the value of m ?

(A) 3
(B) $3\sqrt{3}$
(C) $3\sqrt{6}$
(D) 9
(E) 81

IF YOU FINISH BEFORE TIME IS CALLED, YOU MAY CHECK YOUR WORK ON THIS SECTION ONLY. DO NOT TURN TO ANY OTHER SECTION IN THE TEST.

STOP

Time—25 Minutes
35 Questions

Directions: For each question in this section, select the best answer from among the choices given and fill in the corresponding oval on the answer sheet.

The following sentences test correctness and effectiveness of expression. Part of each sentence or the entire sentence is underlined; beneath each sentence are five ways of phrasing the underlined material. Choice A repeats the original phrasing; the other four choices are different. If you think the original phrasing produces a better sentence than any of the alternatives, select choice A; if not, select one of the other choices.

In making your selection, follow the requirements of standard written English; that is, pay attention to grammar, choice of words, sentence construction, and punctuation. Your selection should result in the most effective sentence—clear and precise—without awkwardness or ambiguity.

EXAMPLE:

Every apple in the baskets <u>are ripe and labeled according to the date it was picked</u>.

(A) are ripe and labeled according to the date it was picked
(B) is ripe and labeled according to the date it was picked
(C) are ripe and labeled according to the date they were picked
(D) is ripe and labeled according to the date they were picked
(E) are ripe and labeled as to the date it was picked

ANSWER:

Ⓐ ● Ⓒ Ⓓ Ⓔ

1 Hearing that the test results exceeded state mandates, <u>a party was thrown by the math teacher</u> for the students.

(A) a party was thrown by the math teacher
(B) a party was thrown
(C) the math teacher was thrown a party
(D) the math teacher threw a party
(E) the math teacher had thrown a party

2 The ragdoll is a breed of very flexible cat, some <u>of whom being</u> abused because they rarely fight, preferring to lounge instead.

(A) of whom being
(B) of which are
(C) of them are
(D) are
(E) to be

3 Elise <u>Ray, the captain of the 2000 Olympic women's gymnastic team before attending</u> the University of Michigan.

(A) Ray, the captain of the 2000 Olympic women's gymnastic team before attending
(B) Ray, who was the captain of the 2000 Olympic women's gymnastic team before attending
(C) Ray who was the captain of the 2000 Olympic women's gymnastic team and who attended
(D) Ray, the captain of the 2000 Olympic women's gymnastic team attending
(E) Ray was the captain of the 2000 Olympic women's gymnastic team before attending

4 George Balanchine was <u>almost as skillful a dancer as he was at choreography</u>.

(A) almost as skillful a dancer as he was at choreography
(B) almost as skillful at dance as he was a choreographer
(C) almost skillful as a dancer and a choreographer
(D) almost as skillful a dancer as at choreography
(E) almost as skillful a dancer as he was a choreographer

5 The Supreme Court's citations of foreign decisions have been derided <u>by opponents, disregarding they say</u> the tenets of the Constitution.

(A) by opponents, disregarding they say
(B) by opponents saying they are showing a disregard
(C) by opponents who say the Court is disregarding
(D) with opponents saying the citations show disregard of
(E) as disregarding, so opponents said, of

GO ON TO THE NEXT PAGE

6 Training to be a professional taste tester means many hours <u>in which they</u> sample foods of many different flavors and textures and record their impressions on several standardized scales.

(A) in which they
(B) by which they
(C) and during those hours trainees
(D) during which trainees
(E) while they

7 Certain constellations have a particular meaning for those people <u>which have a belief in astrology</u>.

(A) which have a belief in astrology
(B) who believe in astrology
(C) whom believe in astrology
(D) that believe in astrology
(E) who believing in astrology

8 <u>Relying on its news, CNN is a television station many people watch.</u>

(A) Relying on its news, CNN is a television station many people watch.
(B) Relying on its news, the television station CNN is the one many people watch.
(C) A television station watched by many people relying on its news is CNN.
(D) Relying on its news, many people watch the television station CNN.
(E) Many people, relying on CNN, and watching it.

9 <u>Although William Howard Taft served as</u> President of the United States from 1909 to 1913; he was not finished with public service, though, and went on to serve as Chief Justice of the Supreme Court from 1921 to 1930.

(A) Although William Howard Taft served as
(B) They elected William Howard Taft
(C) Despite the fact that William Howard Taft served as
(D) William Howard Taft served as
(E) With William Howard Taft serving as

10 Tom hated to watch <u>golf, of which he found the length particularly boring</u>.

(A) golf, of which he found the length particularly boring
(B) golf; he found the length particularly boring
(C) golf, which he found particularly boring
(D) golf, to which he found the length particularly boring
(E) golf; which he found particularly boring in length

11 The government <u>imposed sanctions on a renegade nation last month after they violated</u> the terms of a worldwide arms-control agreement.

(A) imposed sanctions on a renegade nation last month after they violated
(B) imposed sanctions on a renegade nation last month after it was violating
(C) has imposed sanctions on a renegade nation last month after they violated
(D) imposed sanctions on a renegade nation last month after that nation violated
(E) imposed sanctions on a nation of renegades last month after they violated

GO ON TO THE NEXT PAGE

Directions: The following sentences test your ability to recognize grammar and usage errors. Each sentence contains either a single error or no error at all. No sentence contains more than one error. The error, if there is one, is underlined and lettered. If the sentence contains an error, select the one underlined part that must be changed to make the sentence correct. If the sentence is correct, select choice E. In choosing answers, follow the requirements of standard written English.

EXAMPLE:

<u>Whenever</u> one is driving late at night, <u>you</u> must take extra precautions <u>against</u>
    A   B   C
falling asleep <u>at</u> the wheel. <u>No error</u>
           D   E

ANSWER:

12 The scientist <u>conducting</u> the experiment in the
               A
rain forest was less interested in why the

particular species was prevalent <u>than in</u> whether
                                   B
<u>they have</u> <u>violently</u> taken over another species'
  C   D
habitat. <u>No error</u>
        E

13 <u>That</u> his presentation on financial strategy was
   A
criticized <u>savagely</u> by his customers <u>who</u> watched
        B   C
it <u>came</u> as a shock to the analyst. <u>No error</u>
  D   E

14 A downfall in the economy could affect the ballet

season because programs <u>performed</u> in the new
                         A
symphony hall <u>cost</u> twice <u>as much</u> in overhead as
            B   C
<u>the old performance space.</u> <u>No error</u>
             D   E

15 The <u>other</u> cyclists and <u>me</u> <u>immediately</u> started
     A   B   C
pedaling when we heard the whistle <u>blown</u> by the
                                  D
race organizer. <u>No error</u>
              E

16 <u>Although</u> the amount of money in the bank
   A
accounts <u>keep</u> dwindling, the account holders
         B
<u>claim that</u> their finances <u>are improving</u>. <u>No error</u>
   C   D   E

17 Hiring someone <u>to plow</u> my driveway <u>costs</u> a lot of
             A   B
money, but it's <u>infinitely</u> preferable <u>than to do it</u>
             C   D
myself. <u>No error</u>
       E

GO ON TO THE NEXT PAGE

18 Exhausted <u>from our long day</u> of shopping,
              A

<u>Kathy and I decided</u> <u>to treat ourselves</u> to an
      B   C

<u>extravagant</u> lunch. <u>No error</u>
   D   E

19 After the auction, Marsue realized that she <u>purchases</u> a
                                A

painting <u>that</u> was worth <u>far more</u> than she had bid
      B   C

<u>for it</u>. <u>No error</u>
 D   E

20 No one <u>dares</u> to defy Mr. Webb; <u>between</u> all of the
      A   B

members <u>of the faculty</u>, he is the <u>strictest</u>. <u>No error</u>
        C   D   E

21 The store manager <u>telephoned</u> the warehouse
                 A

manager <u>after</u> <u>he failed</u> <u>to deliver</u> the products on
       B   C   D

the correct day. <u>No error</u>
             E

22 During the debate, Jack <u>attended closely</u> to the
                     A

Independent Party candidate's economic plan,

<u>which Jack</u> thought was <u>better structured</u>
   B   C

<u>than the other candidates</u>. <u>No error</u>
     D   E

23 Edward Villella <u>stages</u> ballets <u>that reflect</u> the
          A   B

<u>influence of</u> <u>an earlier</u> choreographer,
   C   D

George Balanchine. <u>No error</u>
           E

24 Many people claim <u>to have seen</u> UFOs, <u>but</u>
            A   B

not one <u>have</u> proved that <u>such objects</u> exist.
      C   D

<u>No error</u>
 E

25 Last year, the company <u>announces</u> Take Your
               A

Daughter to Work Day in an effort <u>to build</u> the
                     B

morale <u>of employees</u> in the head office
      C

<u>during the recession</u>. <u>No error</u>
    D   E

26 Initially intended as a <u>commentary on</u> <u>recently</u> passed
                  A   B

legislation, the editorial <u>provoked</u> new <u>interest of</u> the
               C   D

process of creating ballot initiatives. <u>No error</u>
                    E

27 Seniors <u>which need</u> help with their college
       A

applications <u>can find</u> <u>immediate</u> <u>assistance from</u>
        B   C   D

the Guidance Department. <u>No error</u>
              E

28 Doctors <u>have found that</u> herbal medications,
       A

when combined with a <u>more traditional</u> medical
               B

approach, <u>shortens</u> the healing time <u>for a number</u>
       C   D

of surgical procedures. <u>No error</u>
           E

29 The complex formulas and problems <u>of Algebra II</u>
                         A

<u>caused</u> me <u>more</u> sleepless nights and test anxiety
  B   C

<u>than Algebra I</u>. <u>No error</u>
   D   E

GO ON TO THE NEXT PAGE

Directions: The following passage is an early draft of an essay. Some parts of the passage need to be rewritten.

Read the passage and select the best answer for each question that follows. Some questions are about particular sentences or parts of sentences and ask you to improve sentence structure or word choice. Other questions ask you to consider organization and development. In choosing answers, follow the conventions of standard written English.

Questions 30–35 are based on the following passage.

(1) A few years ago, my high school decided to eliminate music programs. (2) My friends and I disagreed with the decision, and so we developed a pamphlet that discussed our opinions. (3) Many students approached us after reading the pamphlet and said that we changed the way they used to be thinking about music. (4) This made us feel that we were really effecting our curriculum. (5) We hoped our actions would make the school change its policy.

(6) But, we hoped in vain. (7) We weren't allowed to take chorus, band, or string classes. (8) The school said that it was because music wasn't an important skill to develop in comparison to math, English, and science. (9) The development of musical ability affects so many aspects of a person's life. (10) I disagree. (11) Music teaches you to listen for patterns and ideas that aren't in words. (12) Learning how to read music is like learning a second language—it is the same because it's another way to express yourself.
(13) People should know the importance of music education and it is up to students to prove it to them.

30 In context, which is the best version of the underlined portion of sentence 3 (reproduced below)?

Many students approached us after reading the pamphlet and said that we changed the way they used to be thinking about music.

(A) the pamphlet and said that we changed the way they used to think about music
(B) the pamphlet and said that we changed the way they thought about music
(C) the pamphlet and said that we changed the way they think about music
(D) the pamphlet and said that we change the way they think about music
(E) the pamphlet and said that we change the way they used to think about music

31 In context, which is the best version of the underlined portion of sentence 4 (reproduced below)?

This made us feel that we were really effecting our curriculum.

(A) we were really effecting our
(B) we were really influencing on our
(C) we were really having an influence on our
(D) we were really affecting our
(E) we were effecting our

32 In context, what is the best way to deal with sentence 6 (reproduced below)?

But, we hoped in vain.

(A) Leave it as it is.
(B) Change "But" to "However."
(C) Change "we" to "us."
(D) Change "hoped" to "hope."
(E) Change "in vain" to "vainly."

33 Which of the following would be the most suitable sentence to insert immediately after sentence 6?

(A) We were too optimistic.
(B) Our pamphlet was very effective.
(C) The school continued their policies.
(D) The school continued its policy.
(E) The school changed its policy.

34 Sentence 10 would make most sense if placed after:

(A) Sentence 7
(B) Sentence 8
(C) Sentence 11
(D) Sentence 12
(E) Sentence 13

35 In context, which is the best version of the underlined portion of sentence 12 (reproduced below)?

Learning how to read music is like learning a second language— it is the same because it's another way to express yourself.

(A) it is the same because it's another way to
    express yourself
(B) it is the same way to express yourself
(C) music is the same because it's another way to
    express yourself
(D) each are a way to express yourself
(E) it's another way to express yourself

IF YOU FINISH BEFORE TIME IS CALLED, YOU MAY CHECK YOUR WORK ON THIS SECTION ONLY. DO NOT TURN TO ANY OTHER SECTION IN THE TEST.

STOP

Time—25 Minutes
24 Questions

Directions: For each question in this section, select the best answer from among the choices given and fill in the corresponding oval on the answer sheet.

Each sentence below has one or two blanks, each blank indicating that something has been omitted. Beneath the sentence are five words or sets of words labeled A through E. Choose the word or set of words that, when inserted in the sentence, best fits the meaning of the sentence as a whole.

EXAMPLE:

Today's small, portable computers contrast markedly with the earliest electronic computers, which were -------.

(A) effective   (B) invented
  (C) useful   (D) destructive
    (E) enormous

ANSWER:

Ⓐ Ⓑ Ⓒ Ⓓ ●

---

1 As far as the committee was concerned, the ------- with which the braggart interjected his opinion confirmed his -------.

(A) flourish . . mediocrity
(B) reluctance . . humility
(C) ostentation . . pretentiousness
(D) severity . . exhibitionism
(E) ambivalence . . prejudice

2 Many philosophers contend that true enlightenment is found only by ------- those material objects that obstruct one's contemplation of the eternal.

(A) renouncing   (B) affirming
  (C) considering   (D) imbibing
    (E) concealing

3 The cheerfulness with which the administrator spoke to the assembly temporarily hid the ------- of her address; her jovial tenor, however, soon gave way to more sober remarks.

(A) elation   (B) optimism
  (C) comprehension (D) frailty
    (E) gravity

4 The university chancellor finally ------- the students' concerns by showing that there was no tuition increase in the following year's budget.

(A) elicited   (B) triggered
  (C) allayed   (D) derogated
    (E) shifted

5 The biography detailed how the formerly ------- young man became a ------- who caused a great deal of harm before his eventual imprisonment.

(A) innocent . . libertarian
(B) irreproachable . . miscreant
(C) nefarious . . demagogue
(D) malicious . . reprobate
(E) hapless . . leader

6 The ------- effects of the recent record-setting blizzards were somewhat ------- by the series of sunny and pleasant days that followed.

(A) frigid . . exacerbated
(B) stimulating . . alleviated
(C) disastrous . . counterbalanced
(D) intensifying . . aggravated
(E) overwhelming . . challenged

7 Because the Senator typically appears -------, her reticent attitude last evening seemed particularly -------.

(A) sociable . . appropriate
(B) gregarious . . incongruous
(C) distraught . . sympathetic
(D) serious . . irrelevant
(E) pedestrian . . inexplicable

8 In contrast to most of the students, whose faces appeared vacant, the new student maintained a(n) ------- expression throughout the lecture.

(A) gloomy   (B) rapt
  (C) disseminated   (D) imbued
    (E) retiring

GO ON TO THE NEXT PAGE

The passages below are followed by questions based on their content; questions following a pair of related passages may also be based on the relationship between the paired passages. Answer the questions on the basis of what is <u>stated</u> or <u>implied</u> in the passages and in any introductory material that may be provided.

Questions 9–10 are based on the following passage.

By the time it finally roused me, I somehow knew my alarm clock had been beeping for a while. Outside my window, the sky was still dark, faintly illuminated by the
Line stars, a moon shrouded by clouds, and a faded orange
(5) horizon that signaled the city was also just beginning to wake. After a cold shower cleared my drowsy mind of the confusion left by convoluted dreams and hours of sleep, I remembered why I was not still sleeping. I had taken on a paper route. The realization seemed to hit me
(10) like a blow to my stomach, inciting a dull pain of regret that only deepened with the understanding that my every morning would begin just as jarringly as this one.

9 In the first sentence, the author mentions his alarm clock in order to make which point?

(A) He had conscientiously prepared for his paper route.
(B) He was used to waking up early in the morning.
(C) He was lucky to have set the alarm or he would not have awakened in time.
(D) He was so deeply asleep that the alarm could not immediately wake him.
(E) He was not looking forward to waking up so early every morning.

10 In line 8, the words "I remembered why I was not still sleeping" suggest that the author was

(A) disoriented by his early awakening
(B) entirely unenthusiastic about his paper route
(C) a rather forgetful individual
(D) unconcerned with the responsibilities of his paper route
(E) somewhat confused about the details of his new job

Questions 11–12 are based on the following passage.

While he is called the father of the montage—a widely-used cinematic technique that involves a rapid succession of different shots, often superimposed—
Line Russian director Sergei Eisenstein's influence on the
(5) modern movie is considerably more profound than this simple characterization suggests. His seven films, though not a particularly large body of work, contained a clarity and sharpness of composition that made the depth of his plots and the powerful
(10) complexity of his juxtaposed images remarkably accessible to most viewers. In this way, Eisenstein essentially demonstrated to the notoriously pretentious cinematic establishment of his day that the average viewer could not only consume abstract expressions
(15) through film, but that they could enjoy doing so.

11 The author refers to Eisenstein as the "father of the montage" (line 1) in order to

(A) underscore his immense contribution to film
(B) suggest his impact has been underappreciated
(C) explain how his films were so powerful
(D) celebrate his place in cinematic history
(E) imply his influence has been exaggerated

12 The author gives all of the following as reasons why Eisenstein's films were important EXCEPT for their ability to

(A) lucidly communicate complexity
(B) superimpose contrasting shots
(C) entertain with abstraction
(D) empower the average viewer
(E) challenge the cinematic establishment's perceptions

GO ON TO THE NEXT PAGE

Questions 13–24 are based on the following passages.

The following passages are excerpted from two books that discuss fairy tales. Passage 1 was written by a specialist in psychology and children's literature and was published in 1965. Passage 2 was written by a folklore methodologist and was published in 1986.

Passage 1

Most of the stories that our society tells have only enjoyed a comparatively short period of popularity in comparison with the sweep of human history,
Line flaming into popular consciousness in books,
(5) television or film for a period reaching anywhere from a few months to a few centuries. Fads come and go as fickle as the weather, and today's hit may be tomorrow's forgotten relic. But one particular kind of story that our society tells, the fairy tale, has a kind of
(10) popularity that is uniquely persistent. Literally since time immemorial, fairy tales have been told and retold, refined and adapted across generations of human history. Folk tales that spoke to people in some deeper way, and thus proved popular, endured
(15) and were passed down through the ages. Tales that had only temporal and fleeting appeal are long since lost. Since, as we know, it is a truism that time sifts out the literary wheat and discards the chaff, fairy tales can be said to have undergone the longest
(20) process of selection and editing of any stories in human history.

Consider, for example, the story of *Snow White*. Here is reflected the tale of the eternal struggle for supremacy between the generations. The evil mother
(25) queen grows jealous of the competition of the young Snow White for supremacy in the realm of youth and beauty, so she contrives to do away with her rival. The innocent Snow White survives by a twist of whim and circumstance, and then retreats into the
(30) forest—the traditional symbol of the site of psychological change—where she hides among the Seven Dwarves. Small supernatural spirits or homunculi, often depicted in folk tales as tiny elves, spirit men, trolls, or fairies, represent unconscious
(35) forces, and thus Snow White must care for and nurture the Seven Dwarves while she undergoes her psychological transformation. The dwarves' mining activities can be said to symbolize this process of mental delving into the depths in hopes of uncovering
(40) the precious materials of the developing psyche.

Yet Snow White's road to her new identity is not without incident. The breaching of the secure space by the disguised queen mother and Snow White's giving in to the temptation of the apple—
(45) representative of the same youth and beauty that the queen seeks to deprive her of—causes her to fall into the slumberous mock death. Only the prince can deliver Snow White and metaphorically resurrect her with a kiss, itself a motif that suggests
(50) her entry into the identity of a mature person ready to leave the dwarves and forest of the unconscious behind and take on adult responsibilities.

The popularity of this tale, and others like it, across time and in widely-scattered societies
(55) confirms its power in tapping into unconscious forces and common motifs that all humans share. All humans in all ages experience generational rivalry and the impact that it has on patterns of growth and maturity. The specific symbols used to
(60) represent these dynamics are less important than their universality; indeed the very adaptability of the symbolism is what allows tales to remain popular over time. By dramatizing these psychological progressions, the fairy tale helps its audience to
(65) process the ill-understood unconscious psychological forces that are a part of human life. Can it be any wonder that such powerful avenues to the cosmic unconscious can be shown to have remained popular across the eons?

Passage 2

(70) The contention that folklore represents a cosmic tale that encapsulates cross-cultural human universalities in narrative form is naïve in the extreme. The notion that folk tales somehow embody a symbolically encoded map of human
(75) consciousness suffers from a fundamental flaw: it assumes that each tale has a more-or-less consistent form. In fact, the forms of most folk tales that we have today recorded in collections and in the popular media represent nothing more than isolated
(80) snapshots of narratives that have countless forms, many of which are so different as to drastically change the interpretations that some critics want to say are universal.

Consider, for example, the story of *Little Red
(85) Riding Hood.* Some psychological interpretations might conjecture, for example, that this is a tale about obedience and parental authority. Straying

GO ON TO THE NEXT PAGE

from the path in the forest, in this context, might
represent rebelling against that authority, and the
(90) wolf then symbolizes the dangerous unconscious
forces from which parents seek to protect Little Red.
The red color of the riding hood might be seen as
representing the subdued emotions of anger and
hostility. Being consumed by the wolf signifies a
(95) period of isolation and transformation. Finally, the
rescuing huntsman at the end of the story then
symbolizes the return of parental authority to deliver
the innocent child from being metaphorically
consumed by ill-understood emotional states.

(100)   It is an apparently consistent analogy, and one
that is difficult to dispute, until one investigates the
circumstances of the composition and recording of
the version of *Little Red Riding Hood* that we have
today. Earlier editions of the story simply don't have
(105) many of the components that critics would like to
present as so-called "universal symbols." For
example, in the vast majority of the older and
simpler versions of this tale, the story ends after the
wolf eats the girl. So there can be no theme of
(110) parental rescue because, in all but a few of the
examples of this tale, there is no rescue and no kind
huntsman. In some versions the girl even saves
herself, completely contradicting the assumption that
it is a story about rescue. Story elements such as
(115) the path, the hunter, and the happy ending, which
are seen as essential symbolic components of our
interpretation above, were introduced to this ancient
tale by the Brothers Grimm in the 19th century.
Even the introduction of the "symbolic" red garment
(120) dates only from the seventeenth century, when it
was put into the story by Charles Perrault.
    In fact, every fairy tale known to the study of
folklore has so many different versions that there are
encyclopedic reference books to catalog the variations
(125) and the differences between them. A creature that is
an elf in one country and era might
be a troll in another. A magic object represented as a
hat in one version of a tale might be a cloak in ten
other tellings. If folk tales actually represent
(130) universal human truths in symbolic form, the
symbols in them would have to reflect universal
consistency across time. Any attempt to pinpoint a
consistent symbolic meaning or underlying scheme
in such a field of moving, blending, and ever-
(135) changing targets is doomed to fail before it even
begins. Instead, we should embrace all such
variations on a theme, searching for insights into the
cultural conditions which prompt such divergence.

13 In discussing "fairy tales" in lines 17–21, the
author of Passage 1 suggests that

(A) which stories endure and which are forgotten has
nothing to do with the quality of the story
(B) stories written by a single author and not
endlessly retold and edited may well not have
the lasting appeal of fairy tales
(C) many folk tales that spoke deeply to their
audiences have been lost and forgotten over
the ages
(D) folk tales undergo the same degree of selection
and editing as other kinds of literature
(E) the original author of *Snow White* was very
careful with the selection and editing of the
tale

14 According to the author of Passage 1, the
experience of the "motifs" mentioned in line 56 is
shared by "all humans" because

(A) they appear in the tale *Snow White*
(B) they reflect the views of critics
(C) they signify the transition from childhood to
adult identity
(D) they embody unconscious forces that must be
cared for and nurtured
(E) they represent experiences that all humans have
undergone

15 The word "avenues" in line 67 most nearly means

(A) boulevards
(B) beginnings
(C) homecomings
(D) approaches
(E) forces

16 The statement that "there can be no theme of
parental rescue...huntsman" in Passage 2 (lines
109–112) suggests that fairy tales

(A) should make a greater effort to capture
universal human themes
(B) are generally not interested in historical
accuracy
(C) cannot be said to have a single authoritative
form
(D) are usually not concerned with themes of
rescue
(E) were not solidified into final form until the
19th century

GO ON TO THE NEXT PAGE

17 The author of Passage 2 primarily takes issue with critics who extract simple symbolic interpretations from fairy tales because of what he sees as their

(A) disregard for the rigorous principles of modern psychology
(B) naïve view of the complexity of human nature
(C) failure to make proper use of reference materials pertaining to folklore methodology
(D) willingness to assume that minor details of a specific version of a folk tale are universal
(E) unsuccessful attempts to correctly interpret the symbolism of older versions of fairy tales

18 Which of the following conclusions is suggested by the final sentence of Passage 2?

(A) The variations among versions of fairy tales can tell us something about the cultures in which these versions developed.
(B) Folklore methodologists should seek out oral versions of folk tales themselves instead of getting them from books.
(C) The earliest recorded versions of folk tales are more accurate and authoritative than later versions.
(D) Only fairy tales written in modern times can be accurately interpreted.
(E) Fairy tales with many versions are more likely to survive many generations than are those that lack significant variations.

19 The authors of both passages state that fairy tales are

(A) intuitively meaningful
(B) critically misunderstood
(C) historically changeable
(D) symbolically rich
(E) essentially practical

20 With which of the following statements about fairy tales would the authors of both passages most likely agree?

(A) The popularity of fairy tales is due to their deeper meanings.
(B) Fairy tales speak to all humans in the language of universal psychological symbols.
(C) Fairy tales have resulted from a compositional process very different from that of modern literature written by a single author.
(D) The study of folklore is undergoing extensive changes because of new information about different versions of particular tales.
(E) The unique origins of fairy tales makes it possible to create symbolic schemes that link the events depicted in fairy tales with eternal human truths.

21

The author of Passage 1 would probably respond to the statement in lines 77–84 of Passage 2 with the argument that

(A) many modern folk tales originated relatively recently and haven't been subjected to centuries of editing
(B) the changes in the symbolism of more-recent revisions of folk tales are less important psychologically than the broad themes
(C) there is no evidence that the symbolism of folk tales is related to psychological forces
(D) *Snow White* is a poor example to use as evidence because it has changed so much over time
(E) better techniques and methodologies have recently allowed even less-popular tales to survive across time

GO ON TO THE NEXT PAGE

22 Which of the following best describes the primary disagreement that the author of Passage 2 would most likely raise against the statement in Passage 1 (lines 32–37) that "Small supernatural spirits...transformation"?

(A) The psychologist who made this interpretation did not use the encyclopedic catalogs of different versions of this tale.

(B) The popularity of this tale is no indication of its value in expressing a psychological truth.

(C) This version of the tale is not necessarily the most accurate, because it is recent and may have deviated too much from the true version over time.

(D) Small supernatural spirits could represent many things other than unconscious forces.

(E) The specific details in different versions of this folk tale show too much variation to make any consistent interpretations based on this particular version.

23 The author of Passage 1 would most likely reply to the statement in lines 119–121 by

(A) arguing that specific symbols still stem from the underlying psychological structure of the tale

(B) pointing out that the seventeenth and nineteenth centuries were still quite a while ago

(C) agreeing that the red garment probably does not represent aggressive emotions

(D) postulating that the works of Perrault and the Grimms are not valid examples of folklore

(E) stipulating that this particular tale has too many variants to be faithfully interpreted

24 Which symbolic interpretation made by the author of Passage 1 most closely mirrors the interpretation made by the author of Passage 2 in lines 94–95 ("Being consumed...transformation")?

(A) Snow White represents the queen's rival in the realm of youth and beauty.

(B) Being lost in the forest symbolizes a period of separation and change.

(C) Small supernatural homunculi signify unconscious forces.

(D) The prince delivers Snow White from her mock death with a kiss.

(E) The huntsman epitomizes parental authority.

Time— 2 Minutes
1 Questions

Directions: For this section, solve each problem and decide which is the best of the choices given. Fill in the corresponding oval on the answer sheet. You may use any available space for scratchwork.

1. Calculator use is permitted.

2. All numbers used are real numbers.

3. Figures are provided for some problems. All figures are drawn to scale and lie in a plane UNLESS otherwise indicated.

4. Unless otherwise specified, the domain of any function f is assumed to be the set of all real numbers x for which $f(x)$ is a real number.

   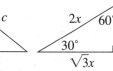

$A = \dfrac{1}{2}bh$ $c^2 = a^2 + b^2$ Special Right Triangles $A = \pi r^2$ $V = \pi r^2 h$ $A = lw$ $V = lwh$

$C = 2\pi r$

The sum of the measures in degrees of the angles of a triangle is 180.
The number of degrees of arc in a circle is 360.
A straight angle has a degree measure of 180.

---

1 If $4p^2 = 36$ and $36 > 5q$, which of the following must be true?

(A) $p^2 > 5q$
(B) $p^2 = 5q$
(C) $4p^2 > 5q$
(D) $4p^2 = 5q$
(E) $4p^2 < 5q$

2 The sum of 7 numbers is greater than 140 and less than 210. Which of the following could be the average (arithmetic mean) of the numbers?

(A) 5
(B) 12
(C) 17
(D) 20
(E) 28

GO ON TO THE NEXT PAGE

3 If $7d < 4r$ and $4r < 8p$, which of the following must be true?

(A) $7d < 8p$
(B) $8p < 7d$
(C) $p < d$
(D) $r = 2p$
(E) $2r = p$

5 If the average (arithmetic mean) of 8 numbers is greater than 10 and less than 12, which of the following could be the sum of the 8 numbers?

(A) 70
(B) 80
(C) 90
(D) 100
(E) 110

Location	Number of Boxes	Number of Toys in Each Box
Basement	4	10
Garage	2	6
Attic	5	7

4 The chart above shows the location of all the toys stored at Joe's house. According to the chart, what is the total number of toys at Joe's house?

(A) 23
(B) 40
(C) 57
(D) 87
(E) 123

6 A certain necklace is made up of beads of the following colors: red, blue, orange, indigo, clear, and silver. The necklace contains 120 beads. According to the pie chart above, how many beads of the necklace are NOT blue?

(A) 20
(B) 24
(C) 92
(D) 96
(E) 100

GO ON TO THE NEXT PAGE

7 The hour hand of a watch rotates 30 degrees every hour. How many complete rotations does the hour hand make in 6 days?

(A) 18
(B) 12
(C) 10
(D) 8
(E) 6

9 Which of the following expressions can be negative?

(A) $\dfrac{x^2}{2}$

(B) $\dfrac{3}{1 + x^2}$

(C) $4x^3$

(D) $(x^3)^2$

(E) $x(x^3 + x^5)$

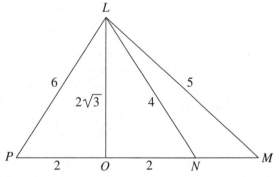

Note: Figure not drawn to scale.

8 Which of the following is a triangle that has angles with degree measures of 30, 60, and 90 ?

(A) $\triangle LMN$
(B) $\triangle LMP$
(C) $\triangle LOP$
(D) $\triangle LMO$
(E) $\triangle LNO$

10 Earth makes one complete rotation about its axis every 24 hours. Assuming it rotates at a constant rate, through how many degrees would Goannaville, Australia rotate from 1:00 P.M. on January 2 to 4:00 P.M. on January 3 ?

(A) 202°
(B) 250°
(C) 350°
(D) 363°
(E) 405°

GO ON TO THE NEXT PAGE

11 If S is the set of all numbers between -3.5 and 3.5, inclusive, T is the set of all prime numbers, and U is the set of all positive integers, then the intersection of S, T, and U contains how many elements?

(A) 0
(B) 1
(C) 2
(D) 3
(E) More than 3

12 Which of the following expressions must be positive for all values of a and b ?

(A) $a + b$
(B) $a^2 - b^2 + 10$
(C) $a^2 + b^2 + 1$
(D) $a^3 + b^3 + 16$
(E) $a^4 + b^2 + a^2$

13 Which of the following expressions is equal to 3^8 when $y = 3^5$?

(A) $\dfrac{y}{3}$

(B) $9y^2$

(C) $\dfrac{y^2}{3}$

(D) $\dfrac{y^2}{9}$

(E) $\dfrac{y^3}{27}$

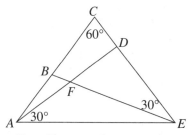

Note: Figure not drawn to scale.

14 In triangle ACE above, $\overline{AD}$ and $\overline{BE}$ are line segments, $\overline{AD}$ is perpendicular to $\overline{CE}$, and $\overline{AD}$ bisects $\angle BAE$. Which of the following is NOT a right triangle?

(A) ABF
(B) ACD
(C) ADE
(D) AFE
(E) BCE

GO ON TO THE NEXT PAGE

15 The initial number of elements in a certain set is p, where $p > 0$. If the number of elements in the set doubles every hour, which of the following represents the total number of elements in the set after exactly 24 hours?

(A) $24p$
(B) $48p$
(C) $2p^{24}$
(D) $(2p)^{24}$
(E) $(2^{24})p$

16 The absolute value of a certain integer is greater than 3 and less than 6. Which of the following could NOT be 2 less than the integer?

(A) -7
(B) -6
(C) 2
(D) 3
(E) 4

IF YOU FINISH BEFORE TIME IS CALLED, YOU MAY CHECK YOUR WORK ON THIS SECTION ONLY. DO NOT TURN TO ANY OTHER SECTION IN THE TEST.

- 50 -

NO TEST MATERIAL ON THIS PAGE

Time—20 Minutes
19 Questions

Directions: For each question in this section, select the best answer from among the choices given and fill in the corresponding oval on the answer sheet.

Each sentence below has one or two blanks, each blank indicating that something has been omitted. Beneath the sentence are five words or sets of words labeled A through E. Choose the word or set of words that, when inserted in the sentence, <u>best</u> fits the meaning of the sentence as a whole.

EXAMPLE:

Today's small, portable computers contrast markedly with the earliest electronic computers, which were ------- .

(A) effective   (B) invented
  (C) useful   (D) destructive
    (E) enormous

ANSWER:
Ⓐ Ⓑ Ⓒ Ⓓ ●

---

1 The editorial highlighted both sides of the ------- ; despite its contentiousness in public discussions, the debate was fairly and objectively outlined in the newspaper.

(A) accord   (B) calamity
  (C) disagreement   (D) disposition
    (E) consensus

2 Although Jane Austen's novels are most often ------- for their eloquence and imagery, they are also highly esteemed for their subtle, yet shrewd ------- the economic and social milieu of the landed gentry of nineteenth century England.

(A) admired . . observations on
(B) denigrated . . metaphors about
(C) respected . . diversity of
(D) inclined . . interpretation of
(E) maligned . . simplicity of

3 From his early, more ------- paintings to his final, most ------- masterworks, the progression of Turner's painting style mirrored the evolution away from Romantic realism and toward increasing degrees of abstraction.

(A) obscure . . explicit
(B) misunderstood . . understated
(C) enthralling . . retrospective
(D) tame . . romantic
(E) traditional . . pioneering

4 Sylvester signed his name with a characteristic ------- that made his signature look more like art than writing.

(A) wince   (B) glimpse
  (C) flourish   (D) nod
    (E) understatement

5 To dissect vital communications, the -------, a specialist in the technology of deciphering messages, typically employs a host of complex mathematical formulas.

(A) entomologist   (B) connoisseur
  (C) cryptologist   (D) statistician
    (E) pathologist

6 Most of the guests found the hotel to be -------, listing the ------- of the amenities as one of the things they disliked the most.

(A) deficient . . paucity
(B) venerable . . expediency
(C) nascent . . petulance
(D) congenial . . convenience
(E) quaint . . antiquity

GO ON TO THE NEXT PAGE

- 52 -

The passage below is followed by questions based on its content. Answer the questions on the basis of what is <u>stated</u> or <u>implied</u> in the passage and in any introductory material that may be provided.

Questions 7–19 are based on the following passage.

This passage is a work of fiction based on the real experiences of Wilma Mankiller, the first female Principal Chief of the Cherokee Nation.

During an interview for a literary magazine, I was asked why my autobiography, titled *Mankiller, A Chief and Her People*, contained so much history of
Line the Cherokee, history that occurred almost five
(5) centuries before I was born. That answer is a very simple one for me to give, but may be difficult to understand. The person that I am has been defined by my people and their experiences, whether it was a week ago or centuries ago. When I ran for Deputy
(10) Chief in 1985, I ran as a Cherokee, not as a Cherokee woman. I was shocked by how much my gender played a role in the election, because it never once entered my mind when I made the decision to run. My decision to run for office was founded on the desire to
(15) help my people recognize their own strength and realize they had the power to rebuild their lives and their communities because they had been able to accomplish these goals in the past.

I am proud to be a Cherokee and I am proud of my
(20) people, both past and present. Everything that has happened in our past has affected our present and will affect our future. But one theme remains constant: survival. Our history has been full of obstacles and hardships, yet we persevere. In the late 1830s, the
(25) Cherokee were forced to relocate from their homelands throughout the Southeast to Indian Territory in what later became Oklahoma. We were stripped of our land, our homes, and our possessions and then forced to walk to the new territory. Many
(30) others may have simply succumbed to the hardships and ceased to exist. Instead, we rebuilt our tribe and our community with a new constitution, a new tribal government including our own judicial system, businesses, schools for both girls and boys, and even
(35) newspapers printed in both Cherokee and English. This renewal occurred within seven years of our arrival in Indian Territory. These accomplishments alone show the limitless tenacity of the Cherokee people.

(40) It becomes even more clear when the story continues and the history of the early 1900s includes the destruction of everything we had rebuilt in the previous fifty years. Our schools and our courts were closed down. Our sovereignty was stripped away.
(45) From 1906 to 1971 we could not even elect our own tribal leaders. But the Cherokees did what we had always done; we survived. This second rebirth took

much longer than the first, but we found the strength to do what had been done before.

(50) You may wonder why I use "we" when I speak of Cherokee history. Again, I return to the idea that as a Cherokee, my tribe's history has defined me, just as it has defined all Cherokee. In fact, some of my personal experiences parallel the experiences of my
(55) ancestors. In 1956, my parents, siblings, and I were moved to California as part of the BIA* relocation program. We were moved away from our family, our tribe, and our community in an effort to improve our lives. Unlike the forced removal of the 1830s,
(60) the program was voluntary, but it had the same effect on the tribe as a whole. It divided us and showed us that the federal government believed we could not improve our lives without aid. But just as my ancestors survived the hardships, so did my
(65) family. We found a new community at the San Francisco Indian Center. We found a place where we belonged and where we could find strength in sharing experiences with other Native Americans.

In 1977, I began working for the Cherokee
(70) Nation as an economic stimulus coordinator. I was charged with the task of getting university training in environmental science and health for as many Cherokee students as possible so that they could return to their communities and provide service for
(75) their people. All around me, I saw a rebuilt Cherokee government working hard to restore the tribe to its earlier glory. One project in particular was a shining example of how the Cherokee are capable of finding and implementing our own
(80) solutions—the Bell Project. Bell was a small rural community where violence was a method of solving problems, where indoor plumbing was a luxury, and where many houses were on the brink of falling down. We entered the community and asked
(85) them what needed to be done and what their dreams for the future included. We asked them to define the problems, then worked with them to decide how they could rebuild their community. As a community, they decided to build a water
(90) system, rehabilitate twenty of their existing houses, and build twenty-five new ones. They would provide volunteer labor while we would provide the materials and technical resources by soliciting financial support for the project.

* Bureau of Indian Affairs

GO ON TO THE NEXT PAGE ➡

(95)   Many people doubted the project would succeed. No one believed the members of the community would work, especially as unpaid volunteers. But I had to believe that, as Cherokee we could follow the paths of our
(100)   ancestors and work to rebuild ourselves. We gave the people of Bell an opportunity to take charge of their own lives and their own future and they accepted it with open arms. I still believe the Bell Project was my most significant achievement for
(105)   the Cherokee Nation. I proved to our tribe that we are all capable of improving our lives and our communities ourselves. It is a very powerful belief; it allows all Cherokees to dream what others would deem impossible and to know that it is very
(110)   possible because we have done it in the past.

7 In lines 1–18, the author achieves each of the following goals EXCEPT

(A) identifying the author's ethnicity
(B) indicating the author's motivation for seeking election as Deputy Chief in 1985
(C) suggesting the role the author's gender played in the 1985 election
(D) describing the influences on the author's self-identity
(E) offering a detailed description of the author's autobiography

8 The author's experience of running for the office of Deputy Chief is significant to her mainly because it

(A) motivated the author to write and publish her autobiography
(B) gave her the chance to prove that a woman could be as effective as a man in the office of Deputy Chief
(C) allowed her to work toward helping Cherokees improve their own lives
(D) gave her the opportunity to work directly on improving the troubled relationship between the U.S. Government and the Cherokee Nation
(E) permitted her to serve as a symbol of the nobility of Cherokee history and culture

9 The list of accomplishments that the Cherokee people achieved after being moved to Oklahoma (lines 31–37) is significant in the passage for which of the following reasons?

I.   It demonstrates that the Cherokee had a sophisticated societal structure.

II. It serves as evidence that the Cherokee were resilient.

III. It shows how the Cherokee were able to benefit from government assistance.

(A) I only
(B) II only
(C) III only
(D) I and II only
(E) I, II, and III

10 The anecdotes in lines 24–31 and lines 55–63 are closely related because

(A) the author cities them as examples of the perseverance of the Cherokee people
(B) the stories are both instances of hardships defeating the Cherokee people
(C) they express the author's horror at the actions of the federal government
(D) they are both examples of forced relocations of native people
(E) they convey the most important influences on the author's identity

11 When the author states that "my tribe's history has defined me, just as it has defined all Cherokee" (lines 52–53), she suggests which of the following about the Cherokee?

(A) They are constantly being moved around to different geographic areas.
(B) They are frequently in dispute with the U.S. government.
(C) The hardships that they have suffered in the past have profoundly affected their lives in the present.
(D) They have the persistence and determination to rebuild their own communities.
(E) Their destiny is to return to their former glory.

GO ON TO THE NEXT PAGE

12 Which of the following best describes the author's attitude toward the BIA relocation program described in lines 55–63?

(A) diffident
(B) dismayed
(C) inspired
(D) agreeable
(E) mystified

13 The author mentions the San Francisco Indian Center (lines 65–66) in order to

(A) show where her family found a community after their relocation to California
(B) illustrate the size of the San Francisco Native American community
(C) describe how the government helped the author's family after their relocation
(D) argue against protecting the Native American community from majority influences
(E) emphasize the need for community centers outside of the Indian tribal lands

14 In line 71, "charged" most nearly means

(A) accused
(B) billed
(C) assigned
(D) electrified
(E) attacked

15 The author refers to the "Cherokee students" in line 73 primarily as examples of Cherokees who

(A) would eventually help coordinate work on the Bell Project
(B) could help spread awareness of Cherokee culture to non-Cherokee people
(C) would contribute to the Cherokee government's economic stimulus efforts
(D) could eventually play a role in the Cherokee tradition of rebuilding the tribe from within
(E) might eventually become involved in the rebuilding of the Cherokee government

16 The Bell Project, lines 80–94, is cited as evidence that the Cherokee should be

(A) aided in solving the problems in their communities
(B) prevented from taking charge of their community projects
(C) provided with materials and resources to improve their communities themselves
(D) held up as examples of outstanding Native Americans
(E) persuaded to build a community water system wherever one is needed

17 In paragraph 6, the author draws a distinction between

(A) volunteering and being forced to do something
(B) helping others and helping yourself
(C) changing your own life and changing the lives of others
(D) following your ancestors and branching out on your own
(E) helping yourself and accepting outside help

18 Which of the following claims is most strongly supported by the author's argument?

(A) More women should run in government elections.
(B) Small-scale volunteer projects work best.
(C) Education is vital to community rebuilding efforts.
(D) Maintaining traditional cultural values is important.
(E) Cherokees should look to their history for inspiration.

19 The primary purpose of the passage is to

(A) determine the role of history in personal identity
(B) persuade readers to cherish their cultural and historical heritage
(C) describe the virtues of the Cherokee people
(D) explain the motivation for including ancestral history in an autobiography
(E) argue against federal assistance for Native Americans

Directions: For each question in this section, select the best answer from among the choices given and fill in the corresponding oval on the answer sheet.

The following sentences test correctness and effectiveness of expression. Part of each sentence or the entire sentence is underlined; beneath each sentence are five ways of phrasing the underlined material. Choice A repeats the original phrasing; the other four choices are different. If you think the original phrasing produces a better sentence than any of the alternatives, select choice A; if not, select one of the other choices.

In making your selection, follow the requirements of standard written English; that is, pay attention to grammar, choice of words, sentence construction, and punctuation. Your selection should result in the most effective sentence—clear and precise—without awkwardness or ambiguity.

EXAMPLE:

Every apple in the baskets <u>are ripe and labeled according to the date it was picked</u>.

(A) are ripe and labeled according to the date it was picked
(B) is ripe and labeled according to the date it was picked
(C) are ripe and labeled according to the date they were picked
(D) is ripe and labeled according to the date they were picked
(E) are ripe and labeled as to the date it was picked

ANSWER:
Ⓐ ● Ⓒ Ⓓ Ⓔ

1 Walt Whitman wrote <u>poems and they express</u> the wonder of both the natural world and the human race.

(A) poems and they express
(B) poems, being the expressions of
(C) poems, they express
(D) poems that express
(E) poems, and expressing in them

2 The press secretary claimed that, although the protesters in the opposing party have made valuable points, <u>the failure is in their not understanding</u> the positive effects of the new policy.

(A) the failure is in their not understanding
(B) the failure they have is in their not understanding
(C) they failed not to understand
(D) they have failed to understand
(E) failing in their understanding of

3 The air pollution levels in California could be reduced by implementing better public-transit systems, encouraging carpools, <u>and inventing new ways</u> to control exhaust fumes from automobiles.

(A) and inventing new ways
(B) and if they invent new ways
(C) also by inventing new ways
(D) and new ways being invented
(E) and if there were new ways

4 <u>Engineered for speed, professional cyclists use special, lighter bikes without brakes and gears for time trials.</u>

(A) Engineered for speed, professional cyclists use special, lighter bikes without brakes and gears for time trials.
(B) Engineered as speedy, professional cyclists use special bikes that are lighter without brakes and gears for time trials.
(C) Engineered for speed, lighter bikes without brakes and gears are used by professional cyclists for time trials.
(D) As engineered for speed, special, lighter bikes, being without brakes and gears are what professional cyclists use for time trials.
(E) Special, lighter bikes engineered without brakes and gears for speed that are used by professional cyclists for time trials.

GO ON TO THE NEXT PAGE

5 Several of Cynthia Murphy's <u>photographs are inspired by the surrealism of rock concerts, taken from</u> dramatic and dizzying low angles.

(A) photographs are inspired by the surrealism of rock concerts, taken from
(B) photographs have their inspiration from the surrealism of rock concerts with
(C) photographs, inspired by the surrealism of rock concerts, are taken from
(D) photographs, which are inspired by the surrealism of rock concerts and which are taken from
(E) photographs, being inspired by the surrealism of rock concerts, taken from

6 <u>The neighborhood, once nearly deserted, is</u> now a bustling, productive community.

(A) The neighborhood, once nearly deserted, is
(B) The neighborhood was once nearly deserted, it is
(C) The neighborhood that once having been nearly deserted is
(D) The neighborhood, because it was once nearly deserted, is
(E) The neighborhood was once nearly deserted, and it is

7 Ernest Hemingway absorbed the culture and events in Paris, where he lived for many years, and <u>these are his observations that are included</u> in his most autobiographical writing.

(A) these are his observations that are included
(B) the inclusion of these, his observations is
(C) his observations having been included
(D) his inclusion of these observations
(E) included his observations

8 Undoubtedly the best rider on our dressage team is Mariah, <u>she has won at least one ribbon in</u> every competition she has ever entered.

(A) she has won at least one ribbon in
(B) having been the winner of at least one ribbon in
(C) which has won at least one ribbon in
(D) who has won at least one ribbon in
(E) they awarded her at least one ribbon in

9 <u>New growth that was being thwarted by the poor quality of the soil, but now they are sprouting several new vines.</u>

(A) New growth that was being thwarted by the poor quality of the soil, but now they are sprouting several new vines.
(B) The poor quality of the soil had thwarted new growth, but the plants are now sprouting several new vines.
(C) New growth was thwarted by the poor quality of the soil, and so now they are sprouting several new vines.
(D) Though the poor quality of the soil had thwarted new growth, the plant is now sprouting several new vines.
(E) Now sprouting several new vines, the plant's poor soil had thwarted new growth.

10 For many a pampered housecat, <u>being cute is more important</u> than being a good hunter.

(A) being cute is more important
(B) having cuteness is more important
(C) there is more importance in cuteness
(D) cuteness has more importance
(E) to be cute is more important

11 The issue we debated <u>which was whether or not to require a minimum lot size for any house built</u> after this year.

(A) which was whether or not to require a minimum lot size for any house built
(B) was whether or not to require a minimum lot size for any house they build
(C) was whether or not to require a minimum lot size for any house built
(D) was the requirement of whether or not a minimum lot size was needed for any house
(E) whether or not to require a minimum lot size for any house built

GO ON TO THE NEXT PAGE

12 You may choose to print your report <u>using the default layout, you may choose to</u> customize your report by clicking on the "custom" icon.

(A) using the default layout, you may choose to
(B) using the default layout, however, you may choose to
(C) using the default layout, yet you may also choose to
(D) using the default layout; you may also
(E) using the default layout; you may have chosen to

13 <u>One of the symptoms of an allergy is when</u> you develop hives on your face or torso.

(A) One of the symptoms of an allergy is when
(B) One of the symptoms of an allergy is that
(C) Symptoms of an allergy include when
(D) One of the symptoms of an allergy includes that
(E) Symptoms of an allergy including that

14 <u>In addition to them we voted on at our last meeting, several issues</u> remain to be decided.

(A) In addition to them we voted on at our last meeting, several issues
(B) As well as them we voted on at our last meeting, several issues
(C) Additional to them we voted on at our last meeting, several issues
(D) In addition to those we voted on at our last meeting, several issues
(E) In addition to them which we voted on at our last meeting, several issues

IF YOU FINISH BEFORE TIME IS CALLED, YOU MAY CHECK YOUR WORK ON THIS SECTION ONLY. DO NOT TURN TO ANY OTHER SECTION IN THE TEST.

SCORING YOUR TEST

For each section (Critical Reading, Math, and Writing) on the SAT, your score will range from 200–800. Your performance on the tests in this book is a good indicator of your abilities and skills.

The scoring information contained here is intended to give an approximate idea of what your performance will be on Test Day. The formulas for calculating your raw score that follow in this book are the same as those the College Board will use to score your SAT.

The raw-to-scaled score conversion tables, however, may differ from the one used to score the SAT that you take. The College Board creates unique raw-to-scaled score conversions for every administration of the SAT. Therefore, practice tests can only approximate the conversion tables that will be used on the real SAT that you take. Nevertheless, the tables in this book are close to the tables that will be used on your test, and will provide you with a good sense of what your score might be at this stage in your preparation.

Step 1: Score Your Essay

First, score your essay, which accounts for approximately 25% of your Writing scaled score; your score on the Multiple Choice questions will account for the remaining 75% or so. For the tests in this book, assign your essay a score of 1–6, which, along with your Multiple Choice score, you will use to arrive at your 200–800 scaled score.

The College Board's website (*www.collegeboard.com*) contains information about the essay and how it is scored.

The following criteria are a good guide:

6 Outstanding—Though it may have a few small errors, the essay is well organized and fully developed with supporting examples. It displays consistent language facility, varied sentence structure, and varied vocabulary.

5 Solid—Though it has occasional errors or lapses in quality, the essay is generally organized and well developed with appropriate examples. It displays language facility, syntactic variety, and varied vocabulary.

4 Adequate—Though it has some flaws, the essay is organized and adequately developed and has some examples. It displays adequate but inconsistent language facility.

3 Limited—The essay does not adequately fulfill the writing assignment and has many flaws. It has inadequate organization and development, along with many errors in grammar or diction (or both). In general, the essay lacks variety.

2 Flawed—The essay demonstrates incompetence with one or more weaknesses. Ideas are vague and thinly developed. It contains frequent errors in grammar and diction and almost no variety.

1 Deficient—The essay demonstrates incompetence with serious flaws. It has no organization, no development, and severe grammar and diction errors. The essay is so seriously flawed that its basic meaning is obscured.

0 Off-Topic—The essay does not follow the assignment.

Step 2: Compute Your Raw Score

Check your answers to the multiple-choice questions against the answer key on the next two pages. Count up the number of answers you got right and the number you got wrong for each section. Do not score Section 5, the Experimental Section. Remember, do not count questions left blank as wrong. Round up to the nearest whole number. Now, plug them in below.

Note: Grid-in questions do not have a wrong-answer penalty, so do not deduct anything for wrong answers.

Critical Reading

	Number Right	Number Wrong	Raw Score
Section 3:	☐	− (.25 × ☐)	= ☐
Section 7:	☐	− (.25 × ☐)	= ☐
Section 9:	☐	− (.25 × ☐)	= ☐
Critical Reading Raw Score		=	☐ (rounded up)

Writing

	Number Right	Number Wrong	Raw Score
Section 6:	☐	− (.25 × ☐)	= ☐
Section 10:	☐	− (.25 × ☐)	= ☐
Writing Multiple-Choice Raw Score		=	☐ (rounded up)

Math

	Number Right	Number Wrong	Raw Score
Section 2:	☐	− (.25 × ☐)	= ☐
Section 4: (QUESTIONS 1–8)	☐	− (.25 × ☐)	= ☐
Section 4: (QUESTIONS 9–18)	☐	− (no wrong answer penalty)	= ☐
Section 8:	☐	− (.25 × ☐)	= ☐
Math Raw Score		=	☐ (rounded up)

PRACTICE TEST 1 ANSWER KEY

CRITICAL READING

Section 3		Section 7		Section 9	
Multiple-Choice Questions		**Multiple-Choice Questions**		**Multiple-Choice Questions**	
	Correct Answer		Correct Answer		Correct Answer
1.	A	1.	C	1.	C
2.	D	2.	A	2.	A
3.	E	3.	E	3.	E
4.	A	4.	C	4.	C
5.	A	5.	B	5.	C
6.	A	6.	C	6.	A
7.	B	7.	B	7.	E
8.	D	8.	B	8.	C
9.	D	9.	D	9.	D
10.	E	10.	A	10.	A
11.	E	11.	B	11.	C
12.	E	12.	D	12.	B
13.	C	13.	B	13.	A
14.	B	14.	E	14.	C
15.	D	15.	D	15.	D
16.	A	16.	C	16.	C
17.	E	17.	D	17.	E
18.	C	18.	A	18.	E
19.	B	19.	C	19.	D
20.	A	20.	C		
21.	E	21.	B		
22.	A	22.	E		
23.	E	23.	A		
24.	D	24.	B		

no. correct	no. correct	no. correct
no. incorrect	no. incorrect	no. incorrect

MATH

Section 2		Section 4		Section 8	
Multiple-Choice Questions		**Multiple-Choice Questions**		**Multiple-Choice Questions**	
	Correct Answer		Correct Answer		Correct Answer
1.	B	1.	C	1.	C
2.	D	2.	D	2.	E
3.	C	3.	C	3.	A
4.	B	4.	C	4.	D
5.	B	5.	E	5.	C
6.	D	6.	D	6.	D
7.	A	7.	B	7.	B
8.	D	8.	C	8.	E
9.	A			9.	C
10.	B			10.	E
11.	E			11.	C
12.	A			12.	C
13.	A			13.	D
14.	E			14.	D
15.	C			15.	E
16.	B			16.	E
17.	E				
18.	E				
19.	C				
20.	D				

no. correct	no. correct	no. correct
no. incorrect	no. incorrect	no. incorrect

Section 4

Student-Produced Response Questions

	Correct Answer
9.	18
10.	23
11.	12
12.	275, 330, or 385
13.	600
14.	24
15.	1
16.	135
17.	5
18.	70

no. correct

	WRITING	
	Section 6	**Section 10**
Essay	**Multiple-Choice Questions**	**Multiple-Choice Questions**
	Correct Answer	Correct Answer
	1. D	1. D
	2. B	2. D
	3. E	3. A
Essay Score*	4. E	4. C
(1–6)	5. C	5. C
	6. D	6. A
	7. B	7. E
	8. D	8. D
	9. D	9. D
	10. B	10. A
	11. D	11. C
	12. C	12. D
	13. E	13. B
	14. D	14. D
	15. B	
	16. B	
	17. D	
	18. E	
	19. A	
	20. B	
	21. C	
	22. D	
	23. E	
	24. C	
	25. A	
	26. D	
	27. A	
	28. C	
	29. D	
	30. B	
	31. D	
	32. B	
	33. D	
	34. B	
	35. E	
	no. correct	no. correct
	no. incorrect	no. incorrect

*To score your essay, see Step 1 on the previous pages. On this Practice Test, your essay score will range from 1 to 6. (Keep in mind that on the actual SAT, your essay will be read by two readers and you will receive a score of 1 to 12 on your score report.)

Step 3: Find Your Scaled Score

To determine your Critical Reading and Math scaled scores, find the raw scores you calculated for these two sections in Step 2 on Tables 1 and 2 on the following page. Next, find the scaled score associated with your raw scores and enter them in the appropriate box in the Scaled Scores table on this page.

To determine your Writing scaled score, use Table 3. First, find the Writing Multiple-Choice raw score you calculated in Step 2 and the essay raw score (1–6) you assigned yourself. Next, locate your Writing Multiple-Choice raw score on the left dimension of Table 3. Then find your essay score along the top. The box associated with this row and column contains your Writing scaled score. Enter it in the appropriate box in the Scaled Scores table below.

The sum of these three scores is your Total Scaled Score.

Scaled Scores	
Critical Reading	
Math	
Writing	
Total	

TABLE 1
Critical Reading Conversion Table

Raw Score	Scaled Score	Raw Score	Scaled Score
67	800	30	500
66	790	29	500
65	770	28	490
64	760	27	480
63	750	26	480
62	740	25	470
61	720	24	470
60	710	23	460
59	700	22	450
58	690	21	450
57	680	20	440
56	670	19	430
55	670	18	430
54	660	17	420
53	650	16	410
52	640	15	410
51	640	14	400
50	630	13	390
49	620	12	380
48	610	11	380
47	610	10	370
46	600	9	360
45	590	8	350
44	590	7	340
43	580	6	330
42	580	5	320
41	570	4	310
40	560	3	300
39	560	2	280
38	550	1	270
37	540	0	250
36	540	−1	250
35	530	−2	240
34	530	−3	230
33	520	−4	220
32	510	−5	210
31	510	−6 and below	200

TABLE 2
Math Conversion Table

Raw Score	Scaled Score	Raw Score	Scaled Score
54	800	24	490
53	780	23	490
52	760	22	480
51	740	21	470
50	730	20	460
49	710	19	460
48	700	18	450
47	690	17	440
46	670	16	430
45	660	15	430
44	650	14	420
43	650	13	410
42	640	12	400
41	630	11	390
40	620	10	380
39	610	9	380
38	600	8	370
37	590	7	360
36	590	6	340
35	580	5	330
34	570	4	320
33	560	3	310
32	560	2	290
31	550	1	280
30	540	0	260
29	530	−1	250
28	520	−2	240
27	520	−3	230
26	510	−4	220
25	500	−5	210
		−6 and below	200

TABLE 3
SAT Score Conversion Table for Writing Composite

		Essay Raw Score						
		0	1	2	3	4	5	6
Writing Multiple-Choice Raw Score	49	670	700	720	740	780	790	800
	48	660	680	700	730	760	780	790
	47	650	670	690	720	750	770	780
	46	640	660	680	710	740	760	770
	45	630	650	670	700	740	750	770
	44	620	640	660	690	730	750	760
	43	600	630	650	680	710	740	750
	42	600	620	640	670	700	730	750
	41	590	610	630	660	690	730	740
	40	580	600	620	650	690	720	740
	39	570	590	610	640	680	710	740
	38	560	590	610	630	670	700	730
	37	550	580	600	630	660	690	720
	36	540	570	590	620	650	680	710
	35	540	560	580	610	640	680	710
	34	530	550	570	600	640	670	700
	33	520	540	560	590	630	660	690
	32	510	540	560	580	620	650	680
	31	500	530	550	580	610	640	670
	30	490	520	540	570	600	630	660
	29	490	510	530	560	590	630	650
	28	480	500	520	550	590	620	640
	27	470	490	510	540	580	610	640
	26	460	490	500	530	570	600	630
	25	450	480	500	520	560	590	620
	24	440	470	490	510	550	580	610
	23	430	460	480	510	540	570	600
	22	430	450	470	500	530	570	590
	21	430	450	470	500	530	570	590
	20	420	440	460	490	520	560	580
	19	410	430	450	480	520	550	570
	18	400	420	440	470	510	540	570
	17	390	420	430	460	500	530	560
	16	380	410	430	450	490	520	550
	15	370	400	420	450	480	510	540
	14	360	390	410	440	470	500	530
	13	360	380	400	430	460	500	520
	12	340	370	390	420	450	490	510
	11	340	360	380	410	450	480	510
	10	330	350	370	400	440	470	500
	9	320	350	360	390	430	460	490
	8	310	340	360	390	420	450	480
	7	300	330	350	380	410	440	470
	6	290	320	340	370	400	430	460
	5	290	310	330	360	390	430	450
	4	280	300	320	350	390	420	450
	3	270	290	310	340	380	410	440
	2	260	280	300	330	370	400	430
	1	250	270	290	320	340	380	410
	0	250	260	280	310	340	370	400
	−1	240	260	270	290	320	360	380
	−2	230	250	260	270	310	340	370
	−3	220	240	250	260	300	330	360
	−4	220	230	240	250	290	320	350
	−5	200	220	230	240	280	310	340
	−6	200	210	220	240	280	310	340
	−7	200	210	220	230	270	300	330
	−8	200	210	220	230	270	300	330
	−9	200	210	220	230	270	300	330
	−10	200	210	220	230	270	300	330
	−11	200	210	220	230	270	300	330

2

PRACTICE TEST 2

For additional practice before Test Day, take this Practice Test under test-like conditions at home or at a Kaplan Center, bubble in your answers on a Kaplan SAT Answer Grid, and have the grid scanned at a Kaplan Center to receive your results.

Scan Code: 1102

Practice Test 2
Answer Sheet

Remove (or photocopy) the following answer sheet and use it to complete the practice test. See the answer key following the test when finished.

Start with number 1 for each bubble-in section. If a section has fewer questions than bubbles, leave the extra bubbles blank.

Use this page to *plan* your essay.

SECTION 2

1. Ⓐ Ⓑ Ⓒ Ⓓ Ⓔ	11. Ⓐ Ⓑ Ⓒ Ⓓ Ⓔ	21. Ⓐ Ⓑ Ⓒ Ⓓ Ⓔ	31. Ⓐ Ⓑ Ⓒ Ⓓ Ⓔ
2. Ⓐ Ⓑ Ⓒ Ⓓ Ⓔ	12. Ⓐ Ⓑ Ⓒ Ⓓ Ⓔ	22. Ⓐ Ⓑ Ⓒ Ⓓ Ⓔ	32. Ⓐ Ⓑ Ⓒ Ⓓ Ⓔ
3. Ⓐ Ⓑ Ⓒ Ⓓ Ⓔ	13. Ⓐ Ⓑ Ⓒ Ⓓ Ⓔ	23. Ⓐ Ⓑ Ⓒ Ⓓ Ⓔ	33. Ⓐ Ⓑ Ⓒ Ⓓ Ⓔ
4. Ⓐ Ⓑ Ⓒ Ⓓ Ⓔ	14. Ⓐ Ⓑ Ⓒ Ⓓ Ⓔ	24. Ⓐ Ⓑ Ⓒ Ⓓ Ⓔ	34. Ⓐ Ⓑ Ⓒ Ⓓ Ⓔ
5. Ⓐ Ⓑ Ⓒ Ⓓ Ⓔ	15. Ⓐ Ⓑ Ⓒ Ⓓ Ⓔ	25. Ⓐ Ⓑ Ⓒ Ⓓ Ⓔ	35. Ⓐ Ⓑ Ⓒ Ⓓ Ⓔ
6. Ⓐ Ⓑ Ⓒ Ⓓ Ⓔ	16. Ⓐ Ⓑ Ⓒ Ⓓ Ⓔ	26. Ⓐ Ⓑ Ⓒ Ⓓ Ⓔ	36. Ⓐ Ⓑ Ⓒ Ⓓ Ⓔ
7. Ⓐ Ⓑ Ⓒ Ⓓ Ⓔ	17. Ⓐ Ⓑ Ⓒ Ⓓ Ⓔ	27. Ⓐ Ⓑ Ⓒ Ⓓ Ⓔ	37. Ⓐ Ⓑ Ⓒ Ⓓ Ⓔ
8. Ⓐ Ⓑ Ⓒ Ⓓ Ⓔ	18. Ⓐ Ⓑ Ⓒ Ⓓ Ⓔ	28. Ⓐ Ⓑ Ⓒ Ⓓ Ⓔ	38. Ⓐ Ⓑ Ⓒ Ⓓ Ⓔ
9. Ⓐ Ⓑ Ⓒ Ⓓ Ⓔ	19. Ⓐ Ⓑ Ⓒ Ⓓ Ⓔ	29. Ⓐ Ⓑ Ⓒ Ⓓ Ⓔ	39. Ⓐ Ⓑ Ⓒ Ⓓ Ⓔ
10. Ⓐ Ⓑ Ⓒ Ⓓ Ⓔ	20. Ⓐ Ⓑ Ⓒ Ⓓ Ⓔ	30. Ⓐ Ⓑ Ⓒ Ⓓ Ⓔ	40. Ⓐ Ⓑ Ⓒ Ⓓ Ⓔ

right in Section 2

wrong in Section 2

SECTION 3

1. Ⓐ Ⓑ Ⓒ Ⓓ Ⓔ	11. Ⓐ Ⓑ Ⓒ Ⓓ Ⓔ	21. Ⓐ Ⓑ Ⓒ Ⓓ Ⓔ	31. Ⓐ Ⓑ Ⓒ Ⓓ Ⓔ
2. Ⓐ Ⓑ Ⓒ Ⓓ Ⓔ	12. Ⓐ Ⓑ Ⓒ Ⓓ Ⓔ	22. Ⓐ Ⓑ Ⓒ Ⓓ Ⓔ	32. Ⓐ Ⓑ Ⓒ Ⓓ Ⓔ
3. Ⓐ Ⓑ Ⓒ Ⓓ Ⓔ	13. Ⓐ Ⓑ Ⓒ Ⓓ Ⓔ	23. Ⓐ Ⓑ Ⓒ Ⓓ Ⓔ	33. Ⓐ Ⓑ Ⓒ Ⓓ Ⓔ
4. Ⓐ Ⓑ Ⓒ Ⓓ Ⓔ	14. Ⓐ Ⓑ Ⓒ Ⓓ Ⓔ	24. Ⓐ Ⓑ Ⓒ Ⓓ Ⓔ	34. Ⓐ Ⓑ Ⓒ Ⓓ Ⓔ
5. Ⓐ Ⓑ Ⓒ Ⓓ Ⓔ	15. Ⓐ Ⓑ Ⓒ Ⓓ Ⓔ	25. Ⓐ Ⓑ Ⓒ Ⓓ Ⓔ	35. Ⓐ Ⓑ Ⓒ Ⓓ Ⓔ
6. Ⓐ Ⓑ Ⓒ Ⓓ Ⓔ	16. Ⓐ Ⓑ Ⓒ Ⓓ Ⓔ	26. Ⓐ Ⓑ Ⓒ Ⓓ Ⓔ	36. Ⓐ Ⓑ Ⓒ Ⓓ Ⓔ
7. Ⓐ Ⓑ Ⓒ Ⓓ Ⓔ	17. Ⓐ Ⓑ Ⓒ Ⓓ Ⓔ	27. Ⓐ Ⓑ Ⓒ Ⓓ Ⓔ	37. Ⓐ Ⓑ Ⓒ Ⓓ Ⓔ
8. Ⓐ Ⓑ Ⓒ Ⓓ Ⓔ	18. Ⓐ Ⓑ Ⓒ Ⓓ Ⓔ	28. Ⓐ Ⓑ Ⓒ Ⓓ Ⓔ	38. Ⓐ Ⓑ Ⓒ Ⓓ Ⓔ
9. Ⓐ Ⓑ Ⓒ Ⓓ Ⓔ	19. Ⓐ Ⓑ Ⓒ Ⓓ Ⓔ	29. Ⓐ Ⓑ Ⓒ Ⓓ Ⓔ	39. Ⓐ Ⓑ Ⓒ Ⓓ Ⓔ
10. Ⓐ Ⓑ Ⓒ Ⓓ Ⓔ	20. Ⓐ Ⓑ Ⓒ Ⓓ Ⓔ	30. Ⓐ Ⓑ Ⓒ Ⓓ Ⓔ	40. Ⓐ Ⓑ Ⓒ Ⓓ Ⓔ

right in Section 3

wrong in Section 3

If sections 2 or 3 of this practice test contain math questions that are not multiple choice, continue to item 9 below. Otherwise, continue to item 9 above.

9.   10.   11.   12.   13.

14.   15.   16.   17.   18.

SECTION 4

1. Ⓐ Ⓑ Ⓒ Ⓓ Ⓔ   11. Ⓐ Ⓑ Ⓒ Ⓓ Ⓔ   21. Ⓐ Ⓑ Ⓒ Ⓓ Ⓔ   31. Ⓐ Ⓑ Ⓒ Ⓓ Ⓔ
2. Ⓐ Ⓑ Ⓒ Ⓓ Ⓔ   12. Ⓐ Ⓑ Ⓒ Ⓓ Ⓔ   22. Ⓐ Ⓑ Ⓒ Ⓓ Ⓔ   32. Ⓐ Ⓑ Ⓒ Ⓓ Ⓔ
3. Ⓐ Ⓑ Ⓒ Ⓓ Ⓔ   13. Ⓐ Ⓑ Ⓒ Ⓓ Ⓔ   23. Ⓐ Ⓑ Ⓒ Ⓓ Ⓔ   33. Ⓐ Ⓑ Ⓒ Ⓓ Ⓔ
4. Ⓐ Ⓑ Ⓒ Ⓓ Ⓔ   14. Ⓐ Ⓑ Ⓒ Ⓓ Ⓔ   24. Ⓐ Ⓑ Ⓒ Ⓓ Ⓔ   34. Ⓐ Ⓑ Ⓒ Ⓓ Ⓔ
5. Ⓐ Ⓑ Ⓒ Ⓓ Ⓔ   15. Ⓐ Ⓑ Ⓒ Ⓓ Ⓔ   25. Ⓐ Ⓑ Ⓒ Ⓓ Ⓔ   35. Ⓐ Ⓑ Ⓒ Ⓓ Ⓔ
6. Ⓐ Ⓑ Ⓒ Ⓓ Ⓔ   16. Ⓐ Ⓑ Ⓒ Ⓓ Ⓔ   26. Ⓐ Ⓑ Ⓒ Ⓓ Ⓔ   36. Ⓐ Ⓑ Ⓒ Ⓓ Ⓔ
7. Ⓐ Ⓑ Ⓒ Ⓓ Ⓔ   17. Ⓐ Ⓑ Ⓒ Ⓓ Ⓔ   27. Ⓐ Ⓑ Ⓒ Ⓓ Ⓔ   37. Ⓐ Ⓑ Ⓒ Ⓓ Ⓔ
8. Ⓐ Ⓑ Ⓒ Ⓓ Ⓔ   18. Ⓐ Ⓑ Ⓒ Ⓓ Ⓔ   28. Ⓐ Ⓑ Ⓒ Ⓓ Ⓔ   38. Ⓐ Ⓑ Ⓒ Ⓓ Ⓔ
9. Ⓐ Ⓑ Ⓒ Ⓓ Ⓔ   19. Ⓐ Ⓑ Ⓒ Ⓓ Ⓔ   29. Ⓐ Ⓑ Ⓒ Ⓓ Ⓔ   39. Ⓐ Ⓑ Ⓒ Ⓓ Ⓔ
10. Ⓐ Ⓑ Ⓒ Ⓓ Ⓔ   20. Ⓐ Ⓑ Ⓒ Ⓓ Ⓔ   30. Ⓐ Ⓑ Ⓒ Ⓓ Ⓔ   40. Ⓐ Ⓑ Ⓒ Ⓓ Ⓔ

right in Section 4

wrong in Section 4

SECTION 5

1. Ⓐ Ⓑ Ⓒ Ⓓ Ⓔ   11. Ⓐ Ⓑ Ⓒ Ⓓ Ⓔ   21. Ⓐ Ⓑ Ⓒ Ⓓ Ⓔ   31. Ⓐ Ⓑ Ⓒ Ⓓ Ⓔ
2. Ⓐ Ⓑ Ⓒ Ⓓ Ⓔ   12. Ⓐ Ⓑ Ⓒ Ⓓ Ⓔ   22. Ⓐ Ⓑ Ⓒ Ⓓ Ⓔ   32. Ⓐ Ⓑ Ⓒ Ⓓ Ⓔ
3. Ⓐ Ⓑ Ⓒ Ⓓ Ⓔ   13. Ⓐ Ⓑ Ⓒ Ⓓ Ⓔ   23. Ⓐ Ⓑ Ⓒ Ⓓ Ⓔ   33. Ⓐ Ⓑ Ⓒ Ⓓ Ⓔ
4. Ⓐ Ⓑ Ⓒ Ⓓ Ⓔ   14. Ⓐ Ⓑ Ⓒ Ⓓ Ⓔ   24. Ⓐ Ⓑ Ⓒ Ⓓ Ⓔ   34. Ⓐ Ⓑ Ⓒ Ⓓ Ⓔ
5. Ⓐ Ⓑ Ⓒ Ⓓ Ⓔ   15. Ⓐ Ⓑ Ⓒ Ⓓ Ⓔ   25. Ⓐ Ⓑ Ⓒ Ⓓ Ⓔ   35. Ⓐ Ⓑ Ⓒ Ⓓ Ⓔ
6. Ⓐ Ⓑ Ⓒ Ⓓ Ⓔ   16. Ⓐ Ⓑ Ⓒ Ⓓ Ⓔ   26. Ⓐ Ⓑ Ⓒ Ⓓ Ⓔ   36. Ⓐ Ⓑ Ⓒ Ⓓ Ⓔ
7. Ⓐ Ⓑ Ⓒ Ⓓ Ⓔ   17. Ⓐ Ⓑ Ⓒ Ⓓ Ⓔ   27. Ⓐ Ⓑ Ⓒ Ⓓ Ⓔ   37. Ⓐ Ⓑ Ⓒ Ⓓ Ⓔ
8. Ⓐ Ⓑ Ⓒ Ⓓ Ⓔ   18. Ⓐ Ⓑ Ⓒ Ⓓ Ⓔ   28. Ⓐ Ⓑ Ⓒ Ⓓ Ⓔ   38. Ⓐ Ⓑ Ⓒ Ⓓ Ⓔ
9. Ⓐ Ⓑ Ⓒ Ⓓ Ⓔ   19. Ⓐ Ⓑ Ⓒ Ⓓ Ⓔ   29. Ⓐ Ⓑ Ⓒ Ⓓ Ⓔ   39. Ⓐ Ⓑ Ⓒ Ⓓ Ⓔ
10. Ⓐ Ⓑ Ⓒ Ⓓ Ⓔ   20. Ⓐ Ⓑ Ⓒ Ⓓ Ⓔ   30. Ⓐ Ⓑ Ⓒ Ⓓ Ⓔ   40. Ⓐ Ⓑ Ⓒ Ⓓ Ⓔ

right in Section 5

wrong in Section 5

If sections 4 or 5 of this practice test contain math questions that are not multiple choice, continue to item 9 below. Otherwise, continue to item 9 above.

9.   10.   11.   12.   13.

14.   15.   16.   17.   18.

SECTION 6

1. Ⓐ Ⓑ Ⓒ Ⓓ Ⓔ	11. Ⓐ Ⓑ Ⓒ Ⓓ Ⓔ	21. Ⓐ Ⓑ Ⓒ Ⓓ Ⓔ	31. Ⓐ Ⓑ Ⓒ Ⓓ Ⓔ		
2. Ⓐ Ⓑ Ⓒ Ⓓ Ⓔ	12. Ⓐ Ⓑ Ⓒ Ⓓ Ⓔ	22. Ⓐ Ⓑ Ⓒ Ⓓ Ⓔ	32. Ⓐ Ⓑ Ⓒ Ⓓ Ⓔ		
3. Ⓐ Ⓑ Ⓒ Ⓓ Ⓔ	13. Ⓐ Ⓑ Ⓒ Ⓓ Ⓔ	23. Ⓐ Ⓑ Ⓒ Ⓓ Ⓔ	33. Ⓐ Ⓑ Ⓒ Ⓓ Ⓔ		
4. Ⓐ Ⓑ Ⓒ Ⓓ Ⓔ	14. Ⓐ Ⓑ Ⓒ Ⓓ Ⓔ	24. Ⓐ Ⓑ Ⓒ Ⓓ Ⓔ	34. Ⓐ Ⓑ Ⓒ Ⓓ Ⓔ		# right in Section 6
5. Ⓐ Ⓑ Ⓒ Ⓓ Ⓔ	15. Ⓐ Ⓑ Ⓒ Ⓓ Ⓔ	25. Ⓐ Ⓑ Ⓒ Ⓓ Ⓔ	35. Ⓐ Ⓑ Ⓒ Ⓓ Ⓔ		
6. Ⓐ Ⓑ Ⓒ Ⓓ Ⓔ	16. Ⓐ Ⓑ Ⓒ Ⓓ Ⓔ	26. Ⓐ Ⓑ Ⓒ Ⓓ Ⓔ	36. Ⓐ Ⓑ Ⓒ Ⓓ Ⓔ		
7. Ⓐ Ⓑ Ⓒ Ⓓ Ⓔ	17. Ⓐ Ⓑ Ⓒ Ⓓ Ⓔ	27. Ⓐ Ⓑ Ⓒ Ⓓ Ⓔ	37. Ⓐ Ⓑ Ⓒ Ⓓ Ⓔ		
8. Ⓐ Ⓑ Ⓒ Ⓓ Ⓔ	18. Ⓐ Ⓑ Ⓒ Ⓓ Ⓔ	28. Ⓐ Ⓑ Ⓒ Ⓓ Ⓔ	38. Ⓐ Ⓑ Ⓒ Ⓓ Ⓔ		# wrong in Section 6
9. Ⓐ Ⓑ Ⓒ Ⓓ Ⓔ	19. Ⓐ Ⓑ Ⓒ Ⓓ Ⓔ	29. Ⓐ Ⓑ Ⓒ Ⓓ Ⓔ	39. Ⓐ Ⓑ Ⓒ Ⓓ Ⓔ		
10. Ⓐ Ⓑ Ⓒ Ⓓ Ⓔ	20. Ⓐ Ⓑ Ⓒ Ⓓ Ⓔ	30. Ⓐ Ⓑ Ⓒ Ⓓ Ⓔ	40. Ⓐ Ⓑ Ⓒ Ⓓ Ⓔ		

SECTION 7

1. Ⓐ Ⓑ Ⓒ Ⓓ Ⓔ	11. Ⓐ Ⓑ Ⓒ Ⓓ Ⓔ	21. Ⓐ Ⓑ Ⓒ Ⓓ Ⓔ	31. Ⓐ Ⓑ Ⓒ Ⓓ Ⓔ		
2. Ⓐ Ⓑ Ⓒ Ⓓ Ⓔ	12. Ⓐ Ⓑ Ⓒ Ⓓ Ⓔ	22. Ⓐ Ⓑ Ⓒ Ⓓ Ⓔ	32. Ⓐ Ⓑ Ⓒ Ⓓ Ⓔ		
3. Ⓐ Ⓑ Ⓒ Ⓓ Ⓔ	13. Ⓐ Ⓑ Ⓒ Ⓓ Ⓔ	23. Ⓐ Ⓑ Ⓒ Ⓓ Ⓔ	33. Ⓐ Ⓑ Ⓒ Ⓓ Ⓔ		
4. Ⓐ Ⓑ Ⓒ Ⓓ Ⓔ	14. Ⓐ Ⓑ Ⓒ Ⓓ Ⓔ	24. Ⓐ Ⓑ Ⓒ Ⓓ Ⓔ	34. Ⓐ Ⓑ Ⓒ Ⓓ Ⓔ		# right in Section 7
5. Ⓐ Ⓑ Ⓒ Ⓓ Ⓔ	15. Ⓐ Ⓑ Ⓒ Ⓓ Ⓔ	25. Ⓐ Ⓑ Ⓒ Ⓓ Ⓔ	35. Ⓐ Ⓑ Ⓒ Ⓓ Ⓔ		
6. Ⓐ Ⓑ Ⓒ Ⓓ Ⓔ	16. Ⓐ Ⓑ Ⓒ Ⓓ Ⓔ	26. Ⓐ Ⓑ Ⓒ Ⓓ Ⓔ	36. Ⓐ Ⓑ Ⓒ Ⓓ Ⓔ		
7. Ⓐ Ⓑ Ⓒ Ⓓ Ⓔ	17. Ⓐ Ⓑ Ⓒ Ⓓ Ⓔ	27. Ⓐ Ⓑ Ⓒ Ⓓ Ⓔ	37. Ⓐ Ⓑ Ⓒ Ⓓ Ⓔ		
8. Ⓐ Ⓑ Ⓒ Ⓓ Ⓔ	18. Ⓐ Ⓑ Ⓒ Ⓓ Ⓔ	28. Ⓐ Ⓑ Ⓒ Ⓓ Ⓔ	38. Ⓐ Ⓑ Ⓒ Ⓓ Ⓔ		# wrong in Section 7
9. Ⓐ Ⓑ Ⓒ Ⓓ Ⓔ	19. Ⓐ Ⓑ Ⓒ Ⓓ Ⓔ	29. Ⓐ Ⓑ Ⓒ Ⓓ Ⓔ	39. Ⓐ Ⓑ Ⓒ Ⓓ Ⓔ		
10. Ⓐ Ⓑ Ⓒ Ⓓ Ⓔ	20. Ⓐ Ⓑ Ⓒ Ⓓ Ⓔ	30. Ⓐ Ⓑ Ⓒ Ⓓ Ⓔ	40. Ⓐ Ⓑ Ⓒ Ⓓ Ⓔ		

If sections 6 or 7 of this practice test contain math questions that are not multiple choice, continue to item 9 below. Otherwise, continue to item 9 above.

9.   10.   11.   12.   13.

14.   15.   16.   17.   18.

SECTION 8

1. Ⓐ Ⓑ Ⓒ Ⓓ Ⓔ	11. Ⓐ Ⓑ Ⓒ Ⓓ Ⓔ	21. Ⓐ Ⓑ Ⓒ Ⓓ Ⓔ	31. Ⓐ Ⓑ Ⓒ Ⓓ Ⓔ
2. Ⓐ Ⓑ Ⓒ Ⓓ Ⓔ	12. Ⓐ Ⓑ Ⓒ Ⓓ Ⓔ	22. Ⓐ Ⓑ Ⓒ Ⓓ Ⓔ	32. Ⓐ Ⓑ Ⓒ Ⓓ Ⓔ
3. Ⓐ Ⓑ Ⓒ Ⓓ Ⓔ	13. Ⓐ Ⓑ Ⓒ Ⓓ Ⓔ	23. Ⓐ Ⓑ Ⓒ Ⓓ Ⓔ	33. Ⓐ Ⓑ Ⓒ Ⓓ Ⓔ
4. Ⓐ Ⓑ Ⓒ Ⓓ Ⓔ	14. Ⓐ Ⓑ Ⓒ Ⓓ Ⓔ	24. Ⓐ Ⓑ Ⓒ Ⓓ Ⓔ	34. Ⓐ Ⓑ Ⓒ Ⓓ Ⓔ
5. Ⓐ Ⓑ Ⓒ Ⓓ Ⓔ	15. Ⓐ Ⓑ Ⓒ Ⓓ Ⓔ	25. Ⓐ Ⓑ Ⓒ Ⓓ Ⓔ	35. Ⓐ Ⓑ Ⓒ Ⓓ Ⓔ
6. Ⓐ Ⓑ Ⓒ Ⓓ Ⓔ	16. Ⓐ Ⓑ Ⓒ Ⓓ Ⓔ	26. Ⓐ Ⓑ Ⓒ Ⓓ Ⓔ	36. Ⓐ Ⓑ Ⓒ Ⓓ Ⓔ
7. Ⓐ Ⓑ Ⓒ Ⓓ Ⓔ	17. Ⓐ Ⓑ Ⓒ Ⓓ Ⓔ	27. Ⓐ Ⓑ Ⓒ Ⓓ Ⓔ	37. Ⓐ Ⓑ Ⓒ Ⓓ Ⓔ
8. Ⓐ Ⓑ Ⓒ Ⓓ Ⓔ	18. Ⓐ Ⓑ Ⓒ Ⓓ Ⓔ	28. Ⓐ Ⓑ Ⓒ Ⓓ Ⓔ	38. Ⓐ Ⓑ Ⓒ Ⓓ Ⓔ
9. Ⓐ Ⓑ Ⓒ Ⓓ Ⓔ	19. Ⓐ Ⓑ Ⓒ Ⓓ Ⓔ	29. Ⓐ Ⓑ Ⓒ Ⓓ Ⓔ	39. Ⓐ Ⓑ Ⓒ Ⓓ Ⓔ
10. Ⓐ Ⓑ Ⓒ Ⓓ Ⓔ	20. Ⓐ Ⓑ Ⓒ Ⓓ Ⓔ	30. Ⓐ Ⓑ Ⓒ Ⓓ Ⓔ	40. Ⓐ Ⓑ Ⓒ Ⓓ Ⓔ

right in Section 8

wrong in Section 8

SECTION 9

1. Ⓐ Ⓑ Ⓒ Ⓓ Ⓔ	11. Ⓐ Ⓑ Ⓒ Ⓓ Ⓔ	21. Ⓐ Ⓑ Ⓒ Ⓓ Ⓔ	31. Ⓐ Ⓑ Ⓒ Ⓓ Ⓔ
2. Ⓐ Ⓑ Ⓒ Ⓓ Ⓔ	12. Ⓐ Ⓑ Ⓒ Ⓓ Ⓔ	22. Ⓐ Ⓑ Ⓒ Ⓓ Ⓔ	32. Ⓐ Ⓑ Ⓒ Ⓓ Ⓔ
3. Ⓐ Ⓑ Ⓒ Ⓓ Ⓔ	13. Ⓐ Ⓑ Ⓒ Ⓓ Ⓔ	23. Ⓐ Ⓑ Ⓒ Ⓓ Ⓔ	33. Ⓐ Ⓑ Ⓒ Ⓓ Ⓔ
4. Ⓐ Ⓑ Ⓒ Ⓓ Ⓔ	14. Ⓐ Ⓑ Ⓒ Ⓓ Ⓔ	24. Ⓐ Ⓑ Ⓒ Ⓓ Ⓔ	34. Ⓐ Ⓑ Ⓒ Ⓓ Ⓔ
5. Ⓐ Ⓑ Ⓒ Ⓓ Ⓔ	15. Ⓐ Ⓑ Ⓒ Ⓓ Ⓔ	25. Ⓐ Ⓑ Ⓒ Ⓓ Ⓔ	35. Ⓐ Ⓑ Ⓒ Ⓓ Ⓔ
6. Ⓐ Ⓑ Ⓒ Ⓓ Ⓔ	16. Ⓐ Ⓑ Ⓒ Ⓓ Ⓔ	26. Ⓐ Ⓑ Ⓒ Ⓓ Ⓔ	36. Ⓐ Ⓑ Ⓒ Ⓓ Ⓔ
7. Ⓐ Ⓑ Ⓒ Ⓓ Ⓔ	17. Ⓐ Ⓑ Ⓒ Ⓓ Ⓔ	27. Ⓐ Ⓑ Ⓒ Ⓓ Ⓔ	37. Ⓐ Ⓑ Ⓒ Ⓓ Ⓔ
8. Ⓐ Ⓑ Ⓒ Ⓓ Ⓔ	18. Ⓐ Ⓑ Ⓒ Ⓓ Ⓔ	28. Ⓐ Ⓑ Ⓒ Ⓓ Ⓔ	38. Ⓐ Ⓑ Ⓒ Ⓓ Ⓔ
9. Ⓐ Ⓑ Ⓒ Ⓓ Ⓔ	19. Ⓐ Ⓑ Ⓒ Ⓓ Ⓔ	29. Ⓐ Ⓑ Ⓒ Ⓓ Ⓔ	39. Ⓐ Ⓑ Ⓒ Ⓓ Ⓔ
10. Ⓐ Ⓑ Ⓒ Ⓓ Ⓔ	20. Ⓐ Ⓑ Ⓒ Ⓓ Ⓔ	30. Ⓐ Ⓑ Ⓒ Ⓓ Ⓔ	40. Ⓐ Ⓑ Ⓒ Ⓓ Ⓔ

right in Section 9

wrong in Section 9

SECTION 10

1. Ⓐ Ⓑ Ⓒ Ⓓ Ⓔ	11. Ⓐ Ⓑ Ⓒ Ⓓ Ⓔ	21. Ⓐ Ⓑ Ⓒ Ⓓ Ⓔ	31. Ⓐ Ⓑ Ⓒ Ⓓ Ⓔ
2. Ⓐ Ⓑ Ⓒ Ⓓ Ⓔ	12. Ⓐ Ⓑ Ⓒ Ⓓ Ⓔ	22. Ⓐ Ⓑ Ⓒ Ⓓ Ⓔ	32. Ⓐ Ⓑ Ⓒ Ⓓ Ⓔ
3. Ⓐ Ⓑ Ⓒ Ⓓ Ⓔ	13. Ⓐ Ⓑ Ⓒ Ⓓ Ⓔ	23. Ⓐ Ⓑ Ⓒ Ⓓ Ⓔ	33. Ⓐ Ⓑ Ⓒ Ⓓ Ⓔ
4. Ⓐ Ⓑ Ⓒ Ⓓ Ⓔ	14. Ⓐ Ⓑ Ⓒ Ⓓ Ⓔ	24. Ⓐ Ⓑ Ⓒ Ⓓ Ⓔ	34. Ⓐ Ⓑ Ⓒ Ⓓ Ⓔ
5. Ⓐ Ⓑ Ⓒ Ⓓ Ⓔ	15. Ⓐ Ⓑ Ⓒ Ⓓ Ⓔ	25. Ⓐ Ⓑ Ⓒ Ⓓ Ⓔ	35. Ⓐ Ⓑ Ⓒ Ⓓ Ⓔ
6. Ⓐ Ⓑ Ⓒ Ⓓ Ⓔ	16. Ⓐ Ⓑ Ⓒ Ⓓ Ⓔ	26. Ⓐ Ⓑ Ⓒ Ⓓ Ⓔ	36. Ⓐ Ⓑ Ⓒ Ⓓ Ⓔ
7. Ⓐ Ⓑ Ⓒ Ⓓ Ⓔ	17. Ⓐ Ⓑ Ⓒ Ⓓ Ⓔ	27. Ⓐ Ⓑ Ⓒ Ⓓ Ⓔ	37. Ⓐ Ⓑ Ⓒ Ⓓ Ⓔ
8. Ⓐ Ⓑ Ⓒ Ⓓ Ⓔ	18. Ⓐ Ⓑ Ⓒ Ⓓ Ⓔ	28. Ⓐ Ⓑ Ⓒ Ⓓ Ⓔ	38. Ⓐ Ⓑ Ⓒ Ⓓ Ⓔ
9. Ⓐ Ⓑ Ⓒ Ⓓ Ⓔ	19. Ⓐ Ⓑ Ⓒ Ⓓ Ⓔ	29. Ⓐ Ⓑ Ⓒ Ⓓ Ⓔ	39. Ⓐ Ⓑ Ⓒ Ⓓ Ⓔ
10. Ⓐ Ⓑ Ⓒ Ⓓ Ⓔ	20. Ⓐ Ⓑ Ⓒ Ⓓ Ⓔ	30. Ⓐ Ⓑ Ⓒ Ⓓ Ⓔ	40. Ⓐ Ⓑ Ⓒ Ⓓ Ⓔ

right in Section 10

wrong in Section 10

ESSAY
Time—25 minutes

The essay gives you an opportunity to show how effectively you can develop and express ideas. You should, therefore, take care to develop your point of view, present your ideas logically and clearly, and use language precisely.

Your essay must be written on the lines provided in your Answer Grid Booklet—you will receive no other paper on which to write. You will have enough space if you write on every line, avoid wide margins, and keep your handwriting to a reasonable size. Remember that people who are not familiar with your handwriting will read what you write. Try to write or print so that what you are writing is legible to those readers.

You have twenty-five minutes to write an essay on the topic assigned below. DO NOT WRITE ON ANOTHER TOPIC. AN OFF-TOPIC ESSAY WILL RECEIVE A SCORE OF ZERO.

Think carefully about the issue presented in the following quotation and the assignment below.

> If you think about disaster, you will get it. Brood about death and you hasten your demise. Think positively and masterfully, with confidence and faith, and life becomes more secure, more fraught with action, richer in achievement and experience...Courage is doing what you're afraid to do. There can be no courage unless you're scared.
>
> Eddie Rickenbacker, adapted from *Selected Writings*

Assignment: Does having courage mean that we have no fear, or that we act despite being afraid? Plan and write an essay in which you develop your point of view on these issues. Support your position with reasoning and examples taken from your reading, studies, experience, or observations.

DO NOT WRITE YOUR ESSAY IN YOUR TEST BOOK.
You will receive credit only for what you write in your Answer Grid Booklet.

BEGIN WRITING YOUR ESSAY ON PAGE 69 OF THIS BOOK
OR ON PAGE 3 OF YOUR KAPLAN SAT ANSWER GRID.

IF YOU FINISH BEFORE TIME IS CALLED, YOU MAY CHECK YOUR WORK ON THIS SECTION ONLY. DO NOT TURN TO ANY OTHER SECTION IN THE TEST.

Time—25 Minutes
24 Questions

Directions: For each question in this section, select the best answer from among the choices given and fill in the corresponding oval on the answer sheet.

Each sentence below has one or two blanks, each blank indicating that something has been omitted. Beneath the sentence are five words or sets of words labeled A through E. Choose the word or set of words that, when inserted in the sentence, best fits the meaning of the sentence as a whole.

EXAMPLE:

Today's small, portable computers contrast markedly with the earliest electronic computers, which were -------.

(A) effective   (B) invented
   (C) useful   (D) destructive
      (E) enormous

ANSWER:
Ⓐ Ⓑ Ⓒ Ⓓ ●

---

1 The author's original manuscript was so ------- that the editor was able to take out a full quarter of the text without compromising the ------- of the paper.

(A) affable . . content
(B) florid . . simplicity
(C) verbose . . heft
(D) concise . . meaning
(E) wordy . . thesis

2 The beauty of freshly painted nails is -------; even the best of manicures will rarely ------- more than a week.

(A) durable . . endure
(B) tactful . . expand
(C) ephemeral . . last
(D) strident . . abide
(E) engaging . . allow

3 The members of the basketball team were ------- upon coming from behind to win their second national title; they celebrated their victory with gusto.

(A) defiant   (B) jubilant
   (C) slothful   (D) odious
      (E) circumspect

4 The elephant, long considered one of the most ------- creatures of the African continent because of the value of its ivory tusks, finally seems to be making some headway in its battle against extinction.

(A) exotic   (B) prevalent
   (C) combative   (D) voracious
      (E) imperiled

5 Sarah found the play to be overly -------, almost ------- in tone.

(A) congenial . . trite
(B) fortuitous . . calamitous
(C) complimentary . . derogatory
(D) sentimental . . maudlin
(E) tactful . . defamatory

GO ON TO THE NEXT PAGE

The passages below are followed by questions based on their content; questions following a pair of related passages may also be based on the relationship between the paired passages. Answer the questions on the basis of what is <u>stated</u> or <u>implied</u> in the passages and in any introductory material that may be provided.

Questions 6–9 are based on the following passages.

Passage 1

Marvin Freeman's groundbreaking new study of the plays of Henrik Ibsen will alter the course of Ibsen scholarship forever. Previously, scholars
Line limited the areas of their studies to a particular
(5) phase of Ibsen's career, since a different scholarly approach seemed to fit each of the phases. Freeman has instead taken on the entirety of Ibsen's work. Happily, this breadth of scholarship does not diminish the depth with which Freeman
(10) explores each work. The career of Ibsen is now liberated from arbitrary divisions and stands before us as a complete picture. It will be years before we can appreciate fully the service that Freeman has rendered.

Passage 2

(15) In his new tome on the plays of Henrik Ibsen, Marvin Freeman presumes to consider all of the 26 plays, a period of writing that spanned some 50 years. This experiment, while yielding some interesting observations, does not serve as a useful
(20) scholarly model. Over the course of Ibsen's career, the playwright's approach evolved so drastically that it is impossible to fully consider all of his works in the confines of a single study. Freeman is forced to simplify where complexity would be
(25) more apt. While Freeman exhibits tremendous dedication to his subject, this devotion ultimately cannot save the project from its own ambition.

6 The author of Passage 2 would most likely regard the approach of the scholars mentioned in lines 3–6 as

(A) of appropriate scope
(B) inferior to that of Freeman
(C) of lasting importance to future generations
(D) unsuitable for Ibsen's career
(E) difficult to assess

7 In Passage 1, the "arbitrary divisions" in line 11 refer to

(A) the unsuccessful scholarly approaches that have been applied to Ibsen's work
(B) the breaks that Ibsen took between writing his plays
(C) a rift that Freeman has created among Ibsen scholars
(D) distinctions between various phases of Ibsen's career
(E) Freeman's dissatisfaction with previous Ibsen scholarship

8 The last sentence of Passage 1 functions primarily to

(A) imply that the book is very difficult to read
(B) highlight the lasting importance of the book
(C) celebrate Freeman's triumph over obstacles
(D) argue that additional scholarship will clarify Freeman's intent
(E) paraphrase the closing argument of Freeman's book

9 The author of Passage 2 implies that Freeman's attempt to write about Ibsen's entire career in a single book is

(A) overwhelming but not idealistic
(B) feasible but not sufficient
(C) admirable but not successful
(D) viable but not important
(E) desirable but not achievable

GO ON TO THE NEXT PAGE

Questions 10–15 are based on the following passage.

In the nineteenth century, the French novelist Gustave Flaubert wrote numerous novels usually categorized as part of the French Realist school. The following is excerpted from an article in a critical journal about his most famous novel, Madame Bovary.

Some critics believe that *Madame Bovary*, itself a well-crafted and engaging novel, has a strange and subversive theme that undermines its own medium:
Line in short, they say that Flaubert's masterpiece of
(5) fiction is a cautionary tale about the dangers of reading novels. As evidence, they point to its unsympathetic protagonist, Emma Bovary, who lives in books, romanticizing the simplest aspects of daily life—eating rich food, buying expensive clothing—as
(10) well as her relationships. Constantly dissatisfied with real life, she becomes cruel, dull-witted, and shortsighted, caring only about immediate physical gratification and material possessions. Her fantasies lead to her downfall; her relationship with her well-
(15) meaning but naïve husband Charles gradually disintegrates, her two adulterous affairs with Leon and Rodolfo end in disaster, her constant borrowing leads her family to financial ruin, and her desire to die in a gloriously dramatic fashion leads instead to an
(20) unexpectedly agonizing three days of death throes. She expects too much from life, and is punished horribly for it.

But is this undercurrent an essential theme in the novel, or simply a byproduct of character and plot?
(25) Are we really to assume that Flaubert thought the novel so dangerous that he wrote a virtual manifesto on the evils of losing oneself in fiction? If this is really the case, why would he choose to disseminate this message in the very medium he so despised (and,
(30) in fact, continued to work in for the rest of his life)?

Certainly Emma's flawed personality, as well as her literary obsession, contributes to her downfall, but it is interesting to note that no other character in the novel reads habitually for pleasure. In fact,
(35) Charles spends the bulk of the novel engaged in the mundane activities of daily life: running a business, tending to family members, maintaining the household. He is naïve, true, but happy, at least until Emma's penchant for romance begins to
(40) interfere with his responsibilities. Therefore, there really are no other appropriate characters with whom to compare her, although we can point out that the novel's non-reading population tends to be a fairly socially responsible group. (It is also interesting to

(45) note that Flaubert hardly uses the sort of clinical, dispassionate language you might expect to see in such a novel; for example, even the most stolid characters are prone to "exclaiming" and "crying" their dialogue.) Perhaps *Madame Bovary*, then, was
(50) not meant to be a criticism of fiction itself, but a caution against allowing suggestible characters like Emma to have access to novels. The permissive environment in the Bovarys' household contributes to their downfall and social ruin; the characters'
(55) unwillingness to check Emma's passions (and even their ignorance of the existence of such a problem) leads to the disintegration of their family.

10 The questions in paragraph 2 suggest the

(A) inability of Flaubert to escape his romantic leanings
(B) failure of Emma to recognize and overcome her flaws
(C) possible contradictory relationship between Flaubert's message and his medium
(D) belief that Flaubert's novel was meant to be a treatise against overly romantic language
(E) ability of Charles to handle the household's financial affairs

11 The author's discussion of "theme" in the second paragraph is most consistent with which of the following statements?

(A) By definition, themes are an inherently important, even essential, part of a well-crafted novel.
(B) Flaubert did not see the inconsistency in writing about the dangers of reading novels within a novel.
(C) Nineteenth-century French novelists were often inconsistent in their examination of themes.
(D) If Charles had interfered with Emma's literary obsession, he could have avoided his family's downfall.
(E) Flaubert did not believe the novel, as a medium, was worth obsessing over.

GO ON TO THE NEXT PAGE

12 In line 36, the author mentions "mundane activities of daily life" primarily in order to

(A) downplay the idea that Emma was justified in fantasizing constantly
(B) explain Flaubert's simultaneous attraction to and repulsion by the arts
(C) provide an example of typical daily activities in a nineteenth-century French household
(D) emphasize that Charles did not read habitually for pleasure by listing his typical daily activities
(E) suggest that Charles did not need to read to find pleasure in his daily life

13 In lines 44–49 the author presents examples of how Flaubert used dialogue in order to

(A) prove that Flaubert himself approved of overly romantic characters
(B) illustrate Flaubert's use of hyperbolic language in a novel that supposedly decries romanticism
(C) suggest that Flaubert may have been unaware of his contradictory use of language
(D) demonstrate the romantic leanings of nineteenth-century French authors in general
(E) provide an example of Emma's shortsightedness

14 The "permissive environment" referred to in lines 52–53 is most accurately paralleled by which of the following situations?

(A) a college student who becomes so obsessed with video games that his schoolwork begins to suffer
(B) an employer overlooking an employee's excessive time off and the resulting loss of productivity
(C) a moviegoer who sees five movies a day
(D) a man who golfs constantly
(E) a teenager's obsession with model airplanes

15 The word "passions" in line 55 most nearly means

(A) romantic relationships
(B) tantrums
(C) obsessions
(D) biases
(E) miseries

Questions 16–24 are based on the following passage.

This passage is excerpted from an article in a popular magazine on scientific advances.

Until recently, patients with progressive diseases that eventually lead to blindness have had little in the way of treatment, let alone a cure. Conditions
Line such as *retinitis pigmentosa* and macular
(5) degeneration still stump doctors, and even the latest treatments, such as prescribing massive doses of Vitamin A, only temporarily slow the progress of the disease in some patients. Currently, there is no failsafe way to reverse or even stop the progress
(10) of these diseases. Mechanical devices such as retinal implants seem to work with only a limited number of patients—really, only those whose vision loss is caused by a retinal disorder.

However, one new treatment is showing some
(15) promise, although it hasn't been thoroughly tested yet. Instead of focusing on dietary solutions, some doctors are attempting to develop an electronic one: a bionic eye that enables the user's brain to translate light impulses and create a virtual black-and-white
(20) "picture" of his or her surroundings. The picture, although accurate, only reflects a very limited field of vision, as if the patient had blinders on. Also, the picture moves fairly slowly, as if the patient were watching a film in very slow motion. But, being able to
(25) locate and identify objects is a definite first step in achieving everyday functional mobility for the visually impaired.

Rather than the glass eye one might imagine, this artificial vision system consists of an elaborate
(30) apparatus that looks like a pair of binoculars, as well as a series of wires that are implanted directly into the patient's brain. The wires electrically stimulate the visual cortex, producing phosphenes, which blind people perceive as small points of light. The device
(35) then maps these phosphenes, gradually training the patient's brain to "see." One major advantage of the system, as opposed to other proposed treatments such as retinal implants, is that it is not condition-specific: patients can use it regardless of the cause of
(40) vision loss. For example, patients with genetic conditions such as *retinitis pigmentosa*, as well as patients with vision loss resulting from illness or accident, can use the device, since it directly stimulates the brain's vision center. In addition, its
(45) construction is fairly flexible and portable (the wires, in fact, are said to be hardly noticeable), and its utilities are far-reaching: one could envision a number of useful additional features, including zoom and night vision functions.

(50) Although the possibilities for this apparatus seem endless, some scientists have raised pressing issues related to its immediate testing, manufacture, and widespread use. As previously mentioned, the device hasn't been tested on a wide range of blind and
(55) visually impaired subjects. In addition, there is some question about the durability of the apparatus: although the plastic currently appears to be biocompatible, there is no evidence that it will stay that way over long periods of time; the material could conceivably
(60) degrade inside the patient's head, causing injury. Multiple surgeries increase the patient's risk of infection, and should the implant move or be violently jerked around, the resulting change in position could cause brain damage. The system,
(65) which is permanently implanted into the brain, is hooked to an external processor bank and thus limits the patient's functional mobility to a certain extent. As an alternative, some scientists suggest that an interior system could be constructed, one that allows
(70) the entire apparatus to be drastically reduced in size and implanted entirely inside the body. Another feasible goal might be a temporary and/or removable device with connectors enabling external application so that the patient can use it at will.

(75) While these issues need to be addressed before further research on human test subjects can be conducted, the fact remains that the usefulness of electrical devices that directly stimulate the visual cortex far outweighs the usefulness of other
(80) neuroprostheses, such as artificial retinas, or non-mechanical treatments, such as vitamins. Further testing needs to be conducted before determining the actual feasibility of the apparatus, although the development—and initial success—of electrical
(85) stimulation represents a major step forward in the fight against vision loss.

GO ON TO THE NEXT PAGE

16 The author most likely refers to retinal implants in lines 10–11 in order to

(A) provide an example of an electronic artificial vision device
(B) describe one way in which mechanical vision devices are limited
(C) imply that all degenerative eye diseases are too advanced for most doctors
(D) describe one extremely effective artificial vision device
(E) argue that all artificial vision systems are ineffective

17 The author suggests in line 25 that the bionic eye is a "definite first step" because

(A) it hasn't been thoroughly tested yet
(B) the limited vision that the device provides permits location and identification of objects
(C) advances in the bionic eye might lead to the development of more-effective retinal implants
(D) it provides a viable alternative to dietary treatments
(E) we can expect that it will someday result in a cure for all forms of blindness

18 In line 26, the author uses the phrase "functional mobility" to refer to the

(A) ability to perform daily activities
(B) usefulness of electrical devices
(C) ability to read road signs
(D) theory that electrical vision devices work better than mechanical ones
(E) practice of locating and moving around objects

19 The author suggests that the uses of the bionic eye are "far-reaching" (line 47) because

(A) the device could be provided with capabilities beyond even those of normal eyesight
(B) a wide variety of visually impaired people could be treated with the device
(C) the devices could be provided at a low cost for people all over the world
(D) improvements in the device would eventually lead to such developments as smaller size, greater durability, and less risk from the implantation surgery
(E) devices that stimulate the visual cortex directly allow a wider field of vision than other types of devices

20 In line 51, "pressing" most nearly means

(A) unyielding
(B) urgent
(C) pushing
(D) arduous
(E) emphasizing

21 The author suggests, in lines 64–67, that the patient's functional mobility could be impaired by the device because

(A) it is only a temporary solution to vision loss
(B) the apparatus can cause injury
(C) electrical stimulation of the brain is dangerous
(D) the system is connected to an external processor
(E) it is not an effective means of repairing vision loss

22 In paragraph 4, the author's reasoning process is best described as

(A) an assertion followed by a list of qualifiers, then alternatives
(B) hypothetical examples followed by an observation
(C) several analyses of a single case from multiple perspectives
(D) a hypothetical situation followed by possible explanations
(E) a description of an actual experiment, then extrapolation based on the results

23 "Application," in line 73, most nearly means

(A) function
(B) attachment
(C) relevance
(D) diligence
(E) request

24 The author believes that "the usefulness of electrical devices that directly stimulate the visual cortex far outweighs the usefulness of other neuroprostheses…" (lines 77–80) because

(A) direct-stimulation devices benefit a much wider range of visually-impaired patients
(B) mass production of artificial retinas is not currently feasible
(C) diet is more helpful than mechanical devices in correcting vision problems
(D) other types of neuroprostheses cause excessive impairment of functional mobility
(E) the initial success of a direct-stimulation device renders all other types of devices obsolete

IF YOU FINISH BEFORE TIME IS CALLED, YOU MAY CHECK YOUR WORK ON THIS SECTION ONLY. DO NOT TURN TO ANY OTHER SECTION IN THE TEST.

STOP

Directions: This section contains two types of questions. You have 25 minutes to complete both types. For questions 1–8, solve each problem and decide which is the best of the choices given. Fill in the corresponding oval on the answer sheet. You may use any available space for scratchwork.

Time—25 Minutes
18 Questions

Notes

1. Calculator use is permitted.

2. All numbers used are real numbers.

3. Figures are provided for some problems. All figures are drawn to scale and lie in a plane UNLESS otherwise indicated.

4. Unless otherwise specified, the domain of any function f is assumed to be the set of all real numbers x for which $f(x)$ is a real number.

Reference Information

  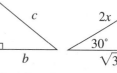

$A = \dfrac{1}{2}bh \qquad c^2 = a^2 + b^2 \qquad \text{Special Right Triangles} \qquad A = \pi r^2 \qquad V = \pi r^2 h \qquad A = lw \qquad V = lwh$

$C = 2\pi r$

The sum of the measures in degrees of the angles of a triangle is 180.
The number of degrees of arc in a circle is 360.
A straight angle has a degree measure of 180.

---

1 If $x + 3x + 5x = -18$, then what is the value of x ?

(A) −168

(B)   −2

(C) $-\dfrac{1}{2}$

(D) $\dfrac{1}{2}$

(E)   2

---

1 quart = 4 cups
5 cups = 40 ounces

2 Based on the information above, how many ounces are equivalent to $\dfrac{3}{8}$ of a quart?

(A) 16
(B) 12
(C) 8
(D) 6
(E) 5

GO ON TO THE NEXT PAGE

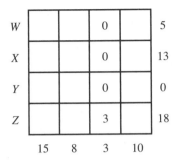

			0		5
W			0		5
X			0		13
Y			0		0
Z			3		18
	15	8	3	10	

3 A 0, 3, or 5 will be placed in each square of the grid above. The sum of the numbers in each row is equal to the number to the right of that row, and the sum of the numbers in each column is equal to the number below that column. For example, the sum of the numbers in the third column is 3, so there is a 3 below the third column. What will row X be when the 0's, 3's and 5's are all entered correctly into the grid?

(A) X | 5 | 3 | 0 | 5 |

(B) X | 5 | 0 | 3 | 5 |

(C) X | 3 | 5 | 0 | 5 |

(D) X | 0 | 3 | 5 | 5 |

(E) X | 5 | 3 | 5 | 0 |

4 For which of the following lists of 5 numbers is the average (arithmetic mean) greater than the median?

(A) 2, 3, 7, 8, 9
(B) 2, 3, 6, 7, 8
(C) 3, 4, 5, 7, 8
(D) 3, 4, 5, 5, 5
(E) 4, 5, 6, 7, 8

5 On a map, the length of the road from Town F to Town G is measured to be 18 inches. On this map, $\frac{1}{4}$ inch represents an actual distance of 10 miles. What is the actual distance, in miles, from Town F to Town G along this road?

(A) 720
(B) 540
(C) 400
(D) 180
(E) 72

6 How many of the prime factors of 42 are greater than 3 ?

(A) Zero
(B) One
(C) Two
(D) Three
(E) Four

GO ON TO THE NEXT PAGE

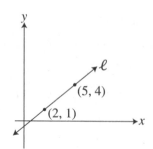

7 In the figure above, what is the *y*-intercept of line ℓ ?

(A) −4
(B) −2
(C) −1
(D) 1
(E) 4

8 If $f(t) = \dfrac{1}{t^{-1} + 1}$ then for what value of *t* does $f(t) = 4$?

(A) $-\dfrac{4}{3}$

(B) $-\dfrac{3}{3}$

(C) $\dfrac{1}{4}$

(D) $\dfrac{1}{3}$

(E) $\dfrac{4}{5}$

GO ON TO THE NEXT PAGE

Directions: For Student-Produced Response questions 9–18, use the grids at the bottom of the answer sheet page on which you have answered questions 1–8.

Each of the remaining 10 questions requires you to solve the problem and enter your answer by marking the ovals in the special grid, as shown in the examples below. You may use any available space for scratchwork.

Answer: 1.25 or $\frac{5}{4}$ or 5/4

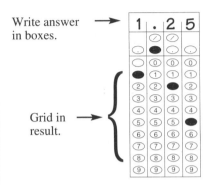

Write answer → in boxes.

Grid in → result.

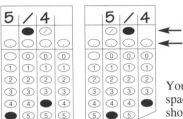

Fraction ← line

Decimal ← point

You may start your answers in any column, space permitting. Columns not needed should be left blank.

Either position is correct.

- It is recommended, though not required, that you write your answer in the boxes at the top of the columns. However, **you will receive credit only for darkening the ovals correctly.**

- Grid only one answer to a question, even though some problems have more than one correct answer.

- Darken no more than one oval in a column.

- No answers are negative.

- **Mixed numbers** cannot be gridded. For example: the number $1\frac{1}{4}$ must be gridded as 1.25 or 5/4.

  (If [1 1 / 4] is gridded, it will be interpreted as $\frac{11}{4}$, not $1\frac{1}{4}$.)

- <u>Decimal Accuracy:</u> Decimal answers must be entered as accurately as possible. For example, if you obtain an answer such as 0.1666. . ., you should record the result as .166 or .167. **Less accurate values such as .16 or .17 are not acceptable.**

Acceptable ways to grid $\frac{1}{6}$ = .1666. . .

---

9 How many $\frac{1}{3}$ pound paperback books together weigh 25 pounds?

10 If $\frac{(2+7)(x-3)}{3} = 8$, what is the value of x ?

GO ON TO THE NEXT PAGE

11 In isosceles triangle XYZ, the measure of angle X is 24°. If angle Y of the triangle measures $s°$, where $s \neq 24$, what is one possible value of s ?

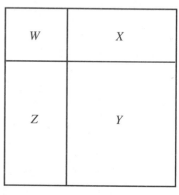

Note: Figure not drawn to scale.

13 In the figure above, the lengths and widths of rectangles W, X, Y, and Z are whole numbers. The areas of rectangles W, X, and Y are 20, 28, and 63, respectively. What is the area of the entire figure?

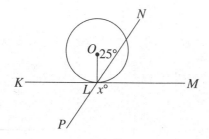

12 In the figure above, $\overline{KM}$ is tangent to circle O at point L. What is the value of x ?

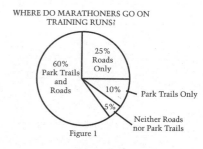

WHERE DO MARATHONERS GO ON TRAINING RUNS?

Figure 1

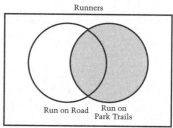

Runners

Figure 2

14 Runners training for the Browerdale Marathon are represented in the circle graph in Figure 1. Figure 2 is another way to illustrate where the runners go on their training runs. If the same 300 runners are represented in both figures, what is the total number of runners represented by the unshaded area inside the circles in Figure 2 ?

GO ON TO THE NEXT PAGE

15 In a laboratory, there were just enough microscopes, test tubes, and calculators so that every 3 students had to share a microscope, every 4 students had to share a test tube, and every 5 students had to share a calculator. If the sum of the number of microscopes, test tubes, and calculators used by the class was 94, how many students were in the class?

17 What is the value of the expression $\left((64)^{\frac{2}{3}} - 9 \right)^2$?

Step 1	Choose a number q less than 100.

Step 2	If q is prime, add 4.	If q is not prime, add 3.

Step 3	Divide the result of step 2 by 3.

Step 4	Find the least integer greater than the result of step 3.

16 In the chart above, if the number q chosen in step 1 is 23, what number will be the result of step 4 ?

18 How many positive integers less than 2,000 are multiples of 7 and equal to 5 times an even integer?

IF YOU FINISH BEFORE TIME IS CALLED, YOU MAY CHECK YOUR WORK ON THIS SECTION ONLY. DO NOT TURN TO ANY OTHER SECTION IN THE TEST.

- 87 -

Time—25 Minutes
35 Questions

Directions: For each question in this section, select the best answer from among the choices given and fill in the corresponding oval on the answer sheet.

The following sentences test correctness and effectiveness of expression. Part of each sentence or the entire sentence is underlined; beneath each sentence are five ways of phrasing the underlined material. Choice A repeats the original phrasing; the other four choices are different. If you think the original phrasing produces a better sentence than any of the alternatives, select choice A; if not, select one of the other choices.

In making your selection, follow the requirements of standard written English; that is, pay attention to grammar, choice of words, sentence construction, and punctuation. Your selection should result in the most effective sentence—clear and precise—without awkwardness or ambiguity.

EXAMPLE:

Every apple in the baskets <u>are ripe and labeled according to the date it was picked</u>.

(A) are ripe and labeled according to the date it was picked
(B) is ripe and labeled according to the date it was picked
(C) are ripe and labeled according to the date they were picked
(D) is ripe and labeled according to the date they were picked
(E) are ripe and labeled as to the date it was picked

ANSWER:
(A) ● (C) (D) (E)

---

1 <u>The little boy spread his toys out on the floor, he</u> began to tell me the about the significance of each of them.

(A) The little boy spread his toys out on the floor, he
(B) The toys, which were spread out on the floor by the little boy, who
(C) The toys were first spread out on the floor by the little boy, then he
(D) After spreading out the toys on the floor, the little boy
(E) The little boy, having spread out the toys on the floor, he

2 A malingerer is <u>when a person feigns illness or other incapacity</u> in order to avoid work or duty.

(A) when a person feigns illness or other incapacity
(B) a person who feigns illness or other incapacity
(C) feigning by a person of illness or other incapacity
(D) if a person feigns illness or other incapacity
(E) illness or other incapacity being feigned by a person

3 As I grow older and gain worldly experience, <u>I realize more and more that one's outward appearance is not nearly as important as your</u> inner happiness.

(A) I realize more and more that one's outward appearance is not nearly as important as your
(B) I realize more and more that one's outward appearance is not nearly as important as one's
(C) then realizing that one's outward appearance is not nearly as important as their
(D) having realized how outward appearance is not nearly as important as
(E) there is my realization about how outward appearance is not nearly as important as

4 Diligently practicing the flute <u>enables flautists to become a better musician</u>.

(A) enables flautists to become a better musician
(B) is enabling to flautists who want to be a better musician
(C) enables flautists to become better musicians
(D) is enabling to flautists in becoming a better musician
(E) enables a flautist to be better musicians

GO ON TO THE NEXT PAGE

5 The average modern cineplex can show more movies than if you combined six or seven old-style movie theaters.

(A) if you combined six or seven old-style movie theaters

(B) when six or seven old-style movie theaters are combined

(C) six or seven old-style movie theaters combined

(D) if six or seven old-style movie theaters were combined with each other

(E) combining six or seven old-style movie theaters

6 Mr. Martin is quite the polyglot; not only does he speak all of the Romance languages fluently, but he is also proficient in various tongues as Sanskrit, Quechua, and Tagalog.

(A) various tongues as

(B) various tongues that are

(C) tongues of such variance as

(D) tongues as various as

(E) a tongue as various as

7 Captured by the Spanish *conquistadores* in 1503, colonization was a development that many of the Incas in Cuzco were distraught by.

(A) colonization was a development that many of the Incas in Cuzco were distraught by

(B) the development of colonization made distraught many of the Incas in Cuzco

(C) many of the Incas in Cuzco were distraught by colonization

(D) many of the Incas in Cuzco felt distraught toward colonization

(E) many of the Incas in Cuzco, distraught by colonization

8 Being nicer and more sincere compared with the other girls in her grade, Shirley was unanimously voted class president all four years of high school.

(A) Being nicer and more sincere compared with

(B) Both nicer and more sincere compared to

(C) Nicer and more sincere than

(D) By being more sincere and nice than

(E) Nicer as well as more sincere, unlike

9 Upon returning to the United States after a semester in France, Marta said that the program had introduced her to the possibilities of both living and study abroad in the future.

(A) had introduced her to the possibilities of both living and study abroad

(B) had introduced her to the possibilities of both living and studying abroad

(C) has supplied the introduction of the possible life abroad along with further study

(D) serves to introduce her to the possibilities of life and of further study abroad both

(E) was her introduction to discovering the possibilities of life abroad or further study

10 Baker, California, which is 200 miles east of Los Angeles and 95 miles southwest of Las Vegas, is the site of the world's largest thermometer.

(A) which is 200 miles east of Los Angeles and 95 miles southwest

(B) found 200 miles east of Los Angeles while also being 95 miles southwest

(C) at a distance of 200 miles east of Los Angeles as well as 95 miles to the southwest

(D) 200 miles east of Los Angeles and it's located 95 miles to the southwest

(E) being 200 miles away from Los Angeles, and 95 miles from the southwest

11 In 1991, Voyageurs National Park banned certain off-road vehicles for environmental concerns specific to Minnesota, there snowmobiling is a popular winter sport.

(A) there

(B) which

(C) where

(D) so

(E) which is a place where

GO ON TO THE NEXT PAGE

The following sentences test your ability to recognize grammar and usage errors. Each sentence contains either a single error or no error at all. No sentence contains more than one error. The error, if there is one, is underlined and lettered. If the sentence contains an error, select the one underlined part that must be changed to make the sentence correct. If the sentence is correct, select choice E. In choosing answers, follow the requirements of standard written English.

EXAMPLE: ANSWER:

<u>Whenever</u> one is driving late at night, <u>you</u> must take extra precautions <u>against</u>
    A   B   C   (A) ● (c) (d) (e)

falling asleep <u>at</u> the wheel. <u>No error</u>
           D   E

12 This resort has trails so <u>dangerous</u> that skiers <u>spotting</u>
                        A   B
them are <u>quick</u> convinced to try <u>easier</u> ones instead.
         C   D
<u>No error</u>
  E

13 Homeopathic remedies, <u>though</u> <u>less widely prescribed</u>
                      A   B
<u>than</u> more traditional medications, <u>is</u> widely gaining
 C   D
acceptance with American physicians. <u>No error</u>
                           E

14 Some students are <u>unable to</u> study for <u>long</u>, uninterrupted
                A   B
periods of time, <u>but</u> this does not mean they are not
          C
capable <u>to get</u> good grades. <u>No error</u>
     D   E

15 <u>Between</u> sixty <u>and</u> seventy-five <u>percent of</u> medical
   A   B   C
students major in biology or chemistry; the rest <u>come</u>
                              D
from other educational backgrounds. <u>No error</u>
                      E

16 The winners <u>of</u> the "Best of Breed" cup and the "Best
        A
in Show" trophy <u>was</u> <u>selected</u> by a panel of breeders
             B   C
<u>from the American Kennel Club.</u> <u>No error</u>
        D   E

17 Home schooling programs, nearly <u>unheard of</u> twenty
                            A
years ago, <u>is</u> now available <u>through</u> <u>many</u> public school
      B   C   D
systems. <u>No error</u>
      E

18 <u>Although</u> the play <u>does not start</u> until eight o'clock, the
   A   B
audience <u>are allowed</u> <u>into</u> the theater at seven-thirty.
        C   D
<u>No error</u>
  E

19 On <u>most</u> commercial airline flights, there <u>is</u> at least six
     A   B
or seven flight attendants, <u>whose</u> job it is <u>to ensure</u>
                  C   D
passenger safety. <u>No error</u>
           E

20 An applicant <u>to an Ivy League college</u> <u>must have</u> an
            A   B
excellent grade point average if <u>they want</u> <u>to be considered</u>
                   C   D
for admission. <u>No error</u>
       E

21 <u>In order to provide</u> better service <u>during</u> the busy
   A   B
summer months, <u>they</u> hire additional help at <u>most</u>
          C   D
stores and restaurants on Cape Cod. <u>No error</u>
                        E

GO ON TO THE NEXT PAGE

22 The district attorney <u>met</u> with the defendant's lawyer
  A
several times before <u>he</u> <u>decided</u> <u>to accept</u> the plea
  B   C   D
agreement. <u>No error</u>
  E

23 <u>Of</u> all the novelists <u>whose books</u> I <u>have read</u>, Jane
  A   B   C
Austen created the <u>most</u> memorable characters.
  D
<u>No error</u>
  E

24 <u>Between</u> tennis <u>and</u> swimming, <u>I think</u> swimming
  A   B   C
provides the <u>best</u> exercise. <u>No error</u>
  D   E

25 <u>My</u> parents <u>would rather</u> take a camping vacation <u>as</u>
  A   B   C
stay in a <u>fancy</u> hotel. <u>No error</u>
  D   E

26 Knowing that you <u>should practice</u> the piano for an
  A
hour <u>every</u> day and <u>to do</u> it are <u>two different things</u>.
  B   C   D
<u>No error</u>
  E

27 Many efforts to conserve water <u>have been made</u> in
  A
local desert communities, <u>but</u> only recently <u>has</u> these
  B   C
efforts had a <u>substantial</u> effect. <u>No error</u>
  D   E

28 <u>In many recipes</u>, butter and margarine can be used
  A
interchangeably, <u>but</u> butter <u>is</u> <u>the best choice</u> when you
  B   C   D
are making drop cookies. <u>No error</u>
  E

29 Eric Clapton, <u>possibly</u> the <u>most gifted</u> guitar player
  A   B
currently performing, <u>wrote and arranged</u> *Layla*,
  C
<u>one of</u> the most enduring rock love songs of all time.
  D
<u>No error</u>
  E

Directions: The following passage is an early draft of an essay. Some parts of the passage need to be rewritten.

Read the passage and select the best answer for each question that follows. Some questions are about particular sentences or parts of sentences and ask you to improve sentence structure or word choice. Other questions ask you to consider organization and development. In choosing answers, follow the conventions of standard written English.

Questions 30–35 are based on the following passage.

(1) Many well-known writers began their professional careers while they were still attending high school or college. (2) Stephen King, for example, not only wrote for his high school newspaper, he also began submitting short stories to science fiction magazines when he was just thirteen years old. (3) Joyce Maynard, another well-known author, had her first book, *Looking Back*, published while she was still in her teens. (4) If you are serious about a career as a writer or journalist, you can submit your work to a number of publications that accept unsolicited manuscripts. (5) It is best, however, to submit a query letter first.

(6) A query letter is a one-page document in which you introduce yourself to the editor of the publication, and ask if they would like to read something you have written. (7) Don't pretend to be a seasoned professional, you won't fool anyone, and your age may actually work to your advantage. (8) Include a paragraph or two outlining the story you've written or the article you'd like to write. (9) If you've taken any creative writing courses, be sure to include that information. (10) If you've won any prizes for your writing or had any of your writings published, tell the editor about that, too. (11) Don't forget to thank the editor for taking the time to read your letter.

(12) You probably won't sell your first story or article, but don't get discouraged. (13) Stephen King didn't sell his first submission either.

30 The sentence that best states the main idea of this passage is

(A) Sentence 1
(B) Sentence 4
(C) Sentence 5
(D) Sentence 6
(E) Sentence 12

31 In the context of the first paragraph, which of the following revisions is most needed in sentence 2?

(A) Omit "for example."
(B) Change "wrote" to "had written."
(C) Change "he also" to "but also."
(D) Change "began" to "begun."
(E) Change "when" to "while."

32 In context, which of the following revisions is most needed in sentence 6?

(A) Change "which" to "that."
(B) Change "and" to "or."
(C) Change "they" to "he or she."
(D) Change "they" to "him or her."
(E) Change "written" to "wrote."

33 Which of the following sentences is best inserted before sentence 7?

(A) Begin by telling the editor a little bit about yourself.
(B) Be sure to spell-check your letter before you send it.
(C) It's always a good idea to write about what you know.
(D) Jane Austen was also quite young when she wrote *Pride and Prejudice* and *Emma*.
(E) Some magazines also accept e-mail submissions.

GO ON TO THE NEXT PAGE

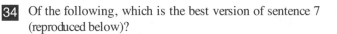
34 Of the following, which is the best version of sentence 7 (reproduced below)?

Don't pretend to be a seasoned professional, you won't fool anyone, and your age may actually work to your advantage.

(A) (As it is now)

(B) Don't pretend to be a seasoned professional, then you won't fool anyone, and your age may actually work to your advantage.

(C) Don't pretend to being a seasoned professional, you won't fool anyone, and your age may actually work to your advantage.

(D) Don't pretend to be a seasoned professional; you won't fool anyone, and your age may actually work to your advantage.

(E) Because you won't fool anyone, don't pretend to be a seasoned professional, your age may actually work to your advantage.

35 What is the best way to combine sentences 9 and 10 (reproduced below)?

If you've taken any creative writing courses, be sure to include that information. If you've won any prizes for your writing or had any of your writings published, tell the editor about that, too.

(A) Any information about creative writing courses you've taken, prizes you've won for your writing or writings of yours that have been published should be told by you to the editor.

(B) Be sure to include any information about any creative writing courses you've taken or any prizes you've won for your writing or any of your writings that you've had published.

(C) Any creative writing courses you've taken should be included, along with any prizes won for your writing or any of your writings that have been published.

(D) If you've taken any creative writing courses, that information should be included, but also any prizes you've won for your writing or any of your writings that have been published.

(E) If you've taken any creative writing courses, won any prizes for your writing, or had any of your writings published, be sure to include that information.

IF YOU FINISH BEFORE TIME IS CALLED, YOU MAY CHECK YOUR WORK ON THIS SECTION ONLY. DO NOT TURN TO ANY OTHER SECTION IN THE TEST.

Time—25 Minutes
24 Questions

Directions: For each question in this section, select the best answer from among the choices given and fill in the corresponding oval on the answer sheet.

Each sentence below has one or two blanks, each blank indicating that something has been omitted. Beneath the sentence are five words or sets of words labeled A through E. Choose the word or set of words that, when inserted in the sentence, best fits the meaning of the sentence as a whole.

EXAMPLE:

Today's small, portable computers contrast markedly with the earliest electronic computers, which were -------.

(A) effective
(B) invented
(C) useful
(D) destructive
(E) enormous

ANSWER:

1 Though many of his books have been ------- readers, John Grisham's writing has been ------- by critics.

(A) loathed by . . mocked
(B) enjoyed by . . lauded
(C) popular with . . derided
(D) ignored by . . ridiculed
(E) associated with . . hailed

2 To relieve the ------- of the interminable lecture, Andreas ------- his notes with drawings of sailboats.

(A) interest . . covered
(B) gall . . surmised
(C) elation . . embellished
(D) excitement . . compounded
(E) tedium . . interspersed

3 The Internet is perhaps the most ------- of media; unlike a book, which needs to be reprinted to correct mistakes, a web page can be corrected and relaunched in a matter of minutes.

(A) itinerant
(B) immutable
(C) terse
(D) affable
(E) malleable

4 Although they expected the continent to be uninhabited, when the first Europeans arrived in Australia they found it already ------- by indigenous people.

(A) abandoned
(B) explored
(C) desired
(D) experienced
(E) populated

5 It was ------- occasion when Nancy Pelosi was elected House Minority Leader in 2002; she is the first woman to hold the position in the history of the Congress.

(A) a momentous
(B) an inexplicable
(C) a fortuitous
(D) an affable
(E) a vapid

6 Although John meant the compliment to be -------, it came out sounding ------- and mocking.

(A) sarcastic . . kind
(B) gracious . . sincere
(C) flattering . . sardonic
(D) satirical . . sharp
(E) quiet . . impressive

7 Having been left in the sun for a week, the bag of garbage gave off a -------, putrid smell when we returned from vacation.

(A) haughty
(B) bombastic
(C) voluble
(D) pallid
(E) noisome

8 Carla's obsession with her soap operas was so ------- that she could not stand to miss a single episode.

(A) acerbic
(B) poignant
(C) untrammeled
(D) derogatory
(E) zealous

GO ON TO THE NEXT PAGE

The passages below are followed by questions based on their content; questions following a pair of related passages may also be based on the relationship between the paired passages. Answer the questions on the basis of what is <u>stated</u> or <u>implied</u> in the passages and in any introductory material that may be provided.

Questions 9–10 are based on the following passage.

There is considerable evidence that irrigation
may have played a pivotal role in the foundation
of the earliest civilizations, such as that of Sumer
Line in the Tigris-Euphrates valley. The reasons for the
(5) influence of irrigation are twofold. The
development of irrigation allowed for extremely
efficient agricultural production, creating the
surplus of food resources that must serve as the
foundation for any civilization. Furthermore,
(10) constructing the elaborate system of canals and
drainage networks was a task of tremendous
complexity. The centers of commerce,
administration, and science that accomplished the
task eventually blossomed into the cities
(15) that served as the cornerstone of Sumerian
civilization.

9 The sentence in lines 4–5 ("The reasons…are
twofold") refers to

(A) a need for a food surplus and a successful
economy
(B) the development of commerce and administration
(C) the construction of elaborate canals and drainage
systems
(D) the establishment of successful agriculture and
the foundation of cities
(E) the complexity and success of the irrigation
systems

As used in line 11, "tremendous" most nearly means

10 (A) wonderful
(B) enormous
(C) intricate
(D) important
(E) moderate

Questions 11–12 are based on the following passage.

The city of Havana stands today as a testament
to its turbulent yet glorious history. This lively
center of all things Cuban looks today much as it did
Line when it was built more than 100 years ago. An
(5) air of distinction and wealth, albeit now somewhat
faded, lingers in its neighborhoods. Spanish architecture,
a symbol of a colonial past, graces the
city, though the paint and plaster of many of the
buildings have chipped and peeled as the years have
(10) passed. Amidst the gentle aging of this great city, it is
the generosity and friendliness of the residents
that have allowed Havana to survive and flourish.

11 The word "air" in line 5 most nearly means

(A) requirement
(B) lack
(C) combination
(D) imitation
(E) impression

12 With which of the following statements would the
writer most likely agree?

(A) Havana is a historic and diverse city.
(B) The citizens of Havana are essential to the
endurance of the city.
(C) The citizens of Havana will never be able to rebuild
the city to its past glory.
(D) The look of Havana has evolved steadily throughout
its history.
(E) Havana is an unusually wealthy city.

GO ON TO THE NEXT PAGE

Questions 13–24 are based on the following passages.

What is the best approach to curriculum and classroom pedagogy for United States public school classrooms? Psychologists, public officials, reformers, and educators have been struggling to answer this question for over a century. The pair of passages that follows represents two opposing opinions on the question.

Passage 1

Recent efforts on the part of some reformers to influence education policy in the public and academic arena have created the danger of a
Line devolution that would do away with a hundred years
(5) of progress in educational methodology. Some proponents of the so-called "instructivist" movement would see our educational institutions return to the days of the factory schools of the nineteenth century, when teachers taught an inflexible,
(10) programmed curriculum to students who learned to regurgitate it by rote, abstracted from any connection with real-world applications or usability and under constant threat of swift punishment for any deviation or intellectual digression. History clearly
(15) demonstrates that such educational arrangements not only fail to foster the divergent and creative thinking vital to success in today's world, but they do not even accomplish the goals they purport to—as the decades of widespread illiteracy and ignorance
(20) that accompanied the practice of such methods can attest. In contrast, the educational approach most pervasive in schools today, known typically as "constructivism," delivers students from the oppression of the factory school model and into the
(25) student-centered environment of communal, hands-on, complex learning.

The constructivist approach to education uses principles of cognitive psychology, particularly the work of Piaget and Erikson, to understand how
(30) students learn and then to design curricula that address those learning patterns. In one famous example, education researcher J. Bruner led students to an understanding of prime numbers by having them sort beans into different sized groups. Through
(35) this sorting exercise, students discovered for themselves the essential principles of multiplication and division. For example, the discovery that some quantities of beans cannot be sorted without some left over beans leads to an understanding of prime

(40) numbers. Researchers tell us that students who come to discover knowledge for themselves in this way— who "construct" knowledge in this pattern—are better able to comprehend, retain, and transfer that knowledge to new contexts. Theorists emphasize
(45) that students subjected to rote memorization of prime numbers and multiplication tables do not incorporate as deep an understanding as students who are led to discover such principles for themselves.

(50) In contrast to the rigidly hierarchic, authoritarian classrooms of the past, the constructivist classroom is collaborative. Facts and principles are always placed in the context of real-world problems or complex projects, and never abstracted from a life
(55) situation to which they are applicable. Learning becomes a social negotiation, highly cooperative, with each student encouraged to contribute. The teacher acts only as a guide and facilitator who creates and maintains the appropriate learning
(60) environment. The course of a lesson is subject to all the errors, false starts, and stalls of student-driven experimentation, but learning acquired this way is ultimately broader and more useful than sets of abstracted facts. The class is capable of transcending
(65) the limits of the curriculum and the expectations of educators alike.

Passage 2

Most people, if they saw it for themselves, would be horrified by the style of "education" that goes on in classrooms across the country today. Gone are the
(70) straight rows, the orderly progress of instruction, the traditional skills and intensive practice that makes for true mastery of school subjects. Instead, observers would see a mishmash of students in circles and groups fumbling around with ill-defined "projects,"
(75) striving to figure out something that they're not instructed in by teachers who aren't even allowed to correct them or tell them when they're wrong. Training and practice in discrete skills is discarded. Assessment as a motivation is de-emphasized in favor
(80) of "facilitating" learning that is "incidental" or "intuitive" to the prescribed activities.

The philosophy that drives this style of education is a hotchpotch of unsubstantiated theory called "constructivism." This approach, which has taken
(85) hold of many classrooms all over the country, flies in the face of common sense. Do constructivists really mean to suggest that knowledge cannot be learned by

GO ON TO THE NEXT PAGE

- 96 -

instruction, or that principles and skills cannot be broken into smaller segments and abstracted from
(90) their contexts for ease of learning? Do they really intend to propose that objective assessment of student learning is impossible or undesirable?

A growing body of evidence, and a few well-publicized fiascos, suggest that constructivists are
(95) strolling down the primrose path. Some emerging studies have failed to show any significant increase in the effectiveness of constructivist methods compared with direct instructional approaches. Moreover, some critics have started
(100) to question whether constructivist ideas are founded on a strong and supportable body of empirical research, or whether the whole approach has been patched together from scraps of cognitive psychology with liberal amounts of
(105) speculation.

Consider, for example, one of the common ways in which a constructivist classroom causes students to waste time. If a pupil needs practice in one specific task that is part of a larger task, that
(110) student might be required to repeat mastered skills unnecessarily, in order to get the opportunity to try out the skill that needs practice. For example, a student who is a skilled writer but needs work on thesis sentences might have to spend weeks working
(115) through an extended project of research and writing in order to get the single opportunity to practice writing a thesis sentence. On the other hand, in a traditional classroom, the learner would receive practice, instruction, and correction in this
(120) one problem area until it was mastered. This is just one of a multitude of instances where constructivism fails to efficiently accomplish what it purports to do: to actually teach.

No one is advocating a reversion to the days of
(125) pointless memorization, drill for its own sake, and draconian discipline. But the unconscionable waste of time, resources and student potential that constructivism supports in the name of progressive education does today's students a
(130) grave disservice.

13 The main goal of Passage 1 is to

(A) identify and summarize a set of fallacies
(B) describe the history of a controversial issue
(C) dispute the significance of recent research
(D) argue for the superiority of a particular approach
(E) advocate for reforms in current educational methods

14 Which of the following is suggested about "some reformers" in Passage 1 (line 1)?

(A) They have some convincing claims supported by strong evidence.
(B) They want all schools to adopt constructivist methodologies.
(C) They intend to retain their widespread control of the school systems.
(D) They want to return education to the model of nineteenth-century factory schools.
(E) They represent no real danger to the state of education.

15 The author of Passage 1 asserts that endeavoring to "understand how students learn" (lines 29–30) would most likely

(A) bring about more debate and discussion about the best path for education
(B) lead to the development of many radically different educational philosophies
(C) result in improved education and teaching approaches
(D) affect the way that studies on student learning are carried out
(E) cause a regression to outdated classroom methodologies

16 The example from the work of J. Bruner (lines 31–40) is included by the author of Passage 1 in order to demonstrate that

(A) teachers can use simple learning aids to help them instruct students in principles of advanced mathematics
(B) understanding of prime numbers is vital to the subsequent learning of multiplication and division
(C) knowledge acquired in this way is easier to reliably transfer to different situations
(D) students are capable of discovering complex concepts on their own through experimentation
(E) schools should return to traditional models of direct teacher instruction

GO ON TO THE NEXT PAGE

17 The author of Passage 2 would most likely respond to the description of the teacher's role in lines 57–60 of Passage 1 with the argument that

(A) teachers need to provide hands-on, collaborative environments that encourage student discovery
(B) students will not learn as accurately or efficiently without a teacher's coaching and correction
(C) research demonstrates that teachers must give direct instruction if students are to master skills
(D) students will tend to waste time, effort, and resources unless teachers strictly discipline and constantly drill them
(E) lessons can be broken down into discrete elements and taught as abstract skills

18 The educational approach that produces the type of classroom described in lines 72–81 of Passage 2 is the same type of educational approach endorsed by

(A) Piaget and Erikson in line 29
(B) the author of Passage 2
(C) "some critics" in line 99
(D) "No one" in line 124
(E) J. Bruner in line 32

19 Lines 79–81 mainly highlight which negative aspect of the constructivist classroom?

(A) Students aren't taught practical skills.
(B) Using grades to reward or punish student performance is discouraged.
(C) The classroom is chaotic and disorganized.
(D) Only students who show high levels of achievement are rewarded.
(E) Students don't receive any feedback on how they're doing.

20 The statement in lines 95–99 of Passage 2 ("Some emerging...approaches") mainly functions to

(A) introduce evidence to support a point
(B) make a transition to a new subject
(C) expand on a theory
(D) contrast two opposing arguments
(E) refute a specific exception

21 According to the author of Passage 2, "some critics" mentioned in line 99 might argue that

(A) constructivist education methodology is firmly based on cognitive psychology
(B) direct instruction methods are based on research results
(C) constructivist approaches waste classroom time and school resources
(D) it is difficult to draw conclusions about educational methods based on research results
(E) additional research would validate the usefulness of the constructivist approach

22 According to Passage 2, both the "students" and the "pupil" specified in line 108 are similar to each other in that they

(A) exhibit strong writing skills but have trouble with transitions and conclusions
(B) are forced by a constructivist classroom to repeat skills they have already mastered
(C) show a high level of skill at working in collaborative and cooperative environments
(D) receive instruction in discrete skills until they can demonstrate mastery of those skills
(E) resent working with other students

23 The passages disagree with each other most strongly on which of the following issues?

(A) whether students learn best by rote memorization
(B) whether constructivist approaches create more false starts and student errors than direct instruction
(C) whether discrete skills should be abstracted from real-world situations
(D) whether research results from cognitive psychology should be used in determining educational approaches
(E) whether knowledge is a cooperative social construction or a constant external truth

GO ON TO THE NEXT PAGE

24 Which of the following best summarizes the attitudes of the two authors toward educational methodologies?

(A) Passage 2 endorses research-based educational approaches, while Passage 1 endorses theoretical, speculative approaches.

(B) Passage 1 makes a case for collaborative, discovery-based curricula, while Passage 2 makes a case for traditional direct instruction.

(C) Passage 2 suggests that writing is best taught as a set of abstracted skills, while Passage 1 suggests that writing is learned through projects and collaboration.

(D) Passage 1 argues for tolerant, permissive classroom environments, while Passage 2 argues for strict, disciplinarian classrooms.

(E) Passage 1 claims that knowledge acquired in collaborative, self-directed activities is easier to retain and transfer, while Passage 2 claims that it is not.

IF YOU FINISH BEFORE TIME IS CALLED, YOU MAY CHECK YOUR WORK ON THIS SECTION ONLY. DO NOT TURN TO ANY OTHER SECTION IN THE TEST.

STOP

Time—25 Minutes
24 Questions

Directions: For each question in this section, select the best answer from among the choices given and fill in the corresponding oval on the answer sheet.

Each sentence below has one or two blanks, each blank indicating that something has been omitted. Beneath the sentence are five words or sets of words labeled A through E. Choose the word or set of words that, when inserted in the sentence, best fits the meaning of the sentence as a whole.

EXAMPLE:

Today's small, portable computers contrast markedly with the earliest electronic computers, which were -------.

(A) effective   (B) invented
  (C) useful   (D) destructive
    (E) enormous

ANSWER:
Ⓐ Ⓑ Ⓒ Ⓓ ●

---

1 Cathedral windows are often -------, composed of thousands of pieces of luminous stained glass.

(A) mysterious   (B) intricate
  (C) sacred   (D) descriptive
    (E) burnished

2 Recent fossil evidence suggests that carnivorous dinosaurs were ------- swimmers, but some paleontologists still think that these dinosaurs ------- the water.

(A) swift . . entered
(B) nervous . . loathed
(C) accomplished . . feared
(D) unskilled . . avoided
(E) natural . . enjoyed

3 Once he had intellectually ------- the difference between regional dialects, Fernando found himself speaking the language ------- .

(A) rejected . . considerately
(B) grasped . . effortlessly
(C) mastered . . implicitly
(D) forgotten . . eloquently
(E) recognized . . ambiguously

4 The international news wire service ------- information -------, so that events are reported all over the world shortly after they happen.

(A) records . . accurately
(B) falsifies . . deliberately
(C) verifies . . painstakingly
(D) disseminates . . rapidly
(E) suppresses . . thoroughly

5 Lacking sacred scriptures or codified -------, Shinto is more properly regarded as a legacy of traditional religious practices and basic values than as a formal system of belief.

(A) followers   (B) boundaries
  (C) dogma   (D) dispositions
    (E) strata

6 We will face the idea of old age with ------- as long as we believe that it invariably brings poverty, isolation, and illness.

(A) regret   (B) apprehension
  (C) enlightenment (D) veneration
    (E) reverence

7 Though a hummingbird weighs less than one ounce, all species of hummingbirds are ------- eaters, maintaining very high body temperatures and ------- many times their weight in food each day.

(A) voracious . . consuming
(B) fastidious . . discarding
(C) hasty . . locating
(D) prolific . . producing
(E) delicate . . storing

8 As a playwright, Pinter is renowned for his mundane settings, his ------- yet poetic dialogue, and his aggressive, often mean-spirited characters.

(A) comprehensive (B) lyrical
  (C) colloquial   (D) ethereal
    (E) affirmative

GO ON TO THE NEXT PAGE

Each passage below is followed by questions based on its content. Answer the questions on the basis of what is <u>stated</u> or <u>implied</u> in each passage and in any introductory material that may be provided.

Questions 9–10 are based on the following passage.

Recently, I casually looked through a journal from my childhood. The pages were filled with ragged cartoons that seemed to have been drawn by
Line someone else. Yet, as I flipped toward the end of
(5) the book, these awkward, almost unrecognizable creations from my past slowly began to come alive with familiarity. One page, covered in a mess of squares and stick figures depicting a billiards game, captured my attention. Suddenly I felt
(10) transported back to my grandparents' musty basement game room, even recalling my older brother's victorious taunts. I turned to the next page eagerly, now exhilarated by a sense of deep connection to this record of bygone years.

9 The author implies that initially he only "casually looked" (line 1) through the childhood journal because

(A) he could not remember the events it described
(B) he was not skilled at drawing
(C) he found its content unfamiliar
(D) he was not interested in his childhood
(E) he was embarrassed by his cartoons

10 The author's purpose in mentioning his brother's "victorious taunts" (line 12) is most likely to

(A) indicate that he had a strained relationship with his brother
(B) imply that this billiards game was particularly memorable
(C) criticize his brother's behavior
(D) suggest the journal recalled painful memories
(E) underscore the journal's ability to powerfully recall the past

Questions 11–12 are based on the following passage.

What plagues both political parties in the United States today is their need to win over the voting public at any cost. Since the average American voter has only
Line an acquaintance with the crucial issues of the day and
(5) an even narrower grasp of the ways in which policy can address them, politicians are forced to mount often-vicious attacks on their competitors to capture the interest of the electorate. Rather than elect the best candidates for the task at hand, the American voter,
(10) election after election, chooses what appears to be the lesser of multiple evils, electing, in effect, the best worst candidate for the job.

11 The plague on both political parties (line 1) could be best described as their

(A) reliance on polls to determine the feelings of the voting public
(B) willingness to attack their closest competitors
(C) need to appeal to an ill-informed electorate
(D) lack of concern for the views of most voters
(E) refusal to appeal to lower-income families

12 The word "acquaintance" in line 4 most nearly means

(A) polite relationship
(B) superficial familiarity
(C) fraught discussion
(D) complex dialogue
(E) nuanced exchange

GO ON TO THE NEXT PAGE

Questions 13–24 are based on the following passage.

This passage, excerpted from an article submitted to an agricultural journal, discusses the growing phenomenon of Community Supported Agriculture farms.

The boom in the market for fresh organic produce since the early 1990s has encouraged the spread of Community Supported Agriculture farms, or CSAs.
Line Modeled after an innovative farming and marketing
(5) concept that originated in Japan in the 1960s, CSAs have grown in popularity in the United States in recent years. Instead of (or in addition to) selling produce at traditional outlets such as farmers' markets or to retailers and restaurants, small farmers grow a wide
(10) variety of crops and sell membership subscriptions to the farm for the season. Members pay a certain amount up front for the subscription and then come to the farm (or to a centrally located pick-up site) each week and receive a selection of the week's harvest. So far, small-
(15) scale CSA farming seems to be a sustainable alternative to traditional agriculture, with many advantages for both producers and consumers.

This arrangement offers clear benefits to small farmers interested in growing a range of fruits or
(20) vegetables. First, it provides greater financial stability than selling at farmers' markets does. Since most CSA subscription payments are due at the beginning of the farming season, farmers have cash on hand in the spring for their initial expenditure on seeds and equipment.
(25) They can anticipate labor costs and other major expenses throughout the season and budget accordingly. In a sense, they have a fixed price for their goods and a guaranteed market, at least for a year at a time.

Second, CSA members share some of the risks
(30) inherent in farming. When growing conditions are favorable, everyone shares in the resulting abundance. In times of drought or when insect infestations or other problems reduce crop yields, everyone receives a bit less. Farmers rely on yields to average out to an
(35) acceptable level over time (otherwise members would be reluctant to renew their subscriptions year after year), but they need not worry unduly if the harvest fluctuates from week to week.

CSA members, in turn, receive the benefit of
(40) guaranteed freshness, since most produce is harvested on the day they pick it up. This is a clear advantage over supermarkets, which may carry produce shipped from afar and stored for a week or more before reaching the consumer. The cost of a subscription, which is based on

(45) the cost of the average number of various fruits and vegetables distributed each week, is usually calculated to be below the retail value of the produce, so financially it is a good deal for members as well.

One potential drawback of the CSA model, from a
(50) member's point of view, is that members have less of a choice as to which vegetables they receive, compared to shopping at a supermarket. Although many farmers give members the option to select whatever they prefer among the items available for the week, members are
(55) allowed to choose only crops that are in season locally. Many members, however, come to prefer eating locally grown, in-season food. As one longtime member noted, "Eating what's in season each week forces you to become aware of the pattern of the seasons and
(60) weather, and it feels great to know you're eating peas that were still on the vine this morning. When such a crop is only available for a short time, you savor it that much more."

This member's comment suggests one of the less
(65) tangible benefits of belonging to a CSA farm: greater awareness of nature and involvement in the cycle of food production. Many CSAs have an open-farm policy where members can visit anytime to see how their food is produced, or just to take a walk or to picnic. They
(70) gain a greater sense of involvement in agriculture and have a chance to talk with the people who grow their food, and farmers get to connect with the people who are, quite literally, eating the fruits of their labor. Some CSAs require or encourage all members to participate in
(75) a short work shift at some time during the season, which further increases members' sense of involvement. These less tangible benefits of CSA membership are, in the end, the reasons many returning members cite for their decision to subscribe year after year. CSA farmers
(80) are thus wise to stress the benefits of involvement with the farm when trying to attract new members.

CSA membership is not for those who place a high value on being able to choose when they want a certain crop or how much of it they need, nor is it for farmers
(85) who prefer to grow abundant quantities of a single crop instead of smaller amounts of a variety of crops. For an increasing number of small organic farmers and consumers, however, the CSA system is uniquely valuable as a model for food production and distribution.

GO ON TO THE NEXT PAGE

13 The first paragraph implies that traditional agricultural practices are

(A) not sustainable for farms of any size
(B) less popular in Japan than in the United States
(C) suitable only for selling at farmers' markets and to retailers and restaurants
(D) advantageous only for consumers and never for farmers
(E) different from some practices used in CSA farming

14 In line 27, "fixed" most nearly means

(A) repaired
(B) restored
(C) constant
(D) preserved
(E) adjusted

15 The reference to "abundance" in line 31 primarily serves to

(A) differentiate between the results of insect infestations and the results of drought
(B) suggest that crop yields average out to a high level over time
(C) contrast risk-taking by farmers with risk-taking by CSA members
(D) describe one potential outcome of risk-sharing among farmers and CSA members
(E) compare the results of CSA farming with the results of traditional agriculture

16 In line 37, the author uses "unduly" to convey the

(A) degree of worry resulting from risk-sharing
(B) futility of trying to increase crop yields
(C) correspondence between worry and crop yields
(D) necessity of predictable harvests
(E) irrationality of some farmers

17 In the paragraph 4, the author indicates that which of the following is an advantage that CSAs hold over supermarkets?

(A) CSA members routinely get produce that has not been stored for long.
(B) CSA members may get produce that is shipped from afar.
(C) The number of various fruits and vegetables distributed each week remains constant.
(D) CSA members can budget their food costs before the farming season begins.
(E) The cost of a subscription is usually calculated to be above retail value.

18 Paragraph 5 indicates that which of the following is an advantage that supermarkets hold over CSAs?

(A) Supermarkets keep on hand larger quantities of a limited number of fruits and vegetables.
(B) Organic produce costs less in supermarkets.
(C) Supermarkets tend to ship and store food for shorter time periods.
(D) Supermarkets provide shoppers with more choice of produce to purchase.
(E) Supermarkets are more convenient to get to than are many farms.

19 The quotation from the CSA member in lines 58–63 emphasizes that the necessity of eating locally grown food is

(A) the primary reason most people choose to become CSA members
(B) a disadvantage of subscribing to a CSA
(C) the most influential factor determining which foods people most enjoy
(D) balanced by the fact that farmers allow members some choice in what to select for the week
(E) not always considered a drawback of CSA membership

20 Which crop would be the most appropriate example to add to the peas mentioned in line 60?

(A) a kind of melon that is ripe when harvested but is usually stored in coolers and distributed gradually over the course of a month
(B) a type of carrot that is widely considered the most flavorful of all root vegetables
(C) a variety of spinach that only grows in early spring and is harvested the same day it is distributed
(D) a kind of tomato that can be grown both in greenhouses and outdoors to yield fruit lasting for four to six months
(E) a type of squash that is harvested all at once and ripens while in storage

GO ON TO THE NEXT PAGE

21 Which of the following are mentioned in the passage as benefits of CSAs for both farmers and members?

   I. They encourage the interaction of farmers with consumers.

  II. They reduce worry about fluctuations in crop yields.

III. They increase financial stability.

(A) I only

(B) III only

(C) I and II only

(D) I and III only

(E) I, II, and III

22 In line 67, the author mentions an "open-farm policy" in order to illustrate that

(A) CSA farms are unique in providing opportunities for consumer involvement in the cycle of food production

(B) one CSA member's comments accurately reflect the values of most other members

(C) connecting with the people who eat their produce is one of the primary goals of CSA farmers

(D) CSA farms provide more intangible benefits than tangible ones

(E) CSA farms provide other benefits to members in addition to guaranteed freshness and lower cost

23 The author of the passage assumes that the reasons cited by returning members for their decision to renew their memberships are

(A) exemplified by the open-farm policy of some non-CSA farms

(B) likely to be important to potential new members as well

(C) unrelated to the more tangible benefits of CSA membership

(D) a result of the fact that subscription price is usually below its assumed retail value

(E) distinct from the reasons new members may want to join a CSA farm

24 The tone of the passage is primarily one of

(A) considered skepticism

(B) tentative reservation

(C) qualified endorsement

(D) robust inquisitiveness

(E) urgent entreaty

IF YOU FINISH BEFORE TIME IS CALLED, YOU MAY CHECK YOUR WORK ON THIS SECTION ONLY. DO NOT TURN TO ANY OTHER SECTION IN THE TEST.

STOP

- 104 -

NO TEST MATERIAL ON THIS PAGE

Notes

1. Calculator use is permitted.

2. All numbers used are real numbers.

3. Figures are provided for some problems. All figures are drawn to scale and lie in a plane UNLESS otherwise indicated.

4. Unless otherwise specified, the domain of any function f is assumed to be the set of all real numbers x for which $f(x)$ is a real number.

Reference Information

$A = \dfrac{1}{2}bh$ $c^2 = a^2 + b^2$ Special Right Triangles $A = \pi r^2$
$C = 2\pi r$

$V = \pi r^2 h$ $A = lw$ $V = lwh$

The sum of the measures in degrees of the angles of a triangle is 180.
The number of degrees of arc in a circle is 360.
A straight angle has a degree measure of 180.

YEARLY PROFITS FOR COMPANY *JKL*

1 According to the graph above, Company *JKL* experienced its smallest increase in yearly profits between which two consecutive years?

(A) 1997 and 1998
(B) 1998 and 1999
(C) 1999 and 2000
(D) 2000 and 2001
(E) 2001 and 2002

2 If $5^{11} = 5^2 \times 5^m$, what is the value of m ?

(A) 11
(B) 10
(C) 9
(D) 5
(E) 3

GO ON TO THE NEXT PAGE

3 If $|x - 6| = 5$, which of the following could be a value of x ?

(A) –6
(B) –5
(C) –1
(D) 1
(E) 5

5 If 12.5 is y percent of 250, what is y percent of 20 ?

(A) 20
(B) 1.25
(C) 1
(D) 0.2
(E) 0.0125

4 Each year, a cyber café charges a base rate of $25.00, an additional $0.30 per visit for the first 50 visits, and $0.10 for every visit after that. How much does the cyber café charge for a year in which 72 visits are made?

(A) $32.20
(B) $36.60
(C) $42.20
(D) $46.60
(E) $47.20

6 For which of the following values of y is $\dfrac{y^2 - 15y + 6}{7 - y}$ undefined?

(A) –7
(B) 4
(C) 7
(D) 16
(E) 23

GO ON TO THE NEXT PAGE

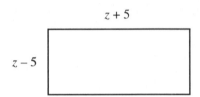

7 If the area of the rectangle above is 39, what is the value of z ?

(A) 8
(B) 13
(C) 18
(D) 20
(E) 25

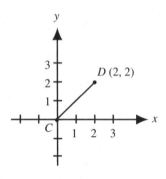

9 In the figure above, line B (not shown) is parallel to $\overline{CD}$ and passes through the point $(0, -1)$. Which of the following points lies on line B ?

(A) $(-2, -1)$
(B) $(-1, -2)$
(C) $(0, 0)$
(D) $(0, 1)$
(E) $(2, 2)$

8 James would like to buy a winter coat that is priced at $124. The price of the coat that James wants to buy is $32 more than he has. In which of the following equations does y represent the number of dollars James has?

(A) $y + 124 = 32$
(B) $y - 124 = 32$
(C) $y - 32 = -124$
(D) $y - 124 = -32$
(E) $y - 32 = 124$

10 If $k(1 - n)(n - k) = 0$, which of the following can be true?

I. $n = 1$
II. $n = k$
III. $k = 0$

(A) I only
(B) III only
(C) I and II only
(D) II and III only
(E) I, II, and III

GO ON TO THE NEXT PAGE

11 What is the diameter of a circle whose area is 16π ?

(A) 2
(B) 4
(C) 8
(D) 4π
(E) 8π

13 What was the initial weight, in pounds, of a person who now weighs 100 pounds and who gained x pounds and then lost y pounds?

(A) $100 - x + y$
(B) $100 + x + y$
(C) $100 - x - y$
(D) $100 + x - y$
(E) $100 - y - x$

$$\begin{array}{r} 5BA \\ + 3B5 \\ \hline A54 \end{array}$$

12 In the addition of two 3-digit numbers above, A and B represent two different digits. What digit does B represent?

(A) 2
(B) 3
(C) 5
(D) 7
(E) 9

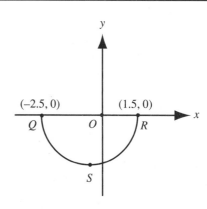

14 On the semicircle shown above, point R is the point with the greatest x-coordinate, and point Q is the point with the least x-coordinate. Point S is the point with the least y-coordinate on the semicircle. What is the y-coordinate of point S ?

(A) -4
(B) -3
(C) -2.5
(D) -2
(E) -1.5

GO ON TO THE NEXT PAGE

$$\frac{1}{2}s, \ s, \ t, \ \frac{3}{2}s, \ 3t$$

15 If the average (arithmetic mean) of the five numbers above is $2t$, what is t in terms of s ?

(A) $\frac{1}{2}s$

(B) $\frac{3}{4}s$

(C) $\quad s$

(D) $2s$

(E) $3s$

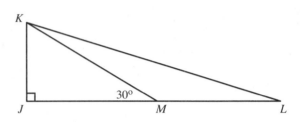

17 In the figure above, the length of JK is 2, and M is the midpoint of JL. What is the length of KL ?

(A) 2
(B) $2\sqrt{3}$
(C) 4
(D) $4\sqrt{3}$
(E) $2\sqrt{13}$

16 The ratio of c to d is 4 to 5, where c and d are positive. If m equals c increased by 25 percent of c, and n equals d decreased by 20 percent of d, what is the value of $\frac{m}{n}$?

(A) $\frac{2}{5}$

(B) $\frac{3}{4}$

(C) $\frac{4}{5}$

(D) $\frac{5}{4}$

(E) $\frac{3}{2}$

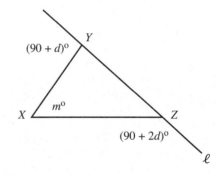

18 In the figure above, side YZ of $\triangle XYZ$ is on line ℓ. What is m in terms of d ?

(A) $\frac{1}{3}d$

(B) $\quad d$

(C) $\quad 2d$

(D) $\quad 3d$

(E) $\quad 180 - d$

GO ON TO THE NEXT PAGE

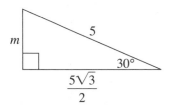

19 What is the value of m ?

(A) 2.5
(B) $2.5\sqrt{3}$
(C) 5
(D) $5\sqrt{2}$
(E) $5\sqrt{3}$

20 For all values of x, let $x\oplus$ be defined by $x\oplus = -x^2 + 3$.
Which of the following is equal to $(x\oplus)\oplus$?

(A) $x^4 - 6x^2 + 6$
(B) $-x^4 + 3$
(C) $-x^4 + 6x^2 - 6$
(D) $-x^4 - 6x^2 - 6$
(E) $-x^4 - 6x^2 + 6$

IF YOU FINISH BEFORE TIME IS CALLED, YOU MAY CHECK YOUR WORK ON
THIS SECTION ONLY. DO NOT TURN TO ANY OTHER SECTION IN THE TEST. **STOP**

Time—20 Minutes
19 Questions

Directions: For each question in this section, select the best answer from among the choices given and fill in the corresponding oval on the answer sheet.

Each sentence below has one or two blanks, each blank indicating that something has been omitted. Beneath the sentence are five words or sets of words labeled A through E. Choose the word or set of words that, when inserted in the sentence, best fits the meaning of the sentence as a whole.

EXAMPLE:

Today's small, portable computers contrast markedly with the earliest electronic computers, which were -------.

(A) effective   (B) invented
  (C) useful   (D) destructive
    (E) enormous

ANSWER:

Ⓐ Ⓑ Ⓒ Ⓓ ●

---

1 Though many exchange students undergo a period of ------- upon arrival in their host countries, in a surprisingly short time they begin to feel much more -------.

(A) disorientation . . comfortable
(B) excitement . . perturbed
(C) boredom . . uninterested
(D) relaxation . . uneasy
(E) shock . . annoyed

2 The trustees could tell that students respected Professor Hamrick's -------; his archaeology lectures were always well attended, and students described him as a(n) ------- in their evaluations.

(A) intelligence . . expert
(B) acumen . . amateur
(C) cruelty . . professional
(D) understanding . . tyrant
(E) authority . . proletarian

3 Because they often spend a lot of time engaged in solitary pursuits, house cats have gained a reputation for being -------.

(A) friendly   (B) interested
  (C) servile   (D) aloof
    (E) affectionate

4 When he was deceived and led into a clever trap, the hero discovered that the villain's ------- was surpassed only by his -------.

(A) interest . . curiosity
(B) invective . . education
(C) generosity . . aversion
(D) mendacity . . wickedness
(E) allure . . narcissism

5 Her infatuation with the idea of living in a castle was evident in her ------- for books about ancient kings and queens.

(A) ambivalence   (B) predilection
  (C) vestige   (D) talent
    (E) ancestry

6 Scrooge is a fictional character known for his obsession with money; this ------- makes him unhappy and unpopular.

(A) veracity   (B) cupidity
  (C) vindictiveness (D) abnegation
    (E) revelation

GO ON TO THE NEXT PAGE

The passage below is followed by questions based on its content. Answer the questions on the basis of what is <u>stated</u> or <u>implied</u> in the passage and in any introductory material that may be provided.

Questions 7–19 are based on the following passage.

The passage that follows is excerpted from a collection of inspirational stories written by adults in which they reflect on their experiences of having immigrated to America in their youth.

It is difficult to describe what it feels like to be different. You know that you are different, and in many ways people let you know that you are
Line different, but it's hard to say exactly what that is
(5) like. Anyone who has been uprooted and moved from his or her homeland knows that it is no small task to take on a new culture. Anyone who doesn't speak the language can tell you how intimidating it is to not even be able to communicate. I am one of these
(10) people, and I can tell you that it is possible to come out at the end of adversity and say that, as hard as it was, you made it.

I grew up in a very small fishing village called Torekov situated on the southwestern coast of
(15) Sweden. The population was only around 1,000, except in the summer when tourists swelled the town to about 3,000 people. In Torekov we went to school with the same group of twenty kids from kindergarten through sixth grade. We became best
(20) friends because we all lived in the same area and spent so much time together. Everything seemed perfect—that is, until my parents announced at the end of my third grade year that they were going to separate.

(25) I felt like everything I had been certain of in my whole life was being torn away. I could not imagine what it would be like to go to sleep without both of my parents to tuck me in. I was the first child out of my twenty classmates whose parents divorced, and it
(30) made me feel like an outcast. No one knew what it was like, even though they said they "understood." I had to resign myself to a new life where I was my mother's daughter on weekdays, and my father's on weekends. Every time I left one of them to go spend
(35) time with the other, it felt like a betrayal, as if I were deserting one of them every time. This went on until the end of my seventh grade year, when my mother came home one day and announced offhand that she was going to marry the American man she
(40) had been seeing, and that we were going to move to America.

Not only would I not see my father during the week, I would not be seeing him at all except during summer breaks from school. In my imagination,

(45) high school in America was like *Beverly Hills 90210,* and every American either lived in Dallas and wore cowboy boots, or was a movie star in Hollywood. This was all I knew, and it did not suggest a world that I wanted to become a part of. Probably what
(50) scared me the most, though, was that before we moved to America, I had only had two years of English language. In Torekov, I had little practice in making new friends. How could I make friends, or even just get my homework done, if I couldn't speak
(55) the language?

After we moved, I started eighth grade. The local middle school seemed colossal. The number of students there was almost as much as the total population of Torekov. I had to spend many hours
(60) on homework every night—probably twice as long as the American students. We had mandatory proficiency testing halfway through the year, and my history teacher told me not to bother studying for the citizenship part of the test because he knew I
(65) wouldn't pass it. It felt humiliating to read a book or work on something else while the other students studied for the test in class. I already felt that everyone looked at me like I was strange—now they seemed angry as well. If only they had known how
(70) hard it was for me to be in a strange country with no friends, speaking a strange language. And then, on top of that, I was being made to feel like I was not good enough in school. I had always been an excellent student in Sweden.

(75) I don't think I invited a single classmate home that entire year. It was difficult to make friends when I didn't know how to talk to them. I continued to work hard, however, and decided to join the band and the basketball team. It was very rewarding to be
(80) able to show the other students that I could contribute to the school. I began to make friends in the band. Once I was around Americans more, I learned the language much better than I had at home with my mom and brother. With my family
(85) it was too expedient for us just to continue to speak Swedish to each other. Once that first year was over, I knew that I could learn to like America. Maybe it would take some time, but I could get through it. I also knew that I would
(90) forever remember my history teacher's expression when I showed him my proficiency test scores. I had passed every single test on the first try.

GO ON TO THE NEXT PAGE

7 In line 8, the narrator suggests that the circumstances she describes are "intimidating" because

(A) people tend to be inconsiderate of those who are from another culture
(B) remaining courageous in the face of struggles is not easy
(C) it is difficult to assimilate into an unfamiliar culture
(D) English is a very challenging language to learn
(E) fear of not being able to communicate discourages attempts at interaction

8 The narrator's main purpose in paragraph 2 is to convey

(A) details about the tourist industry in a Swedish fishing town
(B) the geographic location of Torekov
(C) facts about the grade school system in Sweden
(D) the news about her parents' separation
(E) a sense of how Torekov has a small and closely-knit community

9 The narrator suggests in line 35 that her actions felt like a "betrayal" primarily because

(A) she resented her mother remarrying and taking her away to America
(B) she felt her parents had let her down by separating
(C) she didn't feel it was fair that her mother got more time with her
(D) she felt torn between the affections of her parents
(E) she felt that her father should have gotten custody of her

10 The mother's attitude is primarily characterized in lines 36–41 ("This went on...to America.") as one of

(A) weary pessimism
(B) thoughtless nonchalance
(C) puzzling obscurity
(D) submerged anger
(E) subdued resignation

11 The details about television shows in paragraph 4 are primarily meant to emphasize

(A) how much TV the narrator watched as a child
(B) how popular American TV is in Sweden
(C) where the narrator got her idea of America before she moved there
(D) why the narrator had no time to see her father during the week
(E) that TV became a substitute when the narrator's friends left her

12 The narrator says that she "had little practice in making new friends" (lines 52–53) because

(A) people are not generally very friendly in Sweden
(B) her Swedish schoolmates didn't want to associate with her after her parents' divorce
(C) the yearly arrival and departure of tourists in her home town had made her skeptical about the possibility of lasting friendships
(D) her classmates in Sweden had all known each other from a young age
(E) she spent all her time moving between her father's house and her mother's house

13 The word "colossal" in line 57 implies all of the following meanings EXCEPT

(A) intimidating
(B) expansive
(C) important
(D) monumental
(E) threatening

14 In lines 61–65, the story portrays the narrator's eighth grade history teacher primarily as

(A) embittered toward proficiency testing
(B) pessimistic about the ability of students to learn
(C) unfair in assigning extra homework to the narrator
(D) cynical about the narrator's capabilities
(E) dismissive toward immigrants

15 In line 69, the author implies that the other students feel "angry" as a result of

(A) sympathy with the narrator having been treated badly by the teacher
(B) the perception that the narrator was getting away with doing different work
(C) the narrator's poor command of English
(D) the fact that the narrator received special treatment from everyone in America
(E) the way that the narrator showed herself to be a better student than they were

16 The phrase "too expedient" in line 85 suggests that the narrator's family was

(A) not very good at learning a new language
(B) stubbornly attached to their Swedish culture
(C) inconsiderate toward the narrator's stepfather
(D) misunderstood by their neighbors
(E) indifferent about becoming fluent in English

GO ON TO THE NEXT PAGE

17 The transformation in the narrator's view of what "America" represents in line 45 to what "America" represents in line 88 could be described as having gone from

(A) a movie star dream land to a disappointingly normal place
(B) a symbol of opportunity to the realization of success
(C) an intimidating obligation to a potential home
(D) a path of escape to a set of inevitable consequences
(E) a source of distant inspiration to an unsettling reality

18 The reference to "my history teacher's expression" (line 90) is primarily intended to communicate

(A) that the teacher was narrow-minded and vindictive
(B) the narrator's elation at having passed the proficiency exams on the first try
(C) the newfound sense of belonging that the narrator feels in America
(D) the narrator's feeling of triumph at having defied the teacher's expectations
(E) the teacher's delight in seeing the narrator's favorable test scores

19 The primary purpose of the passage is to

(A) describe the differences between education in Sweden and America
(B) show why the narrator prefers living in Sweden
(C) justify the narrator's difficulty in learning English
(D) demonstrate how determination in the face of difficulties turns out well
(E) examine the emotional impact of feeling like an outsider

IF YOU FINISH BEFORE TIME IS CALLED, YOU MAY CHECK YOUR WORK ON THIS SECTION ONLY. DO NOT TURN TO ANY OTHER SECTION IN THE TEST.

Time—20 Minutes 16 Questions	**Directions:** For this section, solve each problem and decide which is the best of the choices given. Fill in the corresponding oval on the answer sheet. You may use any available space for scratchwork.

Notes

1. Calculator use is permitted.

2. All numbers used are real numbers.

3. Figures are provided for some problems. All figures are drawn to scale and lie in a plane UNLESS otherwise indicated.

4. Unless otherwise specified, the domain of any function f is assumed to be the set of all real numbers x for which $f(x)$ is a real number.

Reference Information

   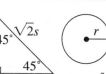

$A = \dfrac{1}{2}bh$ $c^2 = a^2 + b^2$ Special Right Triangles $A = \pi r^2$ $V = \pi r^2 h$ $A = lw$ $V = lwh$

$C = 2\pi r$

The sum of the measures in degrees of the angles of a triangle is 180.
The number of degrees of arc in a circle is 360.
A straight angle has a degree measure of 180.

---

1 The number of bottles of soda Joe buys for a party varies directly with the number of people coming to the party. If Joe bought 9 bottles of soda for a party that 12 people attended, how many bottles of soda would he buy for a party which 8 people attended?

(A) 2
(B) 4
(C) 6
(D) 8
(E) 10

2 If $f(x) = 3x + 7$ and $g(x) = 2x - 5$, at what point does the graph of $f(x)$ intersect the graph of $g(x)$?

(A) (–12, –29)
(B) (–12, 19)
(C) (3, 5)
(D) (5, 5)
(E) (2, 13)

GO ON TO THE NEXT PAGE

- 116 -

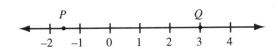

3 Which of the following is the best estimate of the length of $\overline{PQ}$ on the number line above?

(A) 4.5
(B) 4
(C) 2.5
(D) 2
(E) 1.5

4 For every 4,000 snow blowers produced by a snow blower factory, exactly 8 are defective. At this rate, how many snow blowers were produced during a period in which exactly 18 snow blowers were defective?

(A) 4,000
(B) 6,000
(C) 9,000
(D) 12,000
(E) 18,000

5 The figure above will be rotated 180° about point Q in the direction indicated. Which of the following represents the rotated figure?

(A)

(B)

(C)

(D)

(E)

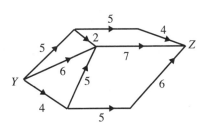

6 In the diagram of train tracks above, the numbers represent the track distance in miles, and the arrows show the only directions in which travel is permitted on the tracks. If the length of the longest route from Y to Z is n miles, and if the length of the shortest route from Y to Z is t miles, then what is the value of $n - t$?

(A) 2
(B) 3
(C) 4
(D) 5
(E) 6

GO ON TO THE NEXT PAGE

7 If $w^3 = x^6y^{15}$ and w, x, and y are positive numbers, then what is the value of w ?

(A) $\dfrac{x^6y^{15}}{3}$

(B) x^2y^{15}

(C) $\dfrac{x^2y^{15}}{3}$

(D) x^2y^5

(E) $\dfrac{x^2y^5}{3}$

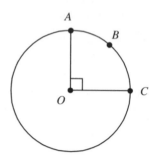

9 The center of the circle is O and the area of region $OABC$ is 4π square inches. What is the circumference of the circle, in inches?

(A) 4
(B) 8
(C) 8π
(D) 16π
(E) 32π

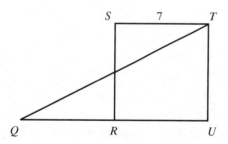

8 In the figure above, if the area of triangle QTU is equal to the area of square $RSTU$, what is the length of segment $\overline{QU}$?

(A)   3

(B) $\dfrac{7}{2}$

(C)   7

(D) 10

(E) 14

$$x, 3x - 4, x + 8, \ldots$$

10 In the increasing sequence above, the first term is x and the difference between any two consecutive terms is 4. What is the value of the fifth term in the sequence?

(A)   8
(B) 16
(C) 20
(D) 24
(E) 40

GO ON TO THE NEXT PAGE

11 If m and n are positive numbers, what percent of $(n + 3)$ is $2m$?

(A) $\dfrac{1}{200m(n + 3)}\%$

(B) $\dfrac{n + 3}{200m}\%$

(C) $\dfrac{100(n + 3)}{2m}\%$

(D) $\left(\dfrac{200m}{n} + 3\right)\%$

(E) $\dfrac{200m}{n + 3}\%$

12 A circle and a triangle are drawn on a piece of paper. Which of the following is the set of the number of possible points that are common to both the circle and the triangle?

(A) {0, 2}
(B) {0, 1, 2, 3}
(C) {2, 4, 6}
(D) {1, 2, 3, 4, 5, 6}
(E) {0, 1, 2, 3, 4, 5, 6}

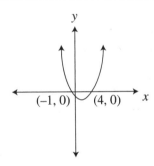

13 $ABCD$ is a rectangle. What is the slope of the line that passes through points A and C ?

(A) $\dfrac{-3}{5}$

(B) $\dfrac{-1}{2}$

(C) $\dfrac{-1}{5}$

(D) $\dfrac{3}{5}$

(E) $\dfrac{2}{3}$

14 Which of the following could be the equation of the parabola in the figure above?

(A) $y = (x - 1)(x - 4)$
(B) $y = (x - 1)(x + 4)$
(C) $y = (x + 1)(x - 4)$
(D) $y = (x + 1)(x + 4)$
(E) $y = 4(x - 1)$

GO ON TO THE NEXT PAGE

15 A quilt has p parallel rows of patches, with 4 patches in each row. If y patches are added to each row, how many patches will then be on the quilt, in terms of p and y ?

(A) $4py$
(B) $4p + y$
(C) $4p + py$
(D) $4p + 4y$
(E) $4 + p + y$

16 Two parallel lines are drawn in a plane. Two additional lines are drawn in the same plane, in such a way that there are exactly three different intersection points between the four lines. Neither of the additional lines is parallel to the two original lines. Into how many non-overlapping regions do these lines divide the plane?

(A) Five
(B) Six
(C) Seven
(D) Eight
(E) Nine

IF YOU FINISH BEFORE TIME IS CALLED, YOU MAY CHECK YOUR WORK ON THIS SECTION ONLY. DO NOT TURN TO ANY OTHER SECTION IN THE TEST. STOP

NO TEST MATERIAL ON THIS PAGE

Time—10 Minutes
14 Questions

Directions: For each question in this section, select the best answer from among the choices given and fill in the corresponding oval on the answer sheet.

The following sentences test correctness and effectiveness of expression. Part of each sentence or the entire sentence is underlined; beneath each sentence are five ways of phrasing the underlined material. Choice A repeats the original phrasing; the other four choices are different. If you think the original phrasing produces a better sentence than any of the alternatives, select choice A; if not, select one of the other choices.

In making your selection, follow the requirements of standard written English; that is, pay attention to grammar, choice of words, sentence construction, and punctuation. Your selection should result in the most effective sentence—clear and precise—without awkwardness or ambiguity.

EXAMPLE:

Every apple in the baskets <u>are ripe and labeled according to the date it was picked</u>.

(A) are ripe and labeled according to the date it was picked
(B) is ripe and labeled according to the date it was picked
(C) are ripe and labeled according to the date they were picked
(D) is ripe and labeled according to the date they were picked
(E) are ripe and labeled as to the date it was picked

ANSWER:
Ⓐ ● Ⓒ Ⓓ Ⓔ

1 Kathy and Allison's new apartment featured a functional fireplace, a deluxe washer and dryer, and <u>there was a sauna in the guest bathroom</u>.

(A) there was a sauna in the guest bathroom
(B) a sauna in the guest bathroom
(C) in the guest bathroom was a sauna
(D) the sauna was in the guest bathroom
(E) a sauna in the guest bathroom was there

2 The corn dog may have been introduced to Americans as early as the 1950s, but the 1962 World's Fair in Seattle <u>has been the first large event to popularize</u> the breaded hot dog on a stick.

(A) has been the first large event to popularize
(B) had been the first large event to popularize
(C) was the first large event having popularized
(D) was the first large event to popularize
(E) having been the first large event to popularize

3 Ms. Harrington's notes for her speech were organized <u>logically but, unfortunately, she got nervous and forgot to use it</u> as a guide.

(A) logically but, unfortunately, she got nervous and forgot to use it
(B) logical but, unfortunately, she got nervous and forgot to use it
(C) logically but, unfortunately, she got nervous and forgot to use them
(D) logical, and there is evidence that she unfortunately got nervous and forgot to use them
(E) logically, and there is evidence that she unfortunately got nervous and forgot to use it

4 Llamas make excellent <u>pets, it is because they are very friendly and are well liked by their owners as a result</u>.

(A) pets, it is because they are very friendly and are well liked by their owners as a result
(B) pets because they are very friendly and are therefore well liked by their owners
(C) pets for the reason that they are very friendly, with resulting owners that like them
(D) pets because of being very friendly and therefore they are well liked by their owners
(E) pets, their friendliness being very great which results in owners that like them

GO ON TO THE NEXT PAGE

5 The kindergarten teacher had the children gather snowflakes to demonstrate that, like people, no two snowflakes <u>is similar enough to justify labeling them</u> exact replicas.

(A) is similar enough to justify labeling them

(B) is similar enough to justify the labeling of them

(C) is similar enough to justify their being labeled

(D) are similar enough to justify the labeling of them

(E) are similar enough to justify labeling them

6 Unlike Parisians, who may bring their dogs into most stores and restaurants, <u>the pets of New Yorkers are usually left outside</u>.

(A) the pets of New Yorkers are usually left outside

(B) a New Yorker's pet is usually left outside

(C) New Yorkers are usually leaving their pets outside

(D) New Yorkers usually leave their pets outside

(E) New Yorkers' pets are usually left outside

7 Even though <u>their structure and alphabet that are</u> not similar to those of Romance languages, Russian has many parallels to French.

(A) their structure and alphabet that are

(B) it has a structure and alphabet that are

(C) they have a structure and alphabet

(D) its structure and alphabet are

(E) there are structures and alphabets that are

8 New cars are offered at substantial discounts several times each <u>year, so they can make room for next season's models</u>.

(A) year, so they can make room for next season's models

(B) year, and they can make room for next season's models

(C) year, since doing so makes room for next season's models

(D) year, and this will make room for next season's models

(E) year, making room for next season's models

9 Hybrid cars are usually viewed as good for the environment, <u>often burning as much gas as regular cars and using</u> the extra energy from the electrical component only as a power boost.

(A) often burning as much gas as regular cars and using

(B) often burning as much gas as regular cars, which use

(C) but they often burn as much gas as regular cars and use

(D) but they often burned as much as regular cars, and that uses

(E) but often burning as much gas as regular cars and using

10 Although the racing bike was designed especially for her, <u>that it still needed a few adjustments did not surprise Melissa</u>.

(A) that it still needed a few adjustments did not surprise Melissa

(B) no surprise resulted when Melissa learned that it still needed a few adjustments

(C) the few adjustments that it still needed did not surprise Melissa

(D) Melissa was not surprised that it still needed a few adjustments

(E) its still needing a few adjustments did not surprise Melissa

11 The idea of a computer in every home once seemed impossible, <u>initially as a result of the fact that computers were so expensive and, in later years, because</u> they seemed unnecessary.

(A) initially as a result of the fact that computers were so expensive and, in later years, because

(B) initially this was because computers were so expensive, and in later years it was due to the fact

(C) initially because computers were so expensive and later because

(D) initially being so expensive, they later

(E) initially because they were more expensive, then later

GO ON TO THE NEXT PAGE

- 123 -

12 Active volcanoes are monitored <u>closely, seismologists observe warning signs to predict when eruptions will occur</u>.

(A) closely, seismologists observe warning signs to predict when eruptions will occur

(B) closely and seismologists observe warning signs to predict when eruptions will occur

(C) closely; seismologists observe warning signs so that they can predict extremely well when eruptions will occur

(D) closely; seismologists observe warning signs to predict when eruptions will occur

(E) closely; because seismologists observe warning signs to predict when eruptions will occur

13 <u>The orchestral arrangement is more famous, and</u> Samuel Barber's *Adagio* was originally written for string quartet.

(A) The orchestral arrangement is more famous, and

(B) The orchestral arrangement is more famous,

(C) The orchestral arrangement is more famous, however

(D) Although the orchestral arrangement is more famous,

(E) Whereby the orchestral arrangement for string is more famous,

14 V-Day is observed on February 14th in cities around the world to celebrate women in general and to promote awareness of women's issues, <u>which includes</u> gender equality and health concerns.

(A) which includes

(B) they include

(C) these include

(D) including

(E) also including

SCORING YOUR TEST

For each section (Critical Reading, Math, and Writing) on the SAT, your score will range from 200–800. Your performance on the tests in this book is a good indicator of your abilities and skills.

The scoring information contained here is intended to give an approximate idea of what your performance will be on Test Day. The formulas for calculating your raw score that follow in this book are the same as those the College Board will use to score your SAT.

The raw-to-scaled score conversion tables, however, may differ from the one used to score the SAT that you take. The College Board creates unique raw-to-scaled score conversions for every administration of the SAT. Therefore, practice tests can only approximate the conversion tables that will be used on the real SAT that you take. Nevertheless, the tables in this book are close to the tables that will be used on your test, and will provide you with a good sense of what your score might be at this stage in your preparation.

Step 1: Score Your Essay

First, score your essay, which accounts for approximately 25% of your Writing scaled score; your score on the Multiple Choice questions will account for the remaining 75% or so. For the tests in this book, assign your essay a score of 1–6, which, along with your Multiple Choice score, you will use to arrive at your 200–800 scaled score.

The College Board's website (*www.collegeboard.com*) contains information about the essay and how it is scored.

The following criteria are a good guide:

6 Outstanding—Though it may have a few small errors, the essay is well organized and fully developed with supporting examples. It displays consistent language facility, varied sentence structure, and varied vocabulary.

5 Solid—Though it has occasional errors or lapses in quality, the essay is generally organized and well developed with appropriate examples. It displays language facility, syntactic variety, and varied vocabulary.

4 Adequate—Though it has some flaws, the essay is organized and adequately developed and has some examples. It displays adequate but inconsistent language facility.

3 Limited—The essay does not adequately fulfill the writing assignment and has many flaws. It has inadequate organization and development, along with many errors in grammar or diction (or both). In general, the essay lacks variety.

2 Flawed—The essay demonstrates incompetence with one or more weaknesses. Ideas are vague and thinly developed. It contains frequent errors in grammar and diction and almost no variety.

1 Deficient—The essay demonstrates incompetence with serious flaws. It has no organization, no development, and severe grammar and diction errors. The essay is so seriously flawed that its basic meaning is obscured.

0 Off-Topic—The essay does not follow the assignment.

Step 2: Compute Your Raw Score

Check your answers to the multiple-choice questions against the answer key on the next two pages. Count up the number of answers you got right and the number you got wrong for each section. Do not score Section 6, the Experimental Section. Remember, do not count questions left blank as wrong. Round up to the nearest whole number. Now, plug them in below.

Note: Grid-in questions do not have a wrong-answer penalty, so do not deduct anything for wrong answers.

Critical Reading

	Number Right		Number Wrong		Raw Score
Section 2:	☐	−	$\left(.25 \times \boxed{}\right)$	=	☐
Section 5:	☐	−	$\left(.25 \times \boxed{}\right)$	=	☐
Section 8:	☐	−	$\left(.25 \times \boxed{}\right)$	=	☐
Critical Reading Raw Score				=	☐
					(rounded up)

Writing

	Number Right		Number Wrong		Raw Score
Section 4:	☐	−	$\left(.25 \times \boxed{}\right)$	=	☐
Section 10:	☐	−	$\left(.25 \times \boxed{}\right)$	=	☐
Writing Multiple-Choice Raw Score				=	☐
					(rounded up)

Math

	Number Right		Number Wrong		Raw Score
Section 3: (QUESTIONS 1–8)	☐	−	$\left(.25 \times \boxed{}\right)$	=	☐
Section 3: (QUESTIONS 9–18)	☐	−	$\left(\text{no wrong answer penalty}\right)$	=	☐
Section 7:	☐	−	$\left(.25 \times \boxed{}\right)$	=	☐
Section 9:	☐	−	$\left(.25 \times \boxed{}\right)$	=	☐
Math Raw Score				=	☐
					(rounded up)

PRACTICE TEST 2 ANSWER KEY

CRITICAL READING			MATH		
Section 2	**Section 5**	**Section 8**	**Section 3**	**Section 7**	**Section 9**
Multiple-Choice Questions	Multiple-Choice Questions	Multiple-Choice Questions	Multiple-Choice Questions	Multiple-Choice Questions	Multiple-Choice Questions
Correct Answer	Correct Answer	Correct Answer	Correct Answer	Correct Answer	Correct Answer
1. E	1. C	1. A	1. B	1. D	1. C
2. C	2. E	2. A	2. B	2. C	2. A
3. B	3. E	3. D	3. A	3. D	3. A
4. E	4. E	4. D	4. C	4. C	4. C
5. D	5. A	5. B	5. A	5. C	5. D
6. A	6. C	6. B	6. B	6. C	6. B
7. D	7. E	7. E	7. C	7. A	7. D
8. B	8. E	8. E	8. A	8. D	8. E
9. C	9. D	9. D		9. B	9. C
10. C	10. B	10. B		10. E	10. C
11. A	11. E	11. C		11. C	11. E
12. D	12. B	12. D		12. D	12. E
13. B	13. D	13. C		13. A	13. A
14. B	14. D	14. D		14. D	14. C
15. C	15. C	15. B		15. A	15. C
16. B	16. D	16. E		16. D	16. E
17. B	17. B	17. C		17. E	
18. A	18. E	18. D		18. D	
19. A	19. B	19. D		19. A	
20. B	20. A			20. C	
21. D	21. E				
22. A	22. B				
23. B	23. C				
24. A	24. B				

no. correct / no. incorrect (Section 3, 7, 9)

no. correct / no. incorrect (Section 2, 5, 8)

Section 3
Student-Produced Response Questions

	Correct Answer
9.	75
10.	17/3 or 5.67
11.	78 or 132
12.	115
13.	156
14.	75
15.	120
16.	10
17.	49
18.	28

no. correct

WRITING

Essay	Section 4 Multiple-Choice Questions		Section 10 Multiple-Choice Questions	
		Correct Answer		Correct Answer
	1.	D	1.	B
	2.	B	2.	D
	3.	B	3.	C
Essay Score* (1–6)	4.	C	4.	B
	5.	C	5.	E
	6.	D	6.	D
	7.	C	7.	D
	8.	C	8.	E
	9.	B	9.	C
	10.	A	10.	D
	11.	C	11.	C
	12.	C	12.	D
	13.	D	13.	D
	14.	D	14.	D
	15.	E		
	16.	B		
	17.	B		
	18.	C		
	19.	B		
	20.	C		
	21.	C		
	22.	B		
	23.	E		
	24.	D		
	25.	C		
	26.	C		
	27.	C		
	28.	D		
	29.	E		
	30.	C		
	31.	C		
	32.	C		
	33.	A		
	34.	D		
	35.	E		

no. correct   no. correct

no. incorrect   no. incorrect

*To score your essay, see Step 1 on the previous pages. On this practice test, your essay score will range from 1 to 6. (Keep in mind that on the actual SAT, your essay will be read by two readers and you will receive a score of 1 to 12 on your score report.)

- 129 -

Step 3: Find Your Scaled Score

To determine your Critical Reading and Math scaled scores, find the raw scores you calculated for these two sections in Step 2 on Tables 1 and 2 on the following page. Next, find the scaled score associated with your raw scores and enter them in the appropriate box in the Scaled Scores table on this page.

To determine your Writing scaled score, use Table 3. First, find the Writing Multiple-Choice raw score you calculated in Step 2 and the essay raw score (1–6) you assigned yourself. Next, locate your Writing Multiple-Choice raw score on the left dimension of Table 3. Then find your essay score along the top. The box associated with this row and column contains your Writing scaled score. Enter it in the appropriate box in the Scaled Scores table below.

The sum of the three scores is your Total Scaled Score.

Scaled Scores	
Critical Reading	
Math	
Writing	
Total	

TABLE 1
Critical Reading Conversion Table

Raw Score	Scaled Score	Raw Score	Scaled Score
67	800	30	500
66	790	29	500
65	770	28	490
64	760	27	480
63	750	26	480
62	740	25	470
61	720	24	470
60	710	23	460
59	700	22	450
58	690	21	450
57	680	20	440
56	670	19	430
55	670	18	430
54	660	17	420
53	650	16	410
52	640	15	410
51	640	14	400
50	630	13	390
49	620	12	380
48	610	11	380
47	610	10	370
46	600	9	360
45	590	8	350
44	590	7	340
43	580	6	330
42	580	5	320
41	570	4	310
40	560	3	300
39	560	2	280
38	550	1	270
37	540	0	250
36	540	–1	250
35	530	–2	240
34	530	–3	230
33	520	–4	220
32	510	–5	210
31	510	–6 and below	200

TABLE 2
Math Conversion Table

Raw Score	Scaled Score	Raw Score	Scaled Score
54	800	24	490
53	780	23	490
52	760	22	480
51	740	21	470
50	730	20	460
49	710	19	460
48	700	18	450
47	690	17	440
46	670	16	430
45	660	15	430
44	650	14	420
43	650	13	410
42	640	12	400
41	630	11	390
40	620	10	380
39	610	9	380
38	600	8	370
37	590	7	360
36	590	6	340
35	580	5	330
34	570	4	320
33	560	3	310
32	560	2	290
31	550	1	280
30	540	0	260
29	530	–1	250
28	520	–2	240
27	520	–3	230
26	510	–4	220
25	500	–5	210
		–6 and below	200

TABLE 3
SAT Score Conversion Table for Writing Composite

Writing Multiple-Choice Raw Score	Essay Raw Score						
	0	**1**	**2**	**3**	**4**	**5**	**6**
49	670	700	720	740	780	790	800
48	660	680	700	730	760	780	790
47	650	670	690	720	750	770	780
46	640	660	680	710	740	760	770
45	630	650	670	700	740	750	770
44	620	640	660	690	730	750	760
43	600	630	650	680	710	740	750
42	600	620	640	670	700	730	750
41	590	610	630	660	690	730	740
40	580	600	620	650	690	720	740
39	570	590	610	640	680	710	740
38	560	590	610	630	670	700	730
37	550	580	600	630	660	690	720
36	540	570	590	620	650	680	710
35	540	560	580	610	640	680	710
34	530	550	570	600	640	670	700
33	520	540	560	590	630	660	690
32	510	540	560	580	620	650	680
31	500	530	550	580	610	640	670
30	490	520	540	570	600	630	660
29	490	510	530	560	590	630	650
28	480	500	520	550	590	620	640
27	470	490	510	540	580	610	640
26	460	490	500	530	570	600	630
25	450	480	500	520	560	590	620
24	440	470	490	510	550	580	610
23	430	460	480	510	540	570	600
22	430	450	470	500	530	570	590
21	430	450	470	500	530	570	590
20	420	440	460	490	520	560	580
19	410	430	450	480	520	550	570
18	400	420	440	470	510	540	570
17	390	420	430	460	500	530	560
16	380	410	430	450	490	520	550
15	370	400	420	450	480	510	540
14	360	390	410	440	470	500	530
13	360	380	400	430	460	500	520
12	340	370	390	420	450	490	510
11	340	360	380	410	450	480	510
10	330	350	370	400	440	470	500
9	320	350	360	390	430	460	490
8	310	340	360	390	420	450	480
7	300	330	350	380	410	440	470
6	290	320	340	370	400	430	460
5	290	310	330	360	390	430	450
4	280	300	320	350	390	420	450
3	270	290	310	340	380	410	440
2	260	280	300	330	370	400	430
1	250	270	290	320	340	380	410
0	250	260	280	310	340	370	400
−1	240	260	270	290	320	360	380
−2	230	250	260	270	310	340	370
−3	220	240	250	260	300	330	360
−4	220	230	240	250	290	320	350
−5	200	220	230	240	280	310	340
−6	200	210	220	240	280	310	340
−7	200	210	220	230	270	300	330
−8	200	210	220	230	270	300	330
−9	200	210	220	230	270	300	330
−10	200	210	220	230	270	300	330
−11	200	210	220	230	270	300	330

PRACTICE TEST 3

For additional practice before Test Day, take this Practice Test under test-like conditions at home or at a Kaplan Center, bubble in your answers on a Kaplan SAT Answer Grid, and have the grid scanned at a Kaplan Center to receive your results.

Scan Code: 1103

Practice Test 3
Answer Sheet

Remove (or photocopy) the following answer sheet and use it to complete the practice test.
See the answer key following the test when finished.

Start with number 1 for each bubble-in section. If a section has fewer questions than bubbles,
leave the extra bubbles blank.

Use this page to *plan* your essay.

SECTION 2

1. Ⓐ Ⓑ Ⓒ Ⓓ Ⓔ 11. Ⓐ Ⓑ Ⓒ Ⓓ Ⓔ 21. Ⓐ Ⓑ Ⓒ Ⓓ Ⓔ 31. Ⓐ Ⓑ Ⓒ Ⓓ Ⓔ
2. Ⓐ Ⓑ Ⓒ Ⓓ Ⓔ 12. Ⓐ Ⓑ Ⓒ Ⓓ Ⓔ 22. Ⓐ Ⓑ Ⓒ Ⓓ Ⓔ 32. Ⓐ Ⓑ Ⓒ Ⓓ Ⓔ
3. Ⓐ Ⓑ Ⓒ Ⓓ Ⓔ 13. Ⓐ Ⓑ Ⓒ Ⓓ Ⓔ 23. Ⓐ Ⓑ Ⓒ Ⓓ Ⓔ 33. Ⓐ Ⓑ Ⓒ Ⓓ Ⓔ
4. Ⓐ Ⓑ Ⓒ Ⓓ Ⓔ 14. Ⓐ Ⓑ Ⓒ Ⓓ Ⓔ 24. Ⓐ Ⓑ Ⓒ Ⓓ Ⓔ 34. Ⓐ Ⓑ Ⓒ Ⓓ Ⓔ
5. Ⓐ Ⓑ Ⓒ Ⓓ Ⓔ 15. Ⓐ Ⓑ Ⓒ Ⓓ Ⓔ 25. Ⓐ Ⓑ Ⓒ Ⓓ Ⓔ 35. Ⓐ Ⓑ Ⓒ Ⓓ Ⓔ
6. Ⓐ Ⓑ Ⓒ Ⓓ Ⓔ 16. Ⓐ Ⓑ Ⓒ Ⓓ Ⓔ 26. Ⓐ Ⓑ Ⓒ Ⓓ Ⓔ 36. Ⓐ Ⓑ Ⓒ Ⓓ Ⓔ
7. Ⓐ Ⓑ Ⓒ Ⓓ Ⓔ 17. Ⓐ Ⓑ Ⓒ Ⓓ Ⓔ 27. Ⓐ Ⓑ Ⓒ Ⓓ Ⓔ 37. Ⓐ Ⓑ Ⓒ Ⓓ Ⓔ
8. Ⓐ Ⓑ Ⓒ Ⓓ Ⓔ 18. Ⓐ Ⓑ Ⓒ Ⓓ Ⓔ 28. Ⓐ Ⓑ Ⓒ Ⓓ Ⓔ 38. Ⓐ Ⓑ Ⓒ Ⓓ Ⓔ
9. Ⓐ Ⓑ Ⓒ Ⓓ Ⓔ 19. Ⓐ Ⓑ Ⓒ Ⓓ Ⓔ 29. Ⓐ Ⓑ Ⓒ Ⓓ Ⓔ 39. Ⓐ Ⓑ Ⓒ Ⓓ Ⓔ
10. Ⓐ Ⓑ Ⓒ Ⓓ Ⓔ 20. Ⓐ Ⓑ Ⓒ Ⓓ Ⓔ 30. Ⓐ Ⓑ Ⓒ Ⓓ Ⓔ 40. Ⓐ Ⓑ Ⓒ Ⓓ Ⓔ

☐ # right in Section 2

☐ # wrong in Section 2

SECTION 3

1. Ⓐ Ⓑ Ⓒ Ⓓ Ⓔ 11. Ⓐ Ⓑ Ⓒ Ⓓ Ⓔ 21. Ⓐ Ⓑ Ⓒ Ⓓ Ⓔ 31. Ⓐ Ⓑ Ⓒ Ⓓ Ⓔ
2. Ⓐ Ⓑ Ⓒ Ⓓ Ⓔ 12. Ⓐ Ⓑ Ⓒ Ⓓ Ⓔ 22. Ⓐ Ⓑ Ⓒ Ⓓ Ⓔ 32. Ⓐ Ⓑ Ⓒ Ⓓ Ⓔ
3. Ⓐ Ⓑ Ⓒ Ⓓ Ⓔ 13. Ⓐ Ⓑ Ⓒ Ⓓ Ⓔ 23. Ⓐ Ⓑ Ⓒ Ⓓ Ⓔ 33. Ⓐ Ⓑ Ⓒ Ⓓ Ⓔ
4. Ⓐ Ⓑ Ⓒ Ⓓ Ⓔ 14. Ⓐ Ⓑ Ⓒ Ⓓ Ⓔ 24. Ⓐ Ⓑ Ⓒ Ⓓ Ⓔ 34. Ⓐ Ⓑ Ⓒ Ⓓ Ⓔ
5. Ⓐ Ⓑ Ⓒ Ⓓ Ⓔ 15. Ⓐ Ⓑ Ⓒ Ⓓ Ⓔ 25. Ⓐ Ⓑ Ⓒ Ⓓ Ⓔ 35. Ⓐ Ⓑ Ⓒ Ⓓ Ⓔ
6. Ⓐ Ⓑ Ⓒ Ⓓ Ⓔ 16. Ⓐ Ⓑ Ⓒ Ⓓ Ⓔ 26. Ⓐ Ⓑ Ⓒ Ⓓ Ⓔ 36. Ⓐ Ⓑ Ⓒ Ⓓ Ⓔ
7. Ⓐ Ⓑ Ⓒ Ⓓ Ⓔ 17. Ⓐ Ⓑ Ⓒ Ⓓ Ⓔ 27. Ⓐ Ⓑ Ⓒ Ⓓ Ⓔ 37. Ⓐ Ⓑ Ⓒ Ⓓ Ⓔ
8. Ⓐ Ⓑ Ⓒ Ⓓ Ⓔ 18. Ⓐ Ⓑ Ⓒ Ⓓ Ⓔ 28. Ⓐ Ⓑ Ⓒ Ⓓ Ⓔ 38. Ⓐ Ⓑ Ⓒ Ⓓ Ⓔ
9. Ⓐ Ⓑ Ⓒ Ⓓ Ⓔ 19. Ⓐ Ⓑ Ⓒ Ⓓ Ⓔ 29. Ⓐ Ⓑ Ⓒ Ⓓ Ⓔ 39. Ⓐ Ⓑ Ⓒ Ⓓ Ⓔ
10. Ⓐ Ⓑ Ⓒ Ⓓ Ⓔ 20. Ⓐ Ⓑ Ⓒ Ⓓ Ⓔ 30. Ⓐ Ⓑ Ⓒ Ⓓ Ⓔ 40. Ⓐ Ⓑ Ⓒ Ⓓ Ⓔ

☐ # right in Section 3

☐ # wrong in Section 3

If sections 2 or 3 of this practice test contain math questions that are not multiple choice, continue to item 9 below. Otherwise, continue to item 9 above.

9.

10.

11.

12.

13.

14.

15.

16.

17.

18.

SECTION 4

1. Ⓐ Ⓑ Ⓒ Ⓓ Ⓔ	11. Ⓐ Ⓑ Ⓒ Ⓓ Ⓔ	21. Ⓐ Ⓑ Ⓒ Ⓓ Ⓔ	31. Ⓐ Ⓑ Ⓒ Ⓓ Ⓔ	
2. Ⓐ Ⓑ Ⓒ Ⓓ Ⓔ	12. Ⓐ Ⓑ Ⓒ Ⓓ Ⓔ	22. Ⓐ Ⓑ Ⓒ Ⓓ Ⓔ	32. Ⓐ Ⓑ Ⓒ Ⓓ Ⓔ	
3. Ⓐ Ⓑ Ⓒ Ⓓ Ⓔ	13. Ⓐ Ⓑ Ⓒ Ⓓ Ⓔ	23. Ⓐ Ⓑ Ⓒ Ⓓ Ⓔ	33. Ⓐ Ⓑ Ⓒ Ⓓ Ⓔ	# right in Section 4
4. Ⓐ Ⓑ Ⓒ Ⓓ Ⓔ	14. Ⓐ Ⓑ Ⓒ Ⓓ Ⓔ	24. Ⓐ Ⓑ Ⓒ Ⓓ Ⓔ	34. Ⓐ Ⓑ Ⓒ Ⓓ Ⓔ	
5. Ⓐ Ⓑ Ⓒ Ⓓ Ⓔ	15. Ⓐ Ⓑ Ⓒ Ⓓ Ⓔ	25. Ⓐ Ⓑ Ⓒ Ⓓ Ⓔ	35. Ⓐ Ⓑ Ⓒ Ⓓ Ⓔ	
6. Ⓐ Ⓑ Ⓒ Ⓓ Ⓔ	16. Ⓐ Ⓑ Ⓒ Ⓓ Ⓔ	26. Ⓐ Ⓑ Ⓒ Ⓓ Ⓔ	36. Ⓐ Ⓑ Ⓒ Ⓓ Ⓔ	
7. Ⓐ Ⓑ Ⓒ Ⓓ Ⓔ	17. Ⓐ Ⓑ Ⓒ Ⓓ Ⓔ	27. Ⓐ Ⓑ Ⓒ Ⓓ Ⓔ	37. Ⓐ Ⓑ Ⓒ Ⓓ Ⓔ	
8. Ⓐ Ⓑ Ⓒ Ⓓ Ⓔ	18. Ⓐ Ⓑ Ⓒ Ⓓ Ⓔ	28. Ⓐ Ⓑ Ⓒ Ⓓ Ⓔ	38. Ⓐ Ⓑ Ⓒ Ⓓ Ⓔ	# wrong in Section 4
9. Ⓐ Ⓑ Ⓒ Ⓓ Ⓔ	19. Ⓐ Ⓑ Ⓒ Ⓓ Ⓔ	29. Ⓐ Ⓑ Ⓒ Ⓓ Ⓔ	39. Ⓐ Ⓑ Ⓒ Ⓓ Ⓔ	
10. Ⓐ Ⓑ Ⓒ Ⓓ Ⓔ	20. Ⓐ Ⓑ Ⓒ Ⓓ Ⓔ	30. Ⓐ Ⓑ Ⓒ Ⓓ Ⓔ	40. Ⓐ Ⓑ Ⓒ Ⓓ Ⓔ	

SECTION 5

1. Ⓐ Ⓑ Ⓒ Ⓓ Ⓔ	11. Ⓐ Ⓑ Ⓒ Ⓓ Ⓔ	21. Ⓐ Ⓑ Ⓒ Ⓓ Ⓔ	31. Ⓐ Ⓑ Ⓒ Ⓓ Ⓔ	
2. Ⓐ Ⓑ Ⓒ Ⓓ Ⓔ	12. Ⓐ Ⓑ Ⓒ Ⓓ Ⓔ	22. Ⓐ Ⓑ Ⓒ Ⓓ Ⓔ	32. Ⓐ Ⓑ Ⓒ Ⓓ Ⓔ	
3. Ⓐ Ⓑ Ⓒ Ⓓ Ⓔ	13. Ⓐ Ⓑ Ⓒ Ⓓ Ⓔ	23. Ⓐ Ⓑ Ⓒ Ⓓ Ⓔ	33. Ⓐ Ⓑ Ⓒ Ⓓ Ⓔ	# right in Section 5
4. Ⓐ Ⓑ Ⓒ Ⓓ Ⓔ	14. Ⓐ Ⓑ Ⓒ Ⓓ Ⓔ	24. Ⓐ Ⓑ Ⓒ Ⓓ Ⓔ	34. Ⓐ Ⓑ Ⓒ Ⓓ Ⓔ	
5. Ⓐ Ⓑ Ⓒ Ⓓ Ⓔ	15. Ⓐ Ⓑ Ⓒ Ⓓ Ⓔ	25. Ⓐ Ⓑ Ⓒ Ⓓ Ⓔ	35. Ⓐ Ⓑ Ⓒ Ⓓ Ⓔ	
6. Ⓐ Ⓑ Ⓒ Ⓓ Ⓔ	16. Ⓐ Ⓑ Ⓒ Ⓓ Ⓔ	26. Ⓐ Ⓑ Ⓒ Ⓓ Ⓔ	36. Ⓐ Ⓑ Ⓒ Ⓓ Ⓔ	
7. Ⓐ Ⓑ Ⓒ Ⓓ Ⓔ	17. Ⓐ Ⓑ Ⓒ Ⓓ Ⓔ	27. Ⓐ Ⓑ Ⓒ Ⓓ Ⓔ	37. Ⓐ Ⓑ Ⓒ Ⓓ Ⓔ	
8. Ⓐ Ⓑ Ⓒ Ⓓ Ⓔ	18. Ⓐ Ⓑ Ⓒ Ⓓ Ⓔ	28. Ⓐ Ⓑ Ⓒ Ⓓ Ⓔ	38. Ⓐ Ⓑ Ⓒ Ⓓ Ⓔ	# wrong in Section 5
9. Ⓐ Ⓑ Ⓒ Ⓓ Ⓔ	19. Ⓐ Ⓑ Ⓒ Ⓓ Ⓔ	29. Ⓐ Ⓑ Ⓒ Ⓓ Ⓔ	39. Ⓐ Ⓑ Ⓒ Ⓓ Ⓔ	
10. Ⓐ Ⓑ Ⓒ Ⓓ Ⓔ	20. Ⓐ Ⓑ Ⓒ Ⓓ Ⓔ	30. Ⓐ Ⓑ Ⓒ Ⓓ Ⓔ	40. Ⓐ Ⓑ Ⓒ Ⓓ Ⓔ	

If sections 4 or 5 of this practice test contain math questions that are not multiple choice, continue to item 9 below. Otherwise, continue to item 9 above.

9.   10.   11.   12.   13.

14.   15.   16.   17.   18.

SECTION 6

1. Ⓐ Ⓑ Ⓒ Ⓓ Ⓔ	11. Ⓐ Ⓑ Ⓒ Ⓓ Ⓔ	21. Ⓐ Ⓑ Ⓒ Ⓓ Ⓔ	31. Ⓐ Ⓑ Ⓒ Ⓓ Ⓔ
2. Ⓐ Ⓑ Ⓒ Ⓓ Ⓔ	12. Ⓐ Ⓑ Ⓒ Ⓓ Ⓔ	22. Ⓐ Ⓑ Ⓒ Ⓓ Ⓔ	32. Ⓐ Ⓑ Ⓒ Ⓓ Ⓔ
3. Ⓐ Ⓑ Ⓒ Ⓓ Ⓔ	13. Ⓐ Ⓑ Ⓒ Ⓓ Ⓔ	23. Ⓐ Ⓑ Ⓒ Ⓓ Ⓔ	33. Ⓐ Ⓑ Ⓒ Ⓓ Ⓔ
4. Ⓐ Ⓑ Ⓒ Ⓓ Ⓔ	14. Ⓐ Ⓑ Ⓒ Ⓓ Ⓔ	24. Ⓐ Ⓑ Ⓒ Ⓓ Ⓔ	34. Ⓐ Ⓑ Ⓒ Ⓓ Ⓔ
5. Ⓐ Ⓑ Ⓒ Ⓓ Ⓔ	15. Ⓐ Ⓑ Ⓒ Ⓓ Ⓔ	25. Ⓐ Ⓑ Ⓒ Ⓓ Ⓔ	35. Ⓐ Ⓑ Ⓒ Ⓓ Ⓔ
6. Ⓐ Ⓑ Ⓒ Ⓓ Ⓔ	16. Ⓐ Ⓑ Ⓒ Ⓓ Ⓔ	26. Ⓐ Ⓑ Ⓒ Ⓓ Ⓔ	36. Ⓐ Ⓑ Ⓒ Ⓓ Ⓔ
7. Ⓐ Ⓑ Ⓒ Ⓓ Ⓔ	17. Ⓐ Ⓑ Ⓒ Ⓓ Ⓔ	27. Ⓐ Ⓑ Ⓒ Ⓓ Ⓔ	37. Ⓐ Ⓑ Ⓒ Ⓓ Ⓔ
8. Ⓐ Ⓑ Ⓒ Ⓓ Ⓔ	18. Ⓐ Ⓑ Ⓒ Ⓓ Ⓔ	28. Ⓐ Ⓑ Ⓒ Ⓓ Ⓔ	38. Ⓐ Ⓑ Ⓒ Ⓓ Ⓔ
9. Ⓐ Ⓑ Ⓒ Ⓓ Ⓔ	19. Ⓐ Ⓑ Ⓒ Ⓓ Ⓔ	29. Ⓐ Ⓑ Ⓒ Ⓓ Ⓔ	39. Ⓐ Ⓑ Ⓒ Ⓓ Ⓔ
10. Ⓐ Ⓑ Ⓒ Ⓓ Ⓔ	20. Ⓐ Ⓑ Ⓒ Ⓓ Ⓔ	30. Ⓐ Ⓑ Ⓒ Ⓓ Ⓔ	40. Ⓐ Ⓑ Ⓒ Ⓓ Ⓔ

☐ # right in Section 6

☐ # wrong in Section 6

SECTION 7

1. Ⓐ Ⓑ Ⓒ Ⓓ Ⓔ	11. Ⓐ Ⓑ Ⓒ Ⓓ Ⓔ	21. Ⓐ Ⓑ Ⓒ Ⓓ Ⓔ	31. Ⓐ Ⓑ Ⓒ Ⓓ Ⓔ
2. Ⓐ Ⓑ Ⓒ Ⓓ Ⓔ	12. Ⓐ Ⓑ Ⓒ Ⓓ Ⓔ	22. Ⓐ Ⓑ Ⓒ Ⓓ Ⓔ	32. Ⓐ Ⓑ Ⓒ Ⓓ Ⓔ
3. Ⓐ Ⓑ Ⓒ Ⓓ Ⓔ	13. Ⓐ Ⓑ Ⓒ Ⓓ Ⓔ	23. Ⓐ Ⓑ Ⓒ Ⓓ Ⓔ	33. Ⓐ Ⓑ Ⓒ Ⓓ Ⓔ
4. Ⓐ Ⓑ Ⓒ Ⓓ Ⓔ	14. Ⓐ Ⓑ Ⓒ Ⓓ Ⓔ	24. Ⓐ Ⓑ Ⓒ Ⓓ Ⓔ	34. Ⓐ Ⓑ Ⓒ Ⓓ Ⓔ
5. Ⓐ Ⓑ Ⓒ Ⓓ Ⓔ	15. Ⓐ Ⓑ Ⓒ Ⓓ Ⓔ	25. Ⓐ Ⓑ Ⓒ Ⓓ Ⓔ	35. Ⓐ Ⓑ Ⓒ Ⓓ Ⓔ
6. Ⓐ Ⓑ Ⓒ Ⓓ Ⓔ	16. Ⓐ Ⓑ Ⓒ Ⓓ Ⓔ	26. Ⓐ Ⓑ Ⓒ Ⓓ Ⓔ	36. Ⓐ Ⓑ Ⓒ Ⓓ Ⓔ
7. Ⓐ Ⓑ Ⓒ Ⓓ Ⓔ	17. Ⓐ Ⓑ Ⓒ Ⓓ Ⓔ	27. Ⓐ Ⓑ Ⓒ Ⓓ Ⓔ	37. Ⓐ Ⓑ Ⓒ Ⓓ Ⓔ
8. Ⓐ Ⓑ Ⓒ Ⓓ Ⓔ	18. Ⓐ Ⓑ Ⓒ Ⓓ Ⓔ	28. Ⓐ Ⓑ Ⓒ Ⓓ Ⓔ	38. Ⓐ Ⓑ Ⓒ Ⓓ Ⓔ
9. Ⓐ Ⓑ Ⓒ Ⓓ Ⓔ	19. Ⓐ Ⓑ Ⓒ Ⓓ Ⓔ	29. Ⓐ Ⓑ Ⓒ Ⓓ Ⓔ	39. Ⓐ Ⓑ Ⓒ Ⓓ Ⓔ
10. Ⓐ Ⓑ Ⓒ Ⓓ Ⓔ	20. Ⓐ Ⓑ Ⓒ Ⓓ Ⓔ	30. Ⓐ Ⓑ Ⓒ Ⓓ Ⓔ	40. Ⓐ Ⓑ Ⓒ Ⓓ Ⓔ

☐ # right in Section 7

☐ # wrong in Section 7

If sections 6 or 7 of this practice test contain math questions that are not multiple choice, continue to item 9 below. Otherwise, continue to item 9 above.

9. ☐ 10. ☐ 11. ☐ 12. ☐ 13. ☐

14. ☐ 15. ☐ 16. ☐ 17. ☐ 18. ☐

SECTION 8

1. Ⓐ Ⓑ Ⓒ Ⓓ Ⓔ	11. Ⓐ Ⓑ Ⓒ Ⓓ Ⓔ	21. Ⓐ Ⓑ Ⓒ Ⓓ Ⓔ	31. Ⓐ Ⓑ Ⓒ Ⓓ Ⓔ
2. Ⓐ Ⓑ Ⓒ Ⓓ Ⓔ	12. Ⓐ Ⓑ Ⓒ Ⓓ Ⓔ	22. Ⓐ Ⓑ Ⓒ Ⓓ Ⓔ	32. Ⓐ Ⓑ Ⓒ Ⓓ Ⓔ
3. Ⓐ Ⓑ Ⓒ Ⓓ Ⓔ	13. Ⓐ Ⓑ Ⓒ Ⓓ Ⓔ	23. Ⓐ Ⓑ Ⓒ Ⓓ Ⓔ	33. Ⓐ Ⓑ Ⓒ Ⓓ Ⓔ
4. Ⓐ Ⓑ Ⓒ Ⓓ Ⓔ	14. Ⓐ Ⓑ Ⓒ Ⓓ Ⓔ	24. Ⓐ Ⓑ Ⓒ Ⓓ Ⓔ	34. Ⓐ Ⓑ Ⓒ Ⓓ Ⓔ
5. Ⓐ Ⓑ Ⓒ Ⓓ Ⓔ	15. Ⓐ Ⓑ Ⓒ Ⓓ Ⓔ	25. Ⓐ Ⓑ Ⓒ Ⓓ Ⓔ	35. Ⓐ Ⓑ Ⓒ Ⓓ Ⓔ
6. Ⓐ Ⓑ Ⓒ Ⓓ Ⓔ	16. Ⓐ Ⓑ Ⓒ Ⓓ Ⓔ	26. Ⓐ Ⓑ Ⓒ Ⓓ Ⓔ	36. Ⓐ Ⓑ Ⓒ Ⓓ Ⓔ
7. Ⓐ Ⓑ Ⓒ Ⓓ Ⓔ	17. Ⓐ Ⓑ Ⓒ Ⓓ Ⓔ	27. Ⓐ Ⓑ Ⓒ Ⓓ Ⓔ	37. Ⓐ Ⓑ Ⓒ Ⓓ Ⓔ
8. Ⓐ Ⓑ Ⓒ Ⓓ Ⓔ	18. Ⓐ Ⓑ Ⓒ Ⓓ Ⓔ	28. Ⓐ Ⓑ Ⓒ Ⓓ Ⓔ	38. Ⓐ Ⓑ Ⓒ Ⓓ Ⓔ
9. Ⓐ Ⓑ Ⓒ Ⓓ Ⓔ	19. Ⓐ Ⓑ Ⓒ Ⓓ Ⓔ	29. Ⓐ Ⓑ Ⓒ Ⓓ Ⓔ	39. Ⓐ Ⓑ Ⓒ Ⓓ Ⓔ
10. Ⓐ Ⓑ Ⓒ Ⓓ Ⓔ	20. Ⓐ Ⓑ Ⓒ Ⓓ Ⓔ	30. Ⓐ Ⓑ Ⓒ Ⓓ Ⓔ	40. Ⓐ Ⓑ Ⓒ Ⓓ Ⓔ

right in Section 8

wrong in Section 8

SECTION 9

1. Ⓐ Ⓑ Ⓒ Ⓓ Ⓔ	11. Ⓐ Ⓑ Ⓒ Ⓓ Ⓔ	21. Ⓐ Ⓑ Ⓒ Ⓓ Ⓔ	31. Ⓐ Ⓑ Ⓒ Ⓓ Ⓔ
2. Ⓐ Ⓑ Ⓒ Ⓓ Ⓔ	12. Ⓐ Ⓑ Ⓒ Ⓓ Ⓔ	22. Ⓐ Ⓑ Ⓒ Ⓓ Ⓔ	32. Ⓐ Ⓑ Ⓒ Ⓓ Ⓔ
3. Ⓐ Ⓑ Ⓒ Ⓓ Ⓔ	13. Ⓐ Ⓑ Ⓒ Ⓓ Ⓔ	23. Ⓐ Ⓑ Ⓒ Ⓓ Ⓔ	33. Ⓐ Ⓑ Ⓒ Ⓓ Ⓔ
4. Ⓐ Ⓑ Ⓒ Ⓓ Ⓔ	14. Ⓐ Ⓑ Ⓒ Ⓓ Ⓔ	24. Ⓐ Ⓑ Ⓒ Ⓓ Ⓔ	34. Ⓐ Ⓑ Ⓒ Ⓓ Ⓔ
5. Ⓐ Ⓑ Ⓒ Ⓓ Ⓔ	15. Ⓐ Ⓑ Ⓒ Ⓓ Ⓔ	25. Ⓐ Ⓑ Ⓒ Ⓓ Ⓔ	35. Ⓐ Ⓑ Ⓒ Ⓓ Ⓔ
6. Ⓐ Ⓑ Ⓒ Ⓓ Ⓔ	16. Ⓐ Ⓑ Ⓒ Ⓓ Ⓔ	26. Ⓐ Ⓑ Ⓒ Ⓓ Ⓔ	36. Ⓐ Ⓑ Ⓒ Ⓓ Ⓔ
7. Ⓐ Ⓑ Ⓒ Ⓓ Ⓔ	17. Ⓐ Ⓑ Ⓒ Ⓓ Ⓔ	27. Ⓐ Ⓑ Ⓒ Ⓓ Ⓔ	37. Ⓐ Ⓑ Ⓒ Ⓓ Ⓔ
8. Ⓐ Ⓑ Ⓒ Ⓓ Ⓔ	18. Ⓐ Ⓑ Ⓒ Ⓓ Ⓔ	28. Ⓐ Ⓑ Ⓒ Ⓓ Ⓔ	38. Ⓐ Ⓑ Ⓒ Ⓓ Ⓔ
9. Ⓐ Ⓑ Ⓒ Ⓓ Ⓔ	19. Ⓐ Ⓑ Ⓒ Ⓓ Ⓔ	29. Ⓐ Ⓑ Ⓒ Ⓓ Ⓔ	39. Ⓐ Ⓑ Ⓒ Ⓓ Ⓔ
10. Ⓐ Ⓑ Ⓒ Ⓓ Ⓔ	20. Ⓐ Ⓑ Ⓒ Ⓓ Ⓔ	30. Ⓐ Ⓑ Ⓒ Ⓓ Ⓔ	40. Ⓐ Ⓑ Ⓒ Ⓓ Ⓔ

right in Section 9

wrong in Section 9

SECTION 10

1. Ⓐ Ⓑ Ⓒ Ⓓ Ⓔ	11. Ⓐ Ⓑ Ⓒ Ⓓ Ⓔ	21. Ⓐ Ⓑ Ⓒ Ⓓ Ⓔ	31. Ⓐ Ⓑ Ⓒ Ⓓ Ⓔ
2. Ⓐ Ⓑ Ⓒ Ⓓ Ⓔ	12. Ⓐ Ⓑ Ⓒ Ⓓ Ⓔ	22. Ⓐ Ⓑ Ⓒ Ⓓ Ⓔ	32. Ⓐ Ⓑ Ⓒ Ⓓ Ⓔ
3. Ⓐ Ⓑ Ⓒ Ⓓ Ⓔ	13. Ⓐ Ⓑ Ⓒ Ⓓ Ⓔ	23. Ⓐ Ⓑ Ⓒ Ⓓ Ⓔ	33. Ⓐ Ⓑ Ⓒ Ⓓ Ⓔ
4. Ⓐ Ⓑ Ⓒ Ⓓ Ⓔ	14. Ⓐ Ⓑ Ⓒ Ⓓ Ⓔ	24. Ⓐ Ⓑ Ⓒ Ⓓ Ⓔ	34. Ⓐ Ⓑ Ⓒ Ⓓ Ⓔ
5. Ⓐ Ⓑ Ⓒ Ⓓ Ⓔ	15. Ⓐ Ⓑ Ⓒ Ⓓ Ⓔ	25. Ⓐ Ⓑ Ⓒ Ⓓ Ⓔ	35. Ⓐ Ⓑ Ⓒ Ⓓ Ⓔ
6. Ⓐ Ⓑ Ⓒ Ⓓ Ⓔ	16. Ⓐ Ⓑ Ⓒ Ⓓ Ⓔ	26. Ⓐ Ⓑ Ⓒ Ⓓ Ⓔ	36. Ⓐ Ⓑ Ⓒ Ⓓ Ⓔ
7. Ⓐ Ⓑ Ⓒ Ⓓ Ⓔ	17. Ⓐ Ⓑ Ⓒ Ⓓ Ⓔ	27. Ⓐ Ⓑ Ⓒ Ⓓ Ⓔ	37. Ⓐ Ⓑ Ⓒ Ⓓ Ⓔ
8. Ⓐ Ⓑ Ⓒ Ⓓ Ⓔ	18. Ⓐ Ⓑ Ⓒ Ⓓ Ⓔ	28. Ⓐ Ⓑ Ⓒ Ⓓ Ⓔ	38. Ⓐ Ⓑ Ⓒ Ⓓ Ⓔ
9. Ⓐ Ⓑ Ⓒ Ⓓ Ⓔ	19. Ⓐ Ⓑ Ⓒ Ⓓ Ⓔ	29. Ⓐ Ⓑ Ⓒ Ⓓ Ⓔ	39. Ⓐ Ⓑ Ⓒ Ⓓ Ⓔ
10. Ⓐ Ⓑ Ⓒ Ⓓ Ⓔ	20. Ⓐ Ⓑ Ⓒ Ⓓ Ⓔ	30. Ⓐ Ⓑ Ⓒ Ⓓ Ⓔ	40. Ⓐ Ⓑ Ⓒ Ⓓ Ⓔ

right in Section 10

wrong in Section 10

ESSAY
Time—25 minutes

The essay gives you an opportunity to show how effectively you can develop and express ideas. You should, therefore, take care to develop your point of view, present your ideas logically and clearly, and use language precisely.

Your essay must be written on the lines provided in your Answer Grid Booklet—you will receive no other paper on which to write. You will have enough space if you write on every line, avoid wide margins, and keep your handwriting to a reasonable size. Remember that people who are not familiar with your handwriting will read what you write. Try to write or print so that what you are writing is legible to those readers.

You have twenty-five minutes to write an essay on the topic assigned below. DO NOT WRITE ON ANOTHER TOPIC. AN OFF-TOPIC ESSAY WILL RECEIVE A SCORE OF ZERO.

Think carefully about the issue presented in the following quotation and the assignment below.

> It is often interesting, in retrospect, to consider the trifling causes that lead to great events. A chance encounter, a thoughtless remark—and the torturous chain reaction of coincidence is set in motion, leading with devious inevitability to some resounding climax.
>
> Patricia Moyes, *Down Among the Dead Men*

Assignment: Do small events lead to catastrophes or are great events initiated by other causes? Plan and write an essay in which you develop your point of view on this issue. Support your position with reasoning and examples taken from your reading, studies, experience, or observations.

DO NOT WRITE YOUR ESSAY IN YOUR TEST BOOK.
You will receive credit only for what you write in your Answer Grid Booklet.

BEGIN WRITING YOUR ESSAY ON PAGE 135 OF THIS BOOK
OR ON PAGE 3 OF YOUR KAPLAN SAT ANSWER GRID.

IF YOU FINISH BEFORE TIME IS CALLED, YOU MAY CHECK YOUR WORK ON THIS SECTION ONLY. DO NOT TURN TO ANY OTHER SECTION IN THE TEST.

- 141 -

Time—25 Minutes
24 Questions

Directions: For each question in this section, select the best answer from among the choices given and fill in the corresponding oval on the answer sheet.

Each sentence below has one or two blanks, each blank indicating that something has been omitted. Beneath the sentence are five words or sets of words labeled A through E. Choose the word or set of words that, when inserted in the sentence, best fits the meaning of the sentence as a whole.

EXAMPLE:

Today's small, portable computers contrast markedly with the earliest electronic computers, which were -------.

(A) effective   (B) invented
   (C) useful   (D) destructive
      (E) enormous

ANSWER:
Ⓐ Ⓑ Ⓒ Ⓓ ●

1 The Hope diamond is ------- by an elaborate alarm system in order to prevent anyone from ------- it.

(A) protected . . stealing
(B) guarded . . noticing
(C) secured . . suppressing
(D) saved . . taking
(E) hidden . . pilfering

2 In addition to her ------- for a larger allowance, the girl also begged her parents to reconsider their ------- about allowing pets in the house.

(A) demand . . consent
(B) petition . . opportunity
(C) refusal . . decision
(D) plea . . reconciliation
(E) request . . stance

3 As frightening political instability loomed, and every day brought more damaging reports of insider trading and fraudulent accounting practices, the value of the stock market -------.

(A) increased   (B) depreciated
   (C) doubled   (D) changed
      (E) denounced

4 Because Greg was so willing to help anyone in need, he quickly became known as the most ------- student in his class.

(A) fortunate   (B) talkative
   (C) philanthropic   (D) resilient
      (E) inconsiderate

5 Many people think today's diseases are harmless compared to the Black Plague of Europe, but the Ebola virus, discovered in 1976, is even more -------.

(A) innocuous   (B) virulent
   (C) common   (D) charitable
      (E) munificent

6 The witness spoke with -------, and talked about even the most personal details of his life without hesitation.

(A) guile   (B) clarity
   (C) diplomacy   (D) candor
      (E) magnanimity

7 Dr. Fobbish was extremely ------- with all people regardless of their age or class, earning her the ------- of everyone she came across; she was even dubbed "Snobbish Fobbish" by the tabloids during her trial for mail fraud and tax evasion.

(A) haughty . . ire
(B) polite . . disdain
(C) sympathetic . . distrust
(D) evasive . . chagrin
(E) supercilious . . admiration

8 The organization's ------- would prove devastating: ------- spending had drained its accounts, and its creditors demanded repayment.

(A) tenacity . . outrageous
(B) thrift . . meager
(C) pariah . . paradoxical
(D) improvidence . . profligate
(E) recklessness . . miserly

GO ON TO THE NEXT PAGE

The passages below are followed by questions based on their content; questions following a pair of related passages may also be based on the relationship between the paired passages. Answer the questions on the basis of what is <u>stated</u> or <u>implied</u> in the passages and in any introductory material that may be provided.

Questions 9–10 are based on the following passage.

Although much about dolphin communication remains a mystery, scientists have discovered three distinct sounds that dolphins frequently make: chirps,
Line clicks, and whistles. Scientists have learned that dolphins
(5) use clicks to create a sonar map, which allows them to navigate and hunt. But apart from possibly transmitting location, the clicks do not appear to serve any communication purpose. Rather, research indicates that dolphins communicate with each other by whistling. This
(10) discovery has necessitated further investigation, as scientists are not yet sure whether the whistles comprise a complex system of linguistic communication or a simple set of sonic cues like the ones used by other animal species.

9 The passage indicates that the whistles mentioned in line 4 are significant in part because they

(A) show that dolphins are capable of expressing emotion
(B) prompt questions about the complexity of dolphin communication
(C) aid dolphins in navigating and hunting
(D) continue to spur research into their unknown purpose
(E) prove that some animals are more intelligent than others

10 The statements in the passage provide evidence that most directly supports the conclusion that

(A) dolphins are not the only animal species that communicates vocally
(B) dolphins never use clicks for communication
(C) dolphins are more intelligent than other animal species
(D) dolphins use a system of communication similar to that of other animal species
(E) dolphins frequently communicate their locations to each other

Questions 11–12 are based on the following passage.

I knew it would come. That precious moment when, stepping out of the airport doors into the atmosphere of a foreign country for the first time, I could breathe in my
Line total displacement and relish the freshness of it all. I had
(5) never known this place, and for that moment only would it be truly new. So there was great anticipation as I pushed eagerly against the last door and felt, suddenly checked by familiarity, the same chilling damp I thought I had left back at home, halfway around the globe. I just
(10) stood there, watching the buses cough out the same exhaust and the rain fall just as it always had.

11 The narrator uses the phrase "So there was great anticipation" (line 6) to express his

(A) nervousness with being so far from home
(B) certainty that everything will feel different
(C) satisfaction with being on his own
(D) eagerness for adventure
(E) confidence that he will enjoy this new place

12 In line 8, "checked" most nearly means

(A) inspected
(B) confirmed
(C) surprised
(D) stopped
(E) examined

GO ON TO THE NEXT PAGE

Questions 13–24 are based on the following passages.

These two passages were written in the early 1990s and present two viewpoints about the ways that the public responds to the results of scientific research.

Passage 1

The way that people in modern industrial societies think about science in the modern world actually tends to cultivate the very unscientific perception that science
Line supplies us with unquestionable facts. If there is one
(5) unquestionable fact about science, it is that science is inherently uncertain. Research consists not so much of a search for truth, as a search for some degree of certainty in an uncertain world. Every research study, every experiment, and every survey incorporates an extensive
(10) statistical analysis that is meant to be taken as qualifying the probability that the results are consistent and reproducible. Yet policy makers, public relations interests, and so-called experts in the popular media continue to treat the results of every latest study as if they
(15) were surefire truths.

History is filled with examples of the fallibility of scientific certainties. From the medieval monks who believed the sun orbited around Earth and the world was only 4,000 years old, to the early twentieth-century
(20) scientists who thought that X-rays were a hoax and that exploding a nuclear bomb would set off a chain reaction that would destroy all matter in the universe, it has been demonstrated repeatedly that science deals primarily with possibilities and is subject to the same prejudices as other
(25) kinds of opinions and beliefs. Yet statistics are complicated, and in our need to feel that we live in a universe of predictable certainties, it is tempting to place our faith in the oversimplified generalities of headlines and sound bites rather than the rigorous application of
(30) probabilities. Ironically, even though the intent of science is to expand the realm of human knowledge, an unfounded prejudice stemming from a desire for scientific constancy can actually discourage inquiry.

Science serves an important practical function;
(35) predictability and reproducibility are vital to making sure that our bridges remain standing, our nuclear power plants run smoothly, and our cars start in the morning so we can drive to work. When these practicalities become everyday occurrences, they tend to encourage a
(40) complacent faith in the reliability and consistency of science. Yet faced with so many simple conveniences, it is important to remember that we depend on the advance of science for our very survival. With progress expanding into those gray areas at the boundaries of scientific
(45) exploration, caution and prudence are just as important as open-mindedness and imagination. As technological advances engage increasingly complex moral questions with the expansion into fields such as genetics, indefinite extension of life, and the potential for inconceivably
(50) potent weapons, an understanding of the limitations of science becomes just as important as an understanding of its strengths.

Passage 2

While it is important that scientific knowledge be taken into consideration in matters of public interest,
(55) such consideration must be tempered with critical rigor. In the early days during the ascendance of science as a practical discipline, the public was inclined to view every new advance with a healthy skepticism—a tendency that has since been unfortunately lost. Yet in the present-day,
(60) and especially where public policy is at issue, response to scientific research needs more than ever to pursue an informed, critical viewpoint. Who performs a research study, what kind of study it is, what kinds of review and scrutiny it comes under, and what interests support it
(65) are every bit as important as its conclusions.

Studies of mass media and public policy reveal that, all too often, scientific findings presented to the public as objective and conclusive are actually funded at two or three degrees of removal by corporate or political
(70) interests with a specific agenda related to the outcome of those findings. Some critics question the issue, for example, of whether a study of the effectiveness of a new drug is more likely to produce favorable results when the study is funded by the pharmaceutical company that
(75) owns the drug patent. In cases where such findings conflict with the interests of the funding parties, analysts sometimes wonder if information was repressed, altered, or given a favorable public relations slant in order to de-emphasize dangerous side effects.

(80) Part of the problem grows from the public's willingness to place blind faith in the authority of science without an awareness of the interests that lie behind the research. Public officials then, in turn, may sometimes be too willing to bend in the face of public or private
(85) political pressure rather than pursuing the best interests of the constituency. Where the safety of individuals is at stake, a precautionary principle of allowing for unpredictable, unforeseen negative effects of technological advances should be pursued. It is the duty
(90) of active citizens of a free society to educate themselves about the real-world application of risk-assessment and statistical analysis, and to resist passive acceptance of the reassurances of self-styled scientific authorities. The most favorable approach to policy decisions based on
(95) realistic assessments finds a middle ground between the alarmism of political "chicken littles" and the recklessness of profit-seeking risk takers.

GO ON TO THE NEXT PAGE

13 The word "qualifying" in line 10 most closely means

(A) improving
(B) succeeding
(C) disproving
(D) modifying
(E) quantifying

14 The author of Passage 2 would probably agree with which of the following statements about the examples of scientific errors (lines 16–22) in Passage 1?

(A) They induced the public to believe blindly in erroneous conclusions.
(B) They reflect the healthy skepticism that people of that time had about science.
(C) They demonstrate the lack of scientific rigor prevalent in the Middle Ages.
(D) They represent errors that may have resulted more from the desires and prejudices of the interests involved than from objective scientific procedure.
(E) They seem silly in hindsight.

15 The author of Passage 1 includes references to the beliefs that the "sun orbited around Earth" and that "X-rays were a hoax" (lines 18–20) as examples of

(A) scientific findings that will be eventually proven true
(B) theories that some scientists still believe
(C) beliefs of scientists that were later discovered to be false
(D) ideas that the public is inclined to believe
(E) viewpoints that experts and the media are still supporting

16 The word "probabilities" in line 30 is used to describe

(A) the results that will most likely take place
(B) the causes of unpredictable occurrences
(C) the study of the likelihood of certain events happening
(D) the range of all possible outcomes
(E) problems that will result from particular actions

17 In lines 42–43, the author points out that "we depend on...very survival" in order to

(A) strengthen the authority of the central thesis
(B) rebut a counterexample
(C) introduce a new line of reasoning
(D) provide reassurance to the reader
(E) emphasize an important argument

18 The author of Passage 2 uses the first paragraph to explain

(A) a new scientific hypothesis
(B) the underlying cause of an issue
(C) a public policy generality
(D) a historical contrast
(E) a catalog of resources

19 The author of Passage 1 would most likely interpret the "public's willingness" described in Passage 2 (lines 80–81) as

(A) symptomatic of widespread skepticism about science
(B) resulting from a desire for scientific certainties
(C) a source of political pressure on public officials
(D) more of a problem in the present than in the past
(E) an indication that the cautious view of science is spreading

20 The phrase "willing to bend...constituency" (lines 84–86) in Passage 2 most nearly means that

(A) the way that politicians view scientific evidence has evolved over time
(B) governments should disregard the results of scientific studies in policy decisions
(C) voters should seek to elect only public officials who understand scientific research
(D) policy makers may sometimes place political interest above scientific findings or benefits to the public
(E) regulations that prevent corporate concerns from pressuring elected officials are often ignored

21 What would the author of Passage 1 say is the biggest obstacle to reaching the solution described by the author of Passage 2 in lines 89–93 ("It is the duty...authorities")?

(A) Policymakers are too willing to bend to public pressure when it comes to regulating scientific research.
(B) The interests that fund research are the same interests that stand to profit by favorable results, making impartiality impossible.
(C) History has shown that science will always be subject to erroneous conclusions.
(D) Unanswered ethical questions are increasingly coming under scrutiny at the forefront of our most advanced scientific research.
(E) Statistics are too abstract when compared with the concrete evidence of technological conveniences.

GO ON TO THE NEXT PAGE

22 The author of Passage 2 uses the reference to "chicken littles" (line 96) in order to

(A) disparage the political leanings of scientific authorities

(B) caricature the overly pessimistic attitudes of some doomsayers

(C) suggest an alternative solution to the alarmism of certain public officials

(D) communicate skepticism over the validity of research findings

(E) imply that most citizens are unable or unwilling to understand the intricacies of science

23 Which of the following most closely describes the respective viewpoints of the author of Passage 1 and the author of Passage 2 toward the results of modern scientific studies?

(A) skepticism and inquisitive distrust

(B) cynicism and optimistic disinterest

(C) urgency and complacent indulgence

(D) anger and resigned acceptance

(E) enthusiasm and informed uncertainty

24 With which of the following statements would the authors of both passages most likely agree?

(A) More government control and regulation are needed to ensure that science serves the best interests of the public.

(B) People should not unquestioningly accept the results of scientific studies.

(C) Society should place less emphasis on modern conveniences and more on understanding the limitations of science.

(D) The results that scientists derive from research are less reliable now than in former times.

(E) Corporations that sponsor research should be forced to disclose their involvement to reduce the chance of bias.

IF YOU FINISH BEFORE TIME IS CALLED, YOU MAY CHECK YOUR WORK ON THIS SECTION ONLY. DO NOT TURN TO ANY OTHER SECTION IN THE TEST.

STOP

- 146 -

NO TEST MATERIAL ON THIS PAGE

Time—25 Minutes
20 Questions

Directions: For this section, solve each problem and decide which is the best of the choices given. Fill in the corresponding oval on the answer sheet. You may use any available space for scratchwork.

Notes

1. Calculator use is permitted.

2. All numbers used are real numbers.

3. Figures are provided for some problems. All figures are drawn to scale and lie in a plane UNLESS otherwise indicated.

4. Unless otherwise specified, the domain of any function f is assumed to be the set of all real numbers x for which $f(x)$ is a real number.

Reference Information

$A = \dfrac{1}{2}bh$ $c^2 = a^2 + b^2$ Special Right Triangles $A = \pi r^2$ $V = \pi r^2 h$ $A = lw$ $V = lwh$

$C = 2\pi r$

The sum of the measures in degrees of the angles of a triangle is 180.
The number of degrees of arc in a circle is 360.
A straight angle has a degree measure of 180.

---

1 If $4x^2 - 6x + 2 = 0$, what is one possible value of x ?

(A) $-\dfrac{1}{2}$

(B) $\dfrac{1}{2}$

(C) 2

(D) 3

(E) 6

2 Steve bought a total of 6 packages of pens, and each package contained either 3 or 7 pens. If exactly 4 of the packages Steve bought contained 7 pens, how many pens did Steve buy?

(A) 21
(B) 28
(C) 30
(D) 34
(E) 42

GO ON TO THE NEXT PAGE

3 The square of the result of adding $7x$ and y is equal to the result of subtracting the square root of $4x$ from y.

Which of the following is an equation for the statement above?

(A) $(7x + y)^2 = (4x - y)^2$
(B) $(7x)2 + y = (4x - y)^2$
(C) $(7x + y)^2 = \sqrt{4x} - y$
(D) $7x + y = y - \sqrt{4x}$
(E) $(7x + y)^2 = y - \sqrt{4x}$

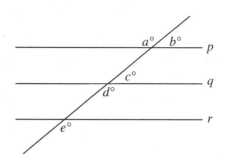

5 In the figure above, lines p, q, and r are all parallel. If $b = 30$, what is the value of $a + c + e$?

(A) 180
(B) 210
(C) 240
(D) 300
(E) 330

4 The three points X, Y, and Z are all on a line in that order. The length of $\overline{XY}$ is 34 and the length of $\overline{YZ}$ is 8 less than the length of $\overline{XY}$. What is the length of $\overline{XZ}$?

(A) 52
(B) 60
(C) 64
(D) 68
(E) 76

6 If $y = -\dfrac{2}{3}$, what is the value of $\dfrac{2}{y} + \dfrac{5}{y + 1}$?

(A) −18
(B) −12
(C)   7
(D)   12
(E)   17

GO ON TO THE NEXT PAGE

7 The area of quadrilateral A is 16 less than 3 times the area of quadrilateral B, and the sum of the areas of quadrilaterals A and B is 24. What is the average (arithmetic mean) of the areas of quadrilaterals A and B ?

(A) 8
(B) 10
(C) 12
(D) 14
(E) 26

9 Which of the following is equal to $(25 \times 10^4) + (5 \times 10^6)$?

(A) 250×10^2
(B) 75×10^4
(C) 525×10^4
(D) 75×10^5
(E) 525×10^6

8 If 750 is 30 percent of y, what is 70 percent of y ?

(A) 1,000
(B) 1,250
(C) 1,500
(D) 1,750
(E) 2,625

10 Box A contains only green disks, blue disks, and orange disks. Box A contains a total of 54 disks, and when choosing a disk at random from box A, the probability of choosing a green disk is $\frac{1}{3}$. All the blue disks and orange disks are taken out of box A and placed in box B, and there is nothing else in box B. If one disk is chosen at random from box B, which of the following could be the probability that the disk chosen is orange?

(A) $\frac{1}{27}$

(B) $\frac{2}{9}$

(C) $\frac{2}{5}$

(D) $\frac{3}{7}$

(E) $\frac{7}{10}$

GO ON TO THE NEXT PAGE

11 Which of the following is the product of exactly three distinct prime numbers?

(A) 18
(B) 20
(C) 105
(D) 125
(E) 210

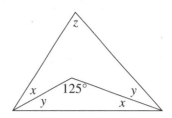

13 In the figure above, what is the value of $z + y + x$?

(A)   55
(B)   70
(C) 110
(D) 125
(E) 140

12 The average (arithmetic mean) of 7 numbers is x. What does $14x$ represent?

(A) 2 times the average of the 7 numbers
(B) $\frac{2}{3}$ times the sum of the 7 numbers
(C) 3 times the average of the 7 numbers
(D) 2 times the sum of the 7 numbers
(E) 4 times the sum of the 7 numbers

14 If $f(x) = 4x + 7$, what is the y-intercept of $f(x)$?

(A) −7
(B) −4
(C)   0
(D)   4
(E)   7

GO ON TO THE NEXT PAGE

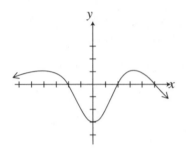

15 The figure above shows the graph of $w(x) - 6$. What is the value of $w(0)$?

(A) −6
(B) −3
(C)   0
(D)   3
(E)   9

16 What is the value of the expression $(-4a^6b^5)^3$?

(A) $-64a^9b^8$
(B) $16a^9b^8$
(C) $-4a^9b^{15}$
(D) $16a^{18}b^{15}$
(E) $-64a^{18}b^{15}$

17 If x and y are positive numbers and $\dfrac{7x}{y} = 3$, then which of the following equations is NOT true?

(A) $\dfrac{x+y}{y} = \dfrac{7}{10}$

(B) $\dfrac{y}{x} = \dfrac{7}{3}$

(C) $\dfrac{4y}{x} + 1 = \dfrac{31}{3}$

(D) $7x - 3y = 0$

(E) $\dfrac{5x + 3y}{x} = 12$

18 If $-4 \leq a \leq 8$ and $-10 \leq b \leq 6$, all the possible values of $2a - b$ are given by which of the following?

(A) $2 \leq 2a - b \leq 6$
(B) $10 \leq 2a - b \leq 14$
(C) $0 \leq 2a - b \leq 4$
(D) $14 \leq 2a - b \leq 18$
(E) $-14 \leq 2a - b \leq 26$

GO ON TO THE NEXT PAGE

19 The first term of a sequence is x and each term after the first term is equal to 5 less than 4 times the previous term. What is the average (arithmetic mean) of the second and third terms?

(A) $8x - 10$
(B) $10x - 15$
(C) $14x - 10$
(D) $16x - 24$
(E) $20x - 30$

20 It takes a crew of 18 workers one hour to assemble a tool shed. If the time required to assemble the shed varies inversely with the number of workers on the crew, how many workers would be required to assemble a tool shed in 40 minutes?

(A) 10
(B) 12
(C) 15
(D) 27
(E) 45

IF YOU FINISH BEFORE TIME IS CALLED, YOU MAY CHECK YOUR WORK ON THIS SECTION ONLY. DO NOT TURN TO ANY OTHER SECTION IN THE TEST.

The following sentences test correctness and effectiveness of expression. Part of each sentence or the entire sentence is underlined; beneath each sentence are five ways of phrasing the underlined material. Choice A repeats the original phrasing; the other four choices are different. If you think the original phrasing produces a better sentence than any of the alternatives, select choice A; if not, select one of the other choices.

In making your selection, follow the requirements of standard written English; that is, pay attention to grammar, choice of words, sentence construction, and punctuation. Your selection should result in the most effective sentence—clear and precise—without awkwardness or ambiguity.

EXAMPLE:

Every apple in the baskets <u>are ripe and labeled according to the date it was picked</u>.

(A) are ripe and labeled according to the date it was picked
(B) is ripe and labeled according to the date it was picked
(C) are ripe and labeled according to the date they were picked
(D) is ripe and labeled according to the date they were picked
(E) are ripe and labeled as to the date it was picked

ANSWER:

Ⓐ ● Ⓒ Ⓓ Ⓔ

1 A civil class action suit, with a large number of plaintiffs suing a single entity, is difficult for a small law firm to try, since <u>they have</u> demands on personnel and time may require years of work by many litigators.

(A) they have
(B) their
(C) these
(D) it has
(E) its

2 If I were to win the 2007 U.S. Open, it <u>will be</u> a miracle.

(A) will be
(B) was
(C) was to be
(D) would be
(E) would have been

3 The United States was allied with the Soviet Union during WWII, <u>although</u> Stalin had previously signed a non-aggression pact with Hitler, the United States was wary of the Soviet Union's fidelity.

(A) although
(B) but because
(C) since
(D) and
(E) therefore

4 Architects in the Middle Ages began to use external supports, known as flying buttresses, to allow them to build taller buildings with large windows, <u>this was an accomplishment that had eluded earlier builders</u>.

(A) this was an accomplishment that had eluded earlier builders
(B) since this accomplishment had eluded earlier builders
(C) the accomplishment earlier builders had eluded
(D) an accomplishment that had eluded earlier builders
(E) it eluded earlier builders as an accomplishment

5 <u>With one</u> of the most popular dances of Mark Morris's career, *L'Allegro, il Penseroso ed il Moderato* is performed often in New York City and around the world.

(A) With one
(B) It is one
(C) Being one
(D) One
(E) As one

Japanese beetles, introduced in Ann Arbor to control local

GO ON TO THE NEXT PAGE

6 insect infestations, are known to bite humans, <u>causing many locals to</u> consider them more harmful than advantageous.

(A) causing many locals to
(B) therefore, many locals
(C) this causes many locals to
(D) which cause many locals to
(E) many locals

Directions for the new laptop are so simple <u>for it to require</u> only a few steps to get the computer running.

7
(A) for it to require
(B) so it required
(C) that it requires
(D) so that it requires
(E) as for it to require

<u>With many babies born</u> just after midnight, the first birth of a new year it is often impossible to identify.

8
(A) With many babies born
(B) Because many babies are born
(C) Because of many babies being born
(D) Considering that there are many babies born
(E) Knowing that many babies are born

9 Amy had decided to leave the party <u>and then she was spotted by Josh, who came</u> over to talk to her.

(A) and then she was spotted by Josh, who came
(B) and then Josh spotted her and he came
(C) when she was spotted by Josh and he came
(D) and Josh spotted her, he came
(E) when Josh spotted her and came

10 Marie Curie, Pierre Curie, and Henri Becquerel were awarded the 1903 Nobel Prize in Physics for their work <u>studying radiation phenomena that he had previously discovered</u>.

(A) studying radiation phenomena that he had previously discovered
(B) studying radiation phenomena that he had discovered previously
(C) studying radiation phenomena that Becquerel had previously discovered
(D) that Becquerel, having studied radiation phenomena, had discovered previously
(E) which, since they had studied radiation phenomena, Becquerel had previously discovered

11 Prehistoric cave paintings were discovered in the Lascaux cave system in France, <u>curators closed the caves to</u> the public in 1963 because the carbon dioxide visitors exhaled was damaging the paintings.

(A) curators closed the caves to
(B) and curators closed them to
(C) which curators close to
(D) curators closing the caves to
(E) which curators closed to

GO ON TO THE NEXT PAGE

The following sentences test your ability to recognize grammar and usage errors. Each sentence contains either a single error or no error at all. No sentence contains more than one error. The error, if there is one, is underlined and lettered. If the sentence contains an error, select the one underlined part that must be changed to make the sentence correct. If the sentence is correct, select choice E. In choosing answers, follow the requirements of standard written English.

EXAMPLE:

Whenever one is driving late at night, you must take extra precautions against
  A   B   C

falling asleep at the wheel. No error
         D   E

ANSWER:

Ⓐ ● Ⓒ Ⓓ Ⓔ

12 In 2005, more than one million college students created
         A

blogs, online journals that allow freedom of personal
              B

expression and are not governed by the rules limiting
                    C   D

materials written for traditional school publications.

No error
  E

13 From its inception as a string of amateur homepages and
  A   B

its current incarnation as a powerful tool of communication,

the Internet has completely changed the manner in which
                               C

both individuals and companies transact business. No error
                          D   E

14 Many critics, and even the editor herself, has admitted
                           A   B

that the quality of the newspaper's local coverage has
  C

declined since the paper was purchased

by a national media conglomerate. No error
             D   E

15 Although generally thought of as docile animals,

hippopotamuses cause more deaths than any other
            A

animal in Africa because a hippopotamus will attack a

boat without warning when it feels its territory or its
     B   C   D

young are threatened. No error
           E

16 Extensive study of atoms' movements have led scientists
                             A

to theories of quantum mechanics, which hold that it is
     B   C

impossible to determine exactly how subatomic particles

move and that the best we can do is make probabilistic
               D

guesses. No error
         E

17 Whenever she walks down the street, Elizabeth,

who is exceedingly beautiful, received admiring
      A   B

glances from others, although she rarely seems to
        C   D

notice. No error
       E

18 Early attempts to produce electricity industrially
                               A

was doomed to failure because, until the discovery of
  B   C   D

alternating current, transporting large amounts of

electricity meant unacceptable current losses. No error
                              E

GO ON TO THE NEXT PAGE

19 Our professor contends that a physicist <u>is having to explain</u>
                                            A
reality using abstract concepts, <u>while</u> a mathematician
                                  B
tries <u>to illustrate</u> abstract concepts <u>by relating them to</u>
      C   D
real life situations. <u>No error</u>
                          E

20 Many novice gun users <u>know</u> to expect <u>a substantial kick</u>
                              A   B
when they fire a gun, <u>yet most are</u> still unprepared for
                       C
the amount of recoil they feel <u>as</u> shooting for the first
                                 D
time. <u>No error</u>
          E

21 <u>To take</u> full advantage of your college education, <u>one</u>
       A   B
<u>should live</u> on campus <u>if possible</u>. <u>No error</u>
   C   D   E

22 The game of Mad Libs <u>is</u> more fun than either charades
                            A
<u>and</u> Trivial Pursuit, since <u>it can be played</u> by as many as
 B   C
thirty people or <u>as few as</u> two. <u>No error</u>
                  D   E

23 Linda was disappointed to discover that, <u>when</u> <u>she awoke</u>
                                                A   B
at eight o'clock, her father was gone, <u>he had left</u> early to
                                         C
catch a <u>flight to</u> Seattle for business. <u>No error</u>
         D   E

24 Paintings <u>by</u> abstract impressionist Jackson Pollock <u>are</u>
                 A   B
better known and <u>more frequently exhibited</u> <u>than his wife</u>,
                  C   D
Lee Krasner. <u>No error</u>
                  E

25 In order to qualify for financial aid, Gwen <u>has</u> to fill out a
                                                   A
detailed application form, submit her high school

transcript, and <u>schedules an appointment</u> <u>for</u> a personal
                 B   C
interview <u>with the dean</u>. <u>No error</u>
           D   E

26 Before 1793, when Eli Whitney <u>invented</u> the cotton gin,
                                      A
cotton was not a profitable crop because the traditional

method used <u>in the separating of</u> seeds <u>from cotton fiber</u>
             B   C
was <u>enormously labor-intensive</u>. <u>No error</u>
     D   E

27 My gold necklace is <u>a piece of</u> jewelry <u>who</u> I <u>get cleaned</u>
                           A   B   C
<u>regularly</u>. <u>No error</u>
 D   E

28 Each of the squad members <u>plays</u> well, <u>but</u> Seth is by far
                                 A   B
<u>the strongest hitter</u> and Eric <u>the faster</u> runner. <u>No error</u>
 C   D   E

29 Chicken cooked on a hot brick, along with <u>several</u> other
                                                 A
Tuscan specialties, <u>are</u> <u>frequently</u> served <u>at</u> traditional
                     B   C   D
Florentine weddings. <u>No error</u>
                         E

GO ON TO THE NEXT PAGE

Directions: The following passage is an early draft of an essay. Some parts of the passage need to be rewritten.

Read the passage and select the best answer for each question that follows. Some questions are about particular sentences or parts of sentences and ask you to improve sentence structure or word choice. Other questions ask you to consider organization and development. In choosing answers, follow the conventions of standard written English.

(1) Compared to most of our country's other Founding Fathers, Thomas Paine is essentially unknown. (2) In fact, there are many Americans who have never even heard of him. (3) Paine was born in 1737, the son of a corseter—a tailor specializing in corsets and other undergarments—and grew up in rural Thetford, England. (4) As a young man, Paine worked as a corseter, sailor, and minister, but only found his true calling when he moved to the British colonies in America.

(5) Paine first gained notoriety as the editor of *Pennsylvania Magazine* and, as political turmoil engulfed the colonies, he became more prominent. (6) In 1776, Paine anonymously published a book called *Common Sense* that argued forcefully for American independence from Britain. (7) The book's popularity spread like wildfire; soon there were 200,000 copies in circulation. (8) Once the war began, Paine published a series of pamphlets called *The Crisis*. (9) These, in the midst of a bloody war, helped keep the morale of the troops up. (10) Thomas Paine is also credited with conceiving the name "The United States of America."

(11) Thomas Paine was an extremely talented writer, Thomas Jefferson and John Adams drew heavily on his work when drafting the Declaration of Independence. (12) Later in life, Paine wrote other, highly controversial works. (13) He was even exiled from England and imprisoned in France for his writings. (14) In 1796, Paine did his part to inspire what would become Social Security. (15) He suggested a system of social insurance for the young and the elderly in his last great work, *Agrarian Justice*.

30 Which is the best version of the underlined portion of sentence 3 (reproduced below)?

Paine was born in 1737, the son of a corseter— a tailor specializing in corsets and other undergarments— and grew up in rural Thetford, England.

(A) (As it is now)
(B) Born in 1737, the son of a corseter
(C) As the son of a corseter, Paine was born in 1737
(D) Having been born in 1737, Paine was the son of a corseter
(E) Paine was born in 1737, he was the son of a corseter

31 Which is the following is the best version of the underlined portion of sentences 8 and 9 (reproduced below)?

Once the war began, Paine published a series of pamphlets called The Crisis. These, in the midst of a bloody war, helped keep the morale of the troops up.

(A) called *The Crisis* so that, in the midst of a bloody war, they
(B) called *The Crisis*, these, in the midst of a bloody war,
(C) called *The Crisis* which, in the midst of a bloody war,
(D) called *The Crisis*, but in the midst of a bloody war, these
(E) called *The Crisis*; furthermore, in the midst of a bloody war, these

32 Which of the following revisions to the underlined portion of sentence 10 (reproduced below) best connects it to the rest of paragraph 2?

Thomas Paine is also credited with conceiving the name "The United States of America."

(A) Since Thomas Paine is also conceived
(B) In addition to his achievements as a writer, Thomas Paine is also credited
(C) Because they also credited him
(D) For example, Thomas Paine is also credited
(E) On the other hand, Thomas Paine is also credited

GO ON TO THE NEXT PAGE

33 In context, which is the best way to deal with sentence 11?

(A) Insert "Since" at the beginning.
(B) Change "when drafting" to "to draft."
(C) Delete "was" and add a comma in its place.
(D) Change "his work" to "him."
(E) Change "drew" to "drawing."

34 Which of the following is the best version of the underlined portions of sentences 14 and 15 (reproduced below)?

In 1796, Paine did his part to inspire what would become Social Security. He suggested a system of social insurance for the young and the elderly in his last great work, "Agrarian Justice."

(A) In 1796, Paine even did his part to inspire what would become Social Security, and he suggested a system of

(B) By doing his part to inspire what would become Social Security, in 1796, Paine suggested a system of

(C) Therefore, Paine suggested a system in 1796 that inspired what would become Social Security, proposing a system of

(D) Thus, in 1796 Paine even did his part to inspire what would become Social Security when he suggested a system of

(E) In 1796, however, Paine did his part to inspire what would become Social Security by suggesting a system of

35 Which sentence, if added at the end of paragraph 3, would provide the best conclusion to both the paragraph and the passage?

(A) In the whole world, there are only five statues honoring Thomas Paine.

(B) No one knows where Thomas Paine is buried.

(C) Given Thomas Paine's contributions to America, he deserves recognition as one of our most important Founding Fathers.

(D) Unfortunately, not enough is known about Thomas Paine to call him a Founding Father.

(E) Paine was also an inventor, patenting his design for a cantilever bridge.

Time—25 Minutes
24 Questions

Directions: For each question in this section, select the best answer from among the choices given and fill in the corresponding oval on the answer sheet.

Each sentence below has one or two blanks, each blank indicating that something has been omitted. Beneath the sentence are five words or sets of words labeled A through E. Choose the word or set of words that, when inserted in the sentence, best fits the meaning of the sentence as a whole.

EXAMPLE:

Today's small, portable computers contrast markedly with the earliest electronic computers, which were -------.

(A) effective   (B) invented
  (C) useful   (D) destructive
    (E) enormous

ANSWER:

Ⓐ Ⓑ Ⓒ Ⓓ ●

1 The despondent look on the face of the widow seemed contagious, and before the night was over everyone wore a ------- expression.

(A) curious   (B) pensive
  (C) joyous   (D) haughty
    (E) morose

2 Although George had no experience speaking in front of large crowds, he was quite ------- and presented his case -------.

(A) well-spoken . . poorly
(B) flustered . . quickly
(C) flabbergasted . . smoothly
(D) articulate . . eloquently
(E) graceful . . awkwardly

3 Many who saw the advance screening were ambivalent about the film's message; although it seemed to glorify violence, in the end the ------- are punished and repent of their evil ways.

(A) actors   (B) characters
  (C) perpetrators   (D) victims
    (E) demagogues

4 Dolores Huerta, one of the founders of the United Farm Workers Union, has been ------- advocate for California's field workers, sometimes traveling up to ten months of the year and sleeping as little as three hours each night.

(A) an elusive   (B) a tireless
  (C) an incognizant   (D) a listless
    (E) a pliant

5 After his English teacher ------- him for his perpetual tardiness, Hank set three different alarms to ensure his ------- arrival at school.

(A) berated . . prepared
(B) depended . . apologetic
(C) reprimanded . . timely
(D) extolled . . opportune
(E) beguiled . . early

GO ON TO THE NEXT PAGE

The passages below are followed by questions based on their content; questions following a pair of related passages may also be based on the relationship between the paired passages. Answer the questions on the basis of what is <u>stated</u> or <u>implied</u> in the passages and in any introductory material that may be provided.

Questions 6–9 are based on the following passages.

Passage 1

When commercial fish farming—a technique that essentially applies the breeding structures used for raising animals on land to the ocean—was first
Line introduced, it was seen as a creative alternative to the
(5) depletion of the world's large finfish and shellfish populations through conventional harvesting methods. New research, however, is beginning to reign in this initial enthusiasm. About 29 million tons of large finfish were farmed in 1997; no doubt a significant contribution
(10) to the world's fish supplies. Yet the cost of this production was roughly 10 million tons of smaller wild fish used as feed, an amount that, if perpetuated, could soon virtually wipe out both the world's supply of small fish and the potential of fish farming.

Passage 2

(15) Our seemingly insatiable appetite for seafood delicacies like smoked salmon, king prawns, and grilled sea bass has inevitably contributed to a sharp reduction in ocean fish populations. As a growing number of commercial boats found themselves frequently returning
(20) to shore with empty nets, it became clear that supply was starting to run significantly short of an ever-increasing demand. But then came a potential solution in the form of a tried and true method of food production: farming. Today, while traditional ocean fisheries remain in
(25) decline, commercial fish farming is booming—and presently premium fish remain on menus across the world. Through ingenuity and flexible thinking, a seemingly doomed resource was made more sustainable.

6 The first sentence of Passage 1 indicates that fish farming was initially considered to be

(A) a complicated technique
(B) an innovative method
(C) a simple improvement on a successful process
(D) environmentally safe
(E) not yet practical

7 The word "sharp" in line 17 most nearly means

(A) piercing
(B) intense
(C) abrupt
(D) appreciable
(E) clear

8 Both passages raise which of the following questions regarding commercial fish farming?

(A) Will fish farming ultimately help or harm wild fish populations?
(B) Is commercial fish farming a sustainable means of food production?
(C) What will happen when wild fish supplies are fully depleted?
(D) Can commercial fish farming meet the growing demand for premium fish?
(E) How can fish farming techniques be made more environmentally kind?

9 The passages differ in their evaluations of commercial fish farming in that Passage 1 focuses on

(A) the relationship between farmed and wild fish populations, whereas Passage 2 addresses the discrepancy between fish supplies and demand
(B) statistics to make an argument, whereas Passage 2 relies more on general predictions
(C) the results of various research studies, whereas Passage 2 relies primarily on data obtained from fisheries
(D) the application of land-based farming techniques to the ocean, whereas Passage 2 considers fish farming as a more unique method
(E) finfish and shellfish populations, whereas Passage 2 addresses fish populations in general

GO ON TO THE NEXT PAGE

Questions 10–15 are based on the following passage.

In 1892 the world-famous British poet and author of The Jungle Book, *Rudyard Kipling, moved with his wife and their children to the New England town of Brattleboro, Vermont. The following is a fanciful account of their arrival and the American townspeople's reaction to them.*

For weeks before the appearance of the great man himself, the town buzzed with smoldering excitement. Every week, it seemed that a new cartload of unexplained
Line goods packed in stenciled crates referring to exotic
(5) locales beyond Keene—even beyond Boston—rolled past the post office and up the hill. Stories came down from the hill, carried by workmen who had built the house itself on Beatty Balestier's old pastureland. There was a room like a long veranda with a roof that opened where
(10) the great man himself would work. There were parlors and dining rooms and sitting rooms and galleries, all to be filled by the mysterious contents of the crates from beyond even New Hampshire. Everyone in town knew that the great man had been born in the mysterious East,
(15) and they could only speculate on what he might keep in the house, which he had exotically dubbed "Naulakha." It was hoped by imaginative children in particular that, although the general opinion was that none of the crates was large enough to contain anything so impressive as an
(20) elephant or tiger, perhaps a few of the larger ones might reasonably contain a panther, a smallish bear, or the odd orangutan.

When the great man himself and his family arrived, though, the tales from the hill proved disappointingly
(25) plain. Not a single python, cobra, or even so much as a common stuffed mongoose presented itself to the workmen who helped with the unpacking. No puzzling tribal souvenirs, books of uncertain content or casks aromatic with exotic spice were in evidence. The newly
(30) hired servants confirmed that the household furnishings were the ordinary accessories of a typical well-to-do family, though perhaps a bit on the ostentatiously luxurious side.

Furthermore, it soon became plain that the great man
(35) himself neither slept with a revolver under his pillow, nor showed any tendency toward daily acts of daring heroism. He turned out to be smaller than expected, with an unusually sloped but mostly indifferent face that one
speedily grew insensitive to. Small boys soon lost interest
(40) in following after the great man's bicycle whenever he pedaled down the hill in his plain brown suit and ordinary hat to pick up commonplace letters from run-of-the-mill lands such as Boston, New York and London. His thick, round spectacles and bristling mustache hid
(45) much of his expression, and he was unusually reserved, or at least uncommunicative, with townspeople who had occasion to speak with him.

Then stories of the great man's outlandish habits began to trickle down the hill, dispensed mainly by
(50) servants with pay in their pockets on their days off at the Back Street tavern. The great man's wife was unsatisfactorily ordinary and American, a bit on the weighty side both in temperament and construction, and plainly in charge of everything that went on in the house
(55) and for some considerable distance around it. The great man himself spent most of his days shut up in the long, skylighted study. Most worrisomely, though, he emerged from the study every evening at dinner time and bizarrely donned his black tie and tails. Then he and his wife—
(60) also dressed for formal evening dining—sat down to a dinner served by manservants only, and they were very particular on that point. They didn't invite any of the prominent townsfolk to dine (to no one's disappointment), but sat there alone, the two of them at the candlelit table
(65) eating from superior china plates and drinking from fine crystal glasses, in silence and entirely in the complete absence of any evident special occasion.

Naturally the town began to feel slighted and a bit unfairly treated in light of their disappointed
(70) expectations. No Rajas arrived amidst their majestic and exotic trains to wend up the hill to visit their childhood blood brother. No mysterious dignitaries uttering unfathomable code phrases crept into town on baffling business. Although none of the native Yankees could have
(75) put their disappointment into words exactly, their visions of dark, sandalwood-scented libraries where great works were generated by mysterious processes and with great and dramatic difficulty had not been at all fulfilled by the beetle-headed personage, his plump and dictatorial wife,
(80) and the ordinary trappings of their lackluster household. All the fire and drama of the great man's works seemed to be somehow impossible in these unexceptional beings and their disappointingly commonplace snobbishness.

GO ON TO THE NEXT PAGE

10 The word "smoldering" in line 2 most nearly means

(A) smoking
(B) expectant
(C) fiery
(D) obscure
(E) noisy

11 The phrase "ordinary accessories" (line 31) suggests that the townspeople were probably disappointed because

(A) the servants were underpaid
(B) there were no exotic animals packed in the crates
(C) they expected that a celebrity would have unusual furnishings in his house
(D) evidence indicated that the newcomers were wealthy
(E) the books were all ordinary

12 In paragraph 3, the author implies that the townspeople lost interest in Kipling primarily because

(A) he looked and acted like an ordinary person
(B) he seldom came to town
(C) he received letters from exotic places
(D) the servants had nothing interesting to say about his habits
(E) small boys stopped chasing him when he rode his bicycle

13 The primary reason that the stories of the Kiplings' dinner habits caused distress among the residents of Brattleboro was that

(A) the townspeople were themselves unable to dress up for dinner
(B) the prominent citizens expected to be invited to eat with them
(C) the residents wanted to imitate the Kiplings' way of eating
(D) the aristocratic ritual made the townspeople feel insulted
(E) the townspeople thought china and crystal should be saved for special occasions

14 The thing about the Kiplings that most disappointed the residents of Brattleboro overall was that the Kiplings

(A) did not bring exotic objects with them
(B) were not friendly and outgoing
(C) were not as interesting as the townspeople had hoped they'd be
(D) did not have unusual visitors
(E) did not come to town very often

15 The primary purpose of this passage is to

(A) demonstrate how the prominent townsfolk shaped the reactions of the rest of the townsfolk
(B) describe the house the Kiplings built in Brattleboro and the furnishings they moved into it
(C) show the daily lives of historical New England townspeople
(D) illustrate the townspeople's reactions to the arrival and presence of the Kiplings
(E) present a case for democratic tolerance and against aristocratic snobbishness

GO ON TO THE NEXT PAGE

Questions 16–24 are based on the following passage.

This passage is about the history and development of contemporary Hawaiian quilts.

Contemporary Hawaiian quilts, such as those created by Marthe Marques and Helen Friend, reflect an eclectic blend of early American quilt making, Hawaiian
Line tradition, island imagery, spiritual influences, current
(5) events, and modern vision. Helen Friend, a recognized contemporary Hawaiian artist, produces quilted artworks inspired by nature's power, Hawaii's natural environment, current events, and historic textiles. Her quilt titled *I ka Ho'okumuana* (In the Beginning) depicts
(10) an aerial view of an erupting volcano constructed of appliquéd red flames set against a black background fabric. This quilt embraces both the past and the future; it clearly falls within the provenance of a traditional Hawaiian quilt, and at the same time it challenges the
(15) boundaries of that definition.

While many historians claim that New England missionaries brought quilting to the islands in 1820, it has been reported that Hawaiian women fashioned decorative bed coverings, called *kapa moe*, long before
(20) the missionaries' arrival. *Kapa moe* were constructed from multiple layers of *tapa*, a paper-like fabric crafted from mulberry bark. The top layer of *tapa* was often dyed and decorated with beautiful geometric designs. The layers, each one comprised of a large piece of fabric,
(25) were stitched together, possibly to provide additional resilience.

With the arrival of the missionaries, Hawaiian quilters were introduced to American materials, quilting methods and designs. The missionaries brought metal needles,
(30) cotton fabrics, and cotton thread to Hawaii. In addition, they taught the native women to work with both patchwork and appliquéd quilting. In patchwork quilting, designs on the quilt's top layer are created by piecing small bits of fabric together to form patterns, then
(35) overstitched with contrasting designs when the layers of the quilt are united. With appliquéd quilts, the quilt's top layer is decorated with pieces of fabric cut to form images and designs. While many patchwork quilts

incorporate small geometric shapes in various colors
(40) aligned to form larger geometric shapes, appliquéd quilting allows quilters to express more natural shapes and images.

Hawaiian women adopted the fabrics, needles, thread, and techniques of the missionary quilters but rejected
(45) the more functional approach of the American quilters. The missionaries employed quilting as a way of indoctrinating their native students with American Protestant ethics such as thrift and patience. In New England, aesthetic appeal was less important than
(50) function; quilts provided warmth on cold winter nights, allowed mothers to teach their daughters basic sewing, and salvaged fabric bits too small for any other household use. In contrast, necessity and frugality were not factors in the construction of a Hawaiian quilt. In the
(55) warm, island climate, blankets were not a necessity and fabric was not cut and sewn into garments similar to those worn by the missionaries. Ornamentation, individual expression, and the cultural context of gift exchange customs were more important aspects that
(60) drove the design and construction of a Hawaiian quilt.

Once the native women had mastered the techniques brought by the missionaries, they integrated the American materials and appliqué method with the designs and inspirations from the traditional *kapa moe*.
(65) These new Hawaiian quilts were fabricated from two solid colors of cloth, the lighter color acting as a background, the darker color creating the curved, symmetrical designs that reflect the flora and fauna indigenous to the islands. Retaining the whole-cloth
(70) method used to manufacture their traditional *kapa moe*, Hawaiian quilters first folded one piece of fabric into fourths or eighths, then cut a pattern out of the folded fabric as if constructing a paper snowflake. Next, this portion of the design was appliquéd onto the background
(75) fabric. Finally, the layers of the quilt were joined together with tiny rows of stitches that repeated the shape of the original design in a closely radiating pattern.

GO ON TO THE NEXT PAGE

16 The ideas expressed in the first two sentences (lines 1–8) have structures that can be described as

(A) defense and rebuttal
(B) assertion and evidence
(C) evidence and conjecture
(D) entreaty and dissent
(E) apology and explanation

17 The author suggests which of the following about the works of Martha Marques and Helen Friend (line 2)?

(A) They integrate traditional culture, early American needlework, and modern imagery.
(B) They should be cherished as exquisite examples of traditional Hawaiian needlework.
(C) They include designs symbolic of the natural flora and fauna of New England.
(D) They ignore the cultural heritage of the Hawaiian islands.
(E) They adopt designs inspired by early American patchwork quilts.

18 In saying that *I ka Ho'okumuana* "embraces both the past and the future" (line 12) the author suggests that the quilt

(A) depicts historical volcanic eruptions
(B) defies practical considerations
(C) avoids traditional practices
(D) adapts established artistic techniques
(E) undermines contemporary aesthetics

19 The author mentions the traditional *kapa moe* (line 19) in order to show that they

(A) are examples of traditional bed coverings inspired by the New England missionaries
(B) explain how modern quilters adopted the methods of their ancestors
(C) can be found in modern Hawaiian households
(D) predated the arrival of missionaries on the islands
(E) are decorated with elaborate geometric designs

20 As used in line 26, "resilience" most nearly means

(A) impermanence
(B) flexibility
(C) lightheartedness
(D) frailty
(E) robustness

21 As used in line 33, "piecing" most nearly means

(A) sewing
(B) cutting up
(C) creating
(D) breaking
(E) replacing

22 The author suggests that native Hawaiian quilters embraced the appliqué technique in particular because of their desire for

(A) quilts with increased durability
(B) American fabrics, needles, and thread
(C) greater range of artistic expression
(D) American Protestant ethics
(E) the ability to align small geometric shapes into larger shapes

23 The author implies which of the following with the statement "aesthetic appeal was less important than function" (lines 49–50)?

(A) The missionaries needed beauty to counteract the hardships they faced.
(B) The missionaries failed to discuss the motivations underlying their quilt making.
(C) The missionaries focused on what a quilt could do rather than on how it looked when they created it.
(D) The missionaries' quilts lacked beauty.
(E) Early American quilt making focused on the functionality of the quilts to the exclusion of other aesthetic concerns.

24 The function of the phrase "constructing a paper snowflake" (line 73) is intended to

(A) describe a traditional Hawaiian quilt design
(B) help the reader visualize the method of creating the quilt's design
(C) illustrate how Hawaiian natives were taught how to sew a quilt
(D) refute how some historians believe traditional *kapa moe* were sewn
(E) explain why Hawaiian quilters use images from nature in their artwork

IF YOU FINISH BEFORE TIME IS CALLED, YOU MAY CHECK YOUR WORK ON THIS SECTION ONLY. DO NOT TURN TO ANY OTHER SECTION IN THE TEST.

STOP

Time—25 Minutes
18 Questions

Directions: This section contains two types of questions. You have 25 minutes to complete both types. For questions 1–8, solve each problem and decide which is the best of the choices given. Fill in the corresponding oval on the answer sheet. You may use any available space for scratchwork.

Notes

1. Calculator use is permitted.

2. All numbers used are real numbers.

3. Figures are provided for some problems. All figures are drawn to scale and lie in a plane UNLESS otherwise indicated.

4. Unless otherwise specified, the domain of any function f is assumed to be the set of all real numbers x for which $f(x)$ is a real number.

Reference Information

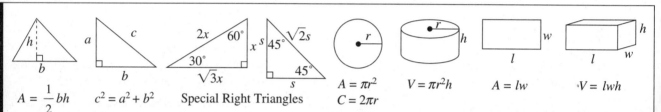

$A = \dfrac{1}{2}bh$ $c^2 = a^2 + b^2$ Special Right Triangles $A = \pi r^2$ $V = \pi r^2 h$ $A = lw$ $V = lwh$
$C = 2\pi r$

The sum of the measures in degrees of the angles of a triangle is 180.
The number of degrees of arc in a circle is 360.
A straight angle has a degree measure of 180.

---

1 Jane owns 7 hats that are all different from one another, and she owns 4 coats that are all different from one another. How many different combinations of one hat and one coat can she choose?

(A) 21
(B) 24
(C) 28
(D) 30
(E) 35

2 If $\dfrac{4}{y-3} = \dfrac{6}{(y-3)z}$ and $y \neq 3$, what is the value of z ?

(A) $\dfrac{1}{3}$

(B) $\dfrac{2}{3}$

(C) $\dfrac{6}{5}$

(D) $\dfrac{3}{2}$

(E) 3

GO ON TO THE NEXT PAGE

9   1   7   5   3

3 What is the smallest number of interchanges of adjacent numbers that needs to be made in the series above so that the first five positive odd integers will be in increasing order?

(A) 5
(B) 6
(C) 7
(D) 10
(E) 12

4 Which of the following is correct if $1 < n < 2$?

(A) $\dfrac{1}{n} < \dfrac{1}{n\sqrt{n}} < \dfrac{1}{n^3}$

(B) $\dfrac{1}{n\sqrt{n}} < \dfrac{1}{n} < \dfrac{1}{n^3}$

(C) $\dfrac{1}{n\sqrt{n}} < \dfrac{1}{n^3} < \dfrac{1}{n}$

(D) $\dfrac{1}{n^3} < \dfrac{1}{n\sqrt{n}} < \dfrac{1}{n}$

(E) $\dfrac{1}{n} < \dfrac{1}{n^3} < \dfrac{1}{n\sqrt{n}}$

5 For all positive numbers x and y, $x \; \text{\small◖}\; y = 2x + \dfrac{3}{y}$.
If c is positive, which of the following is equal to $c \; \text{\small◖}\; \left(\dfrac{2}{c}\right)$?

(A) $\dfrac{5c}{2}$

(B) $\dfrac{7c}{2}$

(C) $5c$

(D) $\dfrac{20c}{3}$

(E) $8c$

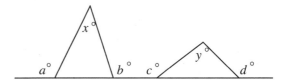

6 In the figure above, six angles are labeled. Which of the following is equal to $x + y$?

(A) $a + b + c + d$

(B) $720 - a - b - c - d$

(C) $a + b + c + d - 180$

(D) $\dfrac{a + b + c + d}{2}$

(E) $a + b + c + d - 360$

GO ON TO THE NEXT PAGE

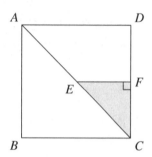

7 In the figure above, point E is the midpoint of $\overline{AC}$. What is the probability that a randomly selected point from the interior of square $ABCD$ will fall within the shaded region?

(A) $\dfrac{1}{8}$

(B) $\dfrac{1}{6}$

(C) $\dfrac{1}{2}$

(D) $\dfrac{\sqrt{2}}{2}$

(E) It cannot be determined from the information given.

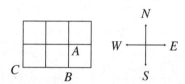

8 The figure above shows a network of streets in Smalltown, which is only three blocks by two blocks. Each intersection has a stop sign for each street approaching it. For example, intersection A requires four stop signs, since four different roads meet. Intersection B requires three stop signs, and intersection C requires just two.

If Largertown is set up in the same manner, but is four blocks by three blocks, how many stop signs are there in Largertown?

(A) 20
(B) 36
(C) 62
(D) 80
(E) 94

GO ON TO THE NEXT PAGE

Directions: For Student-Produced Response questions 9–18, use the grids at the bottom of the answer sheet page on which you have answered questions 1–8.

Each of the remaining 10 questions requires you to solve the problem and enter your answer by marking the ovals in the special grid, as shown in the examples below. You may use any available space for scratchwork.

Answer: 1.25 or $\frac{5}{4}$ or 5/4

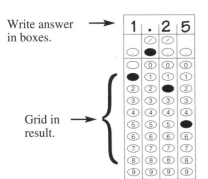

Write answer in boxes.

Grid in result.

Either position is correct.

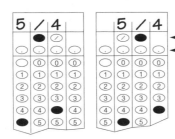

Fraction line

Decimal point

You may start your answers in any column, space permitting. Columns not needed should be left blank.

- It is recommended, though not required, that you write your answer in the boxes at the top of the columns. However, **you will receive credit only for darkening the ovals correctly.**

- Grid only one answer to a question, even though some problems have more than one correct answer.

- Darken no more than one oval in a column.

- No answers are negative.

- **Mixed numbers** cannot be gridded. For example: the number $1\frac{1}{4}$ must be gridded as 1.25 or 5/4.

(If `1 1 / 4` is gridded, it will be interpreted as $\frac{11}{4}$, not $1\frac{1}{4}$.)

- <u>Decimal Accuracy:</u> Decimal answers must be entered as accurately as possible. For example, if you obtain an answer such as 0.1666. . ., you should record the result as .166 or .167. **Less accurate values such as .16 or .17 are not acceptable.**

Acceptable ways to grid $\frac{1}{6}$ = .1666. . .

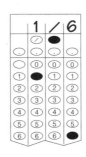  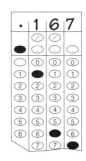

---

9 If set C is the set of all prime numbers and set D is the set of all odd numbers between –10 and 10, what is one number in the intersection of sets C and D ?

$$\begin{array}{r} XXY \\ + XX3 \\ \hline 1{,}548 \end{array}$$

10 X and Y represent digits in the correctly worked arithmetic problem above. What is the value of $X + Y$?

GO ON TO THE NEXT PAGE

11 What is the greatest integer less than 1,000 that has both 5 and 8 as factors?

12 The result of decreasing a positive odd integer n by 20 percent is a number that is between 25 and 33. What is one possible value of n ?

13 A box contains brand A hats, brand B hats, and nothing else. The cost of a brand A hat is $16, the cost of a brand B hat is $7, the ratio of the number of brand A hats to the number of brand B hats is 3 : 4, and the total cost of all the hats in the box is $912. How many brand B hats are in the box?

14 The endpoints of the diameter of a circle in rectangular coordinates are (10, 5) and (10, 21). What is the radius of the circle?

GO ON TO THE NEXT PAGE

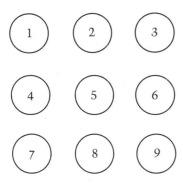

15 Each of the nine disks above is numbered with a different integer among the integers 1 through 9 inclusive. If two different disks are chosen at random from the disks above, what is the probability that the sum of the numbers on the two disks is at least 14 ?

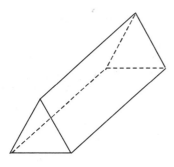

16 The figure above is three-dimensional and has five faces and nine edges. The two triangular faces are parallel. The three other faces are rectangular. How many different pairs of vertices can be connected with line segments that are NOT edges of the figure?

17 In a group of houses, each house is either a two-story or a three-story house. 40 percent of these houses have two stories and 48 percent of all the houses have four or more people living in them. If 70 percent of the two-story houses have three or fewer people living in them, what percent of all the houses are three-story houses with four or more people living in them? (Disregard the percent sign when gridding your answer.)

18 If $q(r) = q^2 - 4q + 8$, what is the value of $q(q(1))$?

Time—25 Minutes
35 Questions

Directions: For each question in this section, select the best answer from among the choices given and fill in the corresponding oval on the answer sheet.

The following sentences test correctness and effectiveness of expression. Part of each sentence or the entire sentence is underlined; beneath each sentence are five ways of phrasing the underlined material. Choice A repeats the original phrasing; the other four choices are different. If you think the original phrasing produces a better sentence than any of the alternatives, select choice A; if not, select one of the other choices.

In making your selection, follow the requirements of standard written English; that is, pay attention to grammar, choice of words, sentence construction, and punctuation. Your selection should result in the most effective sentence—clear and precise—without awkwardness or ambiguity.

EXAMPLE:

Every apple in the baskets <u>are ripe and labeled according to the date it was picked</u>.

(A) are ripe and labeled according to the date it was picked
(B) is ripe and labeled according to the date it was picked
(C) are ripe and labeled according to the date they were picked
(D) is ripe and labeled according to the date they were picked
(E) are ripe and labeled as to the date it was picked

ANSWER:
Ⓐ ● Ⓒ Ⓓ Ⓔ

1 Russia is often used to illustrate the problems with <u>communism, because the government is now democratic,</u> political analysts can explore the rise, fall, and aftereffects of communism on society.

(A) communism, because the government is now democratic
(B) communism, since the government is now democratic
(C) communism, since, with its now democratic government
(D) communism; because the government is now democratic
(E) communism, the democratic government is now democratic; so

2 <u>The conductor took our tickets, he</u> proceeded to explain how to get to the correct station.

(A) The conductor took our tickets, he
(B) The tickets, which were taken by the conductor, then
(C) After taking our tickets, the conductor
(D) The tickets were taken by the conductor, then
(E) The conductor, having taken our tickets, he

3 A lame duck is <u>when an elected official currently holding office will not continue</u> for another term.

(A) when an elected official currently holding office will not continue
(B) an elected official currently holding office who will not continue
(C) when an elected official who currently holds office will not continue
(D) if an elected official currently holding office will not continue
(E) the not continuing of an elected official currently holding office

4 After James, the new student in the class, introduced himself, <u>he realized that one's clothing style is not as important as your</u> personality.

(A) he realized that one's clothing style is not as important as your
(B) he realized that one's clothing style is not as important as one's
(C) he realizes that one's clothing style is not as important as one's
(D) then realizing that one's clothing style is not as important as one's
(E) he realized that his clothing style is not as important as your

GO ON TO THE NEXT PAGE

5 Learning how to sight read <u>helps pianists become a better musician</u>.

(A) helps pianists become a better musician
(B) is helpful to pianists who want to be a better musician
(C) helps pianists become better musicians
(D) helps a pianist become better musicians
(E) is helpful to pianists in becoming a better musician

6 The college dean claimed that <u>the university's not being allocated proper funding by the state, this led</u> to the cancellation of numerous courses.

(A) the university's not being allocated proper funding by the state, this led
(B) the lack of proper funding by the state for the university would lead
(C) when not being allocated proper funding by the state, it leads the university
(D) the failure in allocation of proper funding of the university by the state would lead
(E) the lack of proper funding by the state for the university led

7 Large universities, gathering world-renowned professors, diverse student bodies, and time-honored traditions, have classes on <u>topics as varied as</u> physics, swimming, medieval history, and Russian language.

(A) topics as varied as
(B) topics varied as
(C) topics of such variation as
(D) a topic as varied as
(E) varied topics that encompass

8 Guided by the rules of the French Language Academy, <u>meticulously avoiding new or foreign words is something many French language purists are proud of</u>.

(A) meticulously avoiding new or foreign words is something many French language purists are proud of
(B) the idea of meticulously avoiding new or foreign words is something that makes proud many French language purists
(C) many French language purists, proud of their meticulous avoidance of new or foreign words
(D) many French language purists are proud of meticulously avoiding new or foreign words
(E) new or foreign words are something many French language purists are proud of meticulously avoiding

9 <u>Receiving more publicity and more airplay compared with</u> the Rolling Stones, the Beatles were the first British pop group sensation in the United States.

(A) Receiving more publicity and more airplay compared with
(B) Receiving more publicity and more airplay than
(C) By receiving more publicity and more airplay compared with
(D) Receiving more publicity and more airplay, unlike
(E) Receiving both more publicity and more airplay when being compared to

10 At the presidential debate, each candidate argued that <u>he was equally ready to lead the country through the problems of waging war and to feed the poor</u>.

(A) he was equally ready to lead the country through the problems of waging war and to feed the poor
(B) he had been equally readied to lead the country through the problems of waging war and to feed the poor
(C) he was equally ready to lead the country through the problems of waging war and feeding the poor
(D) they were equally ready to lead the country through the problems of waging war and feeding the poor
(E) he had been just as equally ready to lead the country through the problems of waging war and to feed the poor

11 Cupcakes are not generally thought of as a gourmet food <u>product, but they are treated</u> as such at Magnolia Bakery in Manhattan.

(A) product, but they are treated
(B) product, but being treated
(C) product, but they were treated
(D) product, they are treated
(E) product, being treated

GO ON TO THE NEXT PAGE

The following sentences test your ability to recognize grammar and usage errors. Each sentence contains either a single error or no error at all. No sentence contains more than one error. The error, if there is one, is underlined and lettered. If the sentence contains an error, select the one underlined part that must be changed to make the sentence correct. If the sentence is correct, select choice E. In choosing answers, follow the requirements of standard written English.

EXAMPLE: ANSWER:

<u>Whenever</u> one is driving late at night, <u>you</u> must take extra precautions <u>against</u>   Ⓐ ● Ⓒ Ⓓ Ⓔ
   A   B   C

falling asleep <u>at</u> the wheel. <u>No error</u>
                   D   E

12 If I <u>had given</u> <u>more</u> thought to my essay, I might have
          A   B
succeeded <u>in improving</u> my <u>very</u> low English grade.
                  C   D
<u>No error</u>
   E

13 The tactical squad, after a surprise <u>raid on</u> the rebel army,
                                              A
<u>went into</u> the village <u>heavy armed</u> and was victorious
     B   C
<u>against</u> the remaining soldiers. <u>No error</u>
     D   E

14 In our company, a change <u>in</u> the software system that
                                  A
tracks receivables and overdue accounts <u>were</u> requested
                                             B
<u>by</u> the <u>heads of</u> the accounting and billing departments.
   C   D
<u>No error</u>
   E

15 Most doctors <u>recommend</u> strong <u>antibiotics for</u> heart
                        A   B
patients who <u>are required</u> <u>to undergo dental surgery</u>.
                  C   D
<u>No error</u>
   E

16 Few students <u>cannot hardly</u> <u>maintain</u> a C average in
                        A   B
Advanced Physics, <u>even though</u> faculty members <u>are</u>
                       C   D
available for extra help every day after school. <u>No error</u>
                                                      E

17 The <u>oldest</u> justice currently <u>sitting on</u> the Supreme Court
           A   B
<u>is</u> John Paul Stevens, who was <u>born in</u> 1920. <u>No error</u>
   C   D   E

18 Among American sports legends, Boston's "Curse of the

Bambino" <u>are</u> <u>better</u> known <u>among fans</u> than <u>any other</u>.
              A   B   C   D
<u>No error</u>
   E

19 The archeologist <u>who discovered</u> the mysterious bones at
                             A
the site of the dig was less interested in how they got

there <u>than in</u> whether <u>it was</u> <u>from</u> the Paleocene epoch.
          B   C   D
<u>No error</u>
   E

20 <u>That</u> the small house was purchased so <u>quickly</u> by a
           A   B
couple <u>already approved</u> for a mortgage <u>surprised</u> the real
            C   D
estate agent. <u>No error</u>
                   E

21 Certain parts of New York City always <u>seem</u> dark, even
                                                 A
during the day, <u>because</u> the skyscrapers block out <u>more</u>
                     B   C
of the sun <u>than other cities</u>. <u>No error</u>
                D   E

GO ON TO THE NEXT PAGE

22 The <u>other</u> cast members and <u>me</u> <u>quickly</u> lined up for the
     A   B   C
curtain call <u>we had rehearsed</u> earlier in the day. <u>No error</u>
            D   E

23 <u>Although</u> the number of movie theaters in our town <u>keep</u>
    A   B
growing, my sister <u>insists that</u> she can find nothing <u>to do</u>
                    C   D
on the weekends. <u>No error</u>
                E

24 No group was <u>more involved</u> <u>in raising</u> voter awareness
              A   B
<u>to</u> the bond issues <u>than</u> the Student Government Club.
C   D
<u>No error</u>
   E

25 During 1999, the focus <u>of</u> the computer industry <u>is</u> the
                A   B
development of software <u>that</u> would not only function
                   C
properly in the year 2000, <u>but would also</u> revise existing
                           D
programs to do the same. <u>No error</u>
                    E

26 With <u>less than 15 seconds</u> remaining in the game,
        A
<u>we spotted</u> Jack and Marco on the sidelines where <u>he</u>
   B   C
captured the <u>winning</u> goal on video. <u>No error</u>
          D   E

27 <u>Accused</u> of obstructing justice, the <u>reluctant</u> witness
    A   B
<u>finally testified</u> <u>on the last day</u> of the trial. <u>No error</u>
   C   D   E

28 We had gotten <u>no fewer than</u> five hundred signatures on
                A
our petition <u>when we</u> realized <u>that</u> there was not
             B   C
<u>sufficient enough</u> time to organize a successful protest.
          D
<u>No error</u>
  E

29 A number of <u>writers whose</u> works might <u>otherwise</u>
             A   B
<u>have gone</u> unnoticed were able to publish the books
   C
<u>they wrote</u> through what were known as "vanity presses."
    D
<u>No error</u>
  E

GO ON TO THE NEXT PAGE

Directions: The following passage is an early draft of an essay. Some parts of the passage need to be rewritten.

Read the passage and select the best answer for each question that follows. Some questions are about particular sentences or parts of sentences and ask you to improve sentence structure or word choice. Other questions ask you to consider organization and development. In choosing answers, follow the conventions of standard written English.

(1) Every year, the federal Small Business Administration presents the National Small Business Person of the Year Award to an entrepreneur that has demonstrated both personal achievement and a significant contribution to the national economy. (2) In 1988, this prestigious award was shared by two men who had failed to qualify for an SBA loan when they were starting their company in 1977. (3) Ben Cohen and Jerry Greenfield, undaunted by this setback, had gone ahead and launched their corporation, Ben and Jerry's Homemade, Inc., with $12,000, a correspondence course in ice cream making, and they had a one-year lease on an abandoned gas station in Burlington, Vermont.

(4) The story of Ben and Jerry's, which has been chronicled in numerous magazine articles and two full-length books, can hardly be called typical. (5) Ice cream wasn't even their first product choice. (6) They originally explored the possibility of opening a bagel bakery and delivery service that they planned to call United Bagel Service, the equipment being too expensive. (7) The initial business plan for their ice cream shop called for a location in a rural college town with a warm climate, they ultimately ended up in a rural college town forty miles south of the Canadian border. (8) One thing they settled on early, however, and never considered changing was the company motto: "If it's not fun, why do it?"

30 Which of the following is the best version of sentence 1 (reproduced below)?

Every year, the federal Small Business Administration presents the National Small Business Person of the Year Award to an entrepreneur that has demonstrated both personal achievement and a significant contribution to the national economy.

(A) (As it is now)
(B) Every year, the federal Small Business Administration has presented the National Small Business Person of the Year Award to an entrepreneur that has demonstrated both personal achievement and a significant contribution to the national economy.
(C) Every year, the federal Small Business Administration presents the National Small Business Person of the Year Award to an entrepreneur who has demonstrated both personal achievement and a significant contribution to the national economy.
(D) Every year, the federal Small Business Administration presents the National Small Business Person of the Year Award to an entrepreneur that have demonstrated both personal achievement and a significant contribution to the national economy.
(E) Every year, the federal Small Business Administration presents the National Small Business Person of the Year Award to an entrepreneur that has demonstrated both personal achievement and has made a significant contribution to the national economy.

GO ON TO THE NEXT PAGE

31 Of the following, which is the best version of the underlined portion of sentence 3 (reproduced below)?

Ben Cohen and Jerry Greenfield, undaunted by this setback, had gone ahead and launched their corporation, Ben and Jerry's Homemade, Inc., with $12,000, a correspondence course in ice cream making, and they had a one-year lease on an abandoned gas station in Burlington, Vermont.

(A) (As it is now)
(B) and a one-year lease on an abandoned gas station in Burlington, Vermont
(C) having a one-year lease on an abandoned gas station in Burlington, Vermont
(D) they also had a one-year lease on an abandoned gas station in Burlington, Vermont
(E) they had a one-year lease on an abandoned gas station in Burlington, Vermont as well

32 Which of the following sentences is best inserted at the end of the first paragraph, after sentence 3?

(A) Although it was difficult, they were able to begin production without the Small Business Administration's financial support.
(B) Ben and Jerry's opened their first out-of-state franchise in Maine in 1983.
(C) The original Ben and Jerry's also offered homemade soup and crepes.
(D) By the time they accepted the SBA award from President Ronald Reagan, Ben and Jerry's had more than 80 locations in 18 states, with annual sales of nearly $50 million.
(E) They would later open a manufacturing facility in an old spool and bobbin mill several miles away.

33 Of the following, which is the best version of the underlined portion of sentence 4 (reproduced below)?

The story of Ben and Jerry's, which has been chronicled in numerous magazine articles and two full-length books, can hardly be called typical.

(A) (As it is now)
(B) which have been chronicled in numerous magazine articles and two full-length books
(C) who have been chronicled in numerous magazine articles and two full-length books
(D) having been chronicled in numerous magazine articles and two full-length books
(E) which has been chronicled in both numerous magazine articles as well as two full-length books

34 In context, which of the following is the best version of sentence 6 (reproduced below)?

They originally explored the possibility of opening a bagel bakery and delivery service that they planned to call United Bagel Service, the equipment being too expensive.

(A) (As it is now)
(B) They original explored the possibility of opening a bagel bakery and delivery service that they planned to call United Bagel Service, the equipment being too expensive.
(C) They originally explored the possibility to open a bagel bakery and delivery service that they planned to call United Bagel Service, the equipment being too expensive.
(D) They originally explored the possibility of opening a bagel bakery and delivery service that they planned to call United Bagel Service, the equipment being too expensive.
(E) They originally explored the possibility of opening a bagel bakery and delivery service that they planned to call United Bagel Service, but the equipment was too expensive.

35 In context, what revision is needed in sentence 7?

(A) Change "called" to "calls."
(B) Change "for" to "on."
(C) Insert the word "but" after the comma.
(D) Insert the word "so" after the comma.
(E) Change "ultimately" to "ultimate."

IF YOU FINISH BEFORE TIME IS CALLED, YOU MAY CHECK YOUR WORK ON THIS SECTION ONLY. DO NOT TURN TO ANY OTHER SECTION IN THE TEST.

Time—20 Minutes
19 Questions

Directions: For each question in this section, select the best answer from among the choices given and fill in the corresponding oval on the answer sheet.

Each sentence below has one or two blanks, each blank indicating that something has been omitted. Beneath the sentence are five words or sets of words labeled A through E. Choose the word or set of words that, when inserted in the sentence, best fits the meaning of the sentence as a whole.

EXAMPLE:

Today's small, portable computers contrast markedly with the earliest electronic computers, which were -------.

(A) effective   (B) invented
  (C) useful   (D) destructive
    (E) enormous

ANSWER:
Ⓐ Ⓑ Ⓒ Ⓓ ●

1 The hotel, one of the finest and most expensive in the nation, provides both a pleasant ------- and many -------, including a gym, a swimming pool, and a ballroom.

(A) atmosphere . . amenities
(B) ambiance . . rooms
(C) mood . . extremes
(D) reason . . gratuities
(E) value . . additions

2 Dolphins, though usually friendly, can become ------- when threatened; they will attack if provoked.

(A) amiable   B) aggressive
(C) fearless   (D) docile
(E) strange

3 The mayor is widely known for his -------: even when surrounded by strangers with whom it would seem he has nothing in common, he carries on lengthy conversations.

(A) terseness   (B) infamy
(C) philanthropy   (D) familiarity
(E) volubility

4 According to the magazine article, the former television co-stars put their feud behind them, and this ------- would probably result in a reunion show.

(A) candor   (B) malevolence
(C) adulation   (D) reconciliation
(E) resilience

5 The critic argued that the store's refusal to sell compact discs that contain offensive lyrics is ------- to censorship since, in effect, it compels record labels to alter the ------- of an artistic work.

(A) similar . . inspiration
(B) tantamount . . content
(C) a boon . . meaning
(D) magnanimous . . expression
(E) irreverent . . rancor

6 Pugilist Mike Tyson, the youngest heavyweight champion in history, showed a youthful ------- towards fighting, perhaps because he grew up in a place where such ------- was often required to make it through the day.

(A) proclivity . . pandemonium
(B) inclination . . benevolence
(C) aversion . . violence
(D) antipathy . . anger
(E) predisposition . . belligerence

GO ON TO THE NEXT PAGE

- 178 -

The passage below is followed by questions based on its content. Answer the questions on the basis of what is <u>stated</u> or <u>implied</u> in the passage and in any introductory material that may be provided.

Questions 7–19 are based on the following passage.

The following passage is from a journal that features articles in the field of American studies. It examines the contributions of Reverend Sylvester Graham to the dietary reform movement of the nineteenth century.

It is ironic that one of the men destined to be most influential in his long-term impact on the American diet is now largely forgotten, even by those who enjoy the
Line crackers that still bear his name. Reverend Sylvester
(5) Graham (1795–1851) was lampooned in the press, ridiculed by the public, and scoffed at by medical professionals. Yet his ideas, writings, lectures and influence were instrumental in shaping ideas about food and nutrition that we still hold today.
(10)   The diet of nineteenth-century Americans was not much like that of their modern counterparts. Meat— especially pork—was a main staple of every meal, and what little vegetable and grain people ate was usually fried or drenched in grease, gravy, or fatty sauces. For the
(15) most part, fruits and vegetables were considered not to be very nutritious, and less-nourishing white flour was beginning to displace whole wheat flour as the standard among bread bakers. Long-term, chronic digestive problems were common, and the widespread excessive
(20) consumption of alcoholic beverages was enough of a problem to have spawned the temperance movement.
   After suffering a protracted chronic digestive illness of his own, Reverend Graham began to examine the effects of diet on health. He was exposed to, and influenced by,
(25) the work of the famous English vegetarian Reverend Cowherd. Graham posited that eating meat increased a person's craving for whiskey and other dietary and moral bad habits, and that eliminating meat from the diet led to generally good physical and spiritual health. Graham
(30) wrote and published books and traveled up and down the Atlantic coast giving lectures on his principles of dietary reform. He was reportedly a spellbinding speaker, and thousands attended his seminars, which were part militant sermon and part scientific argument.
(35)   Graham's theories focused on the relationship between proper diet and good physical and spiritual health. His philosophical principle was simple: the decline of humanity since the Garden of Eden had resulted in gluttony, slaughter, and industrial processing
(40) of foods, with the subsequent modern epidemic of poor health and impoverished morals. Graham's prescription for the restoration of humankind to dietary paradise included limiting meals to two per day, eliminating

tobacco, whiskey, and most meat, and leaving foods as
(45) much as possible in their raw, unprocessed state. His own particular obsession was processed white flour, which was just then coming into widespread use in commercial bakeries. Graham railed against the removal of the bran from flour before baking, and was so vehement in his
(50) protestations that some newspapers began to refer to him as "Dr. Bran." The intensity of his stance regarding the ills of meat and white bread was so well known that a Graham speech in Boston once occasioned a riot among groups of local butchers and bakers. Graham's
(55) predilection for dark, coarse cereals eventually came to be connected so closely with him that whole grain products in general took on his name: graham flour, graham bread and the product still known as graham crackers. Practitioners of the "Graham System" came
(60) to be known as "Grahamites."
   Although Graham emphasized the scientific benefits of the Graham System, the system was not actually very scientific. For example, Graham dictated that water—the only beverage allowed in the diet—should never be taken
(65) with meals because he declared that it interfered with digestion. In fact, we know today that liquids are vital to the smooth breakdown of food. But Graham seems never to have actually experimented in order to discover the problems associated with inadequate fluid intake and
(70) digestion. His principles were to a large extent as much involved with the philosophy of morality and goodness prevalent at the time as they were with the tentative results of research on diet and eating that was taking place at the time.
(75)   This connection between good living and good health led to Graham's association with many of the leading social reformers and liberal political organizations of his time. With the cooperation of famous pioneering vegetarians such as Reverend William Metcalfe,
(80) Reverend James Clark, and New York publisher Horace Greeley, Graham participated in the founding of the American Vegetarian Society. Graham's overt opposition to the consumption of whiskey made him a natural ally for the temperance movement. Through his contacts with
(85) prominent abolitionists such as Sojourner Truth, he became involved in the anti-slavery movement. Both the abolitionists and the temperance activists had a great deal of overlap in membership and philosophy with the movement for women's rights and women's suffrage.

GO ON TO THE NEXT PAGE

Line

(90) Through his association with the prominent vegetarian Dr. William Alcott, Graham came to influence William's cousin Bronson Alcott, a founding member of the utopian Fruitlands community and father of novelist Louisa May Alcott.

(95) One of Graham's most lasting influences, however, lies in his impact on Elder Ellen G. White, one of the founders of the Seventh-Day Adventist Church. Although there is no evidence of any direct association between them, Elder White embraced a strikingly

(100) Graham-like combination of moral, spiritual and dietary practices for herself and her congregation after a visit to James Caleb Jackson's Hydropathic Institute in upstate New York. Jackson's views on diet had been influenced by Graham, and Elder White's dietary system included

(105) such edicts as a limit of two meals per day and a preference for whole grain cereals. The Adventist diet became a standard for congregation members of the churches in and around Battle Creek, Michigan. Two Adventists who had grown up eating the whole-grain

(110) diet were breakfast cereal co-inventors Dr. John Harvey Kellogg and William H. Kellogg. Dr. J.H. Kellogg was later to credit Graham with the invention of the idea of scientific eating that not only resulted in the invention of breakfast cereals, but also affected the whole

(115) conception of diet and health as it is understood throughout America today.

7 This passage focuses primarily on Graham's

(A) public reputation
(B) dietary campaign
(C) life history
(D) personal magnetism
(E) theological influence

8 The passage implies that Graham began to study the impact of eating habits (lines 22–24) mostly because he

(A) deplored the increasingly widespread use of white flour
(B) had become ill from eating the normal American diet
(C) was searching for a cure to his craving for whiskey
(D) felt that he needed more spiritual enrichment
(E) wanted to participate in founding the American Vegetarian Society

9 The word "militant" in line 34 most nearly means

(A) enthusiastic
(B) unpopular
(C) regimented
(D) unorthodox
(E) religious

10 The description of Graham's views (lines 35–45) suggests that he was

(A) more troubled by the country's widespread social problems than by the dietary habits of his followers
(B) offended by the use of his name to describe food products
(C) very persuasive in spreading his message and convincing others to follow his dietary system
(D) primarily concerned with the relationship between poor diet and declining morals
(E) enthusiastic about influencing other political and religious leaders

11 The Boston community of butchers and bakers mentioned in line 54 most likely rioted because

(A) they saw Graham's reform agenda as a threat to their economic livelihood
(B) they objected to the influx of Grahamite food reformers into their communities
(C) Graham's prohibitions against eating meat and bread enraged them
(D) they perceived Graham as the forerunner of the temperance and suffrage movements that they felt threatened by
(E) they were incited to riot by the newspaper's treatment of Reverend Graham

12 The phrase "predilection for" in line 55 most nearly means

(A) preference for
(B) insight about
(C) prejudice against
(D) understanding of
(E) power over

13 The discussion of the "Graham System" (lines 61–74) suggests that Graham

(A) saw science as a possible means to restore moral goodness to a declining humanity
(B) completely disregarded the results of the early scientific research on health and diet taking place during his era
(C) did not consistently use scientific methods, even though he claimed to have derived his principles scientifically
(D) believed that liquids interfered with digestion, in spite of scientific studies that suggested the opposite
(E) sometimes changed his mind about dietary reform if new scientific information came to light

GO ON TO THE NEXT PAGE

14 The passage suggests that Graham's prohibition against taking water with meals was probably a result of

(A) a personal chronic illness
(B) a philosophical whim
(C) a drawback of whole grain foods
(D) a moral obligation
(E) a researched analysis

15 The passage suggests which of the following about Sojourner Truth?

(A) She influenced Graham to become involved in the anti-slavery movement.
(B) She contributed a voice of moral authority to the dietary reform interests.
(C) Graham persuaded her to become a vegetarian.
(D) She was deeply concerned with abolition, women's rights, and dietary reform.
(E) Graham encouraged her to spend time at the utopian Fruitlands community.

16 As implied in the passage, Elder Ellen G. White most likely adopted principles from Graham's dietary system because of

(A) James Caleb Jackson's directions
(B) the appealing combination of nutritional and spiritual principles
(C) the desire to discourage consumption of whiskey among Adventists
(D) the widespread popularity of the Graham System
(E) her desire to pass on the dietetic principles to the Kellogg brothers

17 The passage suggests that Graham's views on diet and health most closely corresponded with those of

(A) J. H. Kellogg
(B) Louisa May Alcott
(C) Sojourner Truth
(D) William Kellogg
(E) Reverend Cowherd

18 Which of the following is presented by the passage as the most prominent aspect of the relationship between the ideas of Reverend Graham and the dietary practices of America today?

(A) His invention of breakfast cereal and other processed whole-grain foods changed the dietary patterns of the modern world.
(B) His notion of a careful examination of diet and eating habits foreshadowed the scientific study of nutrition.
(C) He bestowed his name on Graham crackers.
(D) He played a decisive role in shaping the origins of the historic utopian Fruitlands community.
(E) His writings and lectures are still widely read and studied by modern vegetarians.

19 The passage suggests that Graham consistently endorsed the idea that people should consume plenty of

(A) white flour
(B) processed foods
(C) meat
(D) water
(E) raw foods

Time—20 Minutes
16 Questions

Directions: For this section, solve each problem and decide which is the best of the choices given. Fill in the corresponding oval on the answer sheet. You may use any available space for scratchwork.

Notes

1. Calculator use is permitted.

2. All numbers used are real numbers.

3. Figures are provided for some problems. All figures are drawn to scale and lie in a plane UNLESS otherwise indicated.

4. Unless otherwise specified, the domain of any function f is assumed to be the set of all real numbers x for which $f(x)$ is a real number.

Reference Information

$$A = \frac{1}{2}bh \qquad c^2 = a^2 + b^2 \qquad \text{Special Right Triangles} \qquad \begin{array}{c} A = \pi r^2 \\ C = 2\pi r \end{array} \qquad V = \pi r^2 h \qquad A = lw \qquad V = lwh$$

The sum of the measures in degrees of the angles of a triangle is 180.
The number of degrees of arc in a circle is 360.
A straight angle has a degree measure of 180.

---

1 If $f(x) = |x^2 + 10x + 25|$, which of the following is NOT a possible value of $f(x)$?

   I. –5
   II. 0
   III. 5

(A) I only
(B) II only
(C) III only
(D) I and II
(E) II and III

2 If $x = 1$ and $y = -1$, then what is the value of $x^2 + 2xy + y^2$?

(A) –1
(B) 0
(C) 1
(D) 2
(E) 4

GO ON TO THE NEXT PAGE

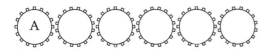

3 In the figure above, 6 gears are placed next to each other such that if one gear turns, all the gears turn. If gear A is turned clockwise, how many of the 6 gears will turn counterclockwise?

(A) 1
(B) 2
(C) 3
(D) 4
(E) 5

5 What percent of all employees at Company X work in the manufacturing department?

(A) 40%
(B) 37.5%
(C) 35%
(D) 30%
(E) 25%

Questions 4 and 5 refer to the following graphs.

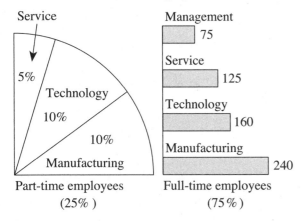

Employees by Department at Company X
100% = 800 employees

Service

5%

Technology
10%

10%

Manufacturing

Part-time employees
(25%)

Management
75

Service
125

Technology
160

Manufacturing
240

Full-time employees
(75%)

6 If $x^2 - 4x - 12 = 0$, what is the value of $2x^2 - 8x$?

(A) 0
(B) 4
(C) 12
(D) 16
(E) 24

4 According to the graphs above, the total number of full-time employees is how many more than the total number of part-time employees at Company X ?

(A) 100
(B) 200
(C) 300
(D) 400
(E) 500

GO ON TO THE NEXT PAGE

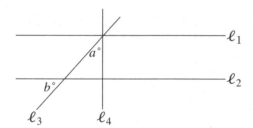

Note: Figure not drawn to scale.

7 In the figure above, ℓ_1 is parallel to ℓ_2, and ℓ_4 is perpendicular to ℓ_2. If ℓ_1, ℓ_3, and ℓ_4 all meet at a single point on ℓ_1, which of the following must be true?

   I. $\ell_1 \perp \ell_4$

   II. $a = b$

   III. $a + b = 90$

(A) I only
(B) II only
(C) I and II only
(D) I and III only
(E) II and III only

8 Which of the following conditions would make $2a - 2b < 0$?

(A) $a = b$
(B) $a > 0$
(C) $b > 0$
(D) $a < b$
(E) $a > b$

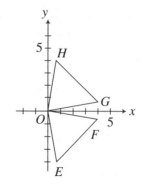

9 In the xy–coordinate system above, which of the following lines has a slope of 1?

(A) Line OE
(B) Line OF
(C) Line OG
(D) Line OH
(E) Line EF

10 If a and b are integers and $2a + 5b = 15$, which of the following CANNOT be a value of b ?

(A) −1
(B)   1
(C)   2
(D)   3
(E)   5

GO ON TO THE NEXT PAGE

11 A certain company employs 25 women and 25 men. Some employees drive to work and the rest take public transportation. If 29 employees drive to work, and exactly 6 men take public transportation, how many women drive to work?

(A) 6
(B) 8
(C) 10
(D) 11
(E) 13

13 If a and b are positive integers, and $a + b = 10$, what is the least possible value of $a - b$?

(A) −10
(B) −9
(C) −8
(D) −6
(E)   0

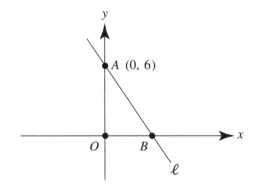

12 In the figure above, if the slope of line ℓ is $-\dfrac{3}{2}$, what is the area of triangle AOB ?

(A) 24
(B) 18
(C) 16
(D) 14
(E) 12

14 If it takes a certain laser printer x minutes to print out y pages, how many minutes would it take this machine to print out $y + 2$ pages?

(A) $x + 2$

(B) $\dfrac{x + 2}{y}$

(C) $\dfrac{x}{y}$

(D) $\dfrac{x(y + 2)}{y}$

(E) $\dfrac{xy}{y + 2}$

GO ON TO THE NEXT PAGE

r, s, t

15 In the sequence above, if each term after the first is x more than the previous term, what is the average of r, s, and t in terms of r and x ?

(A) $r + x$

(B) $r + \dfrac{x}{3}$

(C) $r + \dfrac{2x}{3}$

(D) $\dfrac{r + x}{3}$

(E) $3(r + x)$

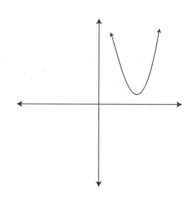

16 The graph above shows the function $f(x)$. Which of the following would be the graph of $f(x - 1)$?

(A) 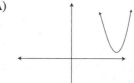 (B)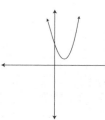

(C) 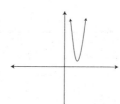 (D)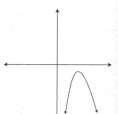

(E)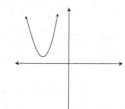

IF YOU FINISH BEFORE TIME IS CALLED, YOU MAY CHECK YOUR WORK ON THIS SECTION ONLY. DO NOT TURN TO ANY OTHER SECTION IN THE TEST.   **STOP**

- 186 -

NO TEST MATERIAL ON THIS PAGE

Time—10 Minutes
14 Questions

Directions: For each question in this section, select the best answer from among the choices given and fill in the corresponding oval on the answer sheet.

The following sentences test correctness and effectiveness of expression. Part of each sentence or the entire sentence is underlined; beneath each sentence are five ways of phrasing the underlined material. Choice A repeats the original phrasing; the other four choices are different. If you think the original phrasing produces a better sentence than any of the alternatives, select choice A; if not, select one of the other choices.

In making your selection, follow the requirements of standard written English; that is, pay attention to grammar, choice of words, sentence construction, and punctuation. Your selection should result in the most effective sentence—clear and precise—without awkwardness or ambiguity.

EXAMPLE:

Every apple in the baskets <u>are ripe and labeled according to the date it was picked</u>.

(A) are ripe and labeled according to the date it was picked
(B) is ripe and labeled according to the date it was picked
(C) are ripe and labeled according to the date they were picked
(D) is ripe and labeled according to the date they were picked
(E) are ripe and labeled as to the date it was picked

ANSWER:
(A) ● (C) (D) (E)

---

1 In the *Lord of the Rings* trilogy, gripping climaxes are mixed with interesting <u>details, and a box office hit was produced</u>.

(A) details, and a box office hit was produced
(B) details; it produced a box office hit
(C) details, and this combination produced a box office hit
(D) details, that combination produced a box office hit
(E) details; thus producing a box office hit

2 Adam Gopnik's book *Paris to the Moon*, <u>like other travel narratives, are</u> based on the similarities and differences of a foreign culture.

(A) like other travel narratives, are
(B) like other travel narratives, is
(C) like other authors, are
(D) like other authors, is
(E) like other authors, were

3 Al Hirschfeld, whose caricatures were often featured in the *New York Times*, became famous for incorporating into all of his drawings his daughter's <u>name, it is Nina</u>.

(A) name, it is Nina
(B) name, which is Nina
(C) name, being Nina
(D) name; the name of his daughter is Nina
(E) name; which is Nina

4 Left in the rubble of the fire on State Street were a red ballet slipper, silver forks, and <u>there were three old TV sets</u>.

(A) there were three old TV sets
(B) three old TV sets
(C) there was three old TV sets
(D) the three TV sets left there were old
(E) three old TV sets were there

GO ON TO THE NEXT PAGE

5 Mary Lou Retton is credited with sparking the growth of gymnastics programs in the country, and she <u>has been the first American gymnast to win</u> the all-around Olympic gold medal.

(A) has been the first American gymnast to win
(B) had been the first American gymnast to win
(C) was the first American gymnast winning
(D) having been the first American gymnast to win
(E) was the first American gymnast to win

6 The salads were prepared <u>carelessly, without enough vegetables in it</u>.

(A) carelessly, without enough vegetables in it
(B) careless, without enough vegetables in it
(C) carelessly, without enough vegetables in them
(D) careless, and there is not enough vegetables in them
(E) carelessly and there are not enough vegetables in them

7 The Transportation Department officials rarely run trains at <u>night, it is because they know it would not be profitable and are hesitant as a consequence</u>.

(A) night, it is because they know it would not be profitable and are hesitant as a consequence
(B) night since they know it would not be profitable, there is a consequent hesitation
(C) night because of knowing it would not be profitable and therefore they are hesitant to do it
(D) night because they know it would not be profitable and are therefore hesitant to do it
(E) night, their knowing that it would not be profitable causes hesitation in it

8 No two of the crimes committed by the inmates <u>was similar enough to justify them being given</u> the same sentence.

(A) was similar enough to justify them being given
(B) was similar enough to justify the giving of them
(C) were similar enough to justify giving them
(D) was similar enough to justify their being given
(E) were similar enough to justify the giving of them

9 Flying over the Grand Canyon, <u>speechless was how Mary found herself, thanks to the majesty of the gorge</u>.

(A) speechless was how Mary found herself, thanks to the majesty of the gorge
(B) speech was beyond Mary, thanks to the majesty of the gorge
(C) the majesty of the gorge left Mary speechless
(D) the gorge was so majestic as to leave Mary speechless
(E) Mary found herself speechless, thanks to the majesty of the gorge

10 <u>Compared to the Americans, the Russian subway</u> is much deeper in the earth.

(A) Compared to the Americans, the Russian subway
(B) Comparing it to the Americans, the Russian subway
(C) Compared to the American subway, the Russian subway
(D) The Russian subway, compared to the Americans
(E) The American subway, when being compared, the Russian subway

11 Yoga is gentler and less stressful than aerobic exercise, but <u>longer is the amount of time it takes to see results</u>.

(A) longer is the amount of time it takes to see results
(B) it takes a longer amount of time to see results
(C) to see results it takes a longer amount of time
(D) there is a longer amount of time to see results
(E) its results take longer to see

12 In *A Civil Action*, Jonathan Harr managed <u>to create</u> a compelling work that not only made the *New York Times* bestseller list, but is also used in law schools around the county.

(A) to create
(B) for creating
(C) in creating
(D) that he created
(E) in the creation of

GO ON TO THE NEXT PAGE

13 Despite borrowing many of his stories from history <u>and myths, with other playwrights providing him with some of his dialogue, William</u> Shakespeare is considered one of the most original writers of all time.

(A) and myths, with other playwrights providing him with some of his dialogue, William

(B) and myths, and on some dialogue of other playwrights, William

(C) and myths, and some of his dialogue from other playwrights, William

(D) and myths, other playwrights provided some of his lines, so William

(E) and myths, other playwrights provided some of his lines, and yet William

14 The prosecutor believed that the criminal defense attorney was successful only because <u>of their witness who lied</u> during his testimony.

(A) of their witness who lied

(B) of their witness lying

(C) the witness who lied

(D) her witness lied

(E) of how their witness lied

SCORING YOUR TEST

For each section (Critical Reading, Math, and Writing) on the SAT, your score will range from 200–800. Your performance on the tests in this book is a good indicator of your abilities and skills.

The scoring information contained here is intended to give an approximate idea of what your performance will be on Test Day. The formulas for calculating your raw score that follow in this book are the same as those the College Board will use to score your SAT.

The raw-to-scaled score conversion tables, however, may differ from the one used to score the SAT that you take. The College Board creates unique raw-to-scaled score conversions for every administration of the SAT. Therefore, practice tests can only approximate the conversion tables that will be used on the real SAT that you take. Nevertheless, the tables in this book are close to the tables that will be used on your test, and will provide you with a good sense of what your score might be at this stage in your preparation.

Step 1: Score Your Essay

First, score your essay, which accounts for approximately 25% of your Writing scaled score; your score on the Multiple Choice questions will account for the remaining 75% or so. For the tests in this book, assign your essay a score of 1–6, which, along with your Multiple Choice score, you will use to arrive at your 200–800 scaled score.

For All Students:

The following criteria are a good guide:

6 **Outstanding**—Though it may have a few small errors, the essay is well organized and fully developed with supporting examples. It displays consistent language facility, varied sentence structure, and varied vocabulary.

5 **Solid**—Though it has occasional errors or lapses in quality, the essay is generally organized and well developed with appropriate examples. It displays language facility, syntactic variety, and varied vocabulary.

4 **Adequate**—Though it has some flaws, the essay is organized and adequately developed and has some examples. It displays adequate but inconsistent language facility.

3 **Limited**—The essay does not adequately fulfill the writing assignment and has many flaws. It has inadequate organization and development, along with many errors in grammar or diction (or both). In general, the essay lacks variety.

2 **Flawed**—The essay demonstrates incompetence with one or more weaknesses. Ideas are vague and thinly developed. It contains frequent errors in grammar and diction and almost no variety.

1 **Deficient**—The essay demonstrates incompetence with serious flaws. It has no organization, no development, and severe grammar and diction errors. The essay is so seriously flawed that its basic meaning is obscured.

0 **Off-Topic**—The essay does not follow the assignment.

Step 2: Compute Your Raw Score

Check your answers to the multiple-choice questions against the answer key on the next two pages. Count up the number of answers you got right and the number you got wrong for each section. Do not score Section 4, the Experimental Section. Remember, do not count questions left blank as wrong. Round up to the nearest whole number. Now, plug them in below.

Note: Grid-in questions do not have a wrong-answer penalty, so do not deduct anything for wrong answers.

Critical Reading

	Number Right	Number Wrong	Raw Score
Section 2:	☐	− (.25 × ☐)	= ☐
Section 5:	☐	− (.25 × ☐)	= ☐
Section 8:	☐	− (.25 × ☐)	= ☐
		Critical Reading Raw Score	= ☐
			(rounded up)

Writing

	Number Right	Number Wrong	Raw Score
Section 7:	☐	− (.25 × ☐)	= ☐
Section 10:	☐	− (.25 × ☐)	= ☐
		Writing Multiple-Choice Raw Score	= ☐
			(rounded up)

Math

	Number Right	Number Wrong	Raw Score
Section 3:	☐	− (.25 × ☐)	= ☐
Section 6: (QUESTIONS 1–8)	☐	− (.25 × ☐)	= ☐
Section 6: (QUESTIONS 9–18)	☐	− (no wrong answer penalty)	= ☐
Section 9:	☐	− (.25 × ☐)	= ☐
		Math Raw Score	= ☐
			(rounded up)

PRACTICE TEST 3 ANSWER KEY

CRITICAL READING					
Section 2		**Section 5**		**Section 8**	
Multiple-Choice Questions		Multiple-Choice Questions		Multiple-Choice Questions	
	Correct Answer		Correct Answer		Correct Answer
1.	A	1.	E	1.	A
2.	E	2.	D	2.	B
3.	B	3.	C	3.	E
4.	C	4.	B	4.	D
5.	B	5.	C	5.	B
6.	D	6.	B	6.	E
7.	A	7.	D	7.	B
8.	D	8.	B	8.	B
9.	B	9.	A	9.	A
10.	A	10.	B	10.	D
11.	B	11.	C	11.	A
12.	D	12.	A	12.	A
13.	D	13.	D	13.	C
14.	D	14.	C	14.	B
15.	C	15.	D	15.	A
16.	C	16.	B	16.	B
17.	E	17.	A	17.	E
18.	D	18.	D	18.	B
19.	B	19.	D	19.	E
20.	D	20.	E		
21.	E	21.	A		
22.	B	22.	C		
23.	A	23.	C		
24.	B	24.	B		

MATH					
Section 3		**Section 6**		**Section 9**	
Multiple-Choice Questions		Multiple-Choice Questions		Multiple-Choice Questions	
	Correct Answer		Correct Answer		Correct Answer
1.	B	1.	C	1.	A
2.	D	2.	D	2.	B
3.	E	3.	C	3.	C
4.	B	4.	D	4.	D
5.	E	5.	B	5.	A
6.	D	6.	E	6.	E
7.	C	7.	A	7.	D
8.	D	8.	C	8.	D
9.	C			9.	E
10.	B			10.	C
11.	C			11.	C
12.	D			12.	E
13.	D			13.	C
14.	E			14.	D
15.	D			15.	A
16.	E			16.	A
17.	A				
18.	E				
19.	B				
20.	D				

no. correct (Section 2)

no. incorrect (Section 2)

no. correct (Section 5)

no. incorrect (Section 5)

no. correct (Section 8)

no. incorrect (Section 8)

no. correct (Section 3)

no. incorrect (Section 3)

no. correct (Section 6)

no. incorrect (Section 6)

no. correct (Section 9)

no. incorrect (Section 9)

Section 6	
Student-Produced Response Questions	
	Correct Answer
9.	3, 5, or 7
10.	12
11.	960
12.	33, 35, 37, 39 or 41
13.	48
14.	8
15.	6/36, 1/6, .166, or .167
16.	6
17.	36
18.	13

no. correct

WRITING

Essay	Section 7 Multiple-Choice Questions		Section 10 Multiple-Choice Questions	
		Correct Answer		Correct Answer
	1.	D	1.	C
	2.	C	2.	B
	3.	B	3.	B
Essay Score* (1–6)	4.	B	4.	B
	5.	C	5.	E
	6.	E	6.	C
	7.	A	7.	D
	8.	D	8.	C
	9.	B	9.	E
	10.	C	10.	C
	11.	A	11.	E
	12.	E	12.	A
	13.	C	13.	C
	14.	B	14.	D
	15.	E		
	16.	A		
	17.	E		
	18.	A		
	19.	C		
	20.	E		
	21.	D		
	22.	B		
	23.	B		
	24.	C		
	25.	B		
	26.	C		
	27.	E		
	28.	D		
	29.	E		
	30.	C		
	31.	B		
	32.	D		
	33.	A		
	34.	E		
	35.	C		

_____
no. correct

_____
no. incorrect

_____
no. correct

_____
no. incorrect

*To score your essay, see Step 1 on the previous pages. On this Practice Test, your essay score will range from 1 to 6. (Keep in mind that on the actual SAT, your essay will be read by two readers and you will receive a score of 1 to 12 on your score report.)

Step 3: Find Your Scaled Score

To determine your Critical Reading and Math scaled scores, find the raw scores you calculated for these two sections in Step 2 on Tables 1 and 2 on the following page. Next, find the scaled score associated with your raw scores and enter them in the appropriate box in the Scaled Scores table on this page.

To determine your Writing scaled score, use Table 3. First, find the Writing Multiple-Choice raw score you calculated in Step 2 and the essay raw score (1–6) you assigned yourself. Next, locate your Writing Multiple-Choice raw score on the left dimension of Table 3. Then find your essay score along the top. The box associated with this row and column contains your Writing scaled score. Enter it in the appropriate box in the Scaled Scores table below.

The sum of the three scores is your Total Scaled Score.

Scaled Scores	
Critical Reading	
Math	
Writing	
Total	

TABLE 1 Critical Reading Conversion Table			
Raw Score	Scaled Score	Raw Score	Scaled Score
67	800	30	500
66	790	29	500
65	770	28	490
64	760	27	480
63	750	26	480
62	740	25	470
61	720	24	470
60	710	23	460
59	700	22	450
58	690	21	450
57	680	20	440
56	670	19	430
55	670	18	430
54	660	17	420
53	650	16	410
52	640	15	410
51	640	14	400
50	630	13	390
49	620	12	380
48	610	11	380
47	610	10	370
46	600	9	360
45	590	8	350
44	590	7	340
43	580	6	330
42	580	5	320
41	570	4	310
40	560	3	300
39	560	2	280
38	550	1	270
37	540	0	250
36	540	−1	250
35	530	−2	240
34	530	−3	230
33	520	−4	220
32	510	−5	210
31	510	−6 and below	200

TABLE 2 Math Conversion Table			
Raw Score	Scaled Score	Raw Score	Scaled Score
54	800	24	490
53	780	23	490
52	760	22	480
51	740	21	470
50	730	20	460
49	710	19	460
48	700	18	450
47	690	17	440
46	670	16	430
45	660	15	430
44	650	14	420
43	650	13	410
42	640	12	400
41	630	11	390
40	620	10	380
39	610	9	380
38	600	8	370
37	590	7	360
36	590	6	340
35	580	5	330
34	570	4	320
33	560	3	310
32	560	2	290
31	550	1	280
30	540	0	260
29	530	−1	250
28	520	−2	240
27	520	−3	230
26	510	−4	220
25	500	−5	210
		−6 and below	200

TABLE 3
SAT Score Conversion Table for Writing Composite

		Essay Raw Score						
		0	1	2	3	4	5	6
	49	670	700	720	740	780	790	800
	48	660	680	700	730	760	780	790
	47	650	670	690	720	750	770	780
	46	640	660	680	710	740	760	770
	45	630	650	670	700	740	750	770
	44	620	640	660	690	730	750	760
	43	600	630	650	680	710	740	750
	42	600	620	640	670	700	730	750
	41	590	610	630	660	690	730	740
	40	580	600	620	650	690	720	740
	39	570	590	610	640	680	710	740
	38	560	590	610	630	670	700	730
	37	550	580	600	630	660	690	720
	36	540	570	590	620	650	680	710
	35	540	560	580	610	640	680	710
	34	530	550	570	600	640	670	700
	33	520	540	560	590	630	660	690
	32	510	540	560	580	620	650	680
	31	500	530	550	580	610	640	670
	30	490	520	540	570	600	630	660
	29	490	510	530	560	590	630	650
	28	480	500	520	550	590	620	640
	27	470	490	510	540	580	610	640
Writing Multiple-Choice Raw Score	26	460	490	500	530	570	600	630
	25	450	480	500	520	560	590	620
	24	440	470	490	510	550	580	610
	23	430	460	480	510	540	570	600
	22	430	450	470	500	530	570	590
	21	430	450	470	500	530	570	590
	20	420	440	460	490	520	560	580
	19	410	430	450	480	520	550	570
	18	400	420	440	470	510	540	570
	17	390	420	430	460	500	530	560
	16	380	410	430	450	490	520	550
	15	370	400	420	450	480	510	540
	14	360	390	410	440	470	500	530
	13	360	380	400	430	460	500	520
	12	340	370	390	420	450	490	510
	11	340	360	380	410	450	480	510
	10	330	350	370	400	440	470	500
	9	320	350	360	390	430	460	490
	8	310	340	360	390	420	450	480
	7	300	330	350	380	410	440	470
	6	290	320	340	370	400	430	460
	5	290	310	330	360	390	430	450
	4	280	300	320	350	390	420	450
	3	270	290	310	340	380	410	440
	2	260	280	300	330	370	400	430
	1	250	270	290	320	340	380	410
	0	250	260	280	310	340	370	400
	−1	240	260	270	290	320	360	380
	−2	230	250	260	270	310	340	370
	−3	220	240	250	260	300	330	360
	−4	220	230	240	250	290	320	350
	−5	200	220	230	240	280	310	340
	−6	200	210	220	240	280	310	340
	−7	200	210	220	230	270	300	330
	−8	200	210	220	230	270	300	330
	−9	200	210	220	230	270	300	330
	−10	200	210	220	230	270	300	330
	−11	200	210	220	230	270	300	330

PRACTICE TEST 4

For additional practice before Test Day, take this Practice Test under test-like conditions at home or at a Kaplan Center, bubble in your answers on a Kaplan SAT Answer Grid, and have the grid scanned at a Kaplan Center to receive your results.

Scan Code: 1104

Practice Test 4
Answer Sheet

Remove (or photocopy) the following answer sheet and use it to complete the practice test. See the answer key following the test when finished.

Start with number 1 for each bubble-in section. If a section has fewer questions than bubbles, leave the extra bubbles blank.

Use this page to *plan* your essay.

SECTION 2

1. Ⓐ Ⓑ Ⓒ Ⓓ Ⓔ	11. Ⓐ Ⓑ Ⓒ Ⓓ Ⓔ	21. Ⓐ Ⓑ Ⓒ Ⓓ Ⓔ	31. Ⓐ Ⓑ Ⓒ Ⓓ Ⓔ
2. Ⓐ Ⓑ Ⓒ Ⓓ Ⓔ	12. Ⓐ Ⓑ Ⓒ Ⓓ Ⓔ	22. Ⓐ Ⓑ Ⓒ Ⓓ Ⓔ	32. Ⓐ Ⓑ Ⓒ Ⓓ Ⓔ
3. Ⓐ Ⓑ Ⓒ Ⓓ Ⓔ	13. Ⓐ Ⓑ Ⓒ Ⓓ Ⓔ	23. Ⓐ Ⓑ Ⓒ Ⓓ Ⓔ	33. Ⓐ Ⓑ Ⓒ Ⓓ Ⓔ
4. Ⓐ Ⓑ Ⓒ Ⓓ Ⓔ	14. Ⓐ Ⓑ Ⓒ Ⓓ Ⓔ	24. Ⓐ Ⓑ Ⓒ Ⓓ Ⓔ	34. Ⓐ Ⓑ Ⓒ Ⓓ Ⓔ
5. Ⓐ Ⓑ Ⓒ Ⓓ Ⓔ	15. Ⓐ Ⓑ Ⓒ Ⓓ Ⓔ	25. Ⓐ Ⓑ Ⓒ Ⓓ Ⓔ	35. Ⓐ Ⓑ Ⓒ Ⓓ Ⓔ
6. Ⓐ Ⓑ Ⓒ Ⓓ Ⓔ	16. Ⓐ Ⓑ Ⓒ Ⓓ Ⓔ	26. Ⓐ Ⓑ Ⓒ Ⓓ Ⓔ	36. Ⓐ Ⓑ Ⓒ Ⓓ Ⓔ
7. Ⓐ Ⓑ Ⓒ Ⓓ Ⓔ	17. Ⓐ Ⓑ Ⓒ Ⓓ Ⓔ	27. Ⓐ Ⓑ Ⓒ Ⓓ Ⓔ	37. Ⓐ Ⓑ Ⓒ Ⓓ Ⓔ
8. Ⓐ Ⓑ Ⓒ Ⓓ Ⓔ	18. Ⓐ Ⓑ Ⓒ Ⓓ Ⓔ	28. Ⓐ Ⓑ Ⓒ Ⓓ Ⓔ	38. Ⓐ Ⓑ Ⓒ Ⓓ Ⓔ
9. Ⓐ Ⓑ Ⓒ Ⓓ Ⓔ	19. Ⓐ Ⓑ Ⓒ Ⓓ Ⓔ	29. Ⓐ Ⓑ Ⓒ Ⓓ Ⓔ	39. Ⓐ Ⓑ Ⓒ Ⓓ Ⓔ
10. Ⓐ Ⓑ Ⓒ Ⓓ Ⓔ	20. Ⓐ Ⓑ Ⓒ Ⓓ Ⓔ	30. Ⓐ Ⓑ Ⓒ Ⓓ Ⓔ	40. Ⓐ Ⓑ Ⓒ Ⓓ Ⓔ

right in Section 2

wrong in Section 2

SECTION 3

1. Ⓐ Ⓑ Ⓒ Ⓓ Ⓔ	11. Ⓐ Ⓑ Ⓒ Ⓓ Ⓔ	21. Ⓐ Ⓑ Ⓒ Ⓓ Ⓔ	31. Ⓐ Ⓑ Ⓒ Ⓓ Ⓔ
2. Ⓐ Ⓑ Ⓒ Ⓓ Ⓔ	12. Ⓐ Ⓑ Ⓒ Ⓓ Ⓔ	22. Ⓐ Ⓑ Ⓒ Ⓓ Ⓔ	32. Ⓐ Ⓑ Ⓒ Ⓓ Ⓔ
3. Ⓐ Ⓑ Ⓒ Ⓓ Ⓔ	13. Ⓐ Ⓑ Ⓒ Ⓓ Ⓔ	23. Ⓐ Ⓑ Ⓒ Ⓓ Ⓔ	33. Ⓐ Ⓑ Ⓒ Ⓓ Ⓔ
4. Ⓐ Ⓑ Ⓒ Ⓓ Ⓔ	14. Ⓐ Ⓑ Ⓒ Ⓓ Ⓔ	24. Ⓐ Ⓑ Ⓒ Ⓓ Ⓔ	34. Ⓐ Ⓑ Ⓒ Ⓓ Ⓔ
5. Ⓐ Ⓑ Ⓒ Ⓓ Ⓔ	15. Ⓐ Ⓑ Ⓒ Ⓓ Ⓔ	25. Ⓐ Ⓑ Ⓒ Ⓓ Ⓔ	35. Ⓐ Ⓑ Ⓒ Ⓓ Ⓔ
6. Ⓐ Ⓑ Ⓒ Ⓓ Ⓔ	16. Ⓐ Ⓑ Ⓒ Ⓓ Ⓔ	26. Ⓐ Ⓑ Ⓒ Ⓓ Ⓔ	36. Ⓐ Ⓑ Ⓒ Ⓓ Ⓔ
7. Ⓐ Ⓑ Ⓒ Ⓓ Ⓔ	17. Ⓐ Ⓑ Ⓒ Ⓓ Ⓔ	27. Ⓐ Ⓑ Ⓒ Ⓓ Ⓔ	37. Ⓐ Ⓑ Ⓒ Ⓓ Ⓔ
8. Ⓐ Ⓑ Ⓒ Ⓓ Ⓔ	18. Ⓐ Ⓑ Ⓒ Ⓓ Ⓔ	28. Ⓐ Ⓑ Ⓒ Ⓓ Ⓔ	38. Ⓐ Ⓑ Ⓒ Ⓓ Ⓔ
9. Ⓐ Ⓑ Ⓒ Ⓓ Ⓔ	19. Ⓐ Ⓑ Ⓒ Ⓓ Ⓔ	29. Ⓐ Ⓑ Ⓒ Ⓓ Ⓔ	39. Ⓐ Ⓑ Ⓒ Ⓓ Ⓔ
10. Ⓐ Ⓑ Ⓒ Ⓓ Ⓔ	20. Ⓐ Ⓑ Ⓒ Ⓓ Ⓔ	30. Ⓐ Ⓑ Ⓒ Ⓓ Ⓔ	40. Ⓐ Ⓑ Ⓒ Ⓓ Ⓔ

right in Section 3

wrong in Section 3

If sections 2 or 3 of this practice test contain math questions that are not multiple choice, continue to item 9 below. Otherwise, continue to item 9 above.

9. 10. 11. 12. 13.

14. 15. 16. 17. 18.

SECTION 4

1. Ⓐ Ⓑ Ⓒ Ⓓ Ⓔ	11. Ⓐ Ⓑ Ⓒ Ⓓ Ⓔ	21. Ⓐ Ⓑ Ⓒ Ⓓ Ⓔ	31. Ⓐ Ⓑ Ⓒ Ⓓ Ⓔ
2. Ⓐ Ⓑ Ⓒ Ⓓ Ⓔ	12. Ⓐ Ⓑ Ⓒ Ⓓ Ⓔ	22. Ⓐ Ⓑ Ⓒ Ⓓ Ⓔ	32. Ⓐ Ⓑ Ⓒ Ⓓ Ⓔ
3. Ⓐ Ⓑ Ⓒ Ⓓ Ⓔ	13. Ⓐ Ⓑ Ⓒ Ⓓ Ⓔ	23. Ⓐ Ⓑ Ⓒ Ⓓ Ⓔ	33. Ⓐ Ⓑ Ⓒ Ⓓ Ⓔ
4. Ⓐ Ⓑ Ⓒ Ⓓ Ⓔ	14. Ⓐ Ⓑ Ⓒ Ⓓ Ⓔ	24. Ⓐ Ⓑ Ⓒ Ⓓ Ⓔ	34. Ⓐ Ⓑ Ⓒ Ⓓ Ⓔ
5. Ⓐ Ⓑ Ⓒ Ⓓ Ⓔ	15. Ⓐ Ⓑ Ⓒ Ⓓ Ⓔ	25. Ⓐ Ⓑ Ⓒ Ⓓ Ⓔ	35. Ⓐ Ⓑ Ⓒ Ⓓ Ⓔ
6. Ⓐ Ⓑ Ⓒ Ⓓ Ⓔ	16. Ⓐ Ⓑ Ⓒ Ⓓ Ⓔ	26. Ⓐ Ⓑ Ⓒ Ⓓ Ⓔ	36. Ⓐ Ⓑ Ⓒ Ⓓ Ⓔ
7. Ⓐ Ⓑ Ⓒ Ⓓ Ⓔ	17. Ⓐ Ⓑ Ⓒ Ⓓ Ⓔ	27. Ⓐ Ⓑ Ⓒ Ⓓ Ⓔ	37. Ⓐ Ⓑ Ⓒ Ⓓ Ⓔ
8. Ⓐ Ⓑ Ⓒ Ⓓ Ⓔ	18. Ⓐ Ⓑ Ⓒ Ⓓ Ⓔ	28. Ⓐ Ⓑ Ⓒ Ⓓ Ⓔ	38. Ⓐ Ⓑ Ⓒ Ⓓ Ⓔ
9. Ⓐ Ⓑ Ⓒ Ⓓ Ⓔ	19. Ⓐ Ⓑ Ⓒ Ⓓ Ⓔ	29. Ⓐ Ⓑ Ⓒ Ⓓ Ⓔ	39. Ⓐ Ⓑ Ⓒ Ⓓ Ⓔ
10. Ⓐ Ⓑ Ⓒ Ⓓ Ⓔ	20. Ⓐ Ⓑ Ⓒ Ⓓ Ⓔ	30. Ⓐ Ⓑ Ⓒ Ⓓ Ⓔ	40. Ⓐ Ⓑ Ⓒ Ⓓ Ⓔ

right in Section 4

wrong in Section 4

SECTION 5

1. Ⓐ Ⓑ Ⓒ Ⓓ Ⓔ	11. Ⓐ Ⓑ Ⓒ Ⓓ Ⓔ	21. Ⓐ Ⓑ Ⓒ Ⓓ Ⓔ	31. Ⓐ Ⓑ Ⓒ Ⓓ Ⓔ
2. Ⓐ Ⓑ Ⓒ Ⓓ Ⓔ	12. Ⓐ Ⓑ Ⓒ Ⓓ Ⓔ	22. Ⓐ Ⓑ Ⓒ Ⓓ Ⓔ	32. Ⓐ Ⓑ Ⓒ Ⓓ Ⓔ
3. Ⓐ Ⓑ Ⓒ Ⓓ Ⓔ	13. Ⓐ Ⓑ Ⓒ Ⓓ Ⓔ	23. Ⓐ Ⓑ Ⓒ Ⓓ Ⓔ	33. Ⓐ Ⓑ Ⓒ Ⓓ Ⓔ
4. Ⓐ Ⓑ Ⓒ Ⓓ Ⓔ	14. Ⓐ Ⓑ Ⓒ Ⓓ Ⓔ	24. Ⓐ Ⓑ Ⓒ Ⓓ Ⓔ	34. Ⓐ Ⓑ Ⓒ Ⓓ Ⓔ
5. Ⓐ Ⓑ Ⓒ Ⓓ Ⓔ	15. Ⓐ Ⓑ Ⓒ Ⓓ Ⓔ	25. Ⓐ Ⓑ Ⓒ Ⓓ Ⓔ	35. Ⓐ Ⓑ Ⓒ Ⓓ Ⓔ
6. Ⓐ Ⓑ Ⓒ Ⓓ Ⓔ	16. Ⓐ Ⓑ Ⓒ Ⓓ Ⓔ	26. Ⓐ Ⓑ Ⓒ Ⓓ Ⓔ	36. Ⓐ Ⓑ Ⓒ Ⓓ Ⓔ
7. Ⓐ Ⓑ Ⓒ Ⓓ Ⓔ	17. Ⓐ Ⓑ Ⓒ Ⓓ Ⓔ	27. Ⓐ Ⓑ Ⓒ Ⓓ Ⓔ	37. Ⓐ Ⓑ Ⓒ Ⓓ Ⓔ
8. Ⓐ Ⓑ Ⓒ Ⓓ Ⓔ	18. Ⓐ Ⓑ Ⓒ Ⓓ Ⓔ	28. Ⓐ Ⓑ Ⓒ Ⓓ Ⓔ	38. Ⓐ Ⓑ Ⓒ Ⓓ Ⓔ
9. Ⓐ Ⓑ Ⓒ Ⓓ Ⓔ	19. Ⓐ Ⓑ Ⓒ Ⓓ Ⓔ	29. Ⓐ Ⓑ Ⓒ Ⓓ Ⓔ	39. Ⓐ Ⓑ Ⓒ Ⓓ Ⓔ
10. Ⓐ Ⓑ Ⓒ Ⓓ Ⓔ	20. Ⓐ Ⓑ Ⓒ Ⓓ Ⓔ	30. Ⓐ Ⓑ Ⓒ Ⓓ Ⓔ	40. Ⓐ Ⓑ Ⓒ Ⓓ Ⓔ

right in Section 5

wrong in Section 5

If sections 4 or 5 of this practice test contain math questions that are not multiple choice, continue to item 9 below. Otherwise, continue to item 9 above.

9. 10. 11. 12. 13.

14. 15. 16. 17. 18.

SECTION 6

1. Ⓐ Ⓑ Ⓒ Ⓓ Ⓔ   11. Ⓐ Ⓑ Ⓒ Ⓓ Ⓔ   21. Ⓐ Ⓑ Ⓒ Ⓓ Ⓔ   31. Ⓐ Ⓑ Ⓒ Ⓓ Ⓔ
2. Ⓐ Ⓑ Ⓒ Ⓓ Ⓔ   12. Ⓐ Ⓑ Ⓒ Ⓓ Ⓔ   22. Ⓐ Ⓑ Ⓒ Ⓓ Ⓔ   32. Ⓐ Ⓑ Ⓒ Ⓓ Ⓔ
3. Ⓐ Ⓑ Ⓒ Ⓓ Ⓔ   13. Ⓐ Ⓑ Ⓒ Ⓓ Ⓔ   23. Ⓐ Ⓑ Ⓒ Ⓓ Ⓔ   33. Ⓐ Ⓑ Ⓒ Ⓓ Ⓔ
4. Ⓐ Ⓑ Ⓒ Ⓓ Ⓔ   14. Ⓐ Ⓑ Ⓒ Ⓓ Ⓔ   24. Ⓐ Ⓑ Ⓒ Ⓓ Ⓔ   34. Ⓐ Ⓑ Ⓒ Ⓓ Ⓔ
5. Ⓐ Ⓑ Ⓒ Ⓓ Ⓔ   15. Ⓐ Ⓑ Ⓒ Ⓓ Ⓔ   25. Ⓐ Ⓑ Ⓒ Ⓓ Ⓔ   35. Ⓐ Ⓑ Ⓒ Ⓓ Ⓔ
6. Ⓐ Ⓑ Ⓒ Ⓓ Ⓔ   16. Ⓐ Ⓑ Ⓒ Ⓓ Ⓔ   26. Ⓐ Ⓑ Ⓒ Ⓓ Ⓔ   36. Ⓐ Ⓑ Ⓒ Ⓓ Ⓔ
7. Ⓐ Ⓑ Ⓒ Ⓓ Ⓔ   17. Ⓐ Ⓑ Ⓒ Ⓓ Ⓔ   27. Ⓐ Ⓑ Ⓒ Ⓓ Ⓔ   37. Ⓐ Ⓑ Ⓒ Ⓓ Ⓔ
8. Ⓐ Ⓑ Ⓒ Ⓓ Ⓔ   18. Ⓐ Ⓑ Ⓒ Ⓓ Ⓔ   28. Ⓐ Ⓑ Ⓒ Ⓓ Ⓔ   38. Ⓐ Ⓑ Ⓒ Ⓓ Ⓔ
9. Ⓐ Ⓑ Ⓒ Ⓓ Ⓔ   19. Ⓐ Ⓑ Ⓒ Ⓓ Ⓔ   29. Ⓐ Ⓑ Ⓒ Ⓓ Ⓔ   39. Ⓐ Ⓑ Ⓒ Ⓓ Ⓔ
10. Ⓐ Ⓑ Ⓒ Ⓓ Ⓔ   20. Ⓐ Ⓑ Ⓒ Ⓓ Ⓔ   30. Ⓐ Ⓑ Ⓒ Ⓓ Ⓔ   40. Ⓐ Ⓑ Ⓒ Ⓓ Ⓔ

□ # right in Section 6

□ # wrong in Section 6

SECTION 7

1. Ⓐ Ⓑ Ⓒ Ⓓ Ⓔ   11. Ⓐ Ⓑ Ⓒ Ⓓ Ⓔ   21. Ⓐ Ⓑ Ⓒ Ⓓ Ⓔ   31. Ⓐ Ⓑ Ⓒ Ⓓ Ⓔ
2. Ⓐ Ⓑ Ⓒ Ⓓ Ⓔ   12. Ⓐ Ⓑ Ⓒ Ⓓ Ⓔ   22. Ⓐ Ⓑ Ⓒ Ⓓ Ⓔ   32. Ⓐ Ⓑ Ⓒ Ⓓ Ⓔ
3. Ⓐ Ⓑ Ⓒ Ⓓ Ⓔ   13. Ⓐ Ⓑ Ⓒ Ⓓ Ⓔ   23. Ⓐ Ⓑ Ⓒ Ⓓ Ⓔ   33. Ⓐ Ⓑ Ⓒ Ⓓ Ⓔ
4. Ⓐ Ⓑ Ⓒ Ⓓ Ⓔ   14. Ⓐ Ⓑ Ⓒ Ⓓ Ⓔ   24. Ⓐ Ⓑ Ⓒ Ⓓ Ⓔ   34. Ⓐ Ⓑ Ⓒ Ⓓ Ⓔ
5. Ⓐ Ⓑ Ⓒ Ⓓ Ⓔ   15. Ⓐ Ⓑ Ⓒ Ⓓ Ⓔ   25. Ⓐ Ⓑ Ⓒ Ⓓ Ⓔ   35. Ⓐ Ⓑ Ⓒ Ⓓ Ⓔ
6. Ⓐ Ⓑ Ⓒ Ⓓ Ⓔ   16. Ⓐ Ⓑ Ⓒ Ⓓ Ⓔ   26. Ⓐ Ⓑ Ⓒ Ⓓ Ⓔ   36. Ⓐ Ⓑ Ⓒ Ⓓ Ⓔ
7. Ⓐ Ⓑ Ⓒ Ⓓ Ⓔ   17. Ⓐ Ⓑ Ⓒ Ⓓ Ⓔ   27. Ⓐ Ⓑ Ⓒ Ⓓ Ⓔ   37. Ⓐ Ⓑ Ⓒ Ⓓ Ⓔ
8. Ⓐ Ⓑ Ⓒ Ⓓ Ⓔ   18. Ⓐ Ⓑ Ⓒ Ⓓ Ⓔ   28. Ⓐ Ⓑ Ⓒ Ⓓ Ⓔ   38. Ⓐ Ⓑ Ⓒ Ⓓ Ⓔ
9. Ⓐ Ⓑ Ⓒ Ⓓ Ⓔ   19. Ⓐ Ⓑ Ⓒ Ⓓ Ⓔ   29. Ⓐ Ⓑ Ⓒ Ⓓ Ⓔ   39. Ⓐ Ⓑ Ⓒ Ⓓ Ⓔ
10. Ⓐ Ⓑ Ⓒ Ⓓ Ⓔ   20. Ⓐ Ⓑ Ⓒ Ⓓ Ⓔ   30. Ⓐ Ⓑ Ⓒ Ⓓ Ⓔ   40. Ⓐ Ⓑ Ⓒ Ⓓ Ⓔ

□ # right in Section 7

□ # wrong in Section 7

If sections 6 or 7 of this practice test contain math questions that are not multiple choice, continue to item 9 below. Otherwise, continue to item 9 above.

9. 10. 11. 12. 13.

14. 15. 16. 17. 18.

SECTION 8

1. Ⓐ Ⓑ Ⓒ Ⓓ Ⓔ	11. Ⓐ Ⓑ Ⓒ Ⓓ Ⓔ	21. Ⓐ Ⓑ Ⓒ Ⓓ Ⓔ	31. Ⓐ Ⓑ Ⓒ Ⓓ Ⓔ
2. Ⓐ Ⓑ Ⓒ Ⓓ Ⓔ	12. Ⓐ Ⓑ Ⓒ Ⓓ Ⓔ	22. Ⓐ Ⓑ Ⓒ Ⓓ Ⓔ	32. Ⓐ Ⓑ Ⓒ Ⓓ Ⓔ
3. Ⓐ Ⓑ Ⓒ Ⓓ Ⓔ	13. Ⓐ Ⓑ Ⓒ Ⓓ Ⓔ	23. Ⓐ Ⓑ Ⓒ Ⓓ Ⓔ	33. Ⓐ Ⓑ Ⓒ Ⓓ Ⓔ
4. Ⓐ Ⓑ Ⓒ Ⓓ Ⓔ	14. Ⓐ Ⓑ Ⓒ Ⓓ Ⓔ	24. Ⓐ Ⓑ Ⓒ Ⓓ Ⓔ	34. Ⓐ Ⓑ Ⓒ Ⓓ Ⓔ
5. Ⓐ Ⓑ Ⓒ Ⓓ Ⓔ	15. Ⓐ Ⓑ Ⓒ Ⓓ Ⓔ	25. Ⓐ Ⓑ Ⓒ Ⓓ Ⓔ	35. Ⓐ Ⓑ Ⓒ Ⓓ Ⓔ
6. Ⓐ Ⓑ Ⓒ Ⓓ Ⓔ	16. Ⓐ Ⓑ Ⓒ Ⓓ Ⓔ	26. Ⓐ Ⓑ Ⓒ Ⓓ Ⓔ	36. Ⓐ Ⓑ Ⓒ Ⓓ Ⓔ
7. Ⓐ Ⓑ Ⓒ Ⓓ Ⓔ	17. Ⓐ Ⓑ Ⓒ Ⓓ Ⓔ	27. Ⓐ Ⓑ Ⓒ Ⓓ Ⓔ	37. Ⓐ Ⓑ Ⓒ Ⓓ Ⓔ
8. Ⓐ Ⓑ Ⓒ Ⓓ Ⓔ	18. Ⓐ Ⓑ Ⓒ Ⓓ Ⓔ	28. Ⓐ Ⓑ Ⓒ Ⓓ Ⓔ	38. Ⓐ Ⓑ Ⓒ Ⓓ Ⓔ
9. Ⓐ Ⓑ Ⓒ Ⓓ Ⓔ	19. Ⓐ Ⓑ Ⓒ Ⓓ Ⓔ	29. Ⓐ Ⓑ Ⓒ Ⓓ Ⓔ	39. Ⓐ Ⓑ Ⓒ Ⓓ Ⓔ
10. Ⓐ Ⓑ Ⓒ Ⓓ Ⓔ	20. Ⓐ Ⓑ Ⓒ Ⓓ Ⓔ	30. Ⓐ Ⓑ Ⓒ Ⓓ Ⓔ	40. Ⓐ Ⓑ Ⓒ Ⓓ Ⓔ

right in Section 8

wrong in Section 8

SECTION 9

1. Ⓐ Ⓑ Ⓒ Ⓓ Ⓔ	11. Ⓐ Ⓑ Ⓒ Ⓓ Ⓔ	21. Ⓐ Ⓑ Ⓒ Ⓓ Ⓔ	31. Ⓐ Ⓑ Ⓒ Ⓓ Ⓔ
2. Ⓐ Ⓑ Ⓒ Ⓓ Ⓔ	12. Ⓐ Ⓑ Ⓒ Ⓓ Ⓔ	22. Ⓐ Ⓑ Ⓒ Ⓓ Ⓔ	32. Ⓐ Ⓑ Ⓒ Ⓓ Ⓔ
3. Ⓐ Ⓑ Ⓒ Ⓓ Ⓔ	13. Ⓐ Ⓑ Ⓒ Ⓓ Ⓔ	23. Ⓐ Ⓑ Ⓒ Ⓓ Ⓔ	33. Ⓐ Ⓑ Ⓒ Ⓓ Ⓔ
4. Ⓐ Ⓑ Ⓒ Ⓓ Ⓔ	14. Ⓐ Ⓑ Ⓒ Ⓓ Ⓔ	24. Ⓐ Ⓑ Ⓒ Ⓓ Ⓔ	34. Ⓐ Ⓑ Ⓒ Ⓓ Ⓔ
5. Ⓐ Ⓑ Ⓒ Ⓓ Ⓔ	15. Ⓐ Ⓑ Ⓒ Ⓓ Ⓔ	25. Ⓐ Ⓑ Ⓒ Ⓓ Ⓔ	35. Ⓐ Ⓑ Ⓒ Ⓓ Ⓔ
6. Ⓐ Ⓑ Ⓒ Ⓓ Ⓔ	16. Ⓐ Ⓑ Ⓒ Ⓓ Ⓔ	26. Ⓐ Ⓑ Ⓒ Ⓓ Ⓔ	36. Ⓐ Ⓑ Ⓒ Ⓓ Ⓔ
7. Ⓐ Ⓑ Ⓒ Ⓓ Ⓔ	17. Ⓐ Ⓑ Ⓒ Ⓓ Ⓔ	27. Ⓐ Ⓑ Ⓒ Ⓓ Ⓔ	37. Ⓐ Ⓑ Ⓒ Ⓓ Ⓔ
8. Ⓐ Ⓑ Ⓒ Ⓓ Ⓔ	18. Ⓐ Ⓑ Ⓒ Ⓓ Ⓔ	28. Ⓐ Ⓑ Ⓒ Ⓓ Ⓔ	38. Ⓐ Ⓑ Ⓒ Ⓓ Ⓔ
9. Ⓐ Ⓑ Ⓒ Ⓓ Ⓔ	19. Ⓐ Ⓑ Ⓒ Ⓓ Ⓔ	29. Ⓐ Ⓑ Ⓒ Ⓓ Ⓔ	39. Ⓐ Ⓑ Ⓒ Ⓓ Ⓔ
10. Ⓐ Ⓑ Ⓒ Ⓓ Ⓔ	20. Ⓐ Ⓑ Ⓒ Ⓓ Ⓔ	30. Ⓐ Ⓑ Ⓒ Ⓓ Ⓔ	40. Ⓐ Ⓑ Ⓒ Ⓓ Ⓔ

right in Section 9

wrong in Section 9

SECTION 10

1. Ⓐ Ⓑ Ⓒ Ⓓ Ⓔ	11. Ⓐ Ⓑ Ⓒ Ⓓ Ⓔ	21. Ⓐ Ⓑ Ⓒ Ⓓ Ⓔ	31. Ⓐ Ⓑ Ⓒ Ⓓ Ⓔ
2. Ⓐ Ⓑ Ⓒ Ⓓ Ⓔ	12. Ⓐ Ⓑ Ⓒ Ⓓ Ⓔ	22. Ⓐ Ⓑ Ⓒ Ⓓ Ⓔ	32. Ⓐ Ⓑ Ⓒ Ⓓ Ⓔ
3. Ⓐ Ⓑ Ⓒ Ⓓ Ⓔ	13. Ⓐ Ⓑ Ⓒ Ⓓ Ⓔ	23. Ⓐ Ⓑ Ⓒ Ⓓ Ⓔ	33. Ⓐ Ⓑ Ⓒ Ⓓ Ⓔ
4. Ⓐ Ⓑ Ⓒ Ⓓ Ⓔ	14. Ⓐ Ⓑ Ⓒ Ⓓ Ⓔ	24. Ⓐ Ⓑ Ⓒ Ⓓ Ⓔ	34. Ⓐ Ⓑ Ⓒ Ⓓ Ⓔ
5. Ⓐ Ⓑ Ⓒ Ⓓ Ⓔ	15. Ⓐ Ⓑ Ⓒ Ⓓ Ⓔ	25. Ⓐ Ⓑ Ⓒ Ⓓ Ⓔ	35. Ⓐ Ⓑ Ⓒ Ⓓ Ⓔ
6. Ⓐ Ⓑ Ⓒ Ⓓ Ⓔ	16. Ⓐ Ⓑ Ⓒ Ⓓ Ⓔ	26. Ⓐ Ⓑ Ⓒ Ⓓ Ⓔ	36. Ⓐ Ⓑ Ⓒ Ⓓ Ⓔ
7. Ⓐ Ⓑ Ⓒ Ⓓ Ⓔ	17. Ⓐ Ⓑ Ⓒ Ⓓ Ⓔ	27. Ⓐ Ⓑ Ⓒ Ⓓ Ⓔ	37. Ⓐ Ⓑ Ⓒ Ⓓ Ⓔ
8. Ⓐ Ⓑ Ⓒ Ⓓ Ⓔ	18. Ⓐ Ⓑ Ⓒ Ⓓ Ⓔ	28. Ⓐ Ⓑ Ⓒ Ⓓ Ⓔ	38. Ⓐ Ⓑ Ⓒ Ⓓ Ⓔ
9. Ⓐ Ⓑ Ⓒ Ⓓ Ⓔ	19. Ⓐ Ⓑ Ⓒ Ⓓ Ⓔ	29. Ⓐ Ⓑ Ⓒ Ⓓ Ⓔ	39. Ⓐ Ⓑ Ⓒ Ⓓ Ⓔ
10. Ⓐ Ⓑ Ⓒ Ⓓ Ⓔ	20. Ⓐ Ⓑ Ⓒ Ⓓ Ⓔ	30. Ⓐ Ⓑ Ⓒ Ⓓ Ⓔ	40. Ⓐ Ⓑ Ⓒ Ⓓ Ⓔ

right in Section 10

wrong in Section 10

ESSAY
Time—25 minutes

The essay gives you an opportunity to show how effectively you can develop and express ideas. You should, therefore, take care to develop your point of view, present your ideas logically and clearly, and use language precisely.

Your essay must be written on the lines provided in your Answer Grid Booklet—you will receive no other paper on which to write. You will have enough space if you write on every line, avoid wide margins, and keep your handwriting to a reasonable size. Remember that people who are not familiar with your handwriting will read what you write. Try to write or print so that what you are writing is legible to those readers.

You have twenty-five minutes to write an essay on the topic assigned below. DO NOT WRITE ON ANOTHER TOPIC. AN OFF-TOPIC ESSAY WILL RECEIVE A SCORE OF ZERO.

Think carefully about the issue presented in the following quotation and the assignment below.

> Our fundamental task as human beings is to seek out connections—to exercise our imaginations. It follows, then, that the basic task of education is the care and feeding of the imagination. Our task as teachers and writers, artists and parents is to nourish the imagination—our own and that of the children entrusted to our care.
>
> Katherine Paterson, adapted from *The Spying Heart*.

Assignment: Should a college education focus on cultivating and encouraging the imagination of students or on teaching basic facts and standards so that we all share a certain amount of common knowledge? Plan and write an essay in which you develop your point of view on these issues. Support your position with reasoning and examples taken from your reading, studies, experience, or observations.

DO NOT WRITE YOUR ESSAY IN YOUR TEST BOOK.
You will receive credit only for what you write in your Answer Grid Booklet.

BEGIN WRITING YOUR ESSAY ON PAGE 201 OF THIS BOOK
OR ON PAGE 3 OF YOUR KAPLAN SAT ANSWER GRID.

IF YOU FINISH BEFORE TIME IS CALLED, YOU MAY CHECK YOUR WORK ON
THIS SECTION ONLY. DO NOT TURN TO ANY OTHER SECTION IN THE TEST.

Directions: This section contains two types of questions. You have 25 minutes to complete both types. For questions 1–8, solve each problem and decide which is the best of the choices given. Fill in the corresponding oval on the answer sheet. You may use any available space for scratchwork.

**Time—25 Minutes
18 Questions**

Notes

1. Calculator use is permitted.

2. All numbers used are real numbers.

3. Figures are provided for some problems. All figures are drawn to scale and lie in a plane UNLESS otherwise indicated.

4. Unless otherwise specified, the domain of any function f is assumed to be the set of all real numbers x for which $f(x)$ is a real number.

Reference Information

$A = \dfrac{1}{2}bh$ $c^2 = a^2 + b^2$ Special Right Triangles

$A = \pi r^2$ $V = \pi r^2 h$ $A = lw$ $V = lwh$

$C = 2\pi r$

The sum of the measures in degrees of the angles of a triangle is 180.
The number of degrees of arc in a circle is 360.
A straight angle has a degree measure of 180.

---

1 If m is a negative number, which of the following must be negative?

(A) $3 - m$
(B) m^2
(C) $3m + 4$
(D) $m^3 + m$
(E) $-5m$

2 If 40 percent of y is 50, what is 20 percent of y ?

(A) 20
(B) 25
(C) 30
(D) 35
(E) 40

GO ON TO THE NEXT PAGE

3 In a single electric circuit, Tom laid four wires, each of which was three inches long. If he had a 30-foot roll of wire when he started and no wire was wasted, which of the following represents the number of inches of wire that was left on the roll after he laid wire in k identical circuits? (1 foot = 12 inches)

(A) $360 - k$

(B) $30 - k$

(C) $30 - 12k$

(D) $\dfrac{30 - k}{12}$

(E) $360 - 12k$

4 For all positive integers x, let $?x?$ be defined as the sum of all the odd integers that are greater than 0 and less than $x + 1$. For example, $?6? = 1 + 3 + 5 = 9$. Which of the following equals $?10? - ?8??$?

(A) $?2?$

(B) $?3?$

(C) $?5?$

(D) $?7?$

(E) $?9?$

5 A number y is decreased by 6 and the result is divided by 6. This result is increased by 6. Finally, that result is multiplied by 6. In terms of y, what is the final result?

(A) $y + 6$

(B) $y - 36$

(C) y

(D) $y + 30$

(E) $\dfrac{y - 6}{6}$

6 One circle has a radius of 1 and another circle has a diameter of 3. What is the ratio of the area of the larger circle to the area of the smaller circle?

(A) $4 : 3$

(B) $3 : 2$

(C) $2 : 1$

(D) $9 : 4$

(E) $3 : 1$

GO ON TO THE NEXT PAGE

7 If $d(w) = \sqrt{w^2 + 1}$ for all real values of w, which of the following is NOT a possible value of $d(w)$?

(A) 0
(B) 1
(C) 4.6
(D) 7.25
(E) 49

8 If $|r + 7| = 6$ and $|2r - 2| = 4$, then what is the value of r ?

(A) −13
(B) −3
(C) −1
(D) 3
(E) 13

GO ON TO THE NEXT PAGE

Directions: For Student-Produced Response questions 9–18, use the grids at the bottom of the answer sheet page on which you have answered questions 1–8.

Each of the remaining 10 questions requires you to solve the problem and enter your answer by marking the ovals in the special grid, as shown in the examples below. You may use any available space for scratchwork.

Answer: 1.25 or $\frac{5}{4}$ or 5/4

Write answer in boxes.

Grid in result.

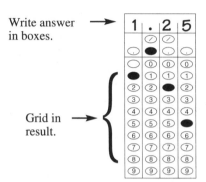

Either position is correct.

Fraction line

Decimal point

You may start your answers in any column, space permitting. Columns not needed should be left blank.

- It is recommended, though not required, that you write your answer in the boxes at the top of the columns. However, **you will receive credit only for darkening the ovals correctly.**

- Grid only one answer to a question, even though some problems have more than one correct answer.

- Darken no more than one oval in a column.

- No answers are negative.

- **Mixed numbers** cannot be gridded. For example: the number $1\frac{1}{4}$ must be gridded as 1.25 or 5/4.

(If $\boxed{1\,1\,/\,4}$ is gridded, it will be interpreted as $\frac{11}{4}$, not $1\frac{1}{4}$.)

- Decimal Accuracy: Decimal answers must be entered as accurately as possible. For example, if you obtain an answer such as 0.1666. . ., you should record the result as .166 or .167. **Less accurate values such as .16 or .17 are not acceptable.**

Acceptable ways to grid $\frac{1}{6}$ = .1666. . .

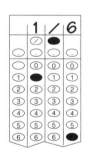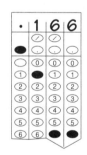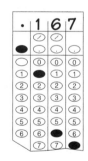

---

9 If $\frac{30}{x+2} = 5$, what is the value of $3x$?

10 If x is a three-digit number that is the product of three consecutive even numbers, what is one possible value of x ?

GO ON TO THE NEXT PAGE

11 If an equilateral triangle with side x has the same perimeter as another triangle with sides 5, 8, and x, what is the value of x ?

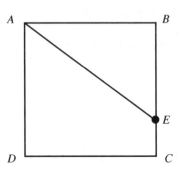

Note: Figure not drawn to scale.

13 Square $ABCD$ has a perimeter of 4 and point E is a point on side BC. What is one possible value of the length of AE ?

12 One full crate holds 48 peaches. If 675 peaches are used to fill as many crates as possible, how many peaches are left over?

$$2, 9, 16, 23, 30,\ldots$$

14 In the sequence above, each term after the first term is 7 more than the previous term. What is the largest 3-digit number that is a term in this sequence?

GO ON TO THE NEXT PAGE

15 If a line that passes through the coordinates $(a + 1, 2a)$ and $(a, 5)$ has a slope of 9, what is the value of a ?

17 The dimensions of a rectangular photograph are $3\frac{1}{2}$ inches long by 2 inches wide. If each dimension is enlarged by 150%, what is the perimeter, in inches, of the new photograph?

16 During a floral shop sale, for every 5 roses purchased, one rose is free. If the cost of one rose is $1.20, how much money is saved by buying 2 dozen roses? (Disregard the $ sign when gridding in your answer.)

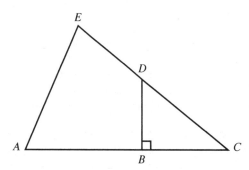

18 In the figure above, $DC = \frac{1}{2} EC$, and $BC = \frac{1}{3} AC$, and the area of $\triangle BDC$ is $\frac{7}{2}$. What is the area of $\triangle ACE$?

Time – 25 Minutes
35 Questions

Directions: For each question in this section, select the best answer from among the choices given and fill in the corresponding oval on the answer sheet.

The following sentences test correctness and effectiveness of expression. Part of each sentence or the entire sentence is underlined; beneath each sentence are five ways of phrasing the underlined material. Choice A repeats the original phrasing; the other four choices are different. If you think the original phrasing produces a better sentence than any of the alternatives, select choice A; if not, select one of the other choices.

In making your selection, follow the requirements of standard written English; that is, pay attention to grammar, choice of words, sentence construction, and punctuation. Your selection should result in the most effective sentence—clear and precise—without awkwardness or ambiguity.

EXAMPLE:

Every apple in the baskets <u>are ripe and labeled according to the date it was picked</u>.

(A) are ripe and labeled according to the date it was picked
(B) is ripe and labeled according to the date it was picked
(C) are ripe and labeled according to the date they were picked
(D) is ripe and labeled according to the date they were picked
(E) are ripe and labeled as to the date it was picked

ANSWER:
Ⓐ ● Ⓒ Ⓓ Ⓔ

1 King Gustavus Adolphus made Sweden a great European military power in the seventeenth <u>century, his armies have defeated</u> Germany and Russia as a result of his new military policies.

(A) century, his armies have defeated
(B) century while his armies had defeated
(C) century, but his armies had been defeating
(D) century, when his armies defeated
(E) century, where his armies were defeating

2 One of the most predictable problems that New England gardeners encounter is rocky <u>soil, another that plagues</u> these gardeners is the destruction of cultivated plants by local wildlife.

(A) soil, another that plagues
(B) soil; another one that plagues
(C) soil, the other, and it plagues
(D) soil; another one which is plaguing
(E) soil and also plaguing

3 Patti LuPone, a famous Broadway performer, is <u>almost as dramatic an actress as she is a singer</u>.

(A) almost as dramatic an actress as she is a singer
(B) almost equally dramatic, whether an actress or a singer
(C) of the same drama as a actress and as a singer, almost
(D) a dramatic singer, with almost as much drama in acting
(E) dramatic as a singer and almost so dramatic in acting

4 <u>Being as there was a heavy rain that</u> soaked their firewood, the campers could not get a fire started.

(A) Being as there was a heavy rain that
(B) With the rain so heavy that it
(C) Due to there being a heavy rain that
(D) The rain was heavy, it
(E) Because the heavy rains

5 <u>Hattie Wyatt Caraway was the first woman to be elected to the U.S. Senate and served for nearly fourteen years.</u>

(A) Hattie Wyatt Caraway was the first woman to be elected to the U.S. Senate and served for nearly fourteen years.
(B) Hattie Wyatt Caraway served for nearly fourteen years, she was the first woman to be elected to the U.S. Senate.
(C) Hattie Wyatt Caraway, serving for nearly fourteen years, being the first woman to be elected to the U.S. Senate.
(D) Hattie Wyatt Caraway, who served for nearly fourteen years, was the first woman to be elected to the U.S. Senate.
(E) Hattie Wyatt Caraway, being the first woman to be elected to the U.S. Senate, and serving for nearly fourteen years.

GO ON TO THE NEXT PAGE

- 214 -

6 Many bikers often fail to use hand signals when sharing a road with cars and other vehicles, in other respects they are cautious riders, however.

(A) Many bikers often fail to use hand signals when sharing a road with cars and other vehicles, in other respects they are cautious riders, however.
(B) Many bikers who are otherwise cautious riders often fail to use hand signals when sharing a road with cars and other vehicles.
(C) Many bikers often fail to use hand signals when sharing a road with cars and other vehicles and are otherwise cautious riders.
(D) Although otherwise cautious riders, many bikers, however, often fail to use hand signals when sharing a road with cars and other vehicles.
(E) Many bikers which often fail to use hand signals when sharing a road with cars and other vehicles are in other respects cautious riders.

7 Folk legends from ancient civilizations continue to fascinate ethnologists which have a belief in gleaning cultural knowledge from them.

(A) which have a belief in gleaning cultural knowledge from them
(B) who believe about cultural knowledge to be gleaned from them
(C) who believe that there is cultural knowledge to be gleaned from them
(D) who believe they hold cultural knowledge and they can glean it from them
(E) that believe that there is cultural knowledge to be gleaned from them

8 Damaging Australia's fragile ecosystem, a nuisance is the quickly multiplying cane toad.

(A) Damaging Australia's fragile ecosystem, a nuisance is the quickly multiplying cane toad.
(B) A nuisance is the quickly multiplying cane toad because of their damaging Australia's fragile ecosystem.
(C) The cane toad, quickly multiplying, damaging Australia's fragile ecosystem, it is a nuisance.
(D) The quickly multiplying cane toad is a nuisance because it damages Australia's fragile ecosystem.
(E) Quickly multiplying is a nuisance of the cane toad damaging Australia's fragile ecosystem.

9 Some scholars argue that the rise of romanticism grew out of a direct and swift reaction to empiricism; they suggest that this shift was more dramatic in literature than either philosophy or science.

(A) either philosophy or science
(B) either philosophy or in science
(C) either in philosophy or science
(D) in either philosophy or science
(E) it was in either philosophy or in science

10 Han liked to read horror stories, of which she found the Edgar Allan Poe tales particularly frightening.

(A) stories, of which she found the Edgar Allan Poe tales particularly frightening
(B) stories; she found the Edgar Allan Poe tales particularly frightening
(C) stories, and it was particularly the Edgar Allan Poe tales that were frightening
(D) stories; the frightening Edgar Allan Poe tales particularly
(E) stories, especially frightening to her were the Edgar Allan Poe tales

11 Hearing that the elementary school did not have a library, a fundraising drive was launched by the district's PTA for the creation of one.

(A) a fundraising drive was launched by the district's PTA for the creation of one
(B) a fundraising drive to create one was launched by the district's PTA
(C) a fundraising drive was launched for the creation of one by the district's PTA
(D) the district's PTA launched a fundraising drive for the creation of one
(E) the district's PTA had launched a fundraising drive for one's creation

GO ON TO THE NEXT PAGE

The following sentences test your ability to recognize grammar and usage errors. Each sentence contains either a single error or no error at all. No sentence contains more than one error. The error, if there is one, is underlined and lettered. If the sentence contains an error, select the one underlined part that must be changed to make the sentence correct. If the sentence is correct, select choice E. In choosing answers, follow the requirements of standard written English.

EXAMPLE: ANSWER:

<u>Whenever</u> one is driving late at night, <u>you</u> must take extra precautions <u>against</u>
   A   B   C

Ⓐ ● Ⓒ Ⓓ Ⓔ

falling asleep <u>at</u> the wheel. <u>No error</u>
         D   E

---

12 The theater department <u>belatedly announced</u> that
                         A

the series of lectures <u>were</u> <u>likely to</u> be postponed
                 B   C

<u>indefinitely</u>. <u>No error</u>
   D   E

13 <u>Only after</u> counting the ballots three times <u>was</u> the
    A   B

election officials able <u>to announce that</u> the mayor
                   C

<u>had been reelected</u>. <u>No error</u>
     D   E

14 As a result of an <u>extremely dedicated</u> group of
                A

fundraisers, our <u>contribution to</u> the United Way
              B

<u>will be</u> twice as much <u>as last year</u>. <u>No error</u>
  C   D   E

15 Our art class decided <u>to paint</u> a series of murals similar
               A

<u>with the ones</u> <u>painted by</u> the environmental artist
   B   C

Wyland <u>in California</u>. <u>No error</u>
      D   E

16 The tremendous commitment that young figure skaters

<u>have to make</u> in order to earn a place on the Olympic
  A

team <u>are impossible</u> <u>without the help</u> and support
     B   C

<u>of their families</u>. <u>No error</u>
    D   E

---

17 <u>Unfortunately</u>, private universities are able to offer larger
  A

scholarships than state schools do <u>and, until</u> our local
                       B

junior colleges receive the same funding <u>as other states</u>,
                           C

this disparity <u>will remain</u>. <u>No error</u>
     D   E

18 We <u>received</u> an overdue notice from the phone
    A

company, but the bill <u>to which</u> <u>it infers</u> is <u>one that</u> we
             B   C   D

already paid. <u>No error</u>
       E

19 <u>Although</u> our new house <u>has</u> hardwood floors, ceramic
  A   B

tile, and wall-to-wall carpeting, I must confess <u>to liking</u>
                               C

the hardwood floors <u>better</u>. <u>No error</u>
         D   E

20 <u>Nearly half</u> of the members <u>of our concert choir</u>
    A   B

graduated in June, <u>and replacing them</u>
               C

<u>has not been</u> easy. <u>No error</u>
  D   E

GO ON TO THE NEXT PAGE

21 The designers of the clothing <u>that was worn</u> at the
                                    A
fashion show <u>includes</u> <u>more than</u> a dozen students <u>who</u>
              B   C   D
had never shown their work before. <u>No error</u>
                                        E

22 Since <u>moving</u> to Maple Drive, we <u>been</u> <u>having</u> trouble
          A   B   C
getting <u>to the bus stop</u> on time. <u>No error</u>
         D   E

23 The federal government <u>provides</u> low-interest
                            A
loans that allow students <u>of deferring</u> payment
                            B
<u>until</u> they graduate and begin <u>to work</u>. <u>No error</u>
 C   D   E

24 The artists <u>participating</u> in the craft show <u>discovered</u>
                A   B
that the benefit of having a booth close to the food

vendors <u>were</u> <u>even greater</u> than they expected.
         C   D
<u>No error</u>
 E

25 <u>In many cases</u>, credit card companies <u>allow</u> their
    A   B
customers to pay their bills online as well as by mail,

<u>since</u> online payments can be processed <u>fastest</u>.
 C   D
<u>No error</u>
 E

26 Of all the restaurants in town, those <u>belonging to</u> the
                                          A
Charlie's chain <u>offers</u> the <u>highest</u> starting salary
                 B   C
<u>for part-time workers</u>. <u>No error</u>
 D   E

27 <u>That</u> the Superbowl was the <u>most</u> highly rated
    A   B
television show last week came as no surprise to

the sponsors <u>whose</u> commercials <u>aired</u> during the
               C   D
broadcast. <u>No error</u>
             E

28 My <u>older</u> sister and <u>me</u> <u>gratefully</u> accepted the ride
        A   B   C
<u>offered</u> by our next-door neighbor. <u>No error</u>
 D   E

29 <u>Although</u> the level of income earned by the
    A
two companies <u>keep</u> rising, their owner
                B
<u>claims that</u> he <u>has not made</u> a profit. <u>No error</u>
 C   D   E

GO ON TO THE NEXT PAGE

Directions: The following passage is an early draft of an essay. Some parts of the passage need to be rewritten.

Read the passage and select the best answer for each question that follows. Some questions are about particular sentences or parts of sentences and ask you to improve sentence structure or word choice. Other questions ask you to consider organization and development. In choosing answers, follow the conventions of standard written English.

Questions 30–35 are based on the following passage.

(1) The twenty-first century has seen a marked increase in the popularity of natural medicines and therapies. (2) The most wide used of these is believed to be the Native American sweat lodge. (3) Nearly every culture has adopted this practice in some form, including the Finnish sauna and the Jewish shvitz. (4) The basic purpose of these therapies is to raise the body's core temperature to between 102 and 106 degrees Fahrenheit. (5) The heat can also ease muscle tension and soreness, the resulting perspiration flushes the system of toxins.

(6) A traditional Native American sweat lodge is built of willow. (7) Its bark is considered to be medicinal. (8) It contains the same analgesic as aspirin. (9) Originally covered with animal skins, the lodges today are more likely to be made with canvas or blankets. (10) Large rocks are heated and brought inside the lodge. (11) Water is then poured over the rocks, filling the lodge with steam.

(12) The original sweat lodge ceremonies, which often included songs, prayers, and chants, were believed to purify not only the body, it also purified the mind. (13) "Healing comes on a spiritual level," wrote Dr. Lewis Mehl-Madrona in his book *Coyote Medicine*. (14) "Ceremony and ritual provide the means of making ourselves available."

30 Of the following, which is the best version of sentence 2 (reproduced below)?

The most wide used of these is believed to be the Native American sweat lodge.

(A) (As it is now)
(B) The more wide used of these is believed to be the Native American sweat lodge.
(C) The more widely used of these is believed to be the Native American sweat lodge.
(D) The most widely used of these is believed to be the Native American sweat lodge.
(E) The most wide used of these is believed to being the Native American sweat lodge.

31 Of the following, which is the best version of sentence 4 (reproduced below)?

The basic purpose of these therapies is to raise the body's core temperature to between 102 and 106 degrees Fahrenheit.

(A) (As it is now)
(B) The basic purpose of these therapies are to raise the body's core temperature to between 102 and 106 degrees Fahrenheit.
(C) The basic purpose of these therapies is to raising the body's core temperature to between 102 and 106 degrees Fahrenheit.
(D) The basic purpose of these therapies are to raising the body's core temperature to between 102 and 106 degrees Fahrenheit.
(E) The basic purpose of these therapies is to raise the body's core temperature to between 102 or 106 degrees Fahrenheit.

32 Which of the following would be the most suitable sentence to insert immediately after sentence 4?

(A) Many Native American remedies are now being prescribed by medical professionals.
(B) Turkey and Russia also have similar forms of heat therapy.
(C) This is approximately three to seven degrees above normal.
(D) At this temperature, bacterial and viral infections within the body cannot easily survive.
(E) This is done with steam.

33 In context, which of the following is best to insert after the comma in sentence 5 (reproduced below)?

The heat can also ease muscle tension and soreness, the resulting perspiration flushes the system of toxins.

(A) however
(B) or
(C) but
(D) and
(E) consequently

34 Which of the following is the best way to combine sentences 6, 7, and 8 (reproduced below) in order to convey clearly the relationship of the ideas?

A traditional Native American sweat lodge is built of willow. Its bark is considered to be medicinal. It contains the same analgesic as aspirin.

(A) A traditional Native American sweat lodge is built of willow, its bark is considered to be medicinal and it contains the same analgesic as aspirin.
(B) A traditional Native American sweat lodge is built of willow, having its bark considered to be medicinal and containing the same analgesic as aspirin.
(C) A traditional Native American sweat lodge, built of willow, has bark that is considered to be medicinal and contains the same analgesic as aspirin.
(D) A traditional Native American sweat lodge, built of willow, with bark considered to be medicinal and containing the same analgesic as aspirin.
(E) A traditional Native American sweat lodge is built of willow; its bark is considered to be medicinal and, indeed, contains the same analgesic as aspirin.

35 In context, what is the best version of the underlined portion of sentence 12 (reproduced below)?

The original sweat lodge ceremonies, which often included songs, prayers, and chants, were believed to purify not only the body, it also purified the mind.

(A) (As it is now)
(B) not the body, but the mind
(C) not only the body, but also the mind
(D) not only the body, but the mind
(E) the body, it also purified the mind

Time—25 Minutes
24 Questions

Directions: For each question in this section, select the best answer from among the choices given and fill in the corresponding oval on the answer sheet.

Each sentence below has one or two blanks, each blank indicating that something has been omitted. Beneath the sentence are five words or sets of words labeled A through E. Choose the word or set of words that, when inserted in the sentence, best fits the meaning of the sentence as a whole.

EXAMPLE:

Today's small, portable computers contrast markedly with the earliest electronic computers, which were -------.

(A) effective   (B) invented
  (C) useful   (D) destructive
    (E) enormous

ANSWER:
Ⓐ Ⓑ Ⓒ Ⓓ ●

---

1 Although animator Walt Disney is best known for his storytelling gifts, his technical innovations, such as the multi-plane camera, are equally -------.

(A) comical   (B) obscure
  (C) generous   (D) notable
    (E) garrulous

2 The use of alternative remedies, such as zinc, to ------- the symptoms of colds has become popular in recent years, even if scientific studies have yet to prove their effectiveness as cures.

(A) alleviate   (B) discover
  (C) energize   (D) exterminate
    (E) augment

3 When the reclusive movie star left the hotel, ------- of burly bodyguards surrounded her to ------- photographers from taking her picture.

(A) an alliance . . protect
(B) a dearth . . circumscribe
(C) a suite . . absorb
(D) a band . . prevent
(E) a debate . . distract

4 Only a handful of people at the publishing house actually knew that Richard Bachman was a ------- adopted by the author Stephen King; the pen name was eventually revealed to the general public.

(A) copyright   (B) tribute
  (C) diminutive   (D) fallacy
    (E) pseudonym

5 The circumspection of the workers around their boss directly contrasts with the ------- of the discussions they have among themselves.

(A) promotion   (B) caution
  (C) frailty   (D) candor
    (E) wariness

GO ON TO THE NEXT PAGE

Each passage below is followed by questions based on its content. Answer the questions on the basis of what is <u>stated</u> or <u>implied</u> in each passage and in any introductory material that may be provided.

Questions 6–7 are based on the following passage.

The Nizhny Novgorod art exhibition in 1896 generated a storm of controversy in Russian newspapers. Of the critics raising their voices on the
Line matter, it is Maxim Gorky who is most remembered.
(5) Although quite young at the time, Gorky's opinions on the exhibit would prove to be remarkably in keeping with his political beliefs later in life. As Gorky saw it, the majority of the art on display had been generated by an economy of exploitation that only rewarded
(10) artists who created works inaccessible to the general population. Gorky took the side of those deriding the artwork as aimed only at the elite.

6 In line 4, the word "matter" most nearly means

(A) value
(B) difficulty
(C) concern
(D) substance
(E) weight

7 The author uses the phrase "Although quite young at the time" (line 5) to emphasize that

(A) Gorky was not qualified to evaluate the exhibit
(B) the artists of the exhibit needed time to develop their talents
(C) opposition to the status quo was driven by a youth movement
(D) Gorky's beliefs were solidified early in his life
(E) Gorky's attitude toward the elite would change as he gained fame

Questions 8–9 are based on the following passage.

By the time I turned ten, my grandfather, a once jovial, loving man, was already grumpily and painfully entering his late eighties. Where before he was prone to
Line sneak up behind me and playfully sprinkle candies into
(5) my unsuspecting lap, as if it were magically raining sweets, later he became fixed upon his old leather recliner, grumbling about the weather and intimidating with snide remarks anyone who dared pass by his gigantic feet. His physical and emotional decline
(10) dragged on unmercifully, as if he himself, in some inexplicable state of self-loathing, wanted to hold onto every last bit of his discomfort before he could pass away peacefully.

8 The narrator's description of his grandfather's feet in line 9 contributes to a sense of the

(A) frightening nature of his grandfather's presence
(B) violence his grandfather was inclined toward
(C) grandfather's self-hatred
(D) grandfather's pitiable situation
(E) narrator's nostalgia for his grandfather's happier days

9 In line 9, "decline" most nearly means

(A) sinking
(B) descent
(C) failure
(D) deterioration
(E) waning

GO ON TO THE NEXT PAGE

Questions 10–16 are based on the following passage.

In this passage, the author discusses the evolution of the attitude of the Greeks toward the newly departed souls of the dead.

In Homer's time, ghosts and spirits were perceived as genial, nonthreatening creatures, prone to gossiping with each other about family members and making
Line long-winded speeches about famous battles and heroic
(5) relatives instead of frightening the living. They rarely bothered anyone, except when the living called on them for advice, and at worst might have been considered annoying pests: *The Iliad* refers to a particular spirit "vanish[ing] as a vapor, gibbering and
(10) whining into the earth." By the time Socrates was executed for atheism and other heretical beliefs, however, the Greeks believed ghosts and spirits were much more solid—even humanlike—beings of mercurial temperament; they also became distinctly
(15) more dangerous, soulless creatures who not only haunted houses, but roamed the streets nightly, terrorizing and occasionally physically harming or even killing anyone who crossed their paths.

One theory suggests that this change in perception
(20) may have actually been a way to control behavior. The Homeric Greeks initially viewed Hades as a dull place populated with dull people, and so the living were inclined to be indifferent towards the dead. Later, when reading, writing, philosophy, art, and drama became
(25) more widespread—in short, when the Greeks became more self-aware and concerned with recording their own ideas and history—they also gradually became fearful about the condition of their own souls in the afterlife. Political turmoil during the rise of the city-
(30) states may also have led to an atmosphere of anxiety and pessimism, which became a fertile breeding ground for supernatural belief among the Greeks. Accordingly, they then began to regulate "proper" behavior through religion, and devise talismanic rituals
(35) to control and manipulate the undead. Around the same time, ghosts suddenly became malevolent entities that could threaten and physically harm. Spirits could still be called upon for advice, but they could also, in turn, call on the living for favors, and demand sacrifices and
(40) other tokens such as coins, wine, and amulets. And Hades—that formerly neutral resting place for all souls—became instead a destination either of peace or punishment, depending both on the departed soul's behavior during life and the mourners' behavior during
(45) the burial. Professional mourners were even hired to wail and gnash their teeth during the burial ceremony, lest the spirit return and complain that the ritual wasn't elaborate enough. Moreover, the dead reached their final destination only after a postmortem otherworldly

(50) journey in which the spirit overcame a series of obstacles. Of course, like everything else, these journeys also became fodder for the Greeks' dramatic supernatural stories.

However, as more than one scholar has pointed out,
(55) the later Greeks postulated more than one theory about the fate of souls after death. Some, believing that the spirit stayed near the corpse, constructed rituals to encourage the benevolence of good spirits and to protect themselves from the malice of bad ones.
(60) Others, as previously mentioned, believed the soul descended to Hades, and a relative minority thought that the spirit died along with the body, leaving no remains—ethereal or otherwise. Spirits were even occasionally invited to Greek parties and festivals.
(65) Some Greeks held more than one belief about the afterlife simultaneously; this inconsistency only led to even more carefully constructed ceremonies and rituals, as the living tried to best each other at communicating with and controlling the dead. As the
(70) Greeks' supernatural belief system became more complex according to their historical and cultural needs, so too did their spirits, transforming into anthropomorphic beings that were at once both familiar and frighteningly arcane.

10 The author most likely includes the quotation from *The Iliad* in lines 9–10 in order to

(A) provide an example of a classical Greek text that specifically mentions a nonthreatening spirit
(B) demonstrate that not all Homeric ghosts threatened others
(C) introduce the idea that the living were often frightened by ghosts
(D) explain how Greeks tried to protect themselves from spirits
(E) suggest that ghosts held a place of social importance in Homer's time

11 In the first paragraph, the author mentions Homer and Socrates in order to

(A) compare their philosophical works
(B) contrast the social climates experienced by each one to illustrate how Greek perceptions of ghosts changed
(C) demonstrate how Homer and Socrates influenced Greek perceptions of ghosts
(D) identify the religious beliefs of two well-known Greek authors
(E) express the author's ambivalence toward religious beliefs in general

GO ON TO THE NEXT PAGE

12 The author describes spirits as having a "mercurial temperament" in line 14 to suggest that

(A) they were perceived as being more humanlike
(B) they continued to be polite and well-mannered
(C) they became more social with the living
(D) the Greeks demanded more from them
(E) they could only be appeased by material items

13 The author includes the examples of "coins, wine, and amulets" in line 40 in order to

(A) exemplify the types of items that later classical ghosts demanded
(B) show that the Greeks often overdramatized ghosts' wishes
(C) suggest that ghosts rarely required human sacrifices
(D) indicate that these spirits did not demand as much as their predecessors
(E) illustrate how demanding Greek ghosts could be

14 In line 41, "neutral" most closely means

(A) nonjudgmental
(B) uncolored
(C) non-acidic
(D) unaffected
(E) unengaged

15 The author mentions "Professional mourners" in line 45 in order to

(A) demonstrate the lengths the living would go to ensure that the dead would not return
(B) prove that the Greeks cared dearly about their dead
(C) illustrate a typical burial ceremony
(D) suggest that the Greeks were inconsistent in their theories about the dead
(E) imply that ghosts' demands were unreasonable

16 The phrase "ethereal or otherwise" (line 63) is used by the author to

(A) question the distinction between material and spiritual remains
(B) suggest that material, not spiritual, remains were left behind
(C) suggest that spiritual, not material, remains were left behind
(D) suggest that neither material nor spiritual remains were left behind
(E) refer to material tokens used to appease the ghosts

GO ON TO THE NEXT PAGE

Questions 17–24 are based on the following passage.

The following passage is excerpted from an article on animal behavior. It discusses the relationship between learning and instinct.

The learning behavior of many mammals is dictated by instinct, but tempered and refined by experience. Very complex behaviors can be learned through
Line individual trial-and-error or practice, as long as that
(5) practice is motivated by instinctive drives. For example, predatory cats aren't born knowing how to hunt, but instinct drives them to stalk, pounce on, and bite things they perceive as prey, and they gradually become more skilled and effective hunters. Wolves aren't born
(10) knowing how to get along with other wolves, but the experience of living in the pack, the correction and support they receive from elders, and the survival instinct that drives them to stay in the pack result in their eventually learning to find their place in the hierarchy
(15) and cooperate in group activities such as hunting and rearing young.

Some kinds of animal learning, however, are not so directly dependent on the need to survive. In the case of primates in particular, evolution seems to have
(20) fostered a behavior pattern that encourages restless experimentation and exploration of the environment apart from the search to fulfill basic needs. Among humans, for example, the discovery of the laws of gravity didn't directly bear on the survival of Isaac
(25) Newton, and the description of the properties of triangles didn't help Pythagoras put food on the table. Although these discoveries may later have indirectly improved the quality of life and survival potential of the discoverers' descendants, the lack of an immediate
(30) survival imperative suggests that experimenting, discovery, and sharing of the benefits of those discoveries have as much to do with enjoyment as with survival.

One nonhuman species for which we have
(35) documented evidence of this behavior is the Japanese snow monkey (*Macaque fuscata*) of the remote mountain forests of Japan. Snow monkeys have a complex society, with each troop organized in a rigid hierarchy, regulated and maintained by the usual range
(40) of primate social behaviors: displays of aggression and submission, mutual grooming, distribution of food based on status, and so forth. Snow monkeys face unusual challenges to survive because of their inhospitable environment. Temperatures may fall as
(45) low as −15° C in deep winter, and when food grows scarce during cold weather the monkeys are often forced to live on tree buds, bark, and the stores of body fat accumulated during summer. Even in warmer months, much of the day of a snow monkey is occupied with the

(50) search for food, the avoidance of predators, and the negotiation of complex social relations with other monkeys.

Yet, in spite of the time and effort it takes to stay alive in their environment, snow monkeys exhibit some
(55) unusually sophisticated recreational behaviors. They are good swimmers, for example, and monkeys living near coastal areas are known to dive for shellfish. Some researchers think that perhaps snow monkeys also swim in thermal hot spring pools in the mountains.
(60) Although skeptics might say these particular behaviors grow from the need to stay warm and fed in harsh conditions, certain theorists believe that the monkeys may be engaging in these activities because they derive some kind of satisfaction that isn't related to the need
(65) for food, warmth, or other biological drives. For example, snow monkeys have also been observed to make snowballs, rolling the snow first in their hands and then enlarging the snowballs by rolling them along the ground, apparently as a social activity.
(70) The most famous case of an activity of this type seeping into snow monkey society was the case of Imo, the monkey who discovered potato washing. Researchers observing snow monkeys in their natural habitat had placed sweet potatoes on the beach to draw
(75) the monkeys out of the woods and into view. Usually the monkeys prepared the potatoes for eating by brushing the dirt off the outside with their hands. But one day a particular snow monkey, a male named Imo, stumbled on the trick of washing the dirt off the potato
(80) in the sea. Other monkeys observed and copied the new trick, and the technique quickly became popular and spread throughout Imo's troop and even to other snow monkey troops. Although one might argue that the practice of potato washing relates to survival, in
(85) fact it isn't necessarily more efficient than removing dirt in other ways. Furthermore, the fact that snow monkeys have been demonstrated to prefer to wash their potatoes in salt water rather than fresh water, perhaps because it improves the flavor, suggests that
(90) the motivation for the behavior has more to do with enjoyment than with survival.

17 The word "tempered" in line 2 is closest in meaning to

(A) angered
(B) hardened
(C) influenced
(D) suppressed
(E) commanded

GO ON TO THE NEXT PAGE

18 Which situation described below would be most similar to the pattern of learning described in paragraph 1?

(A) A hobbyist learns how to knit by reading a book on arts and crafts.

(B) An octopus figures out how to twist the top off of a jar to get at food it can see inside.

(C) A basketball player improves his ability to shoot free throws by practicing every day.

(D) A leafcutter ant hatches knowing how to harvest and store leaves.

(E) Math students learn how to use a geometry formula by watching a teacher demonstrate.

19 In lines 22–26, the author lists famous discoverers primarily in order to

(A) contrast human discoverers with animal discoverers

(B) prove an argument about the way that discoveries benefit later generations

(C) suggest that discoveries are usually accidental

(D) demonstrate that discoveries aren't always inspired by a need to survive

(E) show a contrast between useful discoveries and inconclusive experimentation

20 Which of the following is an example of the principle mentioned in lines 53–55?

(A) Adult lions occasionally leave a wounded antelope alive so that their cubs can practice killing it.

(B) Alligators will respond aggressively to the distress cries of young alligators, even if the young are not their own offspring.

(C) At a certain age, human babies begin to imitate the facial expressions of any adult in their field of view.

(D) Elephants sometimes draw abstract shapes on the ground with a rock or stick held in their trunks.

(E) Howler monkeys use extended, characteristic cries every morning to gather the troop together before setting out to forage for food.

21 The main difference between the opinions of "skeptics" (line 60) and those of "certain theorists" (line 62) is about whether

(A) snow monkeys could survive winter without thermal pools to keep them warm

(B) activities such as diving for shellfish are primarily motivated by the need for survival

(C) washing potatoes is the most efficient way to clean them

(D) making snowballs is a response to a biological drive

(E) snow monkeys are intelligent enough to imitate new ways of doing things

22 The author most likely included the discussion of snow monkeys making snowballs (lines 65–69) in order to suggest that this behavior

(A) serves no survival function

(B) is a social activity

(C) increases manual dexterity

(D) is often engaged in by snow monkeys

(E) is related to a monkey's place in the social hierarchy

23 Which of the following statements is primarily supported by the "most famous case" referred to in line 70?

(A) Mammals living in a remote environment are more difficult to observe.

(B) The more challenges to survival that animals face in their native environment, the more likely they are to creatively seek new discoveries.

(C) Snow monkeys are capable of learning new survival strategies by observation.

(D) Researchers have only recently learned to look for discovery behaviors in snow monkeys.

(E) Snow monkeys demonstrate behaviors not directly related to survival needs.

GO ON TO THE NEXT PAGE

24 The example of the potato washing behavior
(lines 77–91) primarily serves to

(A) explain how a popular theory can be disproved
   by additional findings
(B) show the opposition of certain researchers to
   new data
(C) demonstrate that different explanations might share
   a logical relationship
(D) enlarge the discussion by incorporating an
   alternative explanation
(E) make an argument stronger by including
   supporting evidence

IF YOU FINISH BEFORE TIME IS CALLED, YOU MAY CHECK YOUR WORK ON
THIS SECTION ONLY. DO NOT TURN TO ANY OTHER SECTION IN THE TEST.

STOP

NO TEST MATERIAL ON THIS PAGE

Time—25 Minutes
20 Questions

Directions: For this section, solve each problem and decide which is the best of the choices given. Fill in the corresponding oval on the answer sheet. You may use any available space for scratchwork.

1. Calculator use is permitted.

2. All numbers used are real numbers.

3. Figures are provided for some problems. All figures are drawn to scale and lie in a plane UNLESS otherwise indicated.

4. Unless otherwise specified, the domain of any function f is assumed to be the set of all real numbers x for which $f(x)$ is a real number.

Reference Information

$A = \dfrac{1}{2}bh$ $c^2 = a^2 + b^2$ Special Right Triangles $A = \pi r^2$ $V = \pi r^2 h$ $A = lw$ $V = lwh$
$C = 2\pi r$

The sum of the measures in degrees of the angles of a triangle is 180.
The number of degrees of arc in a circle is 360.
A straight angle has a degree measure of 180.

---

1 If $\dfrac{j-4}{j-2} = 3j$, which of the following must be true?

(A) j is odd.
(B) $j = -1$
(C) j is an integer.
(D) j is not an integer.
(E) $j \neq 2$

2 If n is a positive integer divisible by 7, and if $n < 70$, what is the greatest possible value of n ?

(A) 61
(B) 62
(C) 63
(D) 64
(E) 65

GO ON TO THE NEXT PAGE

3 The letter A is symmetric with respect to only one line, as shown by the dotted line in the figure above. Which of the following letters is NOT symmetric with respect to exactly one line?

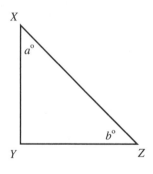

(A) B

(B) C

(C) K

(D) N

(E) Y

5 If $p^2q^2 = 9$ what is the value of $(3 \times \frac{p^2}{q^2} \times q^4)$?

(A) 3
(B) 6
(C) 9
(D) 12
(E) 27

6 If the average (arithmetic mean) of 4, 4, 8, 11, and y is equal to $2y$, what is the value of y ?

(A) 2
(B) 3
(C) 4
(D) 5
(E) 6

4 If $XY = YZ$ and $\angle XYZ$ measures 90° in the figure above, which of the following CANNOT be concluded?

(A) $a = b$
(B) $XZ < XY$
(C) $XY \perp YZ$
(D) $a + b = 90$
(E) $XZ^2 = XY^2 + YZ^2$

GO ON TO THE NEXT PAGE

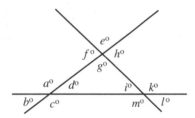

7 Three line segments intersect at various locations in a plane as shown in the figure above. Knowledge of which of the following pairs of angle measures is NOT sufficient for determining all 12 angle measures?

(A) a and g
(B) f and l
(C) i and m
(D) k and b
(E) e and c

8 A computer randomly selects a positive, two-digit number. If the number selected is prime, twice that number is displayed. If the number selected is not prime, the number itself is displayed. If the number displayed is 34, which of the following could have been the number selected?

I. 17
II. 34
III. 68

(A) I only
(B) II only
(C) I and II only
(D) I and III only
(E) I, II, and III

$$BC$$
$$+CB$$
$$\overline{1C4}$$

9 In the correctly worked addition problem above, B and C represent two different, non-zero digits. What digit does B represent?

(A) 3
(B) 4
(C) 5
(D) 7
(E) 9

$$[4 \otimes (7 \spadesuit 5)] + 6 = 14$$

10 In the equation above, $\otimes$ and $\spadesuit$ each represent a different arithmetic operation ($+$, $-$, $\times$, or $\div$). Which of the following equals $4 \otimes (7 \spadesuit 5)$?

(A) $5 \otimes 4$
(B) $5 \spadesuit 4$
(C) $7 \otimes 5$
(D) $2 \otimes (9 \spadesuit 5)$
(E) $9 \spadesuit 5$

GO ON TO THE NEXT PAGE

11 If set R contains 10 distinct even integers and set S contains 10 distinct negative integers, what is the maximum possible number of elements in the intersection of the two sets?

(A) 0
(B) 4
(C) 6
(D) 9
(E) 10

13 The positive difference of two numbers that add up to 3 is p. In terms of p, what is the value of the greater of the two numbers?

(A) $\dfrac{p-3}{2}$

(B) $\dfrac{p}{2}$

(C) $\dfrac{p+3}{2}$

(D) $\dfrac{p}{2}+3$

(E) $\dfrac{2p-3}{2}$

14 How many positive integers that are less than 151 are not the cube of an integer?

(A) 75
(B) 125
(C) 138
(D) 144
(E) 145

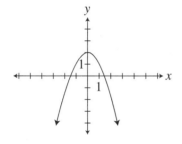

12 Which of the following equations best describes the curve in the figure above?

(A) $y = x^2 - 2$

(B) $y = x^2 + 2$

(C) $y = -x^2$

(D) $y = 1 - x^2$

(E) $y = 2 - x^2$

GO ON TO THE NEXT PAGE

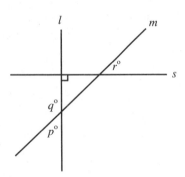

15 In the figure above, if $p = 20$, what is the value of $q + r$?

(A)   70
(B)   90
(C)   130
(D)   160
(E)   230

16 If $x - 5y = 0$, for what value of y is $x = y$?

(A) 0

(B) $\dfrac{1}{5}$

(C) 1

(D) 5

(E) x can never equal y.

17 If the sum of the consecutive integers from -9 to f, inclusive, is 46, what is the value of f?

(A) 10
(B) 13
(C) 26
(D) 39
(E) 55

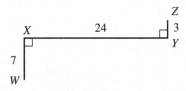

18 The figure above shows the route of Gina's trip from her apartment to her gym. Gina travels 7 miles from W to X, 24 miles from X to Y, and 3 miles from Y to Z. If she were able to travel from W to Z directly, how much shorter, in miles, would the trip be?

(A)   5
(B)   8
(C)   10
(D)   14
(E)   24

GO ON TO THE NEXT PAGE

$$a + \frac{1}{a} = p$$

$$a - \frac{1}{a} = q$$

19 In the equations above, if $a \neq 0$ which of the following must be equal to $p^2 + q^2$?

(A) 4

(B) $2a^2$

(C) $\dfrac{a}{2}$

(D) $2\left(a^2 + \dfrac{1}{a^2}\right)$

(E) $\dfrac{2}{a^2}$

20 If $a^3 = (-x)^2$, which of the following could be true?

I. $a < 0$
II. $a = 0$
III. $a > 0$

(A) II only
(B) III only
(C) I and II only
(D) II and III only
(E) I, II, and III

IF YOU FINISH BEFORE TIME IS CALLED, YOU MAY CHECK YOUR WORK ON THIS SECTION ONLY. DO NOT TURN TO ANY OTHER SECTION IN THE TEST.

STOP

Time—25 Minutes
24 Questions

Directions: For each question in this section, select the best answer from among the choices given and fill in the corresponding oval on the answer sheet.

Each sentence below has one or two blanks, each blank indicating that something has been omitted. Beneath the sentence are five words or sets of words labeled A through E. Choose the word or set of words that, when inserted in the sentence, best fits the meaning of the sentence as a whole.

EXAMPLE:

Today's small, portable computers contrast markedly with the earliest electronic computers, which were -------.

(A) effective   (B) invented
 (C) useful   (D) destructive
    (E) enormous

ANSWER:
Ⓐ Ⓑ Ⓒ Ⓓ ●

---

1 To ------- the seasonal migration of caribou, engineers ------- the trans-Alaska pipeline in over 500 locations to allow large animals access across the pipeline corridor.

(A) banish . . buried
(B) preserve . . elevated
(C) admire . . razed
(D) prevent . . erected
(E) enable . . delivered

2 Most people today think of licorice as candy; however, the ------- properties of the licorice root were once relied on to treat coughs, digestive problems, and insomnia.

(A) somnolent   (B) basic
 (C) sweet   (D) indelible
    (E) medicinal

3 Like all other -------, lionesses give birth to live -------.

(A) mammals . . offspring
(B) reptiles . . shells
(C) creatures . . babies
(D) snakes . . eggs
(E) amphibians . . lakes

4 Amy was nothing like her ------- older brother; she lived a restrained, responsible life close to her childhood home.

(A) ardent   (B) critical
 (C) wayward   (D) charming
    (E) accountable

5 When the election results were announced, the victorious candidate's exhilaration temporarily ------- the recognition of the forthcoming ------- to improve the economic climate of the city.

(A) accepted . . promise
(B) illuminated . . campaign
(C) admitted . . hostility
(D) overshadowed . . struggle
(E) blocked . . inauguration

6 After recovering from a snowboarding accident that resulted in a broken wrist, Vivian was glad to be -------; she could write equally as well with her left hand as with her right hand.

(A) ambidextrous   (B) hapless
 (C) erroneous   (D) sinister
    (E) athletic

7 To attract moviegoers today, film scripts must be both ------- and -------; audiences no longer care to see even their favorite stars spout the usual clichés in the same tired stories.

(A) popular . . indented
(B) well-written . . novel
(C) erudite . . banal
(D) terse . . redundant
(E) original . . trite

8 Sylvie's essay was almost too -------; she may have sacrificed some useful context in her desire to be as concise as possible in explaining her thesis.

(A) diligent   (B) profligate
 (C) equitable   (D) verbose
    (E) terse

GO ON TO THE NEXT PAGE

The passages below are followed by questions based on their content; questions following a pair of related passages may also be based on the relationship between the paired passages. Answer the questions on the basis of what is <u>stated</u> or <u>implied</u> in the passages and in any introductory material that may be provided.

Questions 9–12 are based on the following passages.

Passage 1

Internet access has become an increasingly necessary and invaluable workplace resource for countless American businesses. However, like most
Line technological advancements, this one has also brought
(5) with it significant drawbacks. More specifically, recent survey results released by several workplace watchdog organizations demonstrate that an alarming 60 percent of employees likely visit websites for personal use while at work, a 20 percent increase over the previous
(10) year. In addition—and even more discouraging for management executives charged with keeping productivity levels high—some workplace studies suggest that the average employee spends more than 33 minutes online every day tending to personal needs, a
(15) number supported by usage statistics gathered from many of the most popular shopping and personal care websites themselves.

Passage 2

In the ongoing, and often hushed-up, battle between corporate management and their own employees, new
(20) statistics reveal that a growing number of executives are turning to advanced surveillance techniques to monitor and crack down on so-called "inappropriate" Internet usage at work. Yet, while such methods have proven to be effective at restoring workplace
(25) productivity, some employee advocacy groups have begun to raise serious ethical questions. With 77 percent of American businesses now committed to carefully monitoring the Internet browsing habits of their workforces, the stakes have never been higher. In
(30) particular, while there are numerous arguments both for and against this trend, the legal questions surrounding possible violations of employee privacy rights could be dire.

9 In line 15, "supported" most nearly means

(A) approved
(B) encouraged
(C) defended
(D) confirmed
(E) grounded

10 The author of Passage 2 uses the phrase "the stakes have never been higher" (line 29) to suggest

(A) inappropriate employee Internet usage can threaten the success of a company
(B) workplace productivity levels have decreased significantly
(C) soon nearly 100 percent of companies will use such tactics
(D) many companies could become entangled in legal disputes with their employees
(E) it is illegal for companies to crack down on employee Internet usage

11 The passages differ in tone in that Passage 1 is

(A) purely objective, while Passage 2 firmly supports crackdowns on inappropriate Internet usage
(B) concerned about workplace inefficiencies created by the Internet, while Passage 2 is concerned with the implications of workplace surveillance
(C) sensitive to the needs of employees, while Passage 2 is more concerned with the responsibilities of management
(D) openly critical of employees who visit websites for personal use, while Passage 2 is less subjective
(E) supportive of efforts to limit employee Internet access in the workplace, while Passage 2 indicates the legal ramifications of such limits are too costly

12 Both passages illustrate the idea that Internet access in the workplace

(A) is perhaps not worth all the trouble it can cause
(B) is a necessary resource with manageable consequences
(C) has raised new and challenging problems
(D) may soon become a thing of the past
(E) can seriously hamper workplace productivity

GO ON TO THE NEXT PAGE

Questions 13–24 are based on the following passage.

In the following passage, the author explores some contrasts in the way that Arabs and Americans relate to each other spatially.

In spite of over two thousand years of contact, Westerners and Arabs still do not understand each other. Americans visiting the Middle East are immediately
Line struck by two conflicting sensations. In public, they are
(5) compressed and overwhelmed by smells, crowding, and high noise levels; in Arab homes, Americans are apt to rattle around, feeling somewhat exposed and inadequate because there is too much space.

Proxemics, the study of people's responses to
(10) spatial relationships, can shed a lot of light on these misunderstandings. One of my earliest discoveries in the field of intercultural communication was that the position of the bodies of people in conversation varies from culture to culture. It used to puzzle me that a special
(15) Arab friend seemed unable to walk and talk at the same time. After years in the United States, he could not bring himself to stroll along, facing forward while talking. Our progress would always be arrested while he edged ahead, cutting slightly in front of me and turning sideways so
(20) we could see each other. Once in this position, he would stop. His behavior was explained when I learned that for the Arabs, to view another person peripherally is regarded as impolite. In Arab culture, you are expected to be involved when interacting with friends.

(25) This emphasis on involvement and participation also expresses itself in Arab cities, where the notion of privacy in a public place is a foreign concept. Business transactions in the bazaar, for example, are not just conducted between buyer and seller, but are participated
(30) in by everyone. Anyone who is standing around may join in. If a grownup sees a boy breaking a window, he must stop him even if he doesn't know him. If two men are fighting, the crowd must intervene. On a political level, when a government such as ours fails to intervene when
(35) trouble is brewing, this is construed as taking sides. But given the fact that few people in the world today are even remotely aware of the cultural mold that forms their thoughts, it is normal for Arabs to view our behavior as though it stemmed from their own hidden set of
(40) assumptions.

In the home, the Arab dream is for lots of space, which unfortunately many Arabs cannot afford. Yet when an Arab has space, it is very different from what one finds in most American homes. Spaces inside Arab
(45) upper-middle-class homes are tremendous by our standards. They avoid partitions because Arabs do not like to be alone. The form of the home is such as to hold the family together inside a single protective shell, creating an environment where personalities are
(50) intermingled and take nourishment from each other like the roots and soil. If one is not with people and actively involved in some way, one is deprived of life. An old Arab saying reflects this value: "Paradise without people should not be entered because it is Hell." For this reason,
(55) Arabs in the United States often feel socially and sensorially deprived and long to be back where there is human warmth and contact.

Since there is no physical privacy as we know it in the Arab family, not even a word for privacy, one could
(60) expect that the Arabs might use some other means to be alone. Their way to be alone is to stop talking. Like the English, an Arab who shuts himself off in this way is not indicating that anything is wrong or that he is withdrawing, only that he wants to be alone with his
(65) thoughts or does not want to be intruded upon. One subject I interviewed said that her father would come and go for days at a time without saying a word, and no one in the family thought anything of it. Yet for this very reason, an Arab exchange student visiting a Kansas farm failed to
(70) pick up the cue that his American hosts were mad at him when they gave him the "silent treatment." He only discovered something was wrong when they took him to town and tried forcibly to put him on a bus to Washington, D.C., the headquarters of the exchange
(75) program responsible for his presence in the United States.

13 The main purpose of the passage is to

(A) show how cultural differences resulted in the expulsion of an Arab exchange student from his host home
(B) argue for stronger attempts by Americans to understand unique aspects of other cultures
(C) explain differences in the ways that Arabs and Americans view personal and physical space
(D) discuss Arabs' outlook on the role of privacy in public spaces
(E) criticize the concept of proxemics as it has been applied to Arab peoples

14 According to the passage, the "two conflicting sensations" that Americans experience in the Middle East (line 4) are

(A) understanding and confusion
(B) involvement and participation
(C) friendliness and hostility
(D) crowding and spaciousness
(E) silence and noise

GO ON TO THE NEXT PAGE

15 The author most likely describes the behavior of his Arab friend (lines 14–21) in order to

(A) cite an incident which led to a breakthrough in his research
(B) support the idea that Americans and Arabs cannot communicate with each other
(C) demonstrate that Arabs respond differently to spatial relationships
(D) emphasize the difficulty of learning the customs of other countries
(E) point out the impersonal nature of American cities

16 The author's friend was most likely "unable to walk and talk at the same time" (lines 15–16) because

(A) he was fascinated by American cities
(B) his command of spoken English was poor
(C) he was not familiar with Western customs
(D) he was unaccustomed to talking in public
(E) he did not wish to seem rude

17 The word "arrested" is used in line 18 to mean

(A) apprehended
(B) delayed
(C) anticipated
(D) accelerated
(E) annoyed

18 The phrase "foreign concept" (line 27) is used to indicate that Arabs

(A) prefer not to conduct business transactions in public
(B) regard the right to privacy as an American idea
(C) behave toward friends and strangers in different ways
(D) do not recognize a custom that is common elsewhere
(E) are gradually adjusting to Western ways of life

19 In lines 32–33, the custom of intervening when two men fight is presented as an example of the Arabs'

(A) compassion for strangers
(B) desire to appear polite
(C) respect for law and order
(D) dislike of personal conflict
(E) emphasis on public participation

20 The author most likely regards the Arabs' attitude towards government policy (lines 33–35) as

(A) an effective strategy for resolving international disputes
(B) a typical Western misunderstanding of Arab culture
(C) an overly simplistic approach to the complexities of foreign policy
(D) an understandable reaction, given how little most people know about other cultures
(E) a symptom of the problems involved in Middle Eastern politics

21 According to paragraph 4, the most crucial difference between American homes and Arab homes lies in the

(A) average cost of a house
(B) size of house available
(C) number of occupants housed
(D) use of space inside the house
(E) area of land surrounding the house

22 The word "value" is used in line 53 to mean

(A) belief
(B) cost
(C) number
(D) level
(E) rate

23 Judging from the discussion in paragraph 5, silence in Arab culture is often a way to

(A) resolve arguments between relatives
(B) indicate displeasure with guests
(C) express unhappiness within families
(D) communicate involvement with friends
(E) obtain a psychological form of privacy

24 The author uses the story about the Arab exchange student (lines 68–75) primarily to illustrate that

(A) Arabs visiting the United States often experience homesickness
(B) ignoring other people is rarely an effective form of punishment
(C) silence is not considered unusual in Arab households
(D) Arab and American cultures share a similar sense of humor
(E) it is difficult to recognize anger in foreign cultures

IF YOU FINISH BEFORE TIME IS CALLED, YOU MAY CHECK YOUR WORK ON THIS SECTION ONLY. DO NOT TURN TO ANY OTHER SECTION IN THE TEST.

STOP

<table>
<tr><td>Time—25 Minutes
18 Questions</td><td>Directions: This section contains two types of questions. You have 25 minutes to complete both types. For questions 1–8, solve each problem and decide which is the best of the choices given. Fill in the corresponding oval on the answer sheet. You may use any available space for scratchwork.</td></tr>
</table>

Notes

1. Calculator use is permitted.

2. All numbers used are real numbers.

3. Figures are provided for some problems. All figures are drawn to scale and lie in a plane UNLESS otherwise indicated.

4. Unless otherwise specified, the domain of any function f is assumed to be the set of all real numbers x for which $f(x)$ is a real number.

Reference Information

  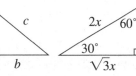 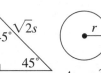

$A = \dfrac{1}{2}bh$ $c^2 = a^2 + b^2$ Special Right Triangles $A = \pi r^2$ $V = \pi r^2 h$ $A = lw$ $V = lwh$

$C = 2\pi r$

The sum of the measures in degrees of the angles of a triangle is 180.
The number of degrees of arc in a circle is 360.
A straight angle has a degree measure of 180.

1 If $a^2 - 16 = 0$, then one possible value of a is:

(A) –8
(B) –4
(C) 0
(D) 2
(E) 16

2 A bookshelf contains b books. After m books are moved to a different shelf, there are l books left. Which of the following is true?

(A) $m = b + l$
(B) $m = b - l$
(C) $m = l - b$
(D) $m = lb$
(E) $m = \dfrac{b}{l}$

GO ON TO THE NEXT PAGE

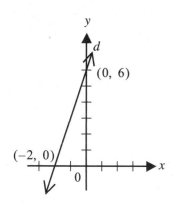

3 In the figure above, what is the slope of line d ?

(A) -3

(B) 3

(C) $-\dfrac{1}{3}$

(D) $\dfrac{1}{3}$

(E) $-\dfrac{1}{6}$

4 For what value of a does $8^2 \times 8^a = 8^{10}$?

(A) 1
(B) 5
(C) 8
(D) 12
(E) 20

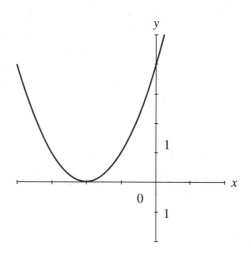

5 The graph of function r is shown above. Which of the following equations could represent r ?

(A) $r(x) = x^2 + 5x + 5$
(B) $r(x) = x^2 + 4x + 4$
(C) $r(x) = x^2 + 3x + 6$
(D) $r(x) = x^2 - 4x - 4$
(E) $r(x) = x^2 + 9x + 1$

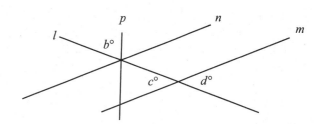

Note: Figure not drawn to scale.

6 In the figure above, line l intersects lines m and n. Line p bisects the angle between lines l and n. If $m \parallel n$ and $b = 50$, then $c + d =$

(A) 160
(B) 170
(C) 180
(D) 200
(E) 240

GO ON TO THE NEXT PAGE

7 If set C contains the positive factors of 45, and set D contains all two-digit numbers with 0 in the units position, how many numbers are in the intersection of the two sets?

(A) None
(B) One
(C) Three
(D) Five
(E) Ten

8 C is the midpoint of line segment $\overline{AE}$, D is the midpoint of line segment $\overline{CE}$, and B is a point between A and C. If $BD = 34$ and $BE = 52$, what is the length of segment $\overline{AB}$?

(A) 17
(B) 18
(C) 19
(D) 20
(E) 21

GO ON TO THE NEXT PAGE

Directions: For Student-Produced Response questions 9–18, use the grids at the bottom of the answer sheet page on which you have answered questions 1–8.

Each of the remaining 10 questions requires you to solve the problem and enter your answer by marking the ovals in the special grid, as shown in the examples below. You may use any available space for scratchwork.

Answer: 1.25 or $\frac{5}{4}$ or 5/4

Write answer in boxes.

Grid in result.

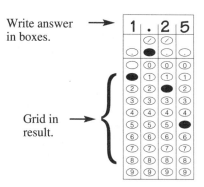

Fraction line

Decimal point

You may start your answers in any column, space permitting. Columns not needed should be left blank.

Either position is correct.

- It is recommended, though not required, that you write your answer in the boxes at the top of the columns. However, **you will receive credit only for darkening the ovals correctly.**

- Grid only one answer to a question, even though some problems have more than one correct answer.

- Darken no more than one oval in a column.

- No answers are negative.

- **Mixed numbers** cannot be gridded. For example: the number $1\frac{1}{4}$ must be gridded as 1.25 or 5/4.

(If [1 1 / 4] is gridded, it will be interpreted as $\frac{11}{4}$, not $1\frac{1}{4}$.)

- Decimal Accuracy: Decimal answers must be entered as accurately as possible. For example, if you obtain an answer such as 0.1666. . ., you should record the result as .166 or .167. **Less accurate values such as .16 or .17 are not acceptable.**

Acceptable ways to grid $\frac{1}{6}$ = .1666. . .

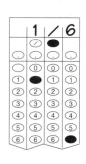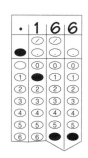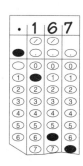

9 Graciella is catering a party and needs 32 pounds of hamburger. How many hamburger patties does she need to buy if a patty weighs $\frac{1}{3}$ of a pound?

10 In $\triangle DEF$, $\angle D$ measures 70°. $\angle E$ measures $a°$, where $a \neq 70$. If $\triangle DEF$ is an isosceles triangle, what is one possible value of a?

GO ON TO THE NEXT PAGE

11 A fish tank is in the shape of a cube. Its edges are 8 inches long. What is the volume of this fish tank, in cubic inches?

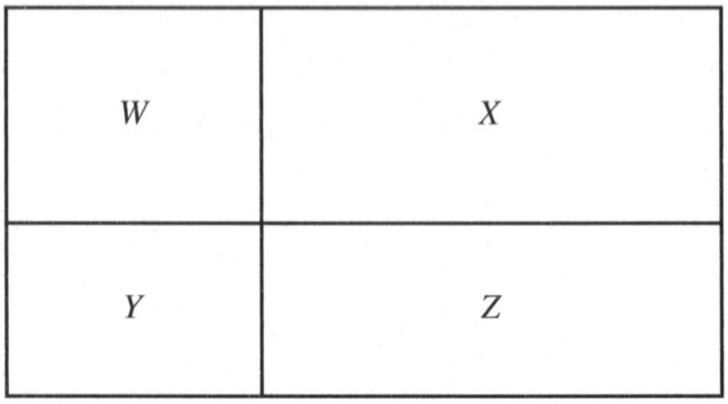

13 In the figure above, the side measures of each of the rectangles W, X, Y, and Z are integers. The areas of rectangles X, Y, and Z are 55, 24, and 44, respectively. What is the sum of the areas of rectangles W, X, Y, and Z ?

12 A number c exists such that c is directly proportional to d. When $c = \dfrac{1}{3}$, $d = \dfrac{1}{8}$. When $c = \dfrac{3}{8}$, what is the value of d ?

$$1, -2, -9, \dots 3n - 2n^2, \dots$$

14 In the sequence above, the expression $3n - 2n^2$ is equivalent to the nth term of the sequence for all positive integers n. What is the positive difference between the 7th and the 8th terms?

GO ON TO THE NEXT PAGE

15 The function $p(z)$ is defined as $p(z) = 2q(z)$, where $q(z) = z - 3$. What is the value of $p(40)$?

16 A drawing studio supplies sketch pads, erasers, and pencils to its artists. Each artist has one pencil, but every 4 artists have to share a sketch pad, and every 3 artists have to share an eraser. If the total number of sketch pads, erasers, and pencils used by the artists is 76, how many artists work in the studio?

TABLE 1

	Monday	Tuesday
Cheese	35	25
Meat	45	50

TABLE 2

	Students	Teachers
Cheese	22	
Meat		37

17 Table 1 above shows the number of cheese and meat sandwiches a college cafeteria sold on Monday and Tuesday. Table 2, which is only partially completed, shows the number of sandwiches purchased by students and teachers during both days. If only students and teachers bought these sandwiches, what is the total number of sandwiches purchased by students during both days?

18 $A(a, 15)$ and $B(17, 50)$ are points in the xy-coordinate plane. If the length of the line segment $\overline{AB}$ is 37, what is one possible value of a ?

Time—20 Minutes
16 Questions

Directions: For this section, solve each problem and decide which is the best of the choices given. Fill in the corresponding oval on the answer sheet. You may use any available space for scratchwork.

Notes

1. Calculator use is permitted.

2. All numbers used are real numbers.

3. Figures are provided for some problems. All figures are drawn to scale and lie in a plane UNLESS otherwise indicated.

4. Unless otherwise specified, the domain of any function f is assumed to be the set of all real numbers x for which $f(x)$ is a real number.

Reference Information

$A = \dfrac{1}{2}bh \qquad c^2 = a^2 + b^2 \qquad$ Special Right Triangles $\qquad A = \pi r^2 \qquad V = \pi r^2 h \qquad A = lw \qquad V = lwh$

$C = 2\pi r$

The sum of the measures in degrees of the angles of a triangle is 180.
The number of degrees of arc in a circle is 360.
A straight angle has a degree measure of 180.

---

1 Within the last year, 6 cats on a farm all had kittens. Two cats had litters of 5 kittens each, and the others all had litters of 4 kittens each. How many kittens were born on the farm over the last year?

(A) 21
(B) 24
(C) 26
(D) 28
(E) 32

2 All of the following are equal to $9x^2$ EXCEPT

(A) $x^2 + 8x^2$
(B) $4x + 5x$
(C) $(9x)(x)$
(D) $(3x)(3x)$
(E) $(-3x)(-3x)$

GO ON TO THE NEXT PAGE

3   A rectangle is cut in half, resulting in squares each of area 25. What is the perimeter of the original rectangle?

(A) 10
(B) 20
(C) 30
(D) 40
(E) 50

5   If set E is $\{A, B, C, 1, 2, 3\}$ and set I is $\{1, 3, 5, A, B, Q\}$, which of the following elements is in the union of the two sets, but not in their intersection?

(A) A
(B) B
(C) 1
(D) 2
(E) 3

4   Jung's average (arithmetic mean) on two biology quizzes is 7. What should Jung's score on the next quiz be in order to have an average of 8 for the three quizzes?

(A) 8
(B) 8.5
(C) 9
(D) 9.5
(E) 10

6   Let x represent the average (arithmetic mean) of a list of test scores. What is the result of multiplying x by the number of scores?

(A) the average of the scores
(B) the highest score
(C) the number of scores
(D) the number of possible scores
(E) the sum of the scores

GO ON TO THE NEXT PAGE

7 What is the length of the hypotenuse of an isosceles right triangle of area 32 ?

(A) 4
(B) $4\sqrt{2}$
(C) 8
(D) $8\sqrt{2}$
(E) $8\sqrt{3}$

8 Set C is made up of a series of consecutive integers whose sum is a positive even number. If the smallest number in the set is –2, what is the least possible number of integers that could be in the set?

(A) 4
(B) 5
(C) 6
(D) 7
(E) 8

9 The spare change on a dresser is composed of pennies, nickels, and dimes. If the ratio of pennies to nickels is $2:3$, and the ratio of pennies to dimes is $3:4$, what is the ratio of nickels to dimes?

(A) $9:8$
(B) $5:7$
(C) $4:5$
(D) $3:4$
(E) $2:3$

10 If $r(b) = \dfrac{b^2 - 7}{b + 7}$, what is the value of $r(7)$?

(A) 0
(B) 3
(C) 4
(D) 7
(E) 12

11 If x is a positive integer, then $5x - x^2$ must be

(A) positive
(B) negative
(C) a multiple of 5
(D) a perfect square
(E) even

12 Lines m and n are parallel. If lines m and n are cut by three different transversals, what is the least number of points of intersection that can occur among the five lines?

(A) Three
(B) Four
(C) Five
(D) Six
(E) Eight

13 While away at school, Eileen receives an allowance of $400 each month, 35 percent of which she uses to pay her bills. If she budgets 30 percent of the remainder for shopping, allots $130 for entertainment, and saves the rest of the money, what percentage of her allowance is she able to save each month?

(A) 2.5%
(B) 13%
(C) 20%
(D) 35%
(E) 52%

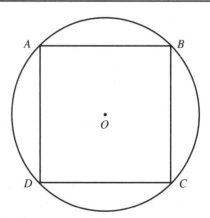

14 Square $ABCD$ is inscribed in the circle with center O. If the area of the square is 36, what is the area of the circle?

(A) 6π
(B) 12π
(C) 18π
(D) 27π
(E) 36π

GO ON TO THE NEXT PAGE

15 If n, p, and x are positive integers, and $\dfrac{n}{p} = \dfrac{2}{x} + 2$, then what is the value of $\dfrac{p}{n}$?

(A) $\dfrac{1}{x + 2}$

(B) $\dfrac{2}{x + 2}$

(C) $\dfrac{x}{2(x + 1)}$

(D) $\dfrac{x}{2} + \dfrac{1}{2}$

(E) $\dfrac{x}{2} + 2$

16 If $x > 0$, then what is the value of $(4^x)(8^x)$?

(A) 2^{9x}
(B) 2^{8x}
(C) 2^{6x}
(D) 2^{5x}
(E) 2^{4x}

IF YOU FINISH BEFORE TIME IS CALLED, YOU MAY CHECK YOUR WORK ON THIS SECTION ONLY. DO NOT TURN TO ANY OTHER SECTION IN THE TEST. **STOP**

NO TEST MATERIAL ON THIS PAGE

Time—20 Minutes
19 Questions

Directions: For each question in this section, select the best answer from among the choices given and fill in the corresponding oval on the answer sheet.

Each sentence below has one or two blanks, each blank indicating that something has been omitted. Beneath the sentence are five words or sets of words labeled A through E. Choose the word or set of words that, when inserted in the sentence, best fits the meaning of the sentence as a whole.

EXAMPLE:

Today's small, portable computers contrast markedly with the earliest electronic computers, which were -------.

(A) effective   (B) invented
(C) useful   (D) destructive
(E) enormous

ANSWER:
Ⓐ Ⓑ Ⓒ Ⓓ ●

1 Jerry's ------- that Jeff was untrustworthy was ------- when Jeff disappeared with the funds earmarked for the prom.

(A) prediction . . contradicted
(B) credibility . . refused
(C) advertisement . . proven
(D) suspicion . . validated
(E) denial . . reinforced

2 The dramatic colors and long plumes of the male bird of paradise may seem to be just -------, but in fact are ------- the courtship rituals of the birds.

(A) attractive . . ancestors of
(B) outstanding . . unneeded in
(C) ornamental . . essential to
(D) romantic . . reliant on
(E) decorative . . reactions to

3 Many national and state parks have no trash cans or recycling bins; to keep the wilderness -------, visitors are encouraged to carry out all materials brought into the parks and leave the area ------- by litter.

(A) unsullied . . endangered
(B) pristine . . unspoiled
(C) pure . . transported
(D) sparse . . crowded
(E) fertile . . depleted

4 The rock group attracts a ------- audience; a surprisingly diverse group of people flocks to their sold-out concerts.

(A) multifarious   (B) mystifying
(C) cacophonous   (D) humane
(E) lyrical

5 Because the tax laws employ ------- language, average taxpayers must often hire accountants to explain the ------- rules and regulations.

(A) lucid . . obscure
(B) esoteric . . absolute
(C) arcane . . impenetrable
(D) insurgent . . economic
(E) terse . . florid

6 To create potpourri, Rachel soaks the dried leaves in ------- made from fragrant plants, such as lavender, rosemary, and thyme.

(A) a synopsis   (B) a convolution
(C) an infusion   (D) a conjecture
(E) an abstinence

GO ON TO THE NEXT PAGE

The passage below is followed by questions based on its content. Answer the questions on the basis of what is <u>stated</u> or <u>implied</u> in the passage and in any introductory material that may be provided.

Questions 7–19 are based on the following passage.

In the following passage, a Polish-American woman ruminates on how the meaning of words like "culture" and "ethnicity" evolved as she grew up in America.

Growing up, I was only tangentially aware that my family's Polish heritage even existed. I knew we had one, certainly; I knew that my great-grandparents had
Line come to America from Poland, I knew that my
(5) grandmother occasionally used Polish words mixed in with her English, and my father taught me about a few traditional Polish dishes, including *pierogies* (mashed potato dumplings) and *golubkies* (stuffed cabbage). Even those, however, were readily obtainable at the
(10) grocery store; *pierogies* were everyday premade lumps of dough you dropped in boiling water, not handmade dumplings created from scratch. Otherwise, it seemed that our heritage rarely affected our day-to-day lives; I didn't even know where in Poland my grandparents
(15) had come from. Moreover, we lived in a predominantly Polish neighborhood, and our homogeneity tended to preclude any pride I could have taken in our ethnic differences. We were chameleons, but we blended so well that our surroundings had essentially become part
(20) of us.

Later, when we moved to a new non-Polish neighborhood two states away, I began to sense for the first time that we really were different. Our accents were different, our slang was different, even our food
(25) was different from our neighbors'. While we were never discriminated against, it was enough to make me feel uneasy and strange about our differences. I became our school's resident "expert" on Polish heritage; other kids expected me to translate English
(30) into Polish at a moment's notice, and describe in detail a country I had never even been to. Instead of chameleons, we were now a brood of bright, awkward butterflies, calling attention to ourselves with every move we made.

(35) Eventually, though, I began to take pride in this part of my background, and I regaled my friends with stories of my grandparents and their friends' exotic-sounding Polish activities (even if I had to make them up). I insisted that my mother keep *pierogies* at all
(40) times in the freezer, in case of unexpected company, and harassed my father for Polish words to teach my friends. (But when I ran out of those, I'd make them up, too.) Regardless of my exaggerations, I was finally taking an interest in our cultural heritage and assuming

(45) some authority about it.

One day I was showing some new friends around our kitchen, describing the meals my mother and grandmother made for our family gatherings. I told them about my grandmother's liberal use of sausage and
(50) sauerkraut; I described in great detail the all-day process of making fresh *pierogies* for special occasions (although my family never had them on holidays, and still only bought them frozen from the grocery store).

And then I told them about *mostaccioli*, a dish we
(55) regularly served during family gatherings.

"What's that?" they said.

"Oh, it's pasta and tomato sauce and meat," I said casually.

"And you have that during the holidays?"

(60) "Yes," I said.

"Oh," they said, "you know that's Italian, right?"

They were right. I had an embarrassing exchange with my mother, who confirmed that *mostaccioli* was indeed an Italian word, and the dish itself—as near as I
(65) could figure out—had nothing whatsoever to do with Poland or the Polish (except for my grandmother, who made it). The more I talked to my mother, the more I realized that my family actually picked and chose their dishes from all kinds of different sources, combining
(70) ingredients from other ethnicities, including Italian, Spanish, German, and French. The foods that I thought made us unique, exotic, and different were, in fact, often culled from various other places and handed down from generation to generation, who modified recipes
(75) along the way. Our cultural heritage was nowhere near as homogeneous as I had originally thought; it had evolved because of factors such as our geographical location and economic circumstances, as well as my elders' creativity. For example, when my mother lived
(80) next door to a German neighbor as a child she learned several German dishes, and mingled them with my grandmother's Polish recipes to create something completely new.

How much of our original cultural heritage had we
(85) actually retained after moving to America? What was "culture" anyway? The more I researched, the more complicated and nebulous this question became. Eventually I began to realize that we, along with our neighbors, family, and friends, were creating a new kind

GO ON TO THE NEXT PAGE

- 251 -

(90) of ethnicity, one that was perhaps never going to be as consistent and unchanging as, in my naive youth, I believed it should be. Instead, we'd borrow the best traits from others as we needed them, and give our own in return.

7 The primary contrast that this passage presents is between

(A) the author's Polish background and her Italian background
(B) the author's beliefs about her heritage and the reality of that heritage
(C) the mother's attitude toward Polish food and the grandmother's attitude toward Italian food
(D) the culture of Polish-Americans and the culture of other kinds of Americans
(E) the way that heritage is viewed in America and the way that it is viewed in other countries

8 The author describes the "predominantly Polish neighborhood" (lines 15–16) in order to make the point that

(A) she was discouraged from taking any pride in her heritage
(B) Polish food was readily available from the local grocery stores
(C) her ethnic similarity with the community made her less aware of her heritage
(D) it wasn't important where in Poland her family had originated
(E) she longed to move to another neighborhood where she could be different

9 The primary purpose of paragraph 1 is to

(A) argue that the author's family didn't have an interest in their heritage
(B) establish that the family's heritage didn't necessarily play a part in their everyday lives
(C) exaggerate the importance of the family's background
(D) provide examples of traditional Polish dishes
(E) describe the author's grandmother

10 The author refers to her family as "chameleons" (line 18) because they

(A) easily blended in with their surroundings
(B) chose food available from their environment
(C) were native to Poland
(D) tried to ignore their surroundings
(E) were transplanted from another country

11 In paragraph 1, the author characterizes her background as

(A) incomplete
(B) exaggerated
(C) prolific
(D) inadequate
(E) unimportant

12 In line 32, "brood" is closest in meaning to

(A) sullenness
(B) worry
(C) group
(D) shelter
(E) protection

13 In lines 32–33, the author describes her family as "bright, awkward butterflies" in order to

(A) imply that her family now felt ashamed of being Polish
(B) demonstrate one way in which her family was discriminated against
(C) indicate that her family could previously be likened to caterpillars
(D) suggest that her family could no longer easily fit in with their surroundings
(E) assign blame to the neighbors who made her feel awkward

14 The "exaggerations" that the author mentions in line 43 are things that

(A) the author had been told by her parents and grandmother
(B) had been handed down as family traditions from Poland
(C) the author was trying to conceal from her friends
(D) did not actually originate in Polish culture
(E) the author was using to respond to social pressure

15 The author uses the word "authority" in line 45 to mean

(A) an assumption that others made about her heritage
(B) a person knowledgeable about culture
(C) her grandmother
(D) her willingness to exaggerate
(E) the right to claim knowledge of a subject

GO ON TO THE NEXT PAGE

- 252 -

16 The fact that the author responds "casually" in line 58 implies that she

(A) does not think much of her non-Polish friends
(B) cares little about Polish culture
(C) has an informal, easygoing personality
(D) is self-conscious about showing friends around her family's kitchen
(E) has become comfortable in her role as an expert on Polish traditions

17 The "embarrassing exchange" in line 62 implies that

(A) the author's mother chided her for lying
(B) the author's mother gave her something in exchange for the *mostaccioli*
(C) the author was mortified about something she had no control over
(D) the author was excited about her new discovery
(E) the author was ashamed when she realized she didn't know as much about her background as she thought

18 What does the author's use of the word "culled" (line 73) suggest about the origins of her family traditions?

(A) They were selected from a variety of non-Polish sources.
(B) They were not as different from the traditions of other families as the author thought.
(C) They shared both German and Polish roots.
(D) They were constructed from unwanted traditions that other cultures had discarded.
(E) They were pieced together at random by coincidence.

19 The discussion of the "complicated…nebulous… question" (line 87) suggests the author's view that

(A) the practice of borrowing from other cultures was perfectly acceptable
(B) neighbors and friends could also be considered "family," along with blood relatives
(C) cultural heritage might not be as quantifiable as the author originally thought
(D) *pierogies* were not authentic Polish food
(E) cultural heritage should always stay consistent and stable

IF YOU FINISH BEFORE TIME IS CALLED, YOU MAY CHECK YOUR WORK ON THIS SECTION ONLY. DO NOT TURN TO ANY OTHER SECTION IN THE TEST.

- 253 -

Time – 10 Minutes
14 Questions

Directions: For each question in this section, select the best answer from among the choices given and fill in the corresponding oval on the answer sheet.

The following sentences test correctness and effectiveness of expression. Part of each sentence or the entire sentence is underlined; beneath each sentence are five ways of phrasing the underlined material. Choice A repeats the original phrasing; the other four choices are different. If you think the original phrasing produces a better sentence than any of the alternatives, select choice A; if not, select one of the other choices.

In making your selection, follow the requirements of standard written English; that is, pay attention to grammar, choice of words, sentence construction, and punctuation. Your selection should result in the most effective sentence—clear and precise—without awkwardness or ambiguity.

EXAMPLE:

Every apple in the baskets <u>are ripe and labeled according to the date it was picked</u>.

(A) are ripe and labeled according to the date it was picked
(B) is ripe and labeled according to the date it was picked
(C) are ripe and labeled according to the date they were picked
(D) is ripe and labeled according to the date they were picked
(E) are ripe and labeled as to the date it was picked

ANSWER:

1 <u>The gallery owner placed the most valuable coins on a velvet tray, she</u> explained to us the provenance of each coin.

(A) The gallery owner placed the most valuable coins on a velvet tray, she
(B) The most valuable coins, which were placed on a velvet tray by the gallery owner, who
(C) The most valuable coins were first placed on a velvet tray by the gallery owner, then she
(D) After placing the most valuable coins on a velvet tray, the gallery owner
(E) The gallery owner, having placed the most valuable coins on a velvet tray, she

2 An assistant coach is <u>when a person works with a sports team</u> in a specialized area.

(A) when a person works with a sports team
(B) a person who works with a sports team
(C) work done by a person with a sports team
(D) if a person works with a sports team
(E) work being done by a person with a sports team

3 After Nora, the main character in Ibsen's *A Doll's House,* is confronted with her husband's true feelings, <u>she recognizes that one's relationships can be as fragile as your</u> image.

(A) she recognizes that one's relationships can be as fragile as your
(B) she recognizes that one's relationships can be as fragile as one's
(C) later recognizing that one's relationships can be as fragile as their
(D) having recognized how relationships are as fragile as one's
(E) there is her recognition about how relationships are as fragile as your

4 Learning the primary colors of pigment <u>helps beginners to become a better painter</u>.

(A) helps beginners to become a better painter
(B) is helpful to beginners who want to be a better painter
(C) helps beginners to become better painters
(D) is helpful to beginners in becoming a better painter
(E) helps a beginner become better painters

GO ON TO THE NEXT PAGE

- 254 -

5 Studies have shown that <u>polar bears' not staying in their natural habitat, this increases</u> the frequency of lethargic behavior.

(A) polar bears' not staying in their natural habitat, this increases

(B) for polar bears who have been removed from their natural habitat, it increases

(C) the act of removing polar bears from their natural habitat would increase

(D) when removing polar bears from their natural environment, it increases

(E) the removal of polar bears from their natural habitat increases

6 The helicopter, offering the advantages of flight without requiring large amounts of space for takeoff and landing, allows relatively easy access to <u>remote places as</u> islands, mountain villages, and snow-bound communities.

(A) remote places as

(B) remote places that are

(C) places of extreme remoteness as

(D) places as remote as

(E) a place as remote as

7 Finally able to walk again after the removal of his cast, <u>restrictive clothing was something Bobby felt uneasy with</u>.

(A) restrictive clothing was something Bobby felt uneasy with

(B) the feeling of restrictive clothing made Bobby uneasy

(C) Bobby felt uneasy in restrictive clothing

(D) the feeling of unease Bobby had in restrictive clothing

(E) Bobby, uneasy in restrictive clothing

8 <u>Being larger and sweeter-tasting compared with</u> other yellow onions, the Texas 1015 has become popular as a sandwich topping and salad ingredient.

(A) Being larger and sweeter-tasting compared with

(B) Both larger and more sweeter tasting compared to

(C) Larger and sweeter-tasting than

(D) By being larger and more sweet than

(E) Larger and sweeter-tasting, unlike

9 The salesman indicated that the many advanced features of the steam iron <u>made it equally suitable for the tasks of pressing and steam</u>.

(A) made it equally suitable for the tasks of pressing and steam

(B) made it equally suitable for the tasks of pressing and steaming

(C) had made the iron suitable for the task of pressing along with the steam setting

(D) makes it suitable for the tasks of pressing and steaming both

(E) were the qualities necessary for the suitability of the iron to the tasks of pressing or steaming

10 <u>Contemporary puppet theater, exploring the essential truths of love and family and maintaining a simplicity of presentation</u>, reflects puppetry's ancient origins.

(A) Contemporary puppet theater, exploring the essential truths of love and family and maintaining a simplicity of presentation

(B) Contemporary puppet theater, through its exploration of the essential truths of love and family and maintaining simplicity in presentation

(C) Since contemporary puppet theater explores the essential truths of love and family and also maintaining a simplicity of presentation, it

(D) Having contemporary puppet theater that explores the essential truths of love and family and maintains a simplicity of presentation, it

(E) Exploring the essential truths of love and family, contemporary puppet theater maintains a simplicity of presentation that also

11 Political commentary is increasingly appearing on the <u>Internet, because its content can be updated quickly</u>, analysts can respond to events almost as they happen.

(A) Internet, because its content can be updated quickly

(B) Internet, since its content can be updated quickly

(C) Internet, with its ability to be updated quickly

(D) Internet; because its content can be updated quickly

(E) Internet; after which its content can be updated quickly, which means

GO ON TO THE NEXT PAGE

12 German playwrights like Bertolt Brecht practiced "alienation": <u>they would intersperse their plays with musical interludes intended to make</u> the audience aware of theatrical devices.

(A) they would intersperse their plays with musical interludes intended to make

(B) he would intersperse his plays with musical interludes to make

(C) they wrote plays, which were interspersed with musical interludes, intended to make

(D) interspersed with musical interludes, their plays intended to make

(E) the interspersing of their plays with musical interludes intended to make

13 This history of the War of the Roses, <u>like other legendary conflicts, are</u> influenced by the point of view of the author.

(A) like other legendary conflicts, are

(B) like those of other legendary conflicts, are

(C) like other legendary conflicts, is

(D) like histories of other legendary conflicts, are

(E) like histories of other legendary conflicts, is

14 Paparazzi and movie stars both attend movie premieres, <u>and the paparazzi would look for movie stars and the stars would promote</u> their films.

(A) and the paparazzi would look for movie stars and the stars would promote

(B) and the paparazzi come to look for movie stars while the stars promote

(C) the paparazzi look for movie stars and the stars are promoting

(D) the paparazzi looking for movie stars while stars would promote

(E) the paparazzi to look for movie stars and the stars to promote

SCORING YOUR TEST

For each section (Critical Reading, Math, and Writing) on the SAT, your score will range from 200–800. Your performance on the tests in this book is a good indicator of your abilities and skills.

The scoring information contained here is intended to give an approximate idea of what your performance will be on Test Day. The formulas for calculating your raw score that follow in this book are the same as those the College Board will use to score your SAT.

The raw-to-scaled score conversion tables, however, may differ from the one used to score the SAT that you take. The College Board creates unique raw-to-scaled score conversions for every administration of the SAT. Therefore, practice tests can only approximate the conversion tables that will be used on the real SAT that you take. Nevertheless, the tables in this book are close to the tables that will be used on your test, and will provide you with a good sense of what your score might be at this stage in your preparation.

Step 1: Score Your Essay

First, score your essay, which accounts for approximately 25% of your Writing scaled score; your score on the Multiple Choice questions will account for the remaining 75% or so. For the tests in this book, assign your essay a score of 1–6, which, along with your Multiple Choice score, you will use to arrive at your 200–800 scaled score.

For All Students:

The following criteria are a good guide:

6 Outstanding—Though it may have a few small errors, the essay is well organized and fully developed with supporting examples. It displays consistent language facility, varied sentence structure, and varied vocabulary.

5 Solid—Though it has occasional errors or lapses in quality, the essay is generally organized and well developed with appropriate examples. It displays language facility, syntactic variety, and varied vocabulary.

4 Adequate—Though it has some flaws, the essay is organized and adequately developed and has some examples. It displays adequate but inconsistent language facility.

3 Limited—The essay does not adequately fulfill the writing assignment and has many flaws. It has inadequate organization and development, along with many errors in grammar or diction (or both). In general, the essay lacks variety.

2 Flawed—The essay demonstrates incompetence with one or more weaknesses. Ideas are vague and thinly developed. It contains frequent errors in grammar and diction and almost no variety.

1 Deficient—The essay demonstrates incompetence with serious flaws. It has no organization, no development, and severe grammar and diction errors. The essay is so seriously flawed that its basic meaning is obscured.

0 Off-Topic—The essay does not follow the assignment.

Step 2: Compute Your Raw Score

Check your answers to the multiple-choice questions against the answer key on the next two pages. Count up the number of answers you got right and the number you got wrong for each section. Do not score Section 7, the Experimental Section. Remember, do not count questions left blank as wrong. Round up to the nearest whole number. Now, plug them in below.

Note: Grid-in questions do not have a wrong-answer penalty, so do not deduct anything for wrong answers.

Critical Reading

	Number Right		Number Wrong		Raw Score
Section 4:	☐	–	(.25 × ☐)	=	☐
Section 6:	☐	–	(.25 × ☐)	=	☐
Section 9:	☐	–	(.25 × ☐)	=	☐
		Critical Reading Raw Score		=	☐
					(rounded up)

Writing

	Number Right		Number Wrong		Raw Score
Section 3:	☐	–	(.25 × ☐)	=	☐
Section 10:	☐	–	(.25 × ☐)	=	☐
		Writing Multiple-Choice Raw Score		=	☐
					(rounded up)

Math

	Number Right		Number Wrong		Raw Score
Section 2: (QUESTIONS 1–8)	☐	–	(.25 × ☐)	=	☐
Section 2: (QUESTIONS 9–18)	☐	–	(no wrong answer penalty)	=	☐
Section 5:	☐	–	(.25 × ☐)	=	☐
Section 8:	☐	–	(.25 × ☐)	=	☐
		Math Raw Score		=	☐
					(rounded up)

PRACTICE TEST 4 ANSWER KEY

CRITICAL READING					
Section 4		**Section 6**		**Section 9**	
Multiple-Choice Questions		**Multiple-Choice Questions**		**Multiple-Choice Questions**	
	Correct Answer		Correct Answer		Correct Answer
1.	D	1.	B	1.	D
2.	A	2.	E	2.	C
3.	D	3.	A	3.	B
4.	E	4.	C	4.	A
5.	D	5.	D	5.	C
6.	C	6.	A	6.	C
7.	D	7.	B	7.	B
8.	A	8.	E	8.	C
9.	D	9.	D	9.	B
10.	A	10.	D	10.	A
11.	B	11.	B	11.	E
12.	A	12.	C	12.	C
13.	A	13.	C	13.	D
14.	A	14.	D	14.	E
15.	A	15.	C	15.	E
16.	D	16.	E	16.	E
17.	C	17.	B	17.	E
18.	D	18.	D	18.	A
19.	D	19.	E	19.	C
20.	D	20.	D		
21.	B	21.	D		
22.	A	22.	A		
23.	E	23.	E		
24.	E	24.	C		

no. correct _____   no. correct _____   no. correct _____

no. incorrect _____   no. incorrect _____   no. incorrect _____

MATH					
Section 2		**Section 5**		**Section 8**	
Multiple-Choice Questions		**Multiple-Choice Questions**		**Multiple-Choice Questions**	
	Correct Answer		Correct Answer		Correct Answer
1.	D	1.	E	1.	C
2.	B	2.	C	2.	B
3.	E	3.	D	3.	C
4.	C	4.	B	4.	E
5.	D	5.	E	5.	D
6.	D	6.	B	6.	E
7.	A	7.	C	7.	D
8.	C	8.	C	8.	E
		9.	E	9.	A
		10.	D	10.	B
		11.	E	11.	E
		12.	E	12.	B
		13.	C	13.	B
		14.	E	14.	C
		15.	E	15.	C
		16.	A	16.	D
		17.	B		
		18.	B		
		19.	D		
		20.	D		

no. correct _____   no. correct _____   no. correct _____

no. incorrect _____   no. incorrect _____   no. incorrect _____

Section 2	
Student-Produced Response Questions	
	Correct Answer
9.	12
10.	192, 480, or 960
11.	6.5 or 13/2
12.	3
13.	$1 < AE \leq 1.41$
14.	996
15.	7
16.	4.80
17.	27.5 or 55/2
18.	21

no. correct _____

WRITING

Essay	Section 3 Multiple-Choice Questions	Section 10 Multiple-Choice Questions
	Correct Answer	Correct Answer
	1. D	1. D
	2. B	2. B
	3. A	3. B
	4. E	4. C
Essay Score* (1–6)	5. D	5. E
	6. B	6. D
	7. C	7. C
	8. D	8. C
	9. D	9. B
	10. B	10. A
	11. D	11. D
	12. B	12. E
	13. B	13. E
	14. D	14. E
	15. B	
	16. B	
	17. C	
	18. C	
	19. D	
	20. E	
	21. B	
	22. B	
	23. B	
	24. C	
	25. D	
	26. B	
	27. E	
	28. B	
	29. B	
	30. D	
	31. A	
	32. D	
	33. D	
	34. E	
	35. C	
	no. correct	no. correct
	no. incorrect	no. incorrect

*To score your essay, see Step 1 on the previous pages. On this Practice Test, your essay score will range from 1 to 6. (Keep in mind that on the actual SAT, your essay will be read by two readers and you will receive a score of 1 to 12 on your score report.)

Step 3: Find Your Scaled Score

To determine your Critical Reading and Math scaled scores, find the raw scores you calculated for these two sections in Step 2 on Tables 1 and on the following page. Next, find the scaled score associated with your raw scores and enter them in the appropriate box in the Scaled Scores table on this page.

To determine your Writing scaled score, use Table 3. First, find the Writing Multiple-Choice raw score you calculated in Step 2 and the essay raw score (1–6) you assigned yourself. Next, locate your Writing Multiple-Choice raw score on the left dimension of Table 3. Then find your essay score along the top. The box associated with this row and column contains your Writing scaled score. Enter it in the appropriate box in the Scaled Scores table below.

The sum of the three scores is your Total Scaled Score.

Scaled Scores	
Critical Reading	
Math	
Writing	
Total	

TABLE 1 Critical Reading Conversion Table			
Raw Score	Scaled Score	Raw Score	Scaled Score
67	800	30	500
66	790	29	500
65	770	28	490
64	760	27	480
63	750	26	480
62	740	25	470
61	720	24	470
60	710	23	460
59	700	22	450
58	690	21	450
57	680	20	440
56	670	19	430
55	670	18	430
54	660	17	420
53	650	16	410
52	640	15	410
51	640	14	400
50	630	13	390
49	620	12	380
48	610	11	380
47	610	10	370
46	600	9	360
45	590	8	350
44	590	7	340
43	580	6	330
42	580	5	320
41	570	4	310
40	560	3	300
39	560	2	280
38	550	1	270
37	540	0	250
36	540	−1	250
35	530	−2	240
34	530	−3	230
33	520	−4	220
32	510	−5	210
31	510	−6 and below	200

TABLE 2 Math Conversion Table			
Raw Score	Scaled Score	Raw Score	Scaled Score
54	800	24	490
53	780	23	490
52	760	22	480
51	740	21	470
50	730	20	460
49	710	19	460
48	700	18	450
47	690	17	440
46	670	16	430
45	660	15	430
44	650	14	420
43	650	13	410
42	640	12	400
41	630	11	390
40	620	10	380
39	610	9	380
38	600	8	370
37	590	7	360
36	590	6	340
35	580	5	330
34	570	4	320
33	560	3	310
32	560	2	290
31	550	1	280
30	540	0	260
29	530	−1	250
28	520	−2	240
27	520	−3	230
26	510	−4	220
25	500	−5	210
		−6 and below	200

TABLE 3
SAT Score Conversion Table for Writing Composite

		Essay Raw Score						
		0	**1**	**2**	**3**	**4**	**5**	**6**
	49	670	700	720	740	780	790	800
	48	660	680	700	730	760	780	790
	47	650	670	690	720	750	770	780
	46	640	660	680	710	740	760	770
	45	630	650	670	700	740	750	770
	44	620	640	660	690	730	750	760
	43	600	630	650	680	710	740	750
	42	600	620	640	670	700	730	750
	41	590	610	630	660	690	730	740
	40	580	600	620	650	690	720	740
	39	570	590	610	640	680	710	740
	38	560	590	610	630	670	700	730
	37	550	580	600	630	660	690	720
	36	540	570	590	620	650	680	710
	35	540	560	580	610	640	680	710
	34	530	550	570	600	640	670	700
	33	520	540	560	590	630	660	690
	32	510	540	560	580	620	650	680
	31	500	530	550	580	610	640	670
	30	490	520	540	570	600	630	660
	29	490	510	530	560	590	630	650
	28	480	500	520	550	590	620	640
	27	470	490	510	540	580	610	640
	26	460	490	500	530	570	600	630
Writing Multiple-Choice Raw Score	25	450	480	500	520	560	590	620
	24	440	470	490	510	550	580	610
	23	430	460	480	510	540	570	600
	22	430	450	470	500	530	570	590
	21	430	450	470	500	530	570	590
	20	420	440	460	490	520	560	580
	19	410	430	450	480	520	550	570
	18	400	420	440	470	510	540	570
	17	390	420	430	460	500	530	560
	16	380	410	430	450	490	520	550
	15	370	400	420	450	480	510	540
	14	360	390	410	440	470	500	530
	13	360	380	400	430	460	500	520
	12	340	370	390	420	450	490	510
	11	340	360	380	410	450	480	510
	10	330	350	370	400	440	470	500
	9	320	350	360	390	430	460	490
	8	310	340	360	390	420	450	480
	7	300	330	350	380	410	440	470
	6	290	320	340	370	400	430	460
	5	290	310	330	360	390	430	450
	4	280	300	320	350	390	420	450
	3	270	290	310	340	380	410	440
	2	260	280	300	330	370	400	430
	1	250	270	290	320	340	380	410
	0	250	260	280	310	340	370	400
	−1	240	260	270	290	320	360	380
	−2	230	250	260	270	310	340	370
	−3	220	240	250	260	300	330	360
	−4	220	230	240	250	290	320	350
	−5	200	220	230	240	280	310	340
	−6	200	210	220	240	280	310	340
	−7	200	210	220	230	270	300	330
	−8	200	210	220	230	270	300	330
	−9	200	210	220	230	270	300	330
	−10	200	210	220	230	270	300	330
	−11	200	210	220	230	270	300	330

The Look-It-Up Book of
MAMMALS

Patricia Lauber, formerly editor-in-chief of a young people's science magazine and Chief Editor, Science and Mathematics, for a leading children's encyclopedia, is the author of many books for children. She has written three LOOK-IT-UP Books, and has contributed several titles to two other Random House series, Allabout Books and Gateway Books. A graduate of Wellesley College, she now lives in New York City.

Guy Coheleach studied art at the Cooper Union for the Advancement of Science and Art. Since 1963, he has concentrated on wildlife studies and has contributed to various textbooks, an encyclopedia, and several other books. His work also appears regularly in National Audubon Magazine. He now lives in Astoria, New York, with his wife and four children.

The Look-It-Up Book of
MAMMALS

by Patricia Lauber

illustrated by Guy Coheleach

Random House New York

We should like to thank
Ernest P. Walker, Mammalogist Extraordinary,
for his thorough reading of the manuscript
and his most helpful comments.

Library of Congress Catalog Card Number: 67-21916
Manufactured in the United States of America

Printed by Copifyer Lithograph Corp., Cleveland, Ohio
Designed by Janet Townsend

What are Mammals

A grizzly bear is a big creature that walks on land. A bat is a small creature that flies through the air. A blue whale is a giant that spends its whole life in the sea. In many ways these animals are very different from one another. But in certain ways they are alike, for they all belong to the large group of animals called mammals.

All mammals have backbones. All breathe air. And all are warm-blooded. But these facts alone do not make them mammals. (Birds are also warm-blooded, air-breathing animals with backbones. Yet they are not mammals.) Two things are true of mammals that are not true of any other kind of animal.

1. Mammals have fur. Some, such as the musk-ox, are very furry, indeed. Some, such as the elephant, have only a sprinkling of bristly hairs. Some, such as the dolphin, have hair only when they are born. But no other kind of animal has any fur at all.

2. Mammals nurse their young on milk. Mother mammals have special glands in their bodies that produce milk. No other kind of animal does. The very word "mammal" comes from a Latin word for "breast".

Almost all mammals bear living young. But two kinds lay eggs. These are the platypus and the spiny anteaters. Some baby mammals are carried inside their mother's bodies until they are well developed. Others are tiny when they are born and have hardly developed at all. Most of these finish developing in their mother's pouch. This is true, for example, of kangaroos and opossums.

Most of the animals we know best are mammals. Dogs, cats, horses, cows, mice, monkeys, elephants, sheep, deer, and beavers are all mammals. And, as you may know, we are mammals, too. In this book you will find most of the mammals you know— and some you don't know. You will see what a surprising and wonderful group of animals the mammals are.

Aardvarks

Aardvark

An aardvark is a wonderful digger. Its strong legs end in huge claws. The aardvark uses its claws to dig the big burrow in which it lives. It uses them to dig out food—termites, ants, and other insects.

Aardvarks live in many parts of Africa. Some African termites build huge nests of earth above ground. The nests are as hard as concrete. An aardvark can easily rip open a termite nest with its claws. Then it eats the termites. An aardvark has a sticky tongue that reaches out for 12 inches. It gathers termites on its tongue and swallows them. Aardvarks hunt for food at night. They sleep in their burrows by day.

Their chief enemies are lions, leopards, and other meat-eating animals. An aardvark fights by rearing on its hind legs and slashing with its claws. It cannot bite. An aardvark has no teeth in the front of the mouth. The side teeth are peg-shaped and have no roots. An aardvark tries to escape from an enemy by running away or by digging a hole. It can dig a hole very quickly. Then it vanishes into its hole.

A female aardvark has one baby a year. By the time it is 2 weeks old, the baby can go out with its mother at night. At 6 months it is big enough to dig for itself.

The name "aardvark" means earth-pig. Aardvarks look something like big pigs. But they are not pigs. In fact, they have no close relatives.

Alpacas

See Llamas

2

Anteaters

Giant Anteater

The GIANT ANTEATER is a large animal with a bushy tail and a tube-shaped head. It has no teeth. Its mouth is simply a small hole at the end of the snout. Inside the mouth is a long, sticky, wormlike tongue. When feeding, the anteater pokes its snout into a nest of ants or termites. Then it flicks out its tongue. Insects attack the tongue and stick to it. Then the anteater swallows them. It may eat a pound or two of termites at one meal.

An anteater rips open a nest with its claws. The claws are long, sharp hooks. They also serve as weapons. If attacked, an anteater stands on its hind legs and claws its enemy. Because of its claws, the giant anteater must walk on its knuckles. It can gallop if it must. It can also swim. The giant anteater has no fixed home. It spends its time shuffling around with its nose to the ground, looking for food. A mother carries her baby on her back.

The giant anteater has two smaller cousins: the COLLARED ANTEATER and the SILKY ANTEATER. Another name for the silky anteater is the PIGMY ANTEATER.

All three kinds are found only in Central and South America. The smaller anteaters spend much of their time in trees. They are active mostly at night.

Several other animals are also called anteaters. Among these are the SPINY ANTEATERS and the SCALY ANTEATERS, or PANGOLINS. All eat ants and other insects in the same way. But they are not related. The closest relatives of the American anteaters are the armadillos and the sloths. *See also:* PANGOLINS; SPINY ANTEATERS

Collared Anteater

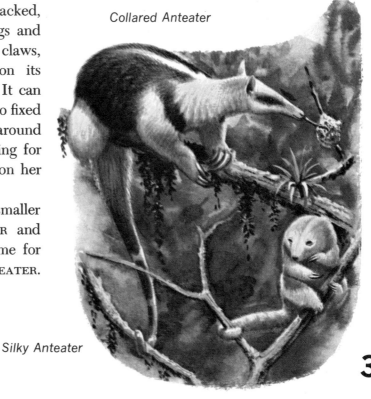

Silky Anteater

Antelopes

Antelopes are graceful, handsome, swift-footed animals. There are about a hundred different antelopes. They come in many sizes and colors. Some live in big herds, while others live alone. Some kinds live in thick forests. Other kinds live in scorching deserts, in swamps, on mountains, or on open plains. All are Old World animals, and most kinds live in Africa. (The pronghorn of North America is sometimes called an antelope. But it is not a true antelope.)

All antelopes have hooves. All are plant-eaters. When feeding, they swallow their food quickly. Later, when they are resting, they chew their cud. That is, they cough up the food, a mouthful at a time. They chew it thoroughly and swallow it again.

Antelopes have horns. Horns are hard and hollow. They grow around cores of bone on the skull. Horns are not shed, as antlers are. In some kinds of antelope, both males and females have horns. In

Gnu

Oryx

Gazelle

Springbok

4

other kinds only the males have horns. In general, antelope horns grow up from the head and then sweep back. But some are as straight as spears. Others grow in spirals or in great curves.

The biggest antelope is the ELAND. A male eland may be 6 feet high at the shoulder and weigh 1,200 pounds. Elands live in small herds on the plains and grasslands of Africa. The smallest antelope is the ROYAL ANTELOPE of West Africa. It is only about 10½ inches high at the shoul-

der. Between these two are all the other sizes of antelope.

GAZELLES are small, graceful antelope of desert regions. The ORYX, which also lives in deserts, has horns like spears. The tiny DUIKERS live in the forests of Africa. So does the rare and beautiful BONGO.

On the plains of Africa you can see many kinds of antelope—HARTEBEESTS, GNUS (or WILDEBEESTS), SABLE ANTELOPE, SPRINGBOKS, and many others.

Impala

Kob

Eland

Duiker

Apes

Gibbon

Chimpanzee

Gorilla

Orangutan

Apes and monkeys belong to one of the main groups of mammals. The name of this group is primates, which means "first." The scientist who named the group said that it was first in importance. He thought so because man is also a primate.

All told, there are about 190 kinds of primate. Except for man, apes are the most highly developed. They are among the most intelligent of mammals.

There are four main kinds of ape: GIBBONS, ORANGUTANS, CHIMPANZEES, and GORILLAS. Gibbons are fairly small. The other three are big. That is why they are called the "great apes."

Apes do not have tails. (Most monkeys do.) They have big jaws and large front teeth. They eat chiefly plant matter— fruits, buds, leaves, and so on. Their eyesight is good, and they can see colors.

Apes are very good at swinging through trees. They can grip the limbs with their hands or their feet. Their feet look much like their hands and the big toe works like a thumb. The great apes also spend a good deal of time on the ground. They cannot swim.

All apes are Old World animals. Chimpanzees and gorillas live in Central Africa. Orangutans live on the islands of Borneo and Sumatra. Gibbons live in Southeast Asia, Sumatra, Java, Borneo, and some smaller islands.

GIBBONS are the smallest of the apes. They stand 3 feet high and weigh 12 to 18 pounds. They have very long arms. In fact, their arms are longer than their legs. A gibbon has a very loud voice. When feeding, it gives low, whistling cries. These are sometimes followed by shrieks and hoots.

On the ground a gibbon hurries awkwardly along. It is most at home in a tree. It is an amazing acrobat. Using each hand as a hook, the gibbon swings from branch to branch. It can swing from one branch to another that is 30 feet away. It can also walk along a tree limb. It grips the limb with its big toes and holds its arms up for balance.

A baby gibbon travels through the trees with its mother. It clings around her waist. She lifts her legs to hold it as she swings.

Gibbons

ORANGUTANS are much bigger than gibbons. A male may be 5 feet tall and weigh 220 pounds. These apes spend much of their time swinging through trees. They can also walk on the ground. When they travel on the ground, they use the sole or side of each foot and the knuckles of their hands. They sleep at night on a platform or nest of limbs. They usually build a new one each night. In rainy weather orangutans cover themselves with large leaves.

These apes are usually gentle and peaceful. But if upset, they are very dangerous. Few animals dare to attack them.

Orangutans seem to be very intelligent. They may be as intelligent as chimpanzees, but it is hard to tell. Unlike chimpanzees, they do not love to show off what they have learned.

See also: CHIMPANZEES; GORILLAS

Orangutan

7

Armadillos

Armadillo

Spanish explorers of the New World discovered many kinds of animals. Among these was one in armor. The Spaniards named it the armadillo, meaning "little armored thing."

As we know today, there are about 20 kinds of armadillo. And some of them are not very little. The largest is the GIANT ARMADILLO. It is 5 feet long from the tip of its nose to the tip of its tail. It may weigh as much as 120 pounds. But some others are small. The smallest of all is the FAIRY ARMADILLO, which is about 5 inches in length. It has pink armor and white fur.

An armadillo's armor is made of horny plates, or shields. They cover the back and sides. The head and tail are also armored. The underside of the body is furred. The back armor is divided into bands, or rings. Skin between the rings serves as hinges. It lets the animal bend. Some armadillos can curl up into a ball when threatened or attacked.

Armadillos are found chiefly in Central and South America. One kind is found in parts of the southern United States.

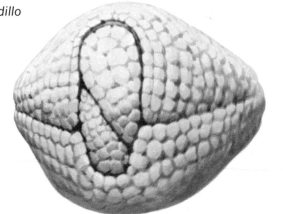

An Armadillo rolled up

This is the NINE-BANDED ARMADILLO. As you can tell by its name, it has nine bands in its back armor. It is about the size of a house cat. This armadillo cannot roll itself up in a ball. If alarmed, it moves very quickly. It hides in thorny bushes or in a hole. It is a good swimmer and can also walk across the bottom of a stream.

Nine-banded armadillos sometimes live in groups. They share a burrow that they have dug. They are most often seen at dusk or at night. They come out then to hunt for insects, small snakes, frogs, and other small creatures. A mother usually has a litter of 4 babies. They are all the same sex and look exactly alike.

Asses

See Donkeys

Baboons

Baboons

Baboons are the largest of the monkeys. A baboon stands 2 to 3 feet tall and weighs between 30 and 90 pounds. These big monkeys spend their days on the ground. They walk on all fours and run in a rocking gallop. At night they sleep in trees. They sleep sitting up.

A baboon spends its whole life sur-

Mandrill (rear)　　　　　　　Mandrill (head)

rounded by other baboons. Baboons live and travel in troops. Such groups can defend themselves against enemies better than a single animal could. There may be 15 to 200 baboons in a troop. Each troop has its own area where it lives. Here it finds water and food. Baboons eat mostly plant food such as grass, fruits, buds, and tender shoots. They may also eat insects, scorpions, birds, and small mammals. By day the troop moves around, feeding and resting. At rest the baboons gather in small groups. Some baboons simply sit. Others groom one another. One picks through the fur of another with its hands. It removes dirt and ticks.

When the troop moves on, the males are at the outside. Meat-eating enemies cannot reach the females and young. An enemy meets the males, who are very brave and very strong. Most meat-eating animals have learned to leave the baboons alone. Only leopards and lions attack them. And only leopards and lions can make baboons take flight into the trees. Baboons often mix with other plant-eating animals. They feed and drink with elephants, giraffes, antelopes, and zebras.

A young baboon rides on its mother's back when the troop is moving. When the troop is resting, it plays with other young baboons. They chase one another, pull tails, and pretend to fight. If a young baboon gets hurt and cries, older baboons come running and stop the playing.

All baboons live in Africa. They have some close relatives there, called MAN-DRILLS and DRILLS. These large monkeys are startling in their looks. Their faces and seat pads are brightly colored. A male mandrill's face is purple, blue, and bright red. His seat pad is red-purple. If you see a mandrill in a zoo, you will remember it well.

10

The badger is probably the fastest digger in North America. If it needs to hide, it digs with all four feet. The earth flies, and the badger vanishes from sight. Then it plugs up the hole behind itself.

The AMERICAN BADGER is a member of the weasel family. It is found from southwestern Canada to northern Mexico. It lives in open country—on plains, prairies, and deserts. It makes its home in a burrow that it digs. In spring a female badger builds a nest of dry grass in her burrow. Here the baby badgers are born. Usually there are 2 in a litter. At first they nurse. Then the mother brings them food. Finally, they follow her on hunting trips. Badgers eat rats, mice, rabbits, birds, snakes, lizards, eggs, and insects. They hunt at night.

If a badger catches something as big as a rabbit, it digs a special burrow. It takes the food into the burrow and stays there for several days. When it has eaten, it moves on. A badger never stays long in one burrow. So it is busy digging a large part of the time. Usually it lives alone. In autumn northern badgers become very fat. They hibernate, or sleep away part of the winter.

About 8 kinds of badger live in the Old World. One of the most interesting is the HONEY BADGER, or RATEL. It lives in Africa and Asia. The honey badger is a fierce fighter. It attacks animals much bigger than itself. Its skin is so tough that a dog cannot bite through it. Also, the skin is loose. The badger can twist inside its skin and bite an enemy that is holding it by the back of the neck.

The honey badger is very fond of honey. In the hot parts of Africa there is a bird called the honey guide. When it finds a bees' nest, it gives a certain call. The badger follows the call and breaks open the nest. Then the badger eats the honey and the bird picks up the crumbs.

American Badger

Bats

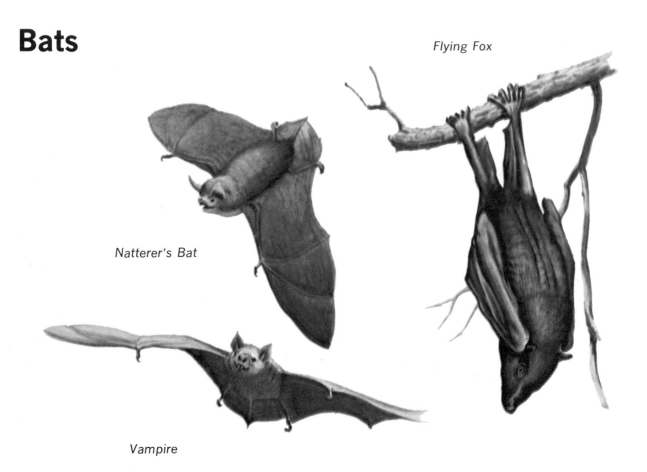

Flying Fox

Natterer's Bat

Vampire

Bat wing

Bats can fly. They are the only mammals that can. A mammal like the "flying" squirrel does not really fly. It glides from tree to tree. Bats are the only mammals that travel through the air with wings.

A bat has a furry, mouse-sized body. Its wings are made of skin that is stretched over bones. The bones are the bat's arms and fingers. The fingers are very long and slender. Only the thumb is not part of the wing. The thumb is short and usually ends in a hooked claw. A bat uses these hooks for climbing.

There are nearly 1,000 kinds of bat. Bats are found almost everywhere except in cold regions. Most are active only at night. That is when they come out to feed. Most kinds eat insects, but some kinds eat fruits. Some prey on frogs, mice, and other small animals. Some feed on the pollen and nectar in flowers. The VAMPIRE BATS feed on blood. They make a small cut with their teeth in the skin of a sleeping animal. Then they lap up some blood.

North American bats eat mostly insects. Sometimes they hunt insects on the ground. More often they capture in-

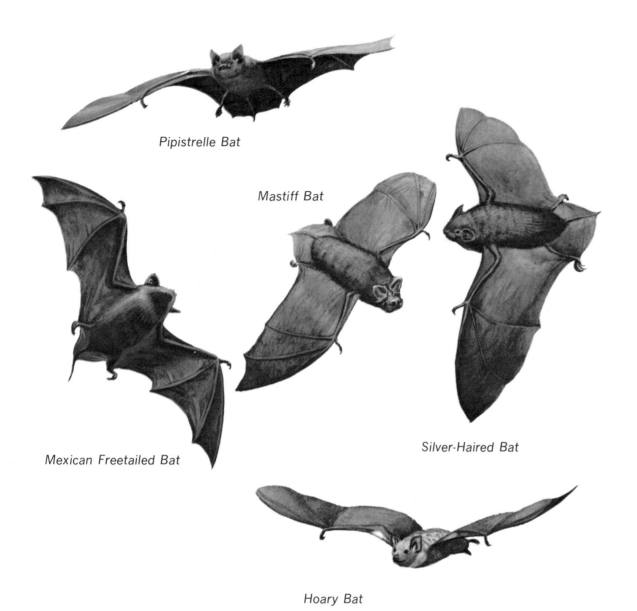

Pipistrelle Bat

Mastiff Bat

Mexican Freetailed Bat

Silver-Haired Bat

Hoary Bat

sects in the air. A bat may catch an insect in its mouth. Or it may "net" one with its wing or the pocket of skin near its tail.

Bats can see at night. But they do not use their eyes for hunting. They use their voices and their ears. A flying bat sends out a steady stream of sounds. Usually the sounds are so high-pitched that human ears cannot hear them. The sounds bounce off insects. The bat hears the echoes and catches the insects. Echoes also keep the bat from flying into things in the dark.

Most bats live in colonies. A small colony of 10 or 12 bats may live in a hollow tree. A large colony of thousands may live in a cave. A bat usually hangs itself up by the claws on its hind feet, but it can hang by its thumbs. It may hang from a

Bats coming home to roost

twig or branch. It may hook into a crack. It is usually head-down or upside down.

Bats cannot live in cold places. Some bats fly hundreds of miles to winter in a warmer climate. Other bats spend the winter in deep caves, where it does not get very cold. These bats go into a winter sleep. They hardly stir until spring comes.

Baby bats are born in late spring or early summer. A mother bat makes a cradle of herself. She hangs by her feet and thumbs, belly-up. The newborn baby rests in this cradle. Within minutes the cradle is no longer needed. The tiny baby can hold onto its mother's fur, using its teeth and claws. It travels with her when she flies off to feed. When the baby becomes too heavy for its mother, it stays home at night. The mother returns at dawn and feeds the baby. By the time it is 6 to 8 weeks old, the young bat goes hunting itself. It may live to be 17 or more years old. Bats have few enemies. Many live to die of old age.

Bears

Bears are big animals with stubby tails and thick legs. They are heavily built, but they can move very fast if they must. A bear can gallop at nearly 30 miles an hour. Bears are usually peaceful animals. But they are very dangerous when they are angry.

Spectacled Bear

Most bears live in the Northern Hemisphere. Only one kind lives south of the equator. This is the SPECTACLED BEAR of South America. There are four main kinds of bear in North America: black bears, grizzly bears, brown bears, and polar bears.

Black Bear with cubs

The AMERICAN BLACK BEAR is not very well named. Only some black bears are black. Others are yellowish, silvery, tan, and cinnamon-colored. One litter may have cubs of several colors. In one small area of southeastern Alaska, the black bears are silver-blue. On islands off British Columbia, they are creamy white. Black bears are found as far north as Alaska and as far south as central Mexico. They are the smallest North American bears.

Bears spend most of their time searching for food, eating, and sleeping. The black bear likes to eat meat best, but it cannot catch big animals. It eats mice, chipmunks, pocket gophers, and woodchucks, as well as fish, birds, eggs, and insects. It fills up on berries, fruits, grass, roots, bark, and bulbs. In summer and autumn the bears stuff themselves and become very fat. Cold weather makes them sleepy and they disappear into their dens. Here they doze away the winter. Around January the bear cubs are born. Usually there are 2 or 3 in a litter. They are born with their eyes shut and are very small. The mother bear goes on dozing, and the cubs nurse.

When spring comes, the mother takes

Grizzly Bear

Brown Bear

her cubs out of the den. Young cubs are very playful. Sometimes the mother joins in their play. But when she tells the cubs to do something, they must obey. If they don't, she cuffs them.

The GRIZZLY BEAR is bigger than the black bear. It has much longer front claws and a hump on its shoulders. Most grizzlies are dark brown or silvery. Their name has to do with their fur. "Grizzly" means that the hairs have light-colored tips. Today grizzlies are found mostly in western Canada and Alaska. Their way of life is much like that of the black bear. But they are skilled at killing deer, elk, and other large game animals.

The big BROWN BEAR is the largest of all the bears. It may weigh almost 2,000 pounds. Brown bears live along the coast of Alaska and on some of the is-lands. They are famous for their skill at catching salmon. A brown bear wades into shallow water and pounces on a salmon. It pins the salmon down with its paws. Then it grasps the fish between its jaws and goes ashore.

POLAR BEARS live around the world in the Arctic. These big bears are always on the move in search of food. The search takes the polar bear onto icebergs and floating chunks of sea ice. From these it hunts walruses and seals. It may travel

Polar Bear

far from the sight of land. A polar bear is a powerful swimmer.

A mother polar bear digs a winter den in hard-packed snow. Her cubs are born here in December or January. Other polar bears do not make dens. They are active the year round.

Beavers

Much of a beaver's life is spent working. A beaver cuts down trees, builds dams and houses, and stores food for winter.

In North America beavers may be found wherever there are trees and ponds or streams. (Some beavers also live in Europe.) A beaver is very much at home in the water. Its thick coat is water-proofed with oil. Its big hind feet are webbed for swimming. Its broad tail serves as a rudder and an oar. When a beaver dives, flaps close in its nostrils and ears. They shut out water. A beaver can stay underwater for 15 minutes at a time.

Beavers are rodents. That is, they are gnawing mammals. The gnawing wears down the teeth. But a rodent's front teeth never stop growing.

A beaver uses its four front teeth for felling a tree. These are big, orange-colored teeth with sharp cutting edges. The beaver circles the tree, cutting out chips. It cuts deeper and deeper until the tree falls. Next the beaver cuts up the tree and drags pieces to the stream.

Several beavers may work together building a dam. They pile branches and logs in the stream. Mud, stones, and drift-wood are added to weight down the branches. At first the dam leaks. But the beavers plaster the holes with mud. They scoop the mud up from the bottom in their arms. The finished dam may be

Beaver

anywhere from a few feet long to more than 100 feet. It is usually 1 to 4 feet high.

Beavers build dams to block streams and make ponds. A beaver needs a pond that is at least 2 to 3 feet deep all year round. In its pond a beaver is safe from enemies. And it has a place to store food.

The beavers usually build a lodge, or house, in their pond. They may build at the edge of the pond or on an island. The lodge is made mostly of branches plastered with mud. It has an air hole in the roof, but the entrances are underwater.

Once the lodge and dam are built, the beavers keep busy repairing them. As they drag branches over the ground, the beavers wear down paths. These are called "tote roads." Sometimes they dig canals from the pond to the tote roads. Then logs can be floated and towed.

Usually you will find a family of beavers living in a lodge. The family is made up of the mother, the father, and the last two litters of young. Just before a new litter is born, the two-year-olds are driven out of the lodge. They are now able to live on their own. The father also leaves for the time being. In late spring 3 to 4 baby beavers are born. The father moves back in. And family life starts again.

In summer beavers eat many kinds of water plants, grasses, roots, and herbs.

Beaver house

Beaver dam

They also eat tender bark, leaves, and buds. They store branches underwater for winter food. When the pond freezes over, the beavers swim under the ice to the food supply. They cut off a branch and take it to the lodge. When they have stripped off its bark, they throw it out.

Beavers have been much trapped for their fur. At one time they became very rare. Now they are protected by law. They are seen again in many parts of North America.

Bison

See Buffaloes

Boars

See Pigs

Bobcats

See Lynxes

19

Buffaloes

Bison

Indian Water Buffalo

The AMERICAN BUFFALO is a huge, shaggy beast with a hump on its shoulders and horns on its head. A bull stands 6 feet high at the shoulder. He can weigh up to 2,000 pounds. Buffalo are usually timid animals, ready to run when they see or smell you. But you cannot count on this. Sometimes a buffalo is bold. It lowers its head and charges.

Buffalo belong to the big family of wild cattle. They live on prairies and in open woodland, where they eat mostly grass. They like to be near water. They need water to drink. They are good swimmers. And in summer they like to wallow in mud. Wallowing helps to get rid of biting flies.

Bulls, cows, and calves graze together the year round. A cow usually has a calf in May. The calf is a lively little creature. It plays tag and follow-the-leader with other calves. It butts its fellows and pushes head-to-head.

At one time huge herds of buffalo roamed North America. There were per-haps 60 million of them. Early settlers and hunters slaughtered them. By 1890 only 500 were left. Fortunately, these buffalo were not killed. They were saved and bred. Today there are several thousand buffalo in the United States and more in Canada.

The American buffalo is sometimes called a BISON. This is its scientific name and a good one. It sets the American animal off from some others that are called buffaloes.

One of those is the WATER BUFFALO of Asia. It is a heavily built animal with curved, pointed horns. In the jungle it fears no living thing and fights fiercely. But it is often bothered by insects. To escape their bites the water buffalo may plaster itself with mud. Or it may escape into water. It stays there for hours with only its nose showing. The water buffalo has been tamed in some countries. It is used as a beast of burden and to pull plows and carts. It is gentle with people it knows but not with strangers.

The one-humped ARABIAN CAMEL is a desert animal. Its nostrils are slits; they can be closed to keep out sand and dust. Thick lashes keep sand out of its eyes. Its hoofed feet are broad and cushioned on the bottom; they are suited to travel across sand. The camel can eat almost any kind of desert plant. If it must go without food, it can for a few days. The hump on the camel's back is a store of fat. The camel's body can draw on the fat for food. Camels need water and will drink even salt water. But if they must, they can go without water for a few days. No one understands exactly how camels do that.

Arabian camels are sometimes called "ships of the desert." With a load of 400 pounds on its back, a camel moves steadily across the desert. Its long legs eat up the miles for hours at a time.

One-humped camels are found in the Near East, the Middle East, and North Africa. None live wild. They all belong to men. Men use them for riding and for carrying goods. Men also get milk, meat, wool, and hides from camels.

The one-humped camel is often called a DROMEDARY. It has a two-humped cousin called the BACTRIAN CAMEL. The Bactrian camel lives in central Asia. There are still some wild Bactrian camels, but many are owned by men. The two-humped camel is easier to ride. A shorter, heavier animal, it is slower than the one-humped camel. It lives in a colder climate and has longer fur.

Arabian Camel, or Dromedary

Bactrian Camel

Caribou

See Reindeer

Cats

The cat that purrs in your lap is a loving pet. But its body is very much like the bodies of the big cats that live wild. Big or small, all cats are made the same way. They are made for hunting.

A cat has keen senses. It hears well and smells well. Like all hunters, it has eyes that look straight forward. (A cow, for example, does not.) In bright light the pupils of the eyes are slits. At night, when the cat hunts, the pupils open wide. They let in much more light. (The eyes also reflect light. That is why a cat's eyes shine in the dark when they catch a gleam of light.)

Dogs are runners who chase their prey. Cats hunt in a different way. They may quietly track their prey, padding along on cushioned feet. Or they may lie hidden, waiting for the prey to pass. Suddenly the cat goes into action. It bounds forward and attacks. Its teeth are made for biting and cutting through flesh. Its feet are armed with sharp, hooked claws. (These are drawn into the paws when not needed.) A cat's are the sharpest claws of any meat-eating mammal. The cat kills and eats. Then it washes itself carefully.

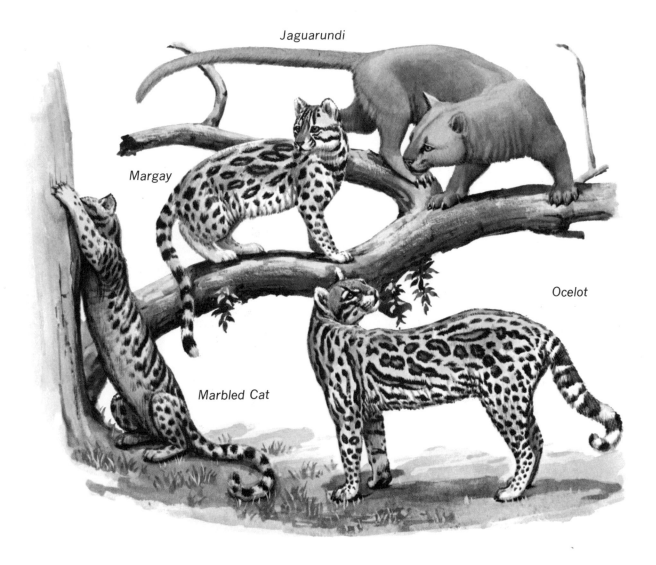

Jaguarundi

Margay

Marbled Cat

Ocelot

22

Like all hunting animals, cats are useful. Without the hunters, the earth would soon be overrun by rats, mice, rabbits, and hoofed mammals. Most kinds of cat hunt alone and live alone. Mothers stay with their young only until the young can hunt for themselves.

Scientists divide the cat family into two main groups. One group is made up of big cats—LIONS, TIGERS, LEOPARDS, and JAGUARS. All of them can roar. The other group is made up of smaller cats. None of them can really roar. MOUNTAIN LIONS, LYNXES, and CHEETAHS are three

such cats. Some of the others are shown in the drawings. Still other small cats live in South America, Africa, and Asia.

One of the small African cats is called the EGYPTIAN or KAFFIR CAT. Our house cats may be partly descended from this kind of cat. The ancient Egyptians tamed the Kaffir cat. From Egypt the cats spread to Europe. There they may have bred with European wildcats. In time the European house cats spread all over the world.

Today there are about nine kinds of DOMESTIC (tame) CAT. The best known

Pallas's Cat

Serval

Leopard Cat

23

Siamese Cat

Tabby

are the familiar short-haired house cats that do not belong to a breed. Then there are eight breeds of cat. Two are long-haired cats: the Persians and Himalayans. Six are short-haired cats: Abyssinians, Burmese, Manx, Russian Blue, Siamese, and Domestic Shorthair.

See also: CHEETAHS; JAGUARS; LEOPARDS; LIONS; LYNXES; MOUNTAIN LIONS; TIGERS

Persian

Cattle

In many parts of the world people raise cattle. Cattle are the familiar cows, bulls, calves, and steers that you see. A grown animal is 3 or 4 feet high at the shoulder and it weighs between 1,000 and 1,800 pounds.

Cattle eat mostly grass. When they are feeding, the grass goes into the first part of the stomach. Later when they are resting, they cough up the grass in mouthfuls. The mouthfuls are called the cud. The cattle chew the cud thoroughly and then swallow it. The cud goes on to the rest of the stomach. Cattle eat for about 8 hours out of the day. During this time a cow can eat some 155 pounds of green grass.

Cattle are raised for meat and milk. Parts of them are also used in making

Guernsey

products such as glue, soap, leather, fat, medicines, and fertilizers.

There are different breeds of cattle. Some give rich or large amounts of milk. The Jerseys, Guernseys, and Holsteins are famous for their milk. Other breeds are raised for beef. The Hereford and Aberdeen Angus are two of these.

People have been raising cattle for at least 5,000 years. Most of today's breeds can be traced in part to a kind of wild cattle called the AUROCHS. The aurochs was once found in many parts of Europe, Asia, and North Africa. It died out 300 to 400 years ago.

In other parts of the world there are other kinds of cattle. Some are wild, and some are bred and raised by men. One of the best known is the YAK. It lives among the high plains and mountains of central Asia. Like all cattle, it has hooves and horns. It is a large, awkward-looking animal. But it climbs well. In Tibet yaks are raised for milk. They are also ridden, driven, and used as pack animals. The yak is sometimes called the grunting ox because of the noise it makes when it is overloaded.

Yak

Aberdeen Angus

Zebu

Holstein

Chamois
See Goats

25

Cheetahs

Cheetahs

Cheetahs are members of the cat family. But a cheetah is somewhat different from other cats. It has very long, slim legs. Its claws are like a dog's—they cannot be pulled back into the paw. They are always out. There is another way in which a cheetah is like a dog. It can be taught to hunt with men. In India cheetahs are trained to chase and bring down antelope.

Antelope are swift animals, but cheetahs are swifter still. They are the fastest of all land animals. They have been clocked at 70 miles an hour. A cheetah can keep up this pace for only 400 or 500 yards. But that is usually enough to let the cheetah catch its prey.

Cheetahs are found in eastern Africa and southern Asia. In the wild, they hunt by daylight and by moonlight. They hunt, catch, and eat antelope, birds, and small mammals such as hares. A mother cheetah has 2 to 4 young in a litter.

When tamed, cheetahs are likely to be gentle and loving.

Chimpanzees

A chimpanzee is one of the great apes. Like all true apes, it has no tail. Like all great apes, it is big and strong. But you can easily tell a chimpanzee from the other apes. All you have to do is look at the ears. If the ape has large ears that stick out from its head, it is a chimpanzee.

Chimpanzees live in the forests of Central Africa. They spend much of their time on the ground. Sometimes they walk on all fours—on their hind feet and the knuckles of their hands. Often they walk upright. By day the chimpanzees move about feeding. They eat mostly fruits, leaves, roots, and other plant matter. But they also catch insects and other small animals. At night each animal builds itself a shelter of branches. The shelter is used for only one night. The shelter may be built in a tree. Or it may be built on the ground in an area where there are no leopards.

Chimpanzees live in small groups. Mother chimpanzees spend their time taking care of their children. The children amuse themselves by climbing and by playing with other chimpanzees. They can touch a new baby. They can ride on the backs of males. They can invite themselves to dinner with another mother and child. Young chimpanzees do what they want to do, yet they are not spoiled. They never whine or whimper. They always obey their mothers. A mother carries her child around until it is about 4 years old. Children stay with their mothers until they are 8 or 9.

After man, chimpanzees are probably the most intelligent mammals. They enjoy change. They are full of curiosity about new things. They seem to puzzle over problems. They build shelters. They invent simple tools and weapons. They are quick to learn. A tame chimpanzee can learn many of the things that a 3-year-old child learns. In captivity some chimpanzees have lived 20 years. Under very good conditions they might live to be 30 or 40.

Chimpanzee

Chipmunks

Chipmunks are bright-eyed little animals that scurry about the woods and open fields. They have stripes on their backs, and they look very much like some of the striped ground squirrels. The best way to tell a chipmunk from a ground squirrel is by its cheeks. If the cheeks are striped, the animal is a chipmunk.

Chipmunks are found only in the Northern Hemisphere. About 17 kinds live in North America. The biggest is the EASTERN CHIPMUNK. It lives in south-

eastern Canada and the eastern United States. Like other chipmunks, it will make friends with you, but it is a shy animal. If you startle it, it goes "chip, chip, chip," and then gives a sort of trill.

The eastern chipmunk can climb trees. But it would rather hunt its food on the ground. It eats seeds, grains, nuts, and berries. Some of the food is eaten at once. Some is gathered and stored for winter. A chipmunk has pouches inside its cheeks, where it can carry food. It

Eastern Chipmunk

darts about, stuffing seeds and nuts into its cheeks. Then it scampers home and unloads its cheek pouches.

Chipmunks live in burrows that they dig under logs or rocks. The burrow has a number of rooms. Some are for storing food. Some are for sleeping. Chipmunks are busy during the day and sleep at night. They also hibernate, or sleep away most of the winter. They wake up from time to time and eat some of the food they have stored. Then they go back to sleep. In spring a mother chipmunk gives birth to 3 to 5 babies.

The other American chipmunks are slightly smaller. They have more stripes and the coloring is slightly different. But their way of life is the same as the eastern chipmunk's.

Western Least Chipmunk

Conies
See Hyraxes; Pikas

Coons
See Raccoons

Cottontails
See Rabbits and Hares

Cougars
See Mountain Lions

The coyote is a member of the dog family. It looks something like a small German shepherd. And it is famous for its evening singing. Around twilight the coyote goes out to sing. It yaps, barks, whines, and howls. Sometimes coyotes also sing at dawn.

Coyotes live only in North America. They are found almost everywhere—from Alaska to Mexico, from the West Coast to the Adirondacks. They are much hunted, because they attack sheep. But they probably do more good than harm. They eat many mice, rats, and rabbits. They are intelligent animals and clever hunters. They seldom run as a pack. But they often hunt in pairs. One coyote chases the prey toward another, which lies hidden. Coyotes do not harm people.

Like wolves, many coyotes mate for life. Before the pups are born, the parents look for a den. It may be a cave, a hollow tree, or the burrow of some other animal. Here 6 to 7 pups are born. The mother stays with the pups and the father brings her food. Later both parents bring food to the pups. And still later the parents teach the pups to hunt.

Coyotes sometimes mate with dogs that live wild. The pups of these animals are called COY-DOGS.

Coyote

Deer

Deer are long-legged, graceful mammals. They live in almost every land area except Australia and Africa south of the Sahara. Deer are found in forests, deserts, swamps, open country, and the frozen lands of the far north.

There are more than 50 kinds of deer. Some kinds are as small as a fox terrier. Some are as big as a horse. Most are middle-sized.

Almost all kinds of male deer have antlers. A male uses his antlers as weapons. He uses them most during the mating season. Then the males often fight one another. Each is trying to gather as many females as possible. After the mating season the antlers are shed. Some of these rot away. Others are eaten by rodents such as porcupines, squirrels, and mice.

Antlers are made of bone. They grow from knobs on the deer's head. While they are growing, the antlers are covered with velvety skin. By late summer, the antlers are full grown. The velvety skin dries up. The deer rubs it off by scraping his antlers against trees and rocks.

Deer are prey for large meat-eating animals. Man also hunts them for their meat and hides. In some places there are no longer many big meat-eaters. Here deer may multiply so fast that there is not enough food for them. Unless there is some hunting of them, many will starve.

Deer are plant-eaters. They belong to the large group of hoofed mammals that chew their cud. When feeding, these mammals gulp down their food. Later they cough up mouthfuls of it and chew these thoroughly.

The WHITE-TAILED DEER is the most common kind in North America. There are several different races of white-tails. A northern one is the biggest, weighing about 300 pounds. The FLORIDA KEY DEER is the smallest; it weighs only 50 to 75 pounds. The white-tail lives in open woodlands. Its name comes from its tail, which is bright white on the underside. Fleeing an enemy, the deer holds its tail up. The flashing white serves as a warning of danger to other deer.

Like other deer, a mother white-tail has 1 or 2 fawns each spring. Baby fawns are weak and unsteady on their legs. They stay hidden, and their mother comes to feed them. She warns them to stay quietly on the ground. The fawns do not begin to follow their mother until they are about 4 weeks old. A fawn's coat is covered with white spots. These help to hide it in the sun and shadows of the woods.

Two other common deer are the MULE DEER and the BLACK-TAILED DEER. They are found in western North America. A mule deer has very large ears. The black-tail is famous for its bounding leaps. It is

Whitetail Deer and fawn

a very fast runner.

The American ELK is a much bigger deer. A male may stand 5 feet tall at the shoulder and weigh up to 600 pounds. Elk live in parts of Canada and the western United States. They move around in herds, feeding on grass and other plants. Elk are sometimes called by their Indian name, which is WAPITI. They are closely related to the RED DEER of Europe. Two other large deer are the MOOSE and the REINDEER.

See also: MOOSE; REINDEER

Caribou

Elk

Black-Tailed Deer

Mule Deer

Moose

31

Dogs

Almost anywhere that you find people you will find dogs. Some are working dogs. They pull sleds, herd sheep, stand guard, or help men hunt. Others are kept as pets. In the United States alone, there are some 26 million pet dogs and working dogs. Some are breeds. Some are a mixture of breeds. All of them are called "domestic dogs." That means they are tame dogs that live with people.

There are also many kinds of wild dog in the world. WOLVES, FOXES, COYOTES, and JACKALS are just a few of the wild dogs. Wild dogs are found in all parts of the world except Antarctica. The largest are the ARCTIC WOLVES.

Dhole

All wild dogs are meat-eaters. They catch and kill other animals for food. Their senses of sight, smell, and hearing are keen. They have long legs and are good runners. Most kinds of wild dog hunt in packs. They may chase their prey for hours. Then they attack. The wild dogs gobble their dinner, stuffing until they can eat no more. If some food is left over, they may bury or hide it to eat later.

Cape Hunting Dog

A wild dog usually has a thick coat of fur, a bushy tail, and pointed ears. At the end of each toe there is a strong claw. A dog's claws are always out. They cannot be drawn back into the paw as a cat's can. The muzzle is broad at the jaws and slender at the nose. Like a domestic dog, the wild dog pants when it is hot. A dog sweats only on the tongue.

Maned Wolf

The wild dogs are intelligent and brave. They are also social animals. This means that they live together in groups. Some kinds seem to mate for life. And a father usually helps to take care of the young.

Some of the wild dogs are well-known.

Bush Dog

Raccoon Dog

Yodeling Dog

Dingo

Others are little-known. The drawings show some of the little-known wild dogs. One wild dog presents something of a mystery. This is the DINGO, which lives in Australia. Scientists do not think it is native to Australia. But they do not know where it came from. Probably the first tribesmen to reach Australia brought the dingo with them. Perhaps they used it for hunting. As time passed, some dingos ran wild. Others stayed with the tribes. Today's tribesmen keep dingos as pets and as hunting dogs. Only one thing seems fairly sure. The dingo must once have been a wild dog that very early people tamed.

Fox Terrier

Basset

Dalmatian

German Shepherd

33

In fact, that is how all our domestic dogs came into being. In the beginning, early man probably feared and hated the wild dogs. The dogs hung around his camp and stole his meat. They hunted the same animals that he did. And so the dogs were enemies. But sometimes a hunter came on a litter of pups. The pups were playful balls of fur. The hunter took them home to his own children. The pups grew up tame. And people began to discover that tame dogs could be useful. They gave warning of danger. They drove other animals away from the camps. They helped in the hunting. The long friendship between dogs and people had begun.

When tribes of people moved around, they met other tribes with other kinds of dogs. The different dogs mated. And pups that were born were not quite like any of the wild dogs. They were a new sort of dog.

In time people learned to breed the sorts of dogs that they wanted. They bred dogs that could run fast or swim well or go after a burrowing animal. In this way different breeds of dog developed. Today there are about 200 breeds in the world. *See also:* COYOTES; FOXES; JACKALS; WOLVES

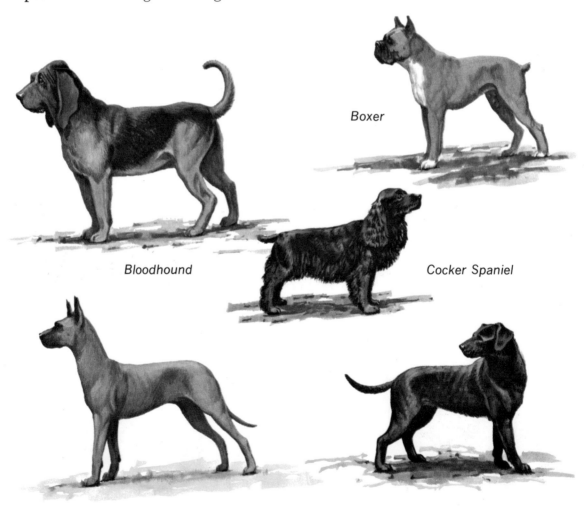

Boxer

Bloodhound

Cocker Spaniel

Great Dane

Labrador Retriever

Dolphins are mammals that live in the sea. A dolphin is born in the sea. It plays, feeds, and sleeps in the sea. It spends its whole life in the sea, for it cannot live on land.

A dolphin swims by moving its powerful tail up and down. And it is an excellent swimmer. Dolphins enjoy playing around ships and riding the bow waves. They can easily keep up with a ship traveling at 25 miles an hour. A dolphin can stay underwater for 4 to 6 minutes. Then it must surface for air. It breathes through its nostrils. These are on the top of its head and are called the blowhole. A cover over the blowhole snaps shut when the dolphin dives.

Many dolphins live along coasts and sometimes swim into bays and the mouths of rivers. Here they can swim at top speed, finding their way in muddy water and at night. They can also find and catch fish, which is what dolphins eat. For a long time scientists did not understand how dolphins could do all this. Then they discovered the answer. A dolphin makes many kinds of noises. One is a clicking sound. A swimming dolphin sends out bursts of clicks. These sounds travel through the water. When they hit a solid object, they bounce off it. The dolphin hears the echoes. The echoes tell the dolphin what lies ahead. That is how it finds food. That is how it avoids hitting things.

A baby dolphin is born tail-first underwater. Its mother pushes it to the surface for its first breath of air. But it is born able to see and to swim. It nurses underwater on milk. At the time it is born, it has a few bristles on its snout. These later fall out. A full-grown dolphin has no hair. A mother dolphin takes very good care of her baby. She is helped by a friend, who acts as the baby's aunt. In fact, dolphins often help one another. If one dolphin is hurt or sick, two others will help to hold it up in the water so that it can breathe.

Another nice thing about dolphins is

Dolphin

Porpoise

that they like people. Dolphins have long made friends with swimmers and fishermen. Most often they have made friends with children. They have played with children in the water and even taken them for rides.

Many dolphins have been kept in aquariums. Perhaps you have seen them there or on TV. Young dolphins are very playful. They make up their own games. Sometimes they play with one another. Sometimes a dolphin teaches its game to people. Dolphins are very intelligent.

Scientists say they are certainly as intelligent as dogs. They may be even more intelligent.

There are many kinds of dolphin in the world. All are members of the whale family. They belong to the branch called toothed whales. They are fairly small— between 5 and 14 feet long. Their closest relatives are the PORPOISES. Dolphins and porpoises are very much alike. They are so much alike that it is hard to tell them apart. Most people call them all by one name—either dolphins or porpoises.

Donkeys

A donkey is a small, long-eared member of the horse family. It is sturdily built. It is sure-footed. And it is hardy. A donkey works well in hot climates. It needs less water than a horse. And it can live on weeds and other foods that would not keep a horse alive. Donkeys can live and work in many places where horses cannot. Donkeys are used for riding and as beasts of burden. They are also used as pack animals in rocky or steep areas. The sure-footed donkey can pick its way safely over ground where a horse might slip and fall.

Pack Donkey

Mule

Hinny

Donkeys have been used by men for thousands of years. They are descended from the wild asses of northern Africa. "Donkey" is simply another name for ass. Usually it means a tamed ass.

Sometimes donkeys and horses mate. If the father is a donkey, the young animal is called a MULE. If the father is a horse, the young animal is called a HINNY. Mules are bigger and stronger than hinnies. Neither mules nor hinnies are able to have young of their own.

Duckbills
See Platypuses

Dugongs
See Sea Cows

Elephants

Once you have seen an elephant, you can never forget it. To begin with, an elephant is very big. It is the biggest land mammal alive. It stands 10 or 11 feet high at the shoulder and may weigh 5 or 6 tons. This mountain of a mammal is clothed in a wrinkled, gray hide. It has legs like pillars and ears like huge fans. Small eyes with long lashes look out at the world from a huge head. And then there is the trunk, which is really the elephant's nose. No other mammal has such a nose —or such a useful nose.

An elephant uses its trunk for eating. It gathers food with its trunk and then stuffs the food into its mouth. Elephants eat plant food. In the wild, an elephant strips branches off trees, pulls up grass, and picks fruit. A big male may eat 300 to 500 pounds of food a day.

An elephant uses its trunk for drinking. It sucks water into the trunk. Then it blows the water into its mouth. It may drink 50 gallons of water a day.

An elephant washes with its trunk. It sucks water into the trunk and then sprays its back. It smells with its trunk. That is how it learns what is going on, for it does not have keen eyes. It tests the ground with its trunk. It examines strange objects with its trunk.

The trunk is used for lifting things. An elephant can pick up a tree trunk that weighs nearly a ton. It can pick up a pea-

37

nut from the floor. If you look closely at the end of the trunk, you will see a fleshy "finger" there. That is what the elephant uses when it picks up something very small.

The trunk is also used for affection. Elephants pat each other when courting. A mother fondles her baby with her trunk.

In the wild, elephants live in herds of 10 to 50 animals. They eat a great deal. So they must travel far and wide to find food. They are good swimmers and often cross large rivers. In fact, the herd is never far from water. In early morning the elephants drink and bathe, rolling and splashing in the water. Then they feed

for several hours. Around noon the herd rests in the shade. Later it goes back to a river or lake and then feeds again. At night some elephants lie down to sleep. But most sleep standing up.

A newborn elephant is a big baby. It is 3 feet high at the shoulder and may weigh 300 pounds. It is also covered with hair. Most of this hair later falls out. A grown elephant has only bristles on its hide. A baby is able to walk an hour or two after it is born. It travels with the herd. It nurses for about 2 years and stays with its mother until it is at least 4. Elephants live a long time. They may live to be 60 or 70.

Most of the elephants in circuses are ASIATIC ELEPHANTS. They come from

Asiatic Elephant

African Elephant

38

India, Ceylon, and Southeast Asia. Sometimes they are called INDIAN ELEPHANTS. Another kind of elephant lives in Africa, south of the Sahara. It is called the AFRICAN ELEPHANT. Many zoos have both kinds.

African and Asian elephants look much alike. But you can tell them apart if you know what to look for. An African elephant has two fingers at the tip of its trunk. Its ears are huge. The Asiatic elephant has one finger at the tip of the trunk. Its ears are smaller.

Elephants are intelligent, strong, and fairly easy to tame. Men have been putting them to work for hundreds of years. In India and Burma they have long been used for many purposes. They are taught to pick up and carry heavy logs. People ride them when hunting tigers.

African Elephants bathing

Elk
See Deer

Ermines
See Weasels

Ferrets

The BLACK-FOOTED FERRET is a member of the weasel family. Now very rare, it lives on the plains and prairies of North America. This is the same area where the prairie dogs live. And the black-footed ferret is found in prairie dog towns. Sometimes it is seen peering out of a prairie dog hole. It is active at dusk and at night. When frightened, it makes a chattering, scolding noise and hisses.

Very little is known about the black-footed ferret. Scientists think it eats prairie dogs. But it has never been seen to do so.

The black-footed ferret is closely related to the Old World polecat. In Europe tame polecats are called ferrets. They are used for hunting rats and rabbits.
See also: POLECATS

Black-Footed Ferret

Fishers

See Martens

Foxes

The RED FOX is a clever animal. Chased by a pack of hounds, the fox runs. But it often escapes by using its wits. It is full of tricks for making the hounds lose the scent. It may leap onto a fence or wall and run along the top. It may run through a shallow brook. It may double back on its own tracks, then leap to one side and run off. While the hounds try to pick up the scent, the fox escapes.

Red foxes are not large animals. They stand about 16 inches high at the shoulder and weigh from 8 to 15 pounds. Most of them have red-gold coats. But some are black or silver. Pups of different colors may be born in the same litter.

Usually 4 to 5 pups are born in the foxes' den. The mother stays with them and the father brings her food. Later both parents bring food to the young. During the summer both parents teach the young to hunt. The red fox uses a den only for

Red Fox

raising its young. The rest of the year it sleeps outdoors. In cold weather it curls up and covers its nose and feet with its tail.

Foxes eat all sorts of small animals. They like mice and rabbits best. But they also eat frogs, eggs, insects, and fruits. They are very fond of raspberries. They help farmers by eating mice and rabbits, but sometimes they eat the farmer's chickens, too. That is why farmers hunt them. Red foxes are also trapped for their fur. And some are raised on fur farms.

The red fox is found in most parts of North America. Other red foxes live in Europe, Asia, and North Africa.

The ARCTIC FOX lives in the far north of North America, Europe, and Asia. Its coat is gray-brown in summer. In autumn the Arctic fox grows a winter coat. Most Arctic foxes grow a white coat. Some grow a smoky-blue coat.

The Arctic fox hunts small mammals and birds in summer. It also eats eggs and berries. In winter the fox eats anything it can find—dead seals, walruses, and whales. Sometimes it goes out on the ice in search of food. For shelter it digs a snug den in the snow.

The Arctic fox is far from shy. It follows people and barks at them. It takes food from the camps of explorers. It also takes all sorts of other things that no fox could eat.

Arctic Fox

Fennec Fox

There are many other kinds of fox. The AMERICAN GRAY FOX can sometimes climb for a few feet into slanting trees. It hugs the trunk with its front legs and pushes itself up with its hind legs. The KIT FOXES and SWIFT FOXES are the smallest ones in North America. They weigh 4 to 5 pounds. The kit fox lives on western plains. The swift fox lives on deserts of the Southwest.

Other kinds of foxes live in other parts of the world. Perhaps the most beautiful one is the FENNEC FOX. It lives in desert areas of northern Africa. It is also the smallest member of the wild dog family. About 16 inches long, it weighs 2 to 4 pounds.

Gibbons

See Apes

Giraffes

A giraffe is the tallest animal in the world. The head of a big male is 18 or 19 feet above the ground. He may weigh more than 2 tons.

This giant animal eats mostly leaves and grass. A giraffe reaches into the branches of a tree. It wraps its very long tongue around some leaves and pulls them into its mouth. Then it nibbles them off. Eating grass is a very different matter. A giraffe has a long neck, but it also has long legs. To eat grass or drink water, it must spread its front legs apart. Only then can its head reach the ground.

Giraffes live in Africa. They are usually seen on dry, sunny plains and along the edges of forests. They move about in

Giraffe

Giraffes

small herds. They are always alert for danger. Their keen eyes and great height give them a good view of the land. If they are alarmed, their long legs carry them off at speeds up to 30 miles an hour. Lions are their chief enemies. If attacked, a giraffe defends itself with its big front hooves.

Both male and female giraffes have horns. The horns are made of bone, and they are covered with skin and hair. When males fight, they butt each other with their heads and necks. Males fight during the mating season. A mother giraffe bears a single baby. At birth the baby is about $6\frac{1}{2}$ feet tall. Young giraffes usually lie down to sleep. But most grown giraffes sleep standing up.

The giraffe has a short-necked relative called the OKAPI. The okapi lives in rain forests of central Africa. It is a shy animal, about the size of a horse. A male has short, hair-covered horns.

Okapi

Goats

Domestic Goat   Ibex

About 8,000 or 9,000 years ago men first began to raise goats. The goats were wild animals that early farmers started to keep in herds. Today there are many breeds of goat. They are raised for meat and for milk, which can be made into butter and cheese. They are raised for hides and for hair. Like the wool of sheep, goat hair can be made into clothing. Cashmere, mohair, and angora are fine wools that are made from goat hairs.

Several kinds of wild goat still live in the Northern Hemisphere. Like wild sheep, they live in rugged mountain country. And they look very much like wild sheep. It is often hard to tell which you are looking at. The best clue is a beard. Male goats have beards. Male sheep do not. The IBEX is one of the best-known Old World goats.

North America has an animal called the ROCKY MOUNTAIN GOAT. It is not a true goat, but is a goat-antelope. Its horns are smaller than a true goat's. Its neck and shoulders are heavier.

The Rocky Mountain goat is found from southern Alaska to northern Idaho. It is slow-moving. But it climbs with sure-footed ease in the steep, rocky places where it lives. Its hooves have a hard,

Chamois

Rocky Mountain Goat

sharp rim. Within the rim is a soft, inner pad. Such feet grip the surface of rocks and ice. The goat feeds on woody plants and may graze on grass.

Kids are born in the spring. One or two are born to a mother each year. Half an hour after its birth, a kid is able to jump about. But the mother keeps it hidden for a few days. She goes off to feed and comes back to nurse the kid. In a few days they join a band of other mothers and their young. The mothers guard their young until the kids are big enough to take care of themselves.

The Rocky Mountain goat is closely related to the CHAMOIS of Europe and Asia Minor. The chamois is a small mammal that lives among high mountain peaks. It is nimble, daring, and graceful. Alarmed, a band of chamois take off in flight. They skim over the mountainside, jumping from one narrow ledge to another.

Gophers

See Pocket Gophers; Squirrels

45

Gorillas

Gorillas

Gorillas are the biggest of the great apes. And they are very big indeed. A male stands about 5½ feet tall. He weighs between 300 and 500 pounds. A growling, angry gorilla is a frightening animal. Almost no other animal will attack it. But usually a gorilla is quiet and shy. It is dangerous only when attacked or threatened.

Gorillas feed mostly on juicy-stemmed plants. But they also eat fruits, leaves, berries, and buds. All climb trees to get food. Females and their young may travel through the trees. Males seldom do. Their great weight makes tree travel dangerous.

On the ground, males often stand upright. But they usually walk on all fours—on their hind feet and the knuckles of their hands.

At night the females build shelters in trees. A male is more likely to build a shelter at the foot of a tree.

Gorillas live in the forests of Central Africa. One kind lives in the lowlands. Another kind lives in mountain forests. There are not many gorillas left today— perhaps about 10,000. They are hunted by natives for their meat and skins. The gorillas you see in zoos and circuses were probably captured as babies.

Grizzly Bears
See Bears

Groundhogs
See Woodchucks

Guinea Pigs

The guinea pig is a native of South America. In spite of its name, it is not a pig. It is one of the rodents, or gnawing mammals. It is a small animal with a plump body, short legs, and no tail. In the wild, guinea pigs live together in burrows. They are shy animals, always ready to take alarm and run. They eat leaves, grain, and other plant food. The Inca Indians of Peru used to raise guinea pigs and eat them.

Today guinea pigs are raised in laboratories all over the world. Scientists use them to study disease and diet and to show how traits are passed down through families. Guinea pigs are good to use in such studies because they breed quickly and often. A mother guinea pig has litters of 3 or 4 young. She may have 5 or 6 litters a year. Each of the young is ready to start breeding at the age of 2 months. Guinea pigs live to be about 8 years old.

Guinea pigs are gentle and do not bite. They are easy to raise if they are fed and kept warm and clean.

Hamsters

A hamster is a small, chubby animal. It has short legs, a stub of a tail, and thick, soft fur. It is a rodent, or gnawing mammal. There are three main types of hamster. All are natives of the Old World. The ones you see in pet shops and zoos are usually golden hamsters. They are native to Syria.

A GOLDEN HAMSTER has huge pouches inside its cheeks. They reach from the lips to the shoulders. A hamster uses the pouches to carry food back to its burrow. When the pouches are filled, the hamster's head and shoulders look very fat. These hamsters eat almost everything—green plants, seeds, fruits, and meat. Like many small creatures, they are most active at night. A mother hamster usually has a litter of 6 or 7 young. She bears several litters a year. A hamster lives to be 2 or 3 years old.

Hamster

Hares

See Rabbits and Hares

Hedgehogs

Hedgehog

A European hedgehog is a small, plump animal about $5\frac{1}{4}$ to 10 inches long. By day it sleeps in the burrow it has dug under a hedge or bush. At night it comes out and searches for food. Many meat-eating animals think a hedgehog would make a tasty meal. But they seldom get a chance to find out, for a hedgehog is a walking pincushion. At the first sign of danger, it rolls itself into a ball. Its furry head, legs, and underside are safely tucked away. An enemy is faced with a ball of needle-sharp quills.

When the enemy goes away, the hedgehog uncurls. It goes on about its business of hunting food. It likes insects best. But it also eats frogs, snails, snakes, young birds, and mice. Sometimes it eats fruits and other vegetable matter. In autumn the hedgehog grows very fat. Its body draws on this fat while the hedge-

Hedgehog quill

hog sleeps away the coldest part of the winter.

Once or twice a year a mother hedgehog has a litter of 5 to 7 young. The young are born with quills, but the quills are soft. They harden within a few weeks. The quills are a form of hair.

There are several kinds of hedgehog. All are found only in the Old World. They are not the same as porcupines. A porcupine is a rodent or gnawing mammal. A hedgehog belongs to the same family as the moles and shrews.

Hippopotamuses

The common hippopotamus has a 4-ton body on short, thick legs. The great body just clears the ground. Small, bulging eyes look out of the huge head. While you watch a hippo at the zoo, it may yawn. The vast, pink mouth opens wide, and you see the animal's tusks. Perhaps the hippo will then decide to take a swim. It lumbers over to its pool and slides into the water. It may stay underwater for a few minutes. Then it may float, with only its eyes and nostrils showing above the water. You see that the bulging eyes and nostrils are useful.

In Africa, where they live, hippos spend much of their time in water. Sometimes they wade about, snorting and bellowing and rooting up food. Sometimes they paddle or float or sink to the bottom. A hippo can stay underwater for as long as half an hour. It is also able to walk about on the bottom of a river or lake.

In many ways, hippos are water animals. A baby hippo is born underwater and nurses underwater. Until it learns to swim, the mother may carry it on her back. A hippo needs to stay moist. Its hide has special pores. They give off a thick, oily, pink stuff called "blood sweat." This thick stuff protects the hide and keeps it from drying out on land.

Common hippos spend the day dozing in or near water. At night they roam about looking for food. They eat mostly grass, but sometimes they raid a farmer's fields. Hippos are much hunted by natives for their flesh and hides. Their tusks are excellent ivory.

A much smaller hippo lives in the forests and swamps of West Africa. It is the PIGMY HIPPOPOTAMUS. This hippo spends much more time on land than the common hippo does.

Hippopotamuses

Hogs

See Pigs

Horses

A fine horse is an intelligent and handsome animal. The graceful body is designed for speed. It is designed for running on hard ground. It is designed for escaping enemies in a burst of speed.

The running muscles are bunched at the tops of the legs. The legs themselves are long and slender. Each ends in a single toe, which is covered by a hard hoof. A horse is always poised on the tips of its toes, ready for flight.

A horse's eyes are set well back on the head. The horse can see all around itself. It can see backward as well as forward, without turning its head. When it puts its long neck and head down, it can easily reach the grass that is its food. At the same time it sees what is happening around it. And it stands ready to run if danger threatens.

A horse looks alert, and it is. Its eyesight is keen. So are its senses of smelling and hearing. The ears twitch, picking up faint sounds. The nostrils gulp in large amounts of air.

Through the ages, their keen senses and long legs have helped horses escape most of their meat-eating enemies.

The horse itself is a plant-eater. It eats mostly coarse grasses. It cuts off a mouthful with its front teeth. It grinds the grass with its back teeth. Grass wears teeth down. That is one reason why an expert can tell the age of a horse by looking at its teeth. Horses are old at 20, but some live to be 30 or 40.

Men first began to capture and tame wild horses about 5,000 years ago. Since then, they have developed many different breeds. Some have been bred for large size. Big and strong, these horses are used for plowing, for pulling loads, and for other heavy work. Some horses are slender and streamlined. They are used for riding, racing, and hunting.

All told, there are about 60 breeds of horse today. The biggest is probably the SHIRE HORSE. This powerful workhorse is nearly 6 feet high at the shoulder and may weigh 2,200 to 2,400 pounds. The smallest is the SHETLAND PONY. (A pony is simply a small horse.) Many Shetlands are less than 3 feet high at the shoulder. They are, however, very strong and hardy.

There are very few true wild horses in the world today. In many places there are herds of horses that live in the wild. But these are horses that men have bred. They have either escaped or been turned loose. This is true of the "wild horses" of the western United States. They are descended from horses that the Spaniards brought to the New World. They are called MUSTANGS, from the Spanish word that means "strayed" or "wild."

Mustang

Przewalski's Horse

Shire

Shetland Pony

Thoroughbred

Pinto

52

In the early 1800's more than a million mustangs ranged the western plains and deserts. Settlers captured and tamed many of the mustangs. Later, ranchers took over the land for cattle. Today only a few hundred mustangs are left.

The mustangs live together in small bands. A band usually roams one area where there is food and water. The band is made up of mares and their young, and it is led by a stallion. Each stallion gathers as many mares as he can for his own band. He may try to steal mares from another band. If he does, a fight takes place. The two stallions scream and rear on their hind legs. They strike with their front hooves and bite with their teeth. The winner takes as many mares as he can and goes on his way. Colts, or foals, are born in spring. Usually a mare has one colt every other year. The young stay with their mothers for about a year. Then the stallion drives them out of the band.

The MONGOLIAN WILD HORSES may be truly wild. Slightly larger than a pony, this horse has a flowing tail and a short mane. It is also called PRZEWALSKI'S HORSE after the Russian explorer who discovered it. No one is sure whether these horses are still of pure stock. They may have bred with other horses that live in the wild. Only a few of them still run wild.

Horses have several close relatives. The best known is the ZEBRA. Another is the WILD ASS of northern and eastern Africa. Still others are the asslike animals of Asia.

See also: DONKEYS; ZEBRAS

Arabian Horse

53

Hyenas

Spotted Hyena

The SPOTTED HYENA is often called the LAUGHING HYENA. It does not really laugh. But it howls, gurgles, and makes a strange cackling noise when it is excited. This hyena is about 3 feet high at the shoulder and may weigh 175 pounds. It looks awkward because its front legs are longer than its hind legs. But it is a swift animal. It can run as fast as 35 or 40 miles an hour.

The spotted hyena lives in a burrow or cave. It sleeps by day. At night it comes out to eat. Like all hyenas, it is a meat-eater with big, strong jaws. It hunts as part of a pack.

People long thought that hyenas were cowards. They were thought to eat mostly what other hunters, such as lions, had left.

New studies show this may not be true. Some, and perhaps all, hyenas are very brave. They attack even large, fierce animals, such as African buffaloes. When the kill is made, the hyenas bark, growl, and shriek. The lions hear the noise and come running. Then there is another fight. If the lions win, they get the meat and the hyenas get the leftovers. If the hyenas win, they get the meat.

There are three kinds of hyena—the spotted, the striped, and the brown hyena. All are found in parts of Africa. The STRIPED HYENA is also found as far east as India. Hyenas look something like ugly dogs. But they are not members of the dog family. They form a separate family of their own.

Striped Hyena

Hyraxes

Rock Hyrax

A hyrax looks somewhat like a rabbit with small ears and short legs. Its toes have flat nails that look like hooves. The soles of the feet are padded and damp. The middle of the sole can be pulled up. This forms a cup that sucks at the surface. A hyrax can stick to almost any surface. It never skids. Hyraxes can climb trees. And they are very good at running over rocks and about cliffs.

There are several kinds of hyrax. All live in the Old World—in Africa and the Middle East. They are sometimes called DASSIES. In the Bible they are called CONIES.

Three kinds of hyrax live in trees. They spend the day in tree hollows or hidden among the leaves. At night they run up and down trees, feeding on leaves, buds, and insects. They are known for the noise they make. It starts as a croaking sound. The croaking becomes louder and louder and ends in a scream.

Six kinds of hyrax live on the ground. They are active by day. They enjoy basking in the sun and rolling in dust. They like to chase one another among the rocks. They are small animals that eat locusts, roots, and bulbs. But they will bite any animal that bothers them. These hyraxes live together in large colonies. They are very noisy, too. They whistle, scream, and chatter. A mother usually has a litter of 3 young. A few hours after birth they are able to run around with the other hyraxes.

Jackals

Jackals belong to the big family of wild dogs. They are Old World animals that live in warm, fairly dry areas. There are several kinds of jackal. But all have the same way of life.

Jackals will eat almost anything—mice, rats, chickens, lambs, goats, lizards, insects, grapes, and sugar cane. They are best known for eating what is left by lions and tigers. When it scents a kill, a jackal goes to the place where the lion or tiger is eating. It sits down and waits.

When the big cat has eaten its fill, the jackal feasts on the remains.

Jackals are stealthy animals. They are seldom seen by people. In areas where people live, the jackal comes out only at night. Then it hunts in family groups or in small packs. When not hunting, a jackal stays by itself.

Like the American coyote, the jackal "sings" in the evening. At sundown it goes out and howls. It gives three or four long wails and then some short yelps.

Jackal

Jack Rabbits *See Rabbits and Hares*

Jaguars

In a zoo it is hard to tell a jaguar from a leopard. They are both big cats. And both have yellow-tan coats with black spots. In the wild you cannot mistake them. Jaguars are found only in the New World, while leopards are found only in the Old World. Jaguars live in many parts of South America and as far north as Mexico. They are the biggest of the New World cats. A male may weigh as much as 250 pounds.

A jaguar likes best to live in a jungle. But it can also live in deserts and on open plains. It is a good climber and swimmer, but it hunts mostly on the ground. It will eat almost anything it can catch—deer and other hoofed mammals, alligators, turtles, and monkeys. It even catches fish. The jaguar crawls out on a limb that overhangs water. It scoops a fish out of the water with its paw. Jaguars rarely attack people. But they do attack man's cattle and sheep.

Young jaguars are born in a den. There may be 2 to 4 of them in a litter. They stay with their mother for about 2 years. Then they are ready to hunt and earn their own living.

Jaguar

Kangaroos

Great Gray Kangaroo

In the cool of early morning the great gray kangaroos feed on grass. The sun rises and the day becomes hot. The great grays rest in the tall grass. They wash themselves. From time to time they rise to scratch themselves or look about. Perhaps one sees something moving—an eagle circling overhead. It gives an alarm thump of its feet. Instantly the others are up and moving. They bound away on their big hind legs.

Hopping slowly, a kangaroo bounces along on its hind legs. It may lazily thump the ground with its tail. Hopping faster, the kangaroo carries its tail in the air. The tail helps to balance the kangaroo and also serves as a rudder. A big kangaroo covers about 25 feet in each leap. It can easily speed along at 20 miles an hour.

The great gray is a big kangaroo. When a male rears up, he can look over a man's head. He may weigh as much as 200 pounds.

A female is smaller and slimmer. Like all kangaroo mothers, she carries her baby in a pouch on her stomach. At birth the baby of a great gray is less than an inch long. All by itself this tiny baby crawls through its mother's fur and scrambles into her pouch. There it clamps onto a nipple and begins to feed. It first leaves the pouch when it is about 4 months old. It tries out its legs and samples some grass. By the time it is 8 months old, it has outgrown the pouch.

Kangaroos belong to the big group of

57

animals called marsupials, or pouched mammals. Almost all these mammals live in Australia and on neighboring islands. There are many types of marsupial. Kangaroos are just one type—and there are 45 to 50 kinds of kangaroo. They are of many sizes.

The heaviest is the GREAT GRAY, or FORESTER, KANGAROO. The RED KANGAROO is taller but more slender. The male is wine-red in color. The female is a soft, smoky-blue.

Red Kangaroo

The smallest kangaroos are only a foot high. They belong to the group called RAT KANGAROOS. Rat kangaroos make nests of grass. They stay in their nests by day and come out at night.

Other kangaroos are small, medium, and large in size. The different kinds are found in all sorts of places—deserts, swamps, woods, rocks, and cliffs. One kind, the TREE KANGAROO, lives in trees. It is a splendid climber and acrobat.

Tree Kangaroo

Koalas

Koala

The koala looks like a teddy bear, but it is not a bear. It is one of the mammals that carry their young in pouches. Koalas are found only in Australia. They are very good at climbing trees. They eat the leaves of eucalyptus trees, which are also called gum trees. A koala eats about 2 pounds of leaves a day. It is not a water-drinker. It gets its water from dew on the leaves and from the leaves themselves.

A mother koala usually has a baby every other year. At birth the baby is less than an inch long. It climbs into its mother's pouch and attaches itself to a nipple. When it grows too big for the pouch, it comes out. It then travels on its mother's back until it is almost as big as she is. When the baby is cold or resting, the mother hugs it in her lap.

A koala has a woolly coat, a black snub nose, and round bushy ears. Its eyes are small and bright. A full-grown koala is $2\frac{1}{2}$ to 3 feet long and weighs about 30 pounds. It is a gentle, quiet animal that never does any harm.

Lemmings

A lemming is like a chubby field mouse with a very short tail. There are four kinds of lemming. All live in the far north of the world. In winter they tunnel under the snow. In summer they live on the surface of the ground or burrow through the soil. They eat grasses, leaves, berries, blossoms, and roots. Female lemmings make nests of grass, moss, and lichens. Several litters of 3 to 9 young are born in a nest each year.

Norway lemmings are famous for the journeys that they make. This is what happens. When there is lots of food, lemmings multiply very quickly. These many, many lemmings gobble up the food. Soon there is little left to eat. Then thousands upon thousands of lemmings set out to find food. Huge bands of them swarm across the land. They travel through swamps, cities, and forests. They swim rivers and lakes. Many die along the way. But many others finally reach the sea. To

Lemming

them the sea is simply more water to cross. Thousands of them plunge in. They swim until they drown.

By this time there are not many lemmings left at home. There is enough food for them. So again the lemmings multiply. And in 3 or 4 years another journey to the sea takes place.

Many other animals are affected by what happens to the lemmings. Lemmings eat the same food as caribou and reindeer. When there are many lemmings, the caribou and reindeer may starve. Lemmings themselves are eaten by many mammals and birds. When there are few lemmings, the animals that prey on them must move south to find food.

Leopards

A leopard is smaller than a lion or a tiger. But it is still one of the big cats. It is about 7 feet long from its nose to the end of its tail. It weighs from 100 to 175 pounds. A leopard is intelligent. It is quick to learn, and it remembers what it has learned. It is a fierce fighter and a dangerous animal.

A leopard is a good climber. It hides among the branches of a tree, waiting for another animal to pass. The leopard leaps on its prey and kills. It may drag its food back into the tree and eat there. On the ground a leopard springs after its prey. It may catch the other animal in a few long leaps. Leopards prey on deer, antelope, monkeys, cattle, sheep, and small animals. They usually hunt alone.

Leopard are found mainly in Africa and Asia. There may still be a few in southeastern Europe.

Most leopards have a bright yellow coat with black spots. You may hear of an animal called a BLACK PANTHER. This is really a leopard that happens to be black. A black leopard can be born in the same litter with spotted leopard cubs. A mother leopard has a litter of 1 to 4 young. They are full grown at the age of 3 years. In a zoo a leopard may live to be 20.

Leopards

Lions

The lion is often called the king of the beasts. He has a thundering roar. He has a mane of long hair on his head and shoulders. And he is a big animal. He stands 3 feet high at the shoulder. He may weigh as much as 500 pounds. (A lioness is smaller and does not have a mane.)

Lions are hunters and meat-eaters. They live in open country and on grassy plains. They hunt hoofed mammals that also live in such areas. Zebras and antelope are their favorite prey. Lions also eat some smaller mammals.

Like the rest of the cat family, lions hunt chiefly at night. A lion pads quietly along on cushioned feet. It can run in spurts of 40 miles an hour. Its powerful muscles carry it through the air in long leaps. A lion attacks with claws and teeth.

Unlike other cats, lions enjoy company. They live together in groups called prides. A pride is a family-sized group. It is made up of several females, one or more males, and a number of young lions. Sometimes the lions hunt together. A male drives the prey to where his mate lies in wait.

When a big kill is made, the lions eat from it for several days. When the food is used up, they kill again. Lions kill only for food or to defend themselves.

A mother lion usually has a litter of about 4 cubs. Unlike other cats, the lion is a good father. He brings food to the lioness. Later he may bring food for the whole family. Young lions do not start to hunt for their own food until they are a year old.

Most lions live in Africa, south of the Sahara. There are also a few lions in northwest India.

Lions are often seen in circuses. They are intelligent animals. They are more friendly than other big cats. So it is fairly easy to teach them tricks. But a lion is never truly tamed. The trainer must always be on guard.

Llamas

Llama

Guanaco

Llamas are members of the camel family. They live in the Andes Mountains of South America. Llamas were first tamed and put to work by the Inca Indians about 2,500 years ago. The llama is much used as a beast of burden. It can carry loads of 200 pounds over the rugged mountains. But like the camel, the llama is a strong-willed animal. If overloaded, it sits down and will not move. If made angry, it spits on the person who annoyed it.

Today's Indians use almost every part of a llama. They eat its meat. They weave its fleece into cloth and make sandals from its hide. They make candles from its fat and braid rope from its long hairs. Llama droppings serve as fuel in a treeless land.

Llamas may be a tamed form of the GUANACO. This wild animal still lives in small herds in the Andes. Guanacos are alert animals that depend on speed for safety. They can run at speeds of up to 35 miles an hour. They eat grass and enjoy bathing in mountain streams. A baby guanaco is able to run as soon as it is born.

Alpaca

The ALPACA may be another tamed form of the guanaco. An alpaca looks like a llama with very long hair. Its woolly coat hangs over its eyes, and the wool of its body may drag on the ground. The alpaca is raised for its wool, which is woven into a very fine cloth.

The VICUÑA is related to the guanaco family. It looks something like a guanaco but is smaller and more slender. Small herds of vicuñas are found high in the Andes. Their silky fleece is highly prized as wool.

Vicuña

Lynxes

Lynxes are cats. But they look rather different from other cats. A lynx has long side whiskers. It has tufts of fur at the tips of its ears. It has a short tail and large feet. Its hind legs are longer than its front legs.

There are several kinds of lynx. Two kinds live in North America. One is the CANADA LYNX. The other is the BOBCAT, which is also called the BAY LYNX or WILDCAT.

Most Canada lynxes live in Alaska and Canada, but some cross the border into Oregon, Colorado, and northern New York. The Canada lynx hunts at night. Its favorite food is the snowshoe hare. This lynx weighs between 20 and 40 pounds. When the ground is covered with snow, its big feet act as snowshoes. It is good at climbing and swimming. A mother has litters of 1 to 4 young.

The bobcat is smaller than the Canada

Canada Lynx

lynx and has a white-tipped tail. It lives in southern Canada, Mexico, and all of the United States except the central and southern Mississippi valley. Bobcats are found in forests, deserts, farmlands, and mountains. They are good swimmers and climbers.

In a night's hunting a bobcat may cover 20 to 25 miles. It is able to attack and kill deer. But mostly it hunts mice, hares, and rabbits. A bobcat catches a rabbit by springing on it.

Manatees

See Sea Cows

Marmots

See Woodchucks

Martens

Bobcat

Martens live in the thick forests of the Northern Hemisphere. They are members of the weasel family and fairly small. A full grown male weighs from $1\frac{1}{2}$ to 4 pounds. Females are even smaller. A female makes her nest in a hollow tree or log and lines it with dry leaves. She bears 2 or 3 young in spring.

A marten sleeps very soundly during part of the day. Then it wakes up full of energy. Quick and graceful, it is excellent at climbing trees. It climbs so fast that it can overtake a squirrel. Red squirrels are what American martens like best to eat. But they also eat other small mammals, insects, berries, and fruits. Martens do not like to be wet. They will stay home and go hungry rather than hunt in bad weather.

The AMERICAN MARTEN is found in Alaska, most of Canada, and parts of the United States. There are several kinds of marten in Europe and Asia. They are highly valued for their fur. The fur is sometimes called sable, and martens themselves may be called SABLES.

Marten

64

The marten has a bigger relative called the FISHER. Fishers live only in North America. Like martens, they live in forests, but they do not climb trees much. Like all the weasel family, they give off a bad scent when frightened. Fishers like to eat porcupines. They bowl the porcupines over and tear open the underside, where there are no quills.

Fisher

Mice and Rats

There are thousands of kinds of mice and rats in the world. They are part of the huge group of gnawing mammals called rodents. A mouse and a rat are much alike. But the smaller ones are usually called mice, while the bigger ones are called rats.

The HOUSE MOUSE is one of the most familiar mice. It is a small, gray-brown animal with a long tail that is almost naked of fur. A hardy little creature it can (and does) live anywhere that people live. The house mouse is a native of the Old World. Stowing away in ships, it arrived in the New World around the time of the American Revolution. Today it is found in almost all parts of North America.

The house mouse builds its nest wherever it can find a safe place. The nest is made of soft shreds of material. The mouse feds on any human food that it can find. It also will try paste, glue, soap, and a number of other things. Nibbling away, house mice do millions of dollars worth of damage a year. They are also a danger to health. They have fleas that carry diseases.

The house mouse can breed all year round. A female starts to mate when she is 40 days old. About 3 weeks later she has a litter of 4 to 7 babies. Then she mates again. Within 2 months the babies from the first litter may have babies of their own.

House Mouse

The FIELD MOUSE is another familiar mouse. It is also called a MEADOW MOUSE or a VOLE. Several kinds of field mice are native to the New World. The common field mouse looks like a house mouse with a short tail.

Field mice are food for almost all meat-eating mammals, birds, snakes, and turtles. Few field mice live to be a year old. But like house mice, they breed very, very quickly. The young are born in a round nest of dry plant material.

Common Field Mouse

The many kinds of field mice eat mostly seeds, plants, and insects. Where there are many field mice, they do great damage to crops.

North America has many other kinds of native mice. One is the HARVEST MOUSE. It weaves a round nest and lives

Harvest Mouse

Deermouse

outdoors. Some kind of DEERMOUSE is found in almost every part of North America. These delicate and beautiful little animals are also called WHITE-FOOTED MICE. They are very nimble. When excited, most kinds drum on the ground with their front feet.

Some kinds of rats are quite small and look like large mice. Others are big. The head and body may be a foot long and the scaly tail even longer than that.

HOUSE RATS—like house mice—live closely with people. Where people go, the rat follows. It crosses the ocean on ships. It travels across the land on trains.

There are two common house rats in North America. Both are natives of the Old World. The BLACK RAT first arrived with the explorers. The BROWN RAT arrived around 1775. Both went westward with the pioneers.

The brown rat is also known as the NORWAY RAT and the HOUSE RAT. It is a big rat with coarse fur and large, naked ears. There is a little hair on its tail, and the tail is shorter than the body. Brown rats breed almost as fast as house mice. This rat is active all year and swims well. It eats garbage, grains, vegetables, meat, packaged foods, soap, eggs, and young birds. It gnaws the covering from electric

Norway Rat

Black Rat

wiring, sometimes causing fires. It needs a lot of drinking water. And it will gnaw through a lead pipe to get water.

The black rat is more slender, and its tail is longer than its body. It is a better climber than the brown rat, and it is very much at home on ships. Together these two rats cause millions of dollars' worth of damage in the world each year. Their fleas have spread diseases over whole continents.

Tamed strains of the brown rat are much used in laboratory studies of medicine. They are also kept as pets. These animals are often white in color.

One of the most interesting New World rats is the WOOD RAT. It is also called the PACK RAT, the TRADE RAT, and the CAVE RAT. It has large hairy ears, soft fur, and a long hairy tail. It eats mostly plant matter. In the West, wood rats build houses that look like small beaver lodges. A house may be on the ground, in a tree, or in a rocky place. Wood rats are collectors. They are very fond of shiny things—coins, watches, spoons, buttons, bits of tinfoil or glass. They pick up shiny things and take them home. (You can find many interesting things in a wood

rat's house.) On the way home, a wood rat may see something else it likes. It lays down what it is carrying and picks up the new thing. That is why it is sometimes called a trade rat.

Wood Rat

Mink

Mink

A mink is a member of the weasel family. It has a long, slender body and short legs. It has soft, thick underfur that is overlaid with long, glistening, dark hairs. Mink are highly valued for their fur. Some are trapped wild for their fur. Others are raised on mink ranches.

There are two main kinds of mink. One lives in the New World and one in the Old World. New World mink are found in Alaska, Canada, and all parts of the United States except the Southwest.

Like the weasel, a mink is a fearless fighter and an expert hunter. It hunts mice, rats, and rabbits. In summer it lives near water. It then hunts muskrats, marsh birds, and young snapping turtles. It eats frogs and shellfish and can catch fish.

Mink are active mostly at night. Sometimes a mink is cornered by an owl, fox, or wildcat. The mink screams, spits, and hisses. It gives off a powerful scent from glands near its tail.

Usually 5 to 8 mink are born in a litter. The young are very playful. They follow their parents until late summer. Then the family breaks up and the young go off on their own.

Moles

Day and night, moles are hard at work digging tunnels. A mole's front legs end in paddlelike hands with big claws. A mole shovels its way through the soil by using its front legs. It digs with a swimming motion something like the breast stroke. The paws dig through the soil and push it backward under the mole's body. When the soil piles up, the mole digs a shaft to the surface. Then it pushes the dirt out. The dirt forms a mound, or molehill.

Gardeners do not like molehills. But moles are often helpful to gardeners. They eat many harmful insects. The hardworking mole may eat its own weight in insects during one day's digging. The digging loosens the soil, which is often good for plants.

An animal that lives underground does not need to see very well. Most moles have small eyes and poor sight. Some kinds cannot see at all. But moles do have excellent senses of touch and smell.

Moles make two sets of tunnels. The tunnels we see are the upper ones. A mole makes these while looking for food. Its back pushes up the soil. The deeper tunnels are 1 to 2 feet below the surface. These connect with the food tunnels and serve as "streets" to the nests.

A mother mole usually has a litter of 2 to 5 young. The young are born in a nest of grass underground.

There are many kinds of mole in the world. The COMMON GARDEN MOLE is found in eastern North America. TOWNS-END'S MOLE lives near the Pacific coast. The strangest mole of all is the AMERICAN STAR-NOSED MOLE. Its nose is surrounded by 22 fleshy "fingers" that grow out like petals on a flower. The star-nosed mole is an expert swimmer and diver. It gathers some of its food in the water. The fleshy fingers are in motion as the mole seeks food.

Common Garden Mole

Townsend's Mole

Star-Nosed Mole

Mongooses

Mongoose

A mongoose is a small mammal that is expert at killing cobras. It will attack these poisonous snakes, which are several times its own length. The mongoose threatens the snake. The snake rears and strikes. The mongoose dodges. The snake strikes again. The mongoose plunges forward. It bites the snake at the back of the head. When the snake is dead, the mongoose eats it.

Mongooses are also good at killing rats. They are kept as rat-killers in some parts of the world. But they can also be a big problem. About 100 years ago mongooses were brought to islands in the West Indies to kill rats. The rats soon moved into the trees. And the mongooses took to eating eggs, chickens, and small animals that men needed. They became as big a pest as the rats. (The United States will not allow anyone to bring a mongoose into the country.)

Most kinds of mongoose live in Africa. Some live in Asia and southern Europe. They make their homes in burrows and are active by day.

Mongooses are members of a large family of meat-eating mammals. All these mammals are native to the Old World. Most are quite small. Many have claws like a cat's that can be drawn back into the paws. Most people have never heard of these mammals. But two you may read about are the CIVETS and GENETS.

Genet

African Civet

Monkeys

There are about 130 kinds of monkey in the world. Of these, 61 kinds are found in Asia and Africa. Together they are called Old World monkeys. The other 69 kinds are found in Central and South America. They are called New World monkeys.

The Old World monkeys all belong to one family. But the different kinds do not look much alike. Tails, snouts, and fur can be long or short. Some kinds have patches of skin that are bright red, blue, or purple. Some live in trees, while others spend most of their time on the ground.

The MACAQUES form a big group of Old World monkeys. Most kinds of macaque are about the size of a fox terrier. All have cheek pouches, where they store and carry food for short times. They live in troops. Strong and brave, they defend themselves well when attacked.

One of the best-known macaques is the RHESUS MONKEY of India. Active and playful, it is a favorite in zoos and circuses. This monkey is also used in medical research—in making polio vaccine, for example.

The BARBARY APE is another famous macaque, which is not an ape but a monkey. It is like an ape only because it has no tail. The Barbary ape lives in North Africa. It also lives on Gibraltar, where it was taken many, many years ago.

Barbary Ape

The CRAB-EATING MACAQUE lives in Malaysia and the Philippines. At low tide, it goes along the beach looking for crabs and other shellfish. It likes to eat them. This long-tailed monkey is a good swimmer and diver. If frightened, a whole tribe may dive into a river and swim across.

Rhesus Monkey

Guenon

Macaque

The PIG-TAILED MACAQUE of Sumatra is easily tamed when young. Natives teach it to climb coconut trees and drop nuts down to them.

Guenon

The GUENONS are another large group of African monkeys. Many kinds have beards. Some have brightly colored fur and skin. These slender monkeys travel through the trees in bands.

Langur

LANGURS are common monkeys in Asia. They are slender monkeys that live mostly in trees. But they can gallop on the ground at speeds up to 23 miles an hour. They eat fruits, flowers, and leaves. They are sometimes called LEAF MONKEYS.

In Borneo there is a very odd-looking monkey. It is called the PROBOSCIS, or LONG-NOSED, MONKEY. A male has a large nose that sticks out from his face. When excited, he makes his nose larger. This monkey's call sounds like the honk of a goose.

Proboscis Monkey

The largest monkeys are the baboons, which live in Africa.
See also: BABOONS

New World monkeys are smaller than their Old World relatives. They are very nimble in trees. And many have tails that can be used for grasping things. Like other monkeys, these eat mainly plant leaves, fruits, insects, and spiders. Most of them sleep during the night and are active by day.

The New World monkeys are grouped in two families.

MARMOSETS and TAMARINS make up one family. These monkeys are all quite small. They use their hands to catch or pick food. One kind has a mane on its head and shoulders. Some have tufts of hair on their ears.

There are many kinds of monkey in the other family. Here are just a few of them.

The DOURICOULI is the only New World monkey that is active at night. Like most night animals, it has very large eyes and sees well in the dark. It runs along tree limbs and leaps from branch to branch. It hunts through trees for fruits, leaves, insects, spiders, birds, and small mammals. It makes about 50 different sounds. Its danger call is "Wook!"

The largest New World monkeys are the HOWLERS. They are famous for their loud howls, which can sometimes be heard 2 miles away. Bands of up to 40 howlers travel among the treetops. A howler's thick, strong tail can be used for grasping limbs or food.

Douricouli

Howler

The UAKARIS are the only short-tailed American monkeys. Small bands of uakaris live among the tops of tall trees. They are much quieter than most monkeys. A uakari has a naked, red face. Its coat may be reddish brown, white, or brown and black.

The skinny SPIDER MONKEYS have very long legs, fingers, and tails. The tail can be used as a fifth hand. These monkeys travel in small groups. Scientists report that spider monkeys break off branches and try to drop them on people below.

Uakari

Spider Monkey

Lemur

The CAPUCHIN MONKEY is active, intelligent, and full of mischief. It is often seen in zoos and circuses. In the wild, these monkeys travel in bands, chattering and shrieking. They are generally good-tempered. But like all monkeys, a capuchin may suddenly fly into a rage and bite a friend.

Other Relatives

There are six families of other mammals that are related to the monkeys. All live only in the Old World. These mammals are less highly developed than the monkeys. Their brains are smaller. They do not have much curiosity. Most cannot use both eyes at the same time to look at one thing.

One family is made up of the TARSIERS. They live on islands of the East Indian region. A tarsier is so small you could hold one in your hand. Tarsiers have huge, owl-like eyes and froglike legs. They have long fingers and toes. At night a tarsier leaps about in bushes and trees, searching for food. Its main food is insects. It watches an insect, then leaps forward and seizes the insect with its hands.

Three families are made up of LEMURS. All live on the island of Madagascar, off eastern Africa. The smallest kind of lemur is the size of a mouse. The largest is the size of a medium-size dog. Most kinds of lemur live in trees.

Another family takes in the LORISES and POTTOS of Africa and Asia. These animals have short ears and short tails (or no tails). They climb trees slowly but surely.

TREE SHREWS make up the sixth family. They are the least highly developed of all. Some of these small animals look rather like squirrels. All have long noses. All have claws on their toes. They eat fruits and insects. When eating, they sit up and hold their food between their hands. "Tree shrews" is not a good name for these mammals. They are not shrews, and many do not live in trees.

Moose

A bull moose is the largest deer on earth. He is a giant who stands 7½ feet high at the shoulder and sometimes weighs up to 1,800 pounds. His antlers alone may weigh 85 pounds. His stiltlike legs are 4½ feet long. Often his long legs are a help in getting food. By standing on his hind legs, he can pull down branches growing 12 feet above the ground. Long legs are also good for wading. And a moose is fond of eating water lilies and other plants that grow in water.

Unlike other deer, the bull moose takes only one mate at a time. During the mating period he is ready to fight any other bull. When he hears one, he goes off at a trot. He swings his antlers, perhaps beating them against trees. A terrible battle may follow, as the two giants fight with their antlers.

Moose are found in Alaska, Canada, and some northern states. The North American moose has a close relative in northern Europe. Europeans call this deer an ELK.

Moose

Mountain Lions

Mountain lions are cats with many names. You may hear them called COUGARS, PANTHERS, and PUMAS. Some of their other names are CATAMOUNTS, PAINTERS, AMERICAN LIONS, and INDIAN DEVILS.

Mountain lions are fairly large cats. Most are 6 to 7 feet long. But from his nose to the tip of his tail, a large male may measure almost 10 feet. He may weigh more than 200 pounds. The mountain lion is a New World cat. Among American cats, only the jaguar is bigger. Mountain lions are now found mostly in western North America and in Central and South America.

The mountain lion usually hunts by night. Moving silently through the dark, it tracks its prey. Nearing, it suddenly bounds forward and kills. Mountain lions usually hunt deer and small mammals. They sometimes prey on horses, cattle, pigs and sheep. That is why they have been much hunted.

In spring a female chooses a cave or ledge for her den. Here her 2 to 4 cubs are born. The mother nurses and washes her cubs. She leaves them only to search for food. Young cubs have light brown fur with dark spots. As they grow older, they shed their spotted fur.

For the first few months the cubs play like kittens. They chase each other. They pounce on pebbles. By the age of 3 months they are eating meat that their mother brings home. Then they start to go hunting with her. They stay with their mother until they are a year or two old.

Mountain Lion

Mouse

See Mice and Rats

Mules

See Donkeys

Musk-oxen

The musk-ox lives in northern Canada and Greenland. It lives through the Arctic winter without shelter. Its big body is covered with thick fur. The outer coat is a layer of long hairs that reach to its ankles. These hairs shed rain and snow. The undercoat is made of fine, soft fur. It is so thick that it keeps the animal warm.

A musk-ox looks clumsy. But it moves easily and quickly on its broad hooves. The hooves spread. Their sharp edges cut into or grip the ground. Musk-oxen can run over crusted snow or rocky ground.

In the short Arctic summer musk-oxen feed on grasses and other plants. When autumn comes, the musk-oxen move into the hills. In some places the wind blows away the snow. Here the musk-oxen feed on dried, frozen plants. They can also paw away snow to find food.

A baby musk-ox is born in April or May. The Arctic is still full of snow and ice and biting winds. The calf huddles beneath its mother for warmth. In summer it learns to eat plants.

Sometimes wolves or bears try to attack musk-oxen. The herd backs into a circle, with their heads facing out. From time to time a bull dashes out to attack the enemy. A man with a rifle is the only enemy musk-oxen cannot defeat.

Musk Ox

Muskrats

A muskrat is a large, sturdy rodent (gnawing mammal). It is found in most parts of North America. It is a native of the New World, but it has been taken to the Old World. Muskrats are valued for their thick, shiny fur.

Muskrats make their homes in marshes, lakes, ponds, rivers, and streams. They swim by paddling with their webbed hind feet. They are very good swimmers. When there is danger, they dive. They can stay underwater for about 12 minutes.

Some muskrats build houses out of reeds. The houses look something like piles of weeds. A house is usually built on an island that the muskrat has made. Underwater tunnels lead to the house.

Other muskrats dig dens in the bank of a stream or pond. A muskrat starts by digging an underwater tunnel. The tunnel leads up into the bank. There the muskrat

Muskrat and young

makes its den. Later it may build more tunnels to the den. Muskrats are preyed on by many meat-eating mammals. Tunnels are the road to safety.

Muskrats eat mostly plants. They also eat clams, fish, and small water creatures. Each muskrat usually lives by itself. A female has several litters of 5 to 7 young each year.

Okapi

See Giraffes

Opossums

The opossum is the only mammal in North America that carries its babies in a pouch. At birth opossum babies are tiny. They are so tiny that 24 would fit in a teaspoon. They climb through their mother's fur into her pouch. Each attaches itself to a nipple. The nipple swells in its mouth. Mother and babies are now firmly attached. The babies stay there feeding.

By the time they are 10 weeks old, the babies are about the size of mice. They can leave the pouch and crawl about. They ride on their mother's back when she goes hunting. As they get bigger, she staggers under their weight. A mother opossum is not a very large animal.

The COMMON, or VIRGINIA, OPOSSUM is about the size of a house cat. Its paws look like tiny hands. They can be used for grasping things. An opossum can hang from a branch by its front feet or its hind feet. The scaly tail is sometimes used as a fifth hand. The tip can be used for grasping things.

Opossums usually live where there are trees. They are good climbers. They may sleep by day in the branches of trees. They also hunt for some of their food in trees. Opossums eat insects, mice, toads, birds, berries, and fruits.

An opossum builds its nest on the ground, often in a hollow stump. To make the nest, the opossum gathers dry leaves.

It picks up the leaves in its mouth. Using its feet, it packs the leaves into a bundle. Then it curls the tip of its tail around the bundle. It carries the bundle in its tail to the nest.

Opossums are famous for playing dead. Faced with danger, an opossum falls over. Its eyes are shut. Its tongue hangs out. It looks dead. The enemy is puzzled by this. Usually it goes away and leaves the opossum alone. Then the opossum recovers and wanders off. People used to think opossums played dead on purpose. Now scientists say this is not so. Threatened, an opossum goes into a state of shock, or faints. It cannot help falling over and looking dead.

The Virginia opossum is found in many parts of the United States and southern Canada. Central and South America have several kinds of opossum. None are found in the Old World.

Opossum

Orangutans
See Apes

Otters

Young or old, river otters like to play. Their favorite kind of play is sliding. In summer they slide down the bank of a stream into the water. In winter they slide on snow. Sometimes a whole family takes turns at sliding.

An otter can move well on land. But it is most at home in the water. Its sturdy body is streamlined for slipping through water. Its broad tail serves as a rudder. Its webbed feet are paddles. A coat of thick fur keeps the otter warm. An otter can cruise at 6 miles an hour. It can go much faster if it must.

Otters are good at fishing. They catch and eat fish, shellfish, frogs, turtles, and similar creatures. They also eat snakes, rabbits, water birds, muskrats, worms, and insects.

Some river otters live on shore. They make dens in hollow logs or under bushes. Most river otters make their den at the edge of the water. The den may have two entrances, one under water and one above. The den is lined with moss and dry leaves. Here 2 or 3 young are born each year. When they are about 3 months old, the mother teaches them to swim. The father helps and also plays with the pups.

There are about 12 kinds of river otter in the world. One kind lives in many parts of North America. Otters are members of the weasel family and are valued for their fur.

River Otters

Sea Otter

The biggest otter is the SEA OTTER. It is found only along the shores of the North Pacific. A full-grown male may be 6 feet long and weigh 75 pounds.

The sea otter spends most of its life afloat. It likes to live near rocky shores where there are beds of the seaweed called kelp.

When it is in a hurry, the sea otter swims on its belly. Mostly it floats on its back. From time to time it stands upright in the water. Shading its eyes with its paws, it looks about. At night it sleeps in the kelp, which keeps the otter from drifting. The sleeping otter may cover its eyes with its paws.

A sea otter eats fish, crabs, mussels, sea urchins, clams, and other kinds of sea life. It dives to find food. While eating, it floats on its back and uses its chest as a table. A young sea otter usually crushes the shells between its back teeth to get at the food inside. An older sea otter may bring up a stone from the bottom. It lays the stone on its chest. Then it opens the shells by pounding them on the stone.

Baby sea otters are born in the water. A mother takes very good care of her baby. She carries it and nurses it on her chest. She plays with it. She tosses it in the air and catches it. She licks it and washes it. When she must dive for food, she leaves the baby hidden in a bed of kelp. Alarmed, she takes the baby under one arm and dives.

Pandas

Giant Panda

The GIANT PANDA is found in the high mountains of southwestern China and eastern Tibet. It is bear-shaped and bear-sized. But its closest relatives are the raccoons.

The giant panda lives in thick forests of bamboo. In winter the black-and-white animal can hardly be seen among the black shadows on the white snow. The panda lives mostly on the ground. It climbs a tree only if chased by an enemy.

Bamboo shoots and roots are the giant panda's main food. (It also eats other plants, fish, and small mammals.) Most of its waking time is spent eating. A giant panda is awake and active for 10 or 12 hours a day. The pads on its front feet can be used to grasp food. They work something like fingers.

The LESSER PANDA is a much smaller animal. It is about the size of a large house cat. It looks something like a raccoon. The lesser panda lives in the forest-covered mountains of northern India and western China. It usually sleeps during the day. Sometimes it sleeps curled up. Then it puts its tail over its head, like a dog or cat. Sometimes it sleeps sitting up. Then it tucks its head between its front paws, like the American raccoon. The lesser panda eats mostly bamboo sprouts, grass, roots, fruits, and acorns. It may also eat eggs, birds, and mice. One or two young are born in spring. The lesser panda is a gentle, friendly animal that tames easily.

Lesser Panda

Pangolins

Pangolin

A pangolin looks like a huge pine cone with a head, tail, and legs. Its underside is soft and furry. The rest of the pangolin is covered with sharp-edged scales. The scales are made of hairs that are stuck together. Hard and horny, they overlap each other.

The scales make excellent armor. When danger threatens, the pangolin rolls itself into a ball. It hooks the end of its tail over a scale. It is almost impossible to open a rolled-up pangolin.

Pangolins eat ants and termites. A pangolin has no teeth, but it does have a long, sticky tongue. It gathers food on its tongue. It rips open termite nests with its long, strong claws.

There are several kinds of pangolin. They live in hot, wet parts of Africa and southeastern Asia. Some live in burrows and some live in trees. A mother pangolin carries her baby on her back or tail.

Pangolins are sometimes called SCALY ANTEATERS.

Panthers

"Panther" is a name used for several kinds of large cat. But it is hard to tell what someone means when he says "panther," unless he uses the scientific name "Panthera." Some scientists use that name to mean all the big cats—lions, tigers, leopards, and jaguars.

Other people use "panther" as another name for the leopard. Some use it only for black leopards. They call these animals black panthers.

Still other people use "panther" as a name for the mountain lion.
See also: LEOPARDS; MOUNTAIN LIONS

Peccaries
See Pigs

Pigs

Domestic Pigs

Young farm pigs are fun to watch. They are friendly, lively, and intelligent. They are very good at discovering how to get out of a pen. Once out, they have a fine romp. And they can run very fast—as you may know if you've chased one. Like all pigs, they love to eat. They plunge their heads and front feet into their food and gobble it down. But they keep themselves clean. Pigs are not dirty animals.

A male pig is called a boar. A female is a sow. "Hogs" is just another name for pigs. Farm pigs are raised for meat. They are easy to fatten up. And a sow has 2 or 3 large litters a year.

FARM PIGS look much like wild pigs. A pig is a hoofed mammal with a barrel-shaped body. Most kinds have a thin covering of bristly hairs. They have a long, pointed head that ends in a flattened snout. The snout is very useful. A pig uses it for pushing things aside and for digging food out of the ground.

Most farm pigs are probably descended

from the wild boar of Europe, Asia, and North Africa. The WILD BOAR stands about 3 feet high at the shoulder and may weigh 350 pounds or more. It has four tusks. Two grow from each jaw. Wild boars eat mostly plant food—roots, nuts, grain, and plant stems. They use their tusks and snouts to dig some of their food out of the ground. Wild boars travel in bands. They are quick-moving and good swimmers. They like to wallow in mud for hours at a time. A female has one or two litters a year. The young are striped, although the parents are not. Later the young shed their striped coats.

Many other kinds of wild pig live in Asia and Africa. One of the strangest looking is the WARTHOG of Africa. It has a big snout and long, curved tusks. Its body is covered with a thick mane of coarse hair. The male has lumps, or "warts," on his face.

There are no true wild pigs in the New World. Certain pigs, called RAZORBACK HOGS, live wild in the southeastern United States. But they are really farm pigs that escaped.

Wild Boar

The New World does have a family of wild, piglike animals called PECCARIES. They are related to pigs. But they are smaller and have a thick coat of bristly hair. When they are frightened, they give off an unpleasant scent. Two kinds of peccary live in Central and South America. One of them is sometimes seen in the United States near the Mexican border. It is called the COLLARED PECCARY.

Warthog

Peccary

Pikas

A pika is a small animal that looks something like a guinea pig. Most pikas live in rocky areas. They make nests among rocks.

A pika spends its time gathering grass, weeds, and other plants. It may even climb a tree and cut twigs from a low branch. This plant material is its food. The pika carries bundles of food back to its nest area. There it makes a kind of haystack, which dries in the sun. The dried plants become the pika's winter food.

Pikas have a whistling call. They give this call during the day and sometimes at night. A pika colony is a rather noisy place.

Pikas have a number of names. They are also called CONIES, ROCK RABBITS, WHISTLING HARES, and HAYMAKERS.

There are several kinds of pika. Most live in mountains of western North America, eastern Europe, and Asia. They are closely related to rabbits and hares.

Pika

Platypuses

The platypus has a furry coat, webbed feet, and a bill that looks like a duck's. The female lays eggs and feeds her young on milk. All told, the platypus is one of the strangest mammals in the world.

A platypus' home is a burrow dug in the bank of a stream. At dawn and at twilight the platypus waddles out to feed. At the water's edge, it closes its beady eyes and dives to the bottom of the stream. Its leathery bill is full of nerve endings. The platypus uses its bill to find small creatures that live in water. Then it comes to the surface and eats what it has found.

A mother digs a special burrow for laying eggs. In it she builds a nest of leaves and grass. She lays two eggs. They have soft shells and are dull white in color. For about two weeks the mother stays curled around her eggs, keeping them warm. She makes only brief trips out of the burrow. Then the babies break out of the eggs. The mother goes off to feed and to clean herself.

At first the babies get no food. Then milk starts to ooze from pores on the mother's stomach. The young lick it off the mother's fur and skin.

The platypus lives only in Tasmania and eastern Australia. It is sometimes called a DUCKBILL.

Platypus

Pocket Gophers

A pocket gopher spends much of its life digging tunnels. It digs with its front teeth and its claws. It uses its four huge front teeth to loosen soil. Its lips close behind the teeth. This way the gopher can gnaw dirt without getting any in its mouth. Once the soil is loose, the gopher digs with its big front claws.

When a gopher is digging, it makes a shaft to the surface. Then it pushes the loose earth to the surface of the ground. When it is not using the shaft, it plugs the opening with dirt. In loose, sandy soil a gopher may tunnel 200 to 300 feet in a single night.

Pocket gophers dig two sets of tunnels: deep ones and shallow ones. The gopher gets its food in the shallow tunnels. It

Pocket Gophers

bites off roots and bulbs that it finds in the tunnels. In each cheek the gopher has a deep, fur-lined pocket. It stuffs food into the pockets with its front paws. Then it carries the food to the deeper tunnel, where it lives. The gopher pushes the food out of the pockets with its paws. It stores the food in the tunnel. The furry pockets can be turned inside out for cleaning.

Pocket gophers are rodents (gnawing mammals). They live only in the Americas. There are many different kinds. Some live as far north as Saskatchewan.

Head of Pocket Gopher

Others live as far south as Panama. There are none in the northeastern United States or in nearby parts of Canada.

Polar bears

See Bears

Polecats

In spite of its name, the polecat is not a cat. It is a member of the weasel family. Like all these animals, it gives off a bad odor when frightened. Polecats are found only in the Old World. (But some people make the mistake of calling a skunk a polecat.)

A polecat is about the size of a house cat. It makes its home in a burrow or among the rocks. The home has one room for a nest. Another room serves as the pantry. The polecat keeps it stocked with things to eat—birds, rats, rabbits, snakes, and frogs.

Baby polecats are born in the spring. They first leave the nest when they are about 6 weeks old. They play like kittens in the sun.

One kind of polecat has been tamed.

It is used in killing rats and rabbits. The polecat's long, slender body fits readily into a rat hole or a rabbit burrow. The polecat drives out the rats or rabbits. They are killed by dogs or are shot. In Europe the tame polecat is called a FERRET. But it is not the same animal as the black-footed ferret of North America.

Polecat

Ponies

See Horses

Porcupines

A porcupine is slow and clumsy on the ground. But any animal that plans to eat the porcupine is in for a surprise. The porcupine's upper side is covered with quills. Alarmed, the porcupine turns its back on the attacker. It raises its quills and swings its tail. The attacker gets a faceful or pawful of quills.

One end of a quill is loosely attached to the porcupine's skin. The other end is pointed and covered with tiny barbs. The quill goes into the other animal easily. But it does not come out easily. The barbs catch in the flesh. (The best way to remove a quill from a dog or cat is with a quick pull of the pliers.) The porcupine never runs out of weapons. It may have 30,000 quills on its back and tail. A quill is a hollow spine—a special form of hair.

One kind of porcupine is found in many parts of North America. It sleeps in a den by day and comes out to eat at night. It is a rodent, or gnawing mammal. It eats buds, twigs, leaves, needles, and the bark of trees. It sometimes kills trees by gnawing at them.

A single baby is born to a mother porcupine in late spring. At birth the baby is furry and its quills are soft. They soon harden.

The North American porcupine can swim. It is very good at climbing trees. There are also porcupines in South America and the Old World. Porcupines are not the same as hedgehogs.

Porcupine quill

Porcupine

Porpoises

See *Dolphins*

Possums

See *Opossums*

Prairie Dogs

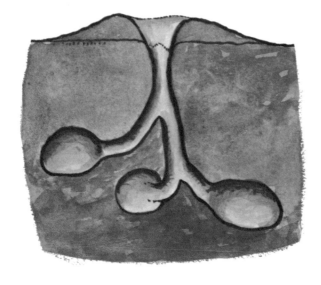

Prairie Dog

A prairie dog is not a dog. It is a rodent, or gnawing mammal. It is a sort of burrowing squirrel, and it is famous for its burrows. There used to be many more prairie dogs. Their burrows formed underground towns, with miles and miles of tunnels and dens. Several thousand prairie dogs lived in each of these towns. Today there are fewer prairie dogs, and the towns are smaller.

A prairie dog spends much of its time taking care of its burrow. The entrance goes almost straight down for 3 to 16 feet. Then it levels off into a tunnel. Rooms open off the tunnel. In one of these a mother makes a grass-lined nest. Here her young are born in late spring. Usually there are 5 young in a litter.

Earth from the tunnels and rooms is piled up around the entrance. It keeps water from running into the tunnels.

Prairie dogs come out by day. They feed on herbs and grass. They have many enemies. Badgers, coyotes, foxes, ferrets, and cats all eat prairie dogs. So do eagles and hawks. So the prairie dogs are always alert. They sit upright and look around. At any sign of danger, they scurry for home. They have several alarm calls. The kind of call tells whether the enemy is coming from the land or the air. There is also an all-clear call. If there is no danger, prairie dogs make a yipping sound, like a bark.

Prairie dogs live only in North America. They are found on western plains and prairies.

The pronghorn is one of the swiftest mammals alive. Covering the ground in great leaps, it can easily travel at 40 miles an hour. It can keep up this pace for about 5 miles.

The pronghorn is sometimes called an antelope. But it is not a true antelope. It is more closely related to sheep. The pronghorn is found only in western North America.

A pronghorn has large, keen eyes. It can see objects several miles away. At any sign of danger, the pronghorn throws up its head and stares. White hairs rise on its rump. They flash in the sun. This is a warning signal. It can be seen by other pronghorns a couple of miles away. In turn, they flash warning signals. All the pronghorns gather in a galloping band.

Running is one way a pronghorn defends itself. It can also fight with its sharp hooves. If chased by a coyote, it will stop and jab at its enemy. The coyote quickly draws back. The pronghorn runs on.

Its horns are hollow and pointed. They grow over cores of bone that are attached to the skull. The pronghorn is the only horned mammal that sheds its horns. (Deer shed their antlers. But antlers are not the same as horns.)

Young pronghorns are born in the spring. A mother usually has a litter of two fawns. By the time they are 4 days old they can run faster than a man. Soon they are nibbling at plants, as their parents do. They grow up in a herd of fawns and mothers.

Pronghorn

See Mountain Lions **Pumas**

Rabbits and Hares

Most people find it very hard to tell rabbits from hares. And no wonder! Both have long ears and short tails. Their front legs are short. Their hind legs are long. They move in hops and leaps. What's more, one kind of animal may be called by the other's name. A jack rabbit, for example, is not a rabbit. It is a hare.

In general, hares are bigger and have longer ears. Their legs are longer and they can jump higher. The young of hares and rabbits are different, too. Baby hares are born with their eyes open. They are covered with fur. And they are able to hop around. Baby rabbits are born with their eyes closed. They have no fur. And they cannot hop. They are helpless babies.

There is still one other difference between hares and rabbits. Hares make their nests in hollows. Most rabbits dig underground burrows. (The cottontail is one of the rabbits that does not.)

There are rabbits and hares in almost every part of the world. In North America the best-known rabbit is the COTTONTAIL. There are many kinds of cottontail. But all are small animals with a fluffy, white tail. Before her babies are born, a mother cottontail finds a hollow or digs one. She lines it with grass and with fur that she pulls from her belly. Usually 4 or 5 babies are born at a time. The mother covers her helpless babies with grass and fur when she goes away to eat. By the time the babies are 2 weeks old, their eyes are open. They are covered with fur. And they are ready to leave the nest. Soon the mother cottontail will have more babies. She has several litters a year.

Cottontail

In Europe the best-known rabbit is the EUROPEAN RABBIT. It looks like a big cottontail. European rabbits dig burrows. Trails lead from the burrows to the feeding grounds, where the rabbits eat grass, leaves, twigs, and buds. Sometimes many rabbits live in the same area, and their trails and burrows are linked. Together all these trails and burrows are called a rabbit warren. Do you remember Peter Rabbit? He was a European rabbit. So are most of the rabbits that people raise in the United States.

JACK RABBITS are hares that live in western North America. There are several kinds. All have very long ears and very long legs. The largest kind is the WHITE-TAILED JACK RABBIT, which weighs between 5 and 8 pounds. It moves along with several short hops and then a long leap. When chased, it can reach a top speed of 40 miles an hour. Every now and then, it leaps up in the air to see where its enemy is.

European Rabbit

Jack Rabbit

93

Some years ago European hares were taken to Ontario. Since then they have spread south into the United States. These large hares are sometimes called jack rabbits.

The VARYING HARE lives in Alaska, Canada, and the northern United States. As winter nears, its fur turns white. The hare can hardly be seen in the snow. This hare has broad hind feet. They act as snowshoes, keeping the animal on top of the snow. The varying hare is also called the SNOWSHOE HARE and the SNOWSHOE RABBIT.

The varying hare is big. The ARCTIC HARE is even bigger. In winter its fur is snow-white except for the tips of its ears. They are black. The Arctic hare lives in northern Alaska, Canada, and Greenland. In the very far north, it may be white all year round.

European Hare

Arctic Hare

Varying Hare

94

Raccoon

It is easy to tell a raccoon when you meet one. This small animal has a black mask across its face, and black and gray rings on its tail. Its paws look like tiny hands. A raccoon can use its paws almost as well as a monkey can. Let loose in a house, a raccoon will search it thoroughly. A raccoon can open bureau drawers, unhook latches, and unscrew jars. Raccoons are intelligent animals and full of curiosity.

A raccoon is a good swimmer and likes to live near water. It uses its fingers to catch fish, frogs, and shellfish. Raccoons also like to eat eggs, birds, insects, mice, nuts, seeds, fruits, and corn on the cob. They are expert at getting the lids off garbage cans and looking for food.

Sometimes raccoons are seen "washing" their food. No one is sure why they do this. They seem to enjoy feeling the food underwater.

The seven kinds of raccoon live only in the Americas. Six live south of the United States. One kind is found from southern Canada through most of the United States. Raccoons are active mostly at night.

A mother raccoon usually has a litter of 4 babies. They are born in a den. The den may be in a hollow tree or under some tree roots. By the time they are 10 to 12 weeks old, the young are leaving the den. They follow their mother and learn how to gather food.

Rats

See Mice and Rats

Reindeer

Reindeer

Reindeer are big, tamed deer of the far north. For thousands of years the people of Lapland have been raising herds of reindeer. And a whole way of life has been built around these herds.

The Lapp, his family, and his herd spend winter in southern Lapland. Here the reindeer feed on twigs. They paw through the snow to get at the mosses and lichens that grow below. Then the winter snows begin to melt. The Lapps move north with the herd to mountain pastures. In autumn they take the herd south. Reindeer pull the family's sleds on these trips. Reindeer carry the packs. Reindeer meat is eaten fresh, frozen, and dried. Reindeer milk is churned into butter and made into cheese. Frozen reindeer blood is carried as food for the dogs. Reindeer hides become warm parkas, trousers, mittens, and moccasins. Reindeer antlers become knife handles and other objects. The family money comes from the sale of reindeer.

Reindeer were first tamed from herds of wild deer that early hunters found in the north. These deer were CARIBOU, and reindeer are simply a tame form of caribou. Herds of them still live in the north today. They are found in the New World and the Old World.

A caribou is a large deer with a mane. Its broad, flat hooves are good for walking on snow and on spongy ground. Both males and females have antlers. (This is true also of reindeer.) Caribou move about in herds. They feed on plants. Their summers are spent in the north, where they eat grasses, willow and birch leaves, berries, and lichens.

Rhinoceroses

African Black Rhinoceros

There are five kinds of rhinoceros. Two live in Africa, one in India, and two on islands of Southeast Asia. All are becoming very rare.

A rhinoceros is a very large mammal. The smallest kind weighs nearly a ton. The largest kind weighs almost 2 tons. A rhino has a huge body on short legs. Its skin is thick and tough and bristly. Some kinds have two horns growing on top of the nose. Other kinds have one horn. The horns are made of hairs that have grown into solid masses.

The best-known rhino is the AFRICAN BLACK RHINOCEROS, which is really brown in color. It lives in East Africa. A full-grown male stands 5 feet high at the shoulder and may weigh 3,000 pounds. If disturbed, the rhino is a fierce fighter. It can charge forward at speeds of up to 30 miles an hour. Almost no other animal will attack a rhinoceros. Man is its chief enemy.

Like all rhinos, the African black is a plant-eater. It feeds on leaves, twigs,

African White Rhinoceros

97

grasses, and other kinds of plants. Its upper lip plucks the food and draws it into the mouth. The rhino lives in a home area where there is food and water. It needs water for drinking. And it loves to wallow in mud—rolling and wading and splashing. It also loves to roll in dust. The black rhino is most active in early morning and early evening. It sleeps during the hot part of the day.

A baby black rhino is born about 18 months after its parents have mated. At birth it may weigh 75 pounds. It stays with its mother for at least 2 years.

Most animals keep away from a rhino. But certain birds alight on a rhino to eat the ticks and insects that get onto it. They also act as lookouts. They chatter and scold when they hear something coming. A rhino itself has good hearing and a keen sense of smell. But it does not see very well.

Indian Rhinoceros

Rodents

When people talk about rodents, they usually mean mice and rats. It is true that mice and rats are rodents. But that is only the beginning of the story. Squirrels, chipmunks, beavers, porcupines, woodchucks, guinea pigs, and hamsters are also rodents. So are many, many other mammals that most people have never heard of. There are thousands of kinds of rodents. Rodents outnumber all the other kinds of mammals in the world.

A rodent is a mammal that gnaws. The many kinds of rodents all have four chisel-shaped front teeth. These are the

Pocket Mouse

gnawing teeth. The upper and lower teeth grind against each other. They keep wearing down into a sharp cutting edge. But the teeth do not wear down to stubs. These four teeth grow throughout a rodent's life.

Rodents are alike in other ways. Most are small animals—the size of a rat or mouse. All eat plant food—roots, bulbs, leaves, fruits, seeds, and nuts. Some also eat eggs and insects and other small animals. Most rodents are short-lived. But in their short lives they have many young.

The pictures show you a few of the rodents you may not have seen.

See also: BEAVERS; CHIPMUNKS; GUINEA PIGS; HAMSTERS; LEMMINGS; MICE and RATS; MUSKRATS; POCKET GOPHERS; PORCUPINES; PRAIRIE DOGS; SQUIRRELS; WOODCHUCKS

Mountain Beaver

Kangaroo Rat

Cavy

Chinchilla

Capybara

Sables

See Martens

99

Sea Cows

In days gone by, sailors used to tell tales of mermaids they had seen. The head and shoulders of the mermaid rose out of the water. Sometimes one was seen cuddling a baby.

These figures were not mermaids but sea cows. And close up they were not very beautiful. A sea cow is a large animal with wrinkled gray skin. The face is covered with bristles. The mouth is wide and drooping. Its front legs are paddle-like flippers. There are no hind legs.

Sea cows are mammals that live in the sea. They are born in the sea. They spend their lives there or in rivers that empty into the sea.

Today there are two main types of sea cow. One is called the MANATEE and the other is called the DUGONG. Both are found only in warm, shallow waters. Both have been much hunted for their flesh and oil. And both are fairly rare.

Some manatees live off western Africa. Others live along the eastern coasts of the Americas. The American manatee is a quiet, slow-moving animal. Full-grown, it measures 8 to 12 feet long and weighs about a ton. It eats huge amounts of grasses and other water plants. The manatee plucks the plants with its lips and grinds them up between its teeth.

The manatee swims by pumping its broad tail up and down. It steers with its flippers. It can swim underwater for long distances. Sometimes it rests on the sea-bottom. It comes up for air several times an hour.

A baby manatee is born underwater. The mother lifts it to the surface on her back. She holds it in her flippers while nursing it. Fishermen say that mother manatees baby-sit for each other. One mother holds both babies while the other mother feeds.

Dugongs look much like manatees. They live in coastal waters of the Indian Ocean and the eastern Pacific.

Manatee

Sea Lions and Fur Seals

Together, the sea lions and the fur seals form a family called the EARED SEALS. All have small, outside ears on their heads. (The true seals do not have outside ears.)

There are 12 kinds of eared seal. The SEA LIONS have thin coats of short, coarse hair. A FUR SEAL has a thick coat of soft underfur topped by coarser hairs. (Fur seals have been much hunted for their fur.)

Every eared seal has a streamlined body with four flippers. The front flippers are longer than the hind flippers. An eared seal swims with its front flippers and steers with its hind flippers. When it leaves the water, it turns its hind flippers forward. It can walk on its flippers, but walking is difficult.

Most eared seals live in herds. They spend much of their time in the water, where they feed mostly on fish. Most eared seals live in the Southern Hemisphere. Four kinds are found off the western coast of North America.

The CALIFORNIA SEA LION is the best-known. This is the trained seal that you see in a zoo or circus. It is able to balance a big rubber ball on its nose. It can play a tune on a row of trumpets. It can sway and dance to music. Sea lions are bright and playful. They love attention and rewards. And so they are easy to train.

The male sea lion is about 8 feet long and weighs 500 to 600 pounds. Like all eared seals, a mother sea lion goes ashore when it is time for her pup to be born. A new-born pup is able to swim but does not wish to do so. The pups first swim in shallow pools near the shore. Later they

California Sea Lion

Steller's Sea Lion

go to sea with their mothers.

The ALASKAN, or NORTHERN, FUR SEAL spends much of the year at sea. The males roam the North Pacific, looking for food. The females travel much farther south, to waters far off the coasts of California and Mexico. In spring the fur seals head for the Pribilof Islands, near Alaska, or for islands near the coast of Asia. By early May the males are gathering on the beaches. Each stakes out a piece of beach as his own. In late June the females begin to arrive. They are almost ready to bear their young. Each male herds as many females as he can onto his beach. The females give birth to their young. Then they mate with the males.

Each pup is nursed by its mother. Several times a week the mother swims out to sea to feed. On her return she is able to find her own pup among the many on the beach. By the time they are 6 or 8 weeks old, the pups can swim. At 4 months they are finding their own food. Soon the females start south again, on the first half of their 6,000-mile round-trip. The pups go off to sea about the same time. But they do not travel with their mothers.

Alaskan Fur Seal

Seals have several names. Sometimes they are called TRUE SEALS. This is to set them off from the sea lions and fur seals. Sometimes they are called HAIR SEALS. This is because their bodies are covered with short, coarse hair. Sometimes they are called EARLESS SEALS. This is because they have no outer ear.

There are 18 kinds of seal, and they are found in many parts of the world. Seals are found in all the oceans. Some have even gone up rivers and taken to living in lakes.

In many ways, all these seals are alike. A seal has four flippers. The hind flippers are longer than the front ones. A seal swims with its hind flippers. It uses its front flippers for turning or balancing in the water. A seal often stands upright in the water. It does this by treading water with its front flippers.

The hind flippers reach out behind the seal. They cannot be turned forward. As a result, a seal cannot walk on its flippers. To move on land, a seal wriggles and hunches. Whenever possible, it rolls or slides. Even so, a seal can move surprisingly fast on land. For a short distance the crab-eater seal can wriggle faster than a man can run.

Most kinds of seal eat fish, shellfish, and small creatures that live in the water. The LEOPARD SEAL of the Antarctic eats other seals and birds. It often captures and eats penguins.

Seals usually live in groups. They leave the water to shelter on rocky or sandy coasts, on islands, or on big pieces of floating ice. Wherever they are, they are within quick reach of the water.

Seals must leave the water to breed and to bear their young. Most kinds of baby seal are born with a thick coat of woolly hair. Within a month, the baby sheds this coat. It grows an adult coat of coarse hair. A baby is born able to swim. But it does not go into the water at first. It stays ashore and nurses for several weeks. Then it starts to swim and to find its own food.

Guadalupe Fur Seal

Harbor Seal

The HARBOR SEAL is the most common kind in the Northern Hemisphere. It is a small seal with a somewhat doglike face. It does a lot of barking and grunting. When it wants to sleep, it crawls out of the water onto a ledge.

The two kinds of ELEPHANT SEAL are the largest. One lives around the Antarctic. The other lives off Mexico. The males may grow to be 20 feet long and weigh 8,000 pounds. A male has a snout, or trunk, about 15 inches long. When there is danger, he blows air into his trunk and trumpets loudly.

Ribbon Seal

Elephant Seal

Sheep

Domestic Sheep

For thousands of years people have been raising sheep for wool, hides, and meat. Today there are about 40 breeds of sheep. Most of them look like the sheep you know. They have long tails and coats of woolly fleece.

There are also several kinds of wild sheep. All live in the Northern Hemisphere. They do not look much like the sheep of farms and ranches. Wild sheep have short tails and coats of stiff hairs.

Two kinds of wild sheep live in North America. One is the ROCKY MOUNTAIN SHEEP, or BIGHORN. It lives in western mountains from Canada to Mexico. The other is the DALL SHEEP. It lives in Alaska and northwestern Canada. It is more slender than the bighorn. Both kinds of sheep have horns. The rams have huge, heavy horns that curl back and around.

These wild sheep live among ledges, cliffs, and steep slopes. They move about with sure-footed swiftness. They plunge down cliffs, leaping 20 feet at a time. They bounce from one ledge to another. Near the bottom they sail off into the air and land on all four feet. Their hooves are slightly hollow and have sharp edges. The hooves cling to rocks and keep the sheep from skidding.

Lambs are born in the spring. The mother sheep leaves the band with which she has been feeding. She climbs to a sheltered place. When the lamb is born, the mother stands guard over it for about a week. Then she takes it to the band. Soon all the lambs are nibbling leaves, grass, and flowers. They play together while the mothers feed and watch out for eagles and other enemies.

Rocky Mountain Goat

Dall Sheep

Shrews

Water Shrew

The PIGMY SHREW is the smallest mammal in North America. It is 3 inches long from the tip of its nose to the tip of its tail. And it weighs less than a dime. This tiny creature lives in Alaska, Canada, and some of the northern and eastern states. Still smaller shrews live in other parts of the world.

There are many, many kinds of shrew. None is very big. Most live on the ground. A few live in burrows and a few live in trees. Some kinds of shrew can swim. The AMERICAN WATER SHREW can skitter across the top of the water.

A shrew spends much of its time scurrying along the ground, hunting for food. It eats insects, such as moths and beetles. It also eats animals that are bigger than itself, such as mice. A tiny shrew eats huge amounts of food. It is a very active animal and its body burns up food quickly. It is also a very nervous animal. A loud noise, such as thunder, can frighten a shrew to death.

Shrews are the only mammals with a poisonous bite. Some of these animals have poison in their saliva. A shrew can kill a mouse by biting it. (The poison does no serious harm to man.)

A female shrew has 2 or 3 litters of young a year. As many as 10 young may be born in a litter. They are born in nests of grass hidden under leaves or logs.

Shrews send out a steady stream of high-pitched sounds. Possibly shrews find their food with these sounds, as bats and dolphins do. When the sounds hit something, they echo. The shrew may hear the echo and so learn where the food is.

Pigmy Shrew

Striped Skunk

Never frighten a skunk. If you meet one, stand still and be quiet. The skunk will probably go on its way. Skunks are easy-going animals. They defend themselves only when threatened. Even then, they give warning first. Faced with danger, a skunk growls and stamps its front feet. Then it raises its bushy tail. If the enemy still advances, the skunk acts quickly. It sprays the enemy with an evil-smelling liquid.

Muscles force the liquid out of two small openings at the base of the tail. A skunk uses only a little of the liquid at a time. It is armed for several shots. And it can hit an enemy that is 12 or 15 feet away. The spray has a terrible smell and taste. It stings the eyes. Usually one shot is enough to send an enemy howling away.

Water will take away the sting. But it won't take away the smell. If your dog is "skunked," scrub him with tomato juice. Then give him a bath. Skunked clothes can be washed in a pail of warm water mixed with a cup of ammonia. (But never use ammonia on a dog or other animal.)

Skunks live only in the Americas. The most common kind in North America is the STRIPED SKUNK. It lives in a hollow log or in a hole in the ground. Sometimes it lives under a building. It comes out at night to look for food. It eats insects, mice, snakes, and frogs. It also likes berries, fruits, grains, and eggs.

From 4 to 7 baby skunks are born at a time. When they are 6 weeks old, they begin to go out. They follow their mother as she looks for food. The family walks single file, with the mother leading her babies, one by one.

The SPOTTED SKUNK is smaller and lives in the United States, Mexico, and Central America. It is playful and full of energy. It can climb up fence posts, trees, and the walls of sheds. If it is threatened, it sometimes walks on its front feet, with its hind feet and tail in the air.

Spotted Skunk

Hooded Skunk

Hognosed Skunk

The HOODED SKUNK looks much like the striped skunk. It lives in the southwestern United States and in Central America. The HOG-NOSED SKUNK lives in the same areas and in South America. It is the largest skunk. It has a snout somewhat like a pig's. It uses its snout and claws to root and dig in the ground for food.

Skunks belong to the weasel family.

Sloths

Sloths live upside down in trees. A sloth has long, hooked claws at the ends of its toes. It hangs by its claws from a branch in a tree. If it must move, it travels slowly, hand over hand. Mostly, though, a sloth sleeps. It sleeps about 18 hours a day, hanging from a branch.

A baby sloth is born while its mother hangs upside down. At first it lives on her chest. Then it hangs from her neck. It finally begins to hang from a branch itself.

A sloth cannot stand up on its legs. On the ground it pulls itself along. But it swims well, with a kind of breast stroke. Sloths defend themselves by biting and clawing.

Sloths are brown or gray in color. But sometimes they appear bright green.

Two-Toed Sloth

This is because tiny green plants grow on the hairs of their fur. A green sloth is almost impossible to see in a tree.

There are two main types of tree sloth. One is called the TWO-TOED SLOTH. It is about as big as a medium-sized dog. It has two huge, curved claws on its hands. Its body is covered with shaggy hair. The sloth has very long arms and no tail. Sometimes its eyes are bright red. The sloth wanders slowly about in trees. It hooks leaves and fruits with a hand and then eats them.

The other type is the THREE-TOED SLOTH. It has three hooked claws on its front hands. It is slightly smaller and even less active. Both types live in the forests of Central and South America.

Three-Toed Sloth

Spiny Anteaters

Left alone, a spiny anteater shuffles along, looking for food. When it finds an ant or termite nest, it tears into the nest with its front claws. Its long, sticky tongue flicks in and out of its mouth. That is how it gathers insects.

If frightened, the spiny anteater buries itself with astounding speed. Digging with all four feet, it quickly sinks out of sight into the ground. An attacker sees only its back. And the back is covered with short, sharp quills.

Spiny Anteater

The spiny anteater is a mammal that lays eggs. A mother grows an extra piece of skin on her underside. It serves as a pouch. She lays one or two eggs. Then she carries the eggs about in her pouch. When they hatch, the mother carries her babies in her pouch. They feed by lapping up milk that oozes out of her skin.

The baby anteaters grow spines, or quills. When they are too spiny for comfort, the mother puts them out of the pouch. She hides them under bushes and comes to feed them. When her pouch is no longer needed, it disappears.

There are two main kinds of spiny anteater. They live in Australia, Tasmania, and New Guinea.

The only other egg-laying mammal is the platypus.

Squirrels

Gray Squirrel

The many, many kinds of squirrel can be sorted out into three main groups. These are the tree squirrels, the ground squirrels, and the so-called flying squirrels, which are really gliders.

TREE SQUIRRELS are the ones you see most often. They are small, long-bodied animals with bushy tails. Its tail is very important to a tree squirrel. The tail acts as a balancer when the squirrel is leaping from branch to branch. It is a warm blanket when the squirrel curls up on a cold night.

Tree squirrels are expert climbers. Most go up a tree trunk at a run. They scamper along branches and leap from tree to tree. A leaping squirrel spreads its legs, flattens its body, and stiffens its tail. It coasts through the air, lands, and is off about its business.

These squirrels make their homes in trees. They prefer a hollow trunk or limb as a home. Sometimes one builds a big nest of leaves and twigs. By day they are very busy looking for food. Tree squirrels eat mostly seeds, nuts, and fruits. Some kinds also eat insects and other small animals. Many kinds gather and store food for winter. Often they store food by burying it. No one is sure how squirrels find this food again. Perhaps they remember where they buried it. Perhaps they find it by smell.

Baby squirrels are born in spring or summer. They stay in the home for a while. Then they come out and play in the sunshine.

The GRAY SQUIRREL is a common North American tree squirrel. It is usually gray, but a few are black.

The RED SQUIRRELS are found in forests of Alaska, Canada, and the United States. They are very "talky" squirrels. They spend some time on the ground and may make burrows.

The FOX SQUIRREL is the largest American tree squirrel. It is found from the East Coast west to Texas and South Dakota. Most of the fox squirrels are reddish brown in color.

Fox Squirrel

GROUND SQUIRRELS are never found in the eastern half of North America. Some live as far east as Ohio, but most live in western North America. Some kinds look very like chipmunks, except that ground squirrels do not have stripes on their cheeks.

Red Squirrel

Columbian Ground Squirrel

13-Striped Ground Squirrel

Most ground squirrels dig burrows or live among rocks. Many kinds go into a deep winter sleep. These squirrels eat mostly plants, seeds, and insects. They are sometimes called gophers.

One of the prettiest of these is the THIRTEEN-STRIPED GROUND SQUIRREL. It lives on prairies of the Middle West, where it is up and busy early in the day. It usually rests at mid-day.

FLYING SQUIRRELS do not fly. They glide. They cannot fly because they do not have wings. This is how they glide.

A flying squirrel climbs to a high place. It leaps into the air and spreads its legs wide. On each side of its body there is a large piece of furry skin. When the squirrel leaps, these pieces of skin are spread and stretched between the front and back legs. The squirrel glides through the air like a paper airplane. It balances itself with its tail. It steers by raising or lowering its legs. It can glide 125 feet without trouble.

Flying squirrels are found in many parts of North America. But they are seldom seen because they are active only at night.

See also: CHIPMUNKS; RODENTS

Flying Squirrel

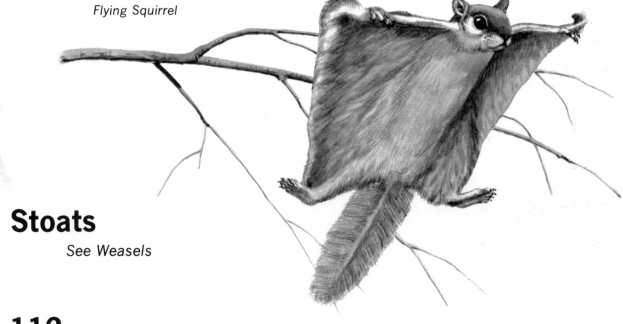

Stoats

See Weasels

Tapirs

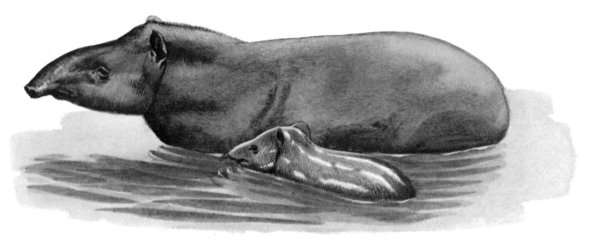

South American Tapir

Tapirs are found in Central and South America and in Southeast Asia. There are three kinds of tapir in the New World and one in Asia.

A tapir looks something like a big pig with a very long snout. The snout and upper lips are drawn out into a sort of short trunk. A tapir eats plants that grow in water. It also eats grasses, twigs, and fruits.

Tapirs are shy, timid animals. They usually live alone or in pairs. They roam around at night feeding. They usually walk with their heads down and their snouts on the ground. They are good at climbing hills, running, sliding, wading, diving, and swimming. They enjoy splashing in water and wallowing in mud. Their chief enemies are the big cats—jaguars in the New World and tigers in Asia.

A baby tapir is the same shape as its mother. But it wears a brightly patterned coat. As the baby grows up, it sheds this coat. It then looks like its parents.

Tapirs are hoofed mammals. Their closest relatives are the horses and the rhinoceroses.

Tapir

Tigers

Siberian Tiger

Tigers live mostly in the forests of Asia. The largest ones live in the cold, snowy north. These are the SIBERIAN TIGERS. A big male may be more than 10 feet from his nose to the end of his tail. He may weigh 600 to 650 pounds. This tiger has long, thick fur that is pale in color. In warmer parts of Asia the tigers are smaller and more brightly colored. The tiger you usually see in a ZOO or circus is an INDIAN TIGER. Sometimes it is called the BENGAL TIGER. It is a big handsome cat.

A tiger is hard to see in its forest home. Its stripes blend with the shadows and streaks of sunshine. A tiger likes to be near water. It needs water to drink. It also bathes in water and is a good swimmer. It hides by day and hunts by night.

A tiger usually hunts alone. It moves silently and quickly. It springs with ease and may cover 15 feet in one leap. Tigers hunt deer, wild pigs, and other hoofed mammals. Near villages tigers prey on cattle and goats. When a tiger has killed, it carries the victim to some hidden spot. There the tiger eats its fill. It may feed on the same animal for several days.

Usually 2 to 4 tiger cubs are born at a time. They are not ready to hunt for themselves until they are about a year old. By then they have learned to lie in wait and spring on a passing animal.

In zoos tigers sometimes breed with lions. If the father is a tiger, the young are called TIGONS. If the father is a lion, they are called LIGERS.

Indian Tiger

Vicuñas

See Llamas

Voles

See Mice and Rats

114

Walruses

A walrus is a mammal of the sea. It has flippers instead of legs. The front flippers are long and oarlike. The walrus swims with them. Its top speed is about 15 miles an hour. Out of the water, a walrus can waddle along on all four flippers. It can also run. In this it is like its relatives the sea lions and fur seals.

A grown walrus is 8 to 12 feet long. It may weigh almost 3,000 pounds. It has only a few stiff hairs on its wrinkled hide. But it has a large mustache. The mustache is part of the walrus' sense of touch. It is useful for feeling things on the bottom of the ocean. That is where a walrus searches for food. A grown walrus also has two long tusks—teeth that grow down from the upper jaw. A walrus uses its tusks to defend itself. It uses them when it hauls itself out of the water onto ice. And it uses them when feeding. A walrus feeds by sinking to the bottom and digging in the mud and sand with its tusks. It digs for clams and other kinds of sea life. It cracks the shells between its back teeth.

Herds of walruses live in the Arctic Ocean. They are noisy animals that fill the air with bellowing and trumpeting. They spend part of their time in the water and part out. They haul themselves out onto rocky coasts, islands, and floating ice.

A baby walrus is born out of the water. It first goes to sea on its mother's neck. It clings with its flippers as she swims and dives. The young walrus nurses for about 2 years. By then it has grown teeth and tusks and can dig its own food.

Walruses are hunted by killer whales and polar bears. Their other enemy is man. Eskimos hunt walruses for their meat, fat, hides and tusks.

Walrus

Wapiti
See Deer

Warthogs
See Pigs

Weasels

All weasels are small, and all are fierce fighters. A weasel will attack animals its own size. It will attack smaller animals. And it will attack animals that are much bigger than it is. A weasel will even attack a man who happens to be standing between the weasel and its meal. Weasels are in turn eaten by larger mammals and birds.

A weasel has a long, slender body. It can slip into any burrow or hole that is big enough for its head. Some weasels can follow a mouse into its home. Weasels have entered chicken coops through knotholes. Some weasels are farm pests because of the chickens that they kill. But on the whole weasels are helpful to man. They keep down the numbers of mice, rats, and rabbits.

There are about a dozen kinds of weasel. Three are found in the New World. (The same three are also found in the Old World.) One of these is the SHORT-TAILED WEASEL, which is called a STOAT in the Old World. It is about the size of a chip-munk, but longer. The young are born in a ready-made den—a hollow under a log or stump, a rockpile, or a chipmunk den. Usually 4 to 7 young are born in a litter. This weasel is found in much of North America. In autumn many short-tailed weasels shed their brown coats. They grow white coats that hide them in the snow. When it turns white, the short-tailed weasel is called an ERMINE. Its fur is highly valued.

The LEAST WEASEL is about 10 inches long and may weigh as little as 1 ounce. It is found in Alaska, most of Canada, and some northern parts of the United States. This tiny weasel takes over a mouse nest and lines it with mouse fur. Like all weasels, it has scent glands at the base of its tail. It gives off an unpleasant odor when frightened.

The LONG-TAILED WEASEL is found from southern Canada into South America. It lives in fairly open areas and is active mostly at night. It is excellent at catching mice and rats.

Long-Tailed Weasel

Ermine

Least Weasel

Short-Tailed Stoat

Sulphur Bottom or Blue Whale

The BLUE WHALE is the largest animal in the world. It is between 70 and 100 feet long and weighs up to 125 tons. This giant mammal is found in the cold waters of the Arctic and the Antarctic. It feeds on tiny shrimplike creatures called krill. In a single meal a blue whale may eat some 5 million krill, weighing 2 tons.

There are about 90 kinds of whale. Scientists divide them into TOOTHED WHALES and BALEEN, or MUSTACHE, WHALES. The blue whale belongs to the baleen whales. These whales do not have teeth. Instead, they have long blades of horny material hanging from the upper jaw inside the mouth. The material is called baleen, or whalebone. A baleen whale takes in a mouthful of water and krill. Then it forces the water out through the baleen. The baleen acts as a strainer. The water goes out, but the food stays in the mouth.

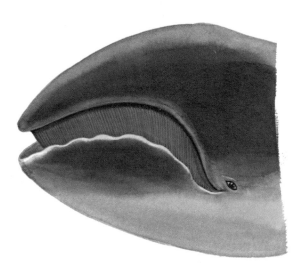

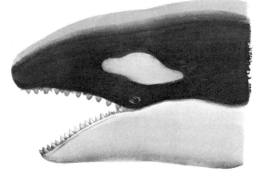

Toothed Whale

Baleen Whale

117

The largest numbers of krill are found in very cold waters. And that is where blue whales spend most of their time. But a mother swims thousands of miles to warmer waters before her baby is born. Like all whales, she swims by moving her broad tail up and down. At birth the baby is about 25 feet long. Under its skin is a thick layer of fat called blubber. This keeps whales warm. They are not covered with fur but have only a sprinkling of bristles.

Most baleen whales are very large. Scientists divide them in three groups: the FIN WHALES, the GRAY WHALE, and the RIGHT WHALES. The right whales were named in the early days of whaling. To whalers, they were the "right" whales to go after. They were slow swimmers. They did not fight when harpooned. They stayed afloat when killed. And they yielded large amounts of oil and whalebone. As a result, the right whales were almost wiped out.

Right Whale

Humpback Whale

Gray Whale

118

All the baleen whales have two blow-holes on top of the head. The blowholes snap shut when the whale dives. They open when the whale surfaces to breathe. When a whale surfaces, it spouts. Many people think the whale is blowing water out of its lungs. But this is not so. The whale blows out a great lungful of warm, moist breath. When this breath meets the colder air, it condenses into water.

The toothed whales have only one blow-hole. And they are mostly smaller than the mustache whales. Only one toothed whale is really big. This is the giant SPERM WHALE, which is 44 to 60 feet long. It is the only source of ambergris. This waxy matter forms inside the whale, perhaps because of an upset stomach. It is used in making perfume.

Most of the toothed whales are DOL-PHINS and PORPOISES. All but a few are quite small—less than 15 feet long. One of the big dolphins is the PILOT WHALE. Another is the KILLER WHALE. Killer

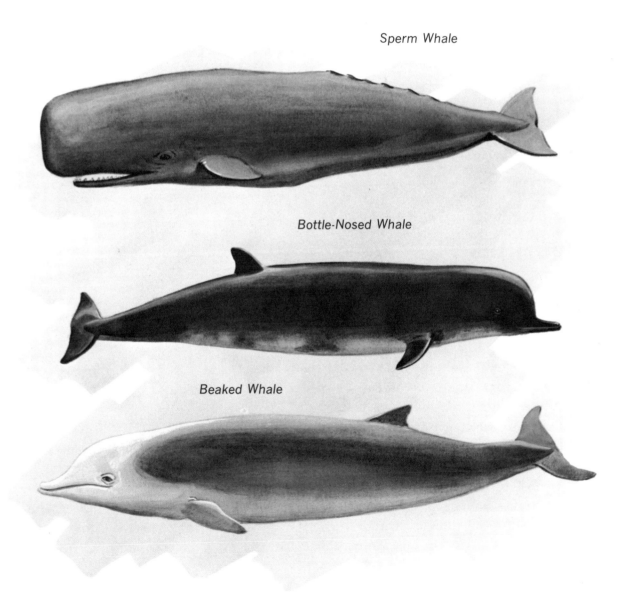

Sperm Whale

Bottle-Nosed Whale

Beaked Whale

119

whales are sometimes about 30 feet long. They are big, strong, and cunning. The other toothed whales eat fish and shellfish. The killer whale is the only one that eats warm-blooded prey. It eats small mustache whales, porpoises, seals, and penguins.

See also: DOLPHINS

Killer Whale

Wildcats

See Lynxes

Wolverines

A wolverine is a shaggy animal of the weasel family. It is found around the world in the far north.

Wolverine

The wolverine is not large—it weighs only 25 to 40 pounds. But it is fearless. It will attack almost any other animal. It drives bears and mountain lions from their kills, which it eats itself. It kills caribou and mountain sheep by leaping on them from a cliff or tree. It is strong enough to kill even elk and moose that are trapped in deep snow.

A wolverine usually lives by itself. It is active either day or night all year round. It sleeps and hunts, sleeps and hunts.

Each wolverine has its own area where it lives and hunts. Little is known about the family life.

Eskimos like to use wolverine fur on their parka hoods. Only a little moisture from the breath freezes on this fur. And it can easily be brushed off. This is not true of other kinds of fur.

Wolves

Once there were wolves in most parts of the Northern Hemisphere. They were different sizes and colors. But most were the kind we call the GRAY, or TIMBER, WOLF. Men, however, have always feared wolves. So wherever men have gone, they have killed wolves. There are very few wolves left in Europe. Some packs still roam northern Asia.

The gray wolf has been killed off in North America except in the unsettled parts of Canada and Alaska. It is seen almost nowhere else. Another kind, the RED WOLF, may be seen in the southern United States. It lives in a few wild parts of Louisiana, eastern Texas, and Arkansas. The red wolf is smaller than the gray. Its coat is usually reddish, but it can be black. Black pups may be born in the same litter with red pups.

The gray wolf looks like a heavily built German shepherd dog. In color it is usu-ally gray or tawny. But in the far north, its coat is pure white. Gray wolves are big, strong, and intelligent.

Wolves seem to mate for life. Wolf pups are born in early spring. They are born in a den that may be a cave or a burrow. Usually there are 4 to 6 pups in a litter. The mother and pups stay in the den. The pups nurse, and the father brings food to the mother. He stands guard outside the den.

When the pups are a month old, they start to leave the den and play outside. Soon they are eating solid food. Then both parents are kept busy finding food for their hungry, growing young. During the summer the pups learn to hunt by following their parents. By autumn they are able to hunt by themselves. But they usually stay with their parents for 2 or 3 years. During this time the parents have another litter or two of pups.

Red Wolves

Wolves hunt in packs. A pack is usually a family group. It is made up of a mother and father and the young from one or more litters. Sometimes relatives join the pack. Sometimes two different families join forces.

The pack follows wolf trails in its hunting. The trails reach over a wide area. A wolf pack on the hunt may travel several hundred miles. The wolves live wherever they happen to be. They have no fixed home. But they do go back to one area each year to bear their young.

Wolves are chiefly meat-eaters. Eyes, ears, and noses alert, they search for game. They eat what they find. In the far north they track caribou, attacking the young and the strays. Farther south they eat deer, moose, and other large hoofed mammals. If they find sheep and cattle, they will attack those. Wolves also hunt hares, rats, mice, squirrels, and other small mammals. They will eat insects and fruits.

Wolves may track their prey for hours. They move in a tireless trot, which they can keep up for miles. Finally, several wolves attack. Then the pack swarms over the prey and eats its fill. A wolf can eat 15 pounds of meat at a time. Leftover food is sometimes buried and eaten later.

Scientists think that our dogs are mostly descended from wolves. Wolves are also closely related to coyotes.

122

In early morning the woodchuck leaves its burrow. It feeds on grass, clover, and other plants. Belly full, it stretches out in the shade and dozes. In late afternoon it feeds again. Then it goes back to its burrow. A woodchuck is a plump, somewhat lazy animal. It is a pest in the garden, but it makes a nice pet.

The burrow usually has several doors. One is a drop hole that goes straight down for a couple of feet. If startled, a woodchuck gives a shrill whistle. It may vanish down its drop hole. The woodchuck's burrow has several rooms. In one of them a mother woodchuck has 4 or 5 babies each spring.

In autumn a woodchuck grows very fat. When cold weather comes, it tucks itself away in its burrow. It sleeps through the winter. Its body draws on the fat for food.

The woodchuck is also called a GROUND-HOG. The story goes that it wakes up and comes out of its burrow on February 2. If the sun is shining, the animal sees its shadow. It goes back to sleep for six more weeks. And that means there will be six more weeks of winter. If the day is cloudy, the animal does not see its shadow. It does not go back to sleep. And that means an early spring. There is really no truth in this story. But February 2 is called Groundhog Day.

The woodchuck lives in most of Canada. In the United States it lives east of the Mississippi but not in the deep South. It has two close relatives in the West. They are called MARMOTS or ROCK CHUCKS. Other kinds of marmot live in the Old World, north of the equator.

Woodchuck

Yaks

See Cattle

Zebras

A zebra is a type of wild horse that is found only in Africa. Zebras live in herds. The herds are usually small, with 10 or 12 members. As they move about grazing on grass, zebras often mix with other kinds of animals. They have even been seen feeding with ostriches. In the dry seasons zebras travel far, looking for grass and water. Then they may band together in big herds of up to a thousand.

Zebras are shy animals. When frightened, they run. They can run very fast—up to 40 miles an hour. But they will also fight to defend themselves. A zebra kicks backward with its hind feet and forward with its front feet. Its hooves can deliver powerful blows. Zebras also bite. Lions are about the only animals that attack zebras. Zebras are always on the lookout for this enemy. They have very good eyes and a keen sense of smell. A zebra's stripes can also be a help. In tall grass or in forests the stripes blend with the shadows. A zebra is very hard to see.

There are three main kinds of zebra. The biggest is called GREVY'S ZEBRA. It stands about $4\frac{1}{2}$ feet high at the shoulder and weighs between 500 and 600 pounds. The most common zebra is BURCHELL'S ZEBRA. It is found in many parts of Africa. The MOUNTAIN ZEBRA of South Africa is the rarest.

Many people have tried to tame zebras. Usually they have failed.

Burchell's Zebra

Grevy's Zebra

Mountain Zebra

The Orders of Living Mammals

There are many, many kinds of living things. To deal with them, scientists have sorted them into groups. The living things within each group are somehow alike.

One huge group is called the Animal Kingdom. Its members can be as different as a butterfly and an elephant. But they are all animals. In that way they are alike.

Within the Animal Kingdom the mammals form a large group. This group is called a class. Its members can be as different as an otter and an elephant. But all mother mammals have glands that produce milk. The young feed on the milk. In that way all mammals are

alike. Then, too, almost all mammals have hair. That is another way they are alike. No other class of animal has hair or produces milk.

The class of mammals is made up of 18 smaller groups. These groups are called orders. The members of each order are somehow alike and somehow related. (Orders in turn are made up of smaller groups of more closely related mammals.)

The list that follows gives you the name of each order. It tells you how the members of an order are alike. And it arranges by order many of the mammals in this book.

Monotremata	This order is made up of egg-laying mammals. They are found only in Australia and neighboring islands. MEMBERS: *platypuses 86–87, spiny anteaters 109–110.*
Marsupialia	At birth the young of this order are tiny. They have only started to develop. Most of the mothers have pouches. Except for opossums, these mammals are found only in Australia and neighboring islands. SOME MEMBERS: *kangaroos 57–58, koalas 59, opossums 78–79.*
Insectivora	These are small, short-legged, insect-eating mammals. SOME MEMBERS: *hedgehogs 48, moles 68–69, shrews 106.*
Dermoptera	The members of this order are squirrel-sized mammals of Southeast Asia. They are sometimes called flying lemurs, but that is not a very good name. They are not lemurs, and they cannot fly. A better name is colugo. Colugos live in trees, where they feed on leaves and fruits. They are active at night. Although they cannot fly, they glide from tree to tree. MEMBERS: *colugos, or flying lemurs*
Chiroptera	The members of this order have wings. They are the only mammals that can truly fly. MEMBERS: *bats 12–14.*
Primates	This is the order to which man belongs. Apes and monkeys also belong to it. The order contains the most intelligent of living creatures. It also contains several much less highly developed mammals. Almost all members have hands that work like man's. MEMBERS: *man, apes 6–7 (also chimpanzees 26–27, gorillas 46), monkeys 71–74 (also baboons 9–10), lower primates (tarsiers, lemurs, lorises, pottos, tree shrews) 74.*
Edentata	The mammals in this order either have no teeth or have simple, peglike teeth. MEMBERS: *anteaters 3, armadillos 8, sloths 108–109.*

Pholidota	This small order is made up of mammals armored with large, hard scales that overlap one another. The mammals defend themselves by rolling up. MEMBERS: *pangolins 83.*
Lagomorpha	The mammals in this order have two pairs of front teeth in the upper jaw. A small pair grows behind the large front pair. Most members of the order have long hind legs and long ears. MEMBERS: *pikas 86, rabbits and hares 92–94.*
Rodentia	This huge order contains about half of all the land mammals. The members are gnawing mammals, with four chisel-shaped front teeth. SOME MEMBERS: *rodents 98–99 (also beavers 17–19, chipmunks 27–28, guinea pigs 47, hamsters 47, lemmings 59–60, mice and rats 65–67, muskrats 77–78, pocket gophers 87–88, porcupines 89, prairie dogs 90, squirrels 110–112, woodchucks 123).*
Cetacea	The members of this order are water-dwelling mammals with fish-like shapes and little or no hair. MEMBERS: *dolphins 35–36, whales 117–120.*
Carnivora	This is the order of flesh-eating mammals. MEMBERS: *cats 22–24 (also cheetahs 26, jaguars 56, leopards 60, lions 61, mountain lions 75–76, tigers 114), dogs 32–34 (also coyotes 29, foxes 40–42, jackals 55–56, wolves 121–122), hyenas 54, bears 15–17, raccoons 95, coatis, and pandas 82, weasels 116 (also badgers 11, ferrets 40, martens 64–65, mink 68, otters 80–81, polecats 88, skunks 107–108, weasels 116, wolverines 120), civets 70 and mongooses 70, seals 103–104, sea lions 101–102, and walruses 115.*
Tubulidentata	This small order contains only the aardvarks. They are long-snouted, long-clawed, insect eating mammals. Their tube-shaped teeth have no roots. MEMBERS: *aardvarks 2.*
Proboscidea	Today's members are the elephants—huge mammals with trunks. MEMBERS: *elephants 37–39.*
Hyracoidea	The members are small, active mammals with hooves. MEMBERS: *hyraxes 55.*
Sirenia	The members are large, water-dwelling mammals with flippers, paddle-shaped tails, and no hind legs. MEMBERS: *sea cows 100.*
Perissodactyla	This order contains the hoofed mammals with an odd number of toes on each hind foot. MEMBERS: *horses 50-53 (also donkeys 36–37, zebras 124), rhinoceroses 97–98, tapirs 113.*
Artiodactyla	This is a large order of hoofed mammals with an even number of toes on each foot. SOME MEMBERS: *pigs 84–85, peccaries 85, and hippopotamuses 49, camels 21 and llamas 62–63, chevrotains, deer 29–31 (also moose 75, reindeer 96), giraffes 42–43, pronghorns 91, cattle-like mammals (buffaloes 20, cattle 24–25, goats 44–45, musk-oxen 76–77, Old World antelopes 4–5, sheep 105).*

Index

A

Aardvarks, 2
Aberdeen Angus cattle, 25
Abyssinian cats, 24
Africa, mammals of
  aardvarks, 2
  antelopes, 4, 5
  baboons, 10, 72
  Barbary apes, 71
  camels (dromedaries), 21
  cheetahs, 26
  chimpanzees, 6, 26
  duikers, 5
  elephants, 39
  foxes, 41, 42
  giraffes, 42
  gorillas, 6, 46
  hippopotamuses, 49
  honey badgers, 11
  hyenas, 54
  hyraxes, 55
  leopards, 60
  lemurs, 74
  lions, 61
  mongooses, 70
  monkeys, 71, 72
  okapis, 43
  pottos, 74
  rhinoceroses, 97–98
  warthogs, 85
  wild asses, 53
  wild pigs, 85
  zebras, 124
Alaskan fur seals, 102
Alpacas, 62–63
American badgers, 11
American black bears, 15
American buffaloes, 20
American gray foxes, 42
American lions (mountain lions),
  23, 75–76
American martens, 64
American star-nosed moles, 69
American water shrews, 106
Anteaters, 3, 83, 109–110
  scaly, 83
  spiny, 109–110
Antelopes, 4–5, 26, 61
Apes, 6–7
  See also: Chimpanzees,
    Gorillas

Arabian camels, 21
Arctic foxes, 41
Arctic hares, 94
Arctic, mammals of
  Arctic foxes, 41
  Arctic hares, 94
  black bears, 15
  brown bears, 16
  caribous, 60, 96
  ermines, 116
  fur seals, 101–102
  grizzly bears, 16
  lemmings, 59–60
  musk-oxen, 76
  polar bears, 15, 16, 16–17,
    115
  reindeer, 96
  sea lions, 101–102
  seals, 103–104
  walruses, 115
  whales, 117–120
  wolverines, 120
  wolves, 32
Armadillos, 3, 8
Asia, mammals of
  camels, 21
  cats, small, 23
  cheetahs, 26
  elephants, 38–39
  foxes, 41
  gibbons, 6
  golden hamsters, 47
  honey badgers, 11
  hyenas, 54
  hyraxes, 55
  leopards, 60
  lions, 61
  lorises, 74
  macaques, 71, 72
  martens, 64
  mongooses, 70
  monkeys, 71, 72
  orangutans, 96
  pandas, 82
  pikas, 86
  proboscis monkeys, 72
  rhesus monkeys, 71
  rhinoceroses, 97
  spiny anteaters, 110
  tapirs, 113
  tigers, 114

  water buffaloes, 20
  wild pigs, 85
  yaks, 25
Asiatic elephants, 38–39
Asses (donkeys), 36–37
Aurochs, 25
Australia, mammals of
  dingos, 33
  kangaroos, 58
  koalas, 59
  marsupials, 58, 59
  platypuses, 87
  spiny anteaters, 110

B

Baboons, 9–10, 72
Bactrian camels, 21
Badgers, 11
Baleen (mustache) whales, 117,
  118–119, 120
Barbary apes, 71
Bats, 12–14
Bay lynxes (bobcats), 63, 64
Bears, 15–17
Beavers, 17–19
Bengal tigers, 114
Bighorns, 105
Bisons, 20
Black bears, 15
Black-footed ferrets, 40, 88
Black panthers, 60
Black rats, 66, 67
Black rhinoceroses, African, 97–
  98
Black-tailed deer, 30
Blowholes of whales, 119
Blue whales, 117, 118
Boars, 84, 85
Bobcats, 63, 64
Bongos, 5
Brown bears, 15, 16
Brown hyenas, 54
Brown rats, 66
Buffaloes, 20
Bull moose, 75
Burchell's zebras, 124
Burmese cats, 24

C

California sea lions, 101
Camels, 21

Capuchin monkeys, 74
Caribous, 60, 96
Catamounts (mountain lions), 23, 75–76
Cats, domestic, 22–24
Cats, wild, 22–23
    See also: Cheetahs, Jaguars, Leopards, Lions, Lynxes, Mountain lions, Panthers, Tigers
Cattle, 20, 24–25, 76–77, 127
Cave rats, 67
Central America, mammals of
    anteaters, 3
    armadillos, 8
    badgers, 11
    black bears, 15
    bobcats, 64
    coyotes, 29
    jaguars, 56
    monkeys, 71
    mountain lions, 75
    opossums, 79
    peccaries, 85
    pocket gophers, 88
    Rocky Mountain sheep, 105
    skunks, 107, 108
    sloths, 109
    tapirs, 113
Chamois, 45
Cheetahs, 23, 26
Chimpanzees, 6, 7, 26–27
Chipmunks, 27–28
Civets, 70
Collared anteaters, 3
Collared peccaries, 85
Common garden moles, 69
Common opossums, 79
Conies, 55, 86
Coons (raccoons), 95
Cottontails, 92
Cougars (mountain lions), 23, 75–76
Coy-dogs, 29
Coyotes, 29, 32, 91, 122
Crab-eating macaques, 71

D

Dall sheep, 105
Dassies, 55
Deer, 29–31

    See also: Moose, Reindeer
Deer mice, 66
Dingos, 33
Dogs, domestic, 32, 34, 122
Dogs, wild, 32, 33
    See also: Coyotes, Foxes, Jackals, Wolves
Dolphins, 35–36, 119
Domestic cats, 22–24
Domestic dogs, 32, 34, 122
Donkeys, 36–37
Douroucoulis, 73
Drills, 10
Dromedaries, 21
Duckbills (platypuses), 86–87
Dugongs, 100
Duikers, 5

E

Eared seals, 101–102
Earless seals, 103–104
Eastern chipmunks, 27
Egg-laying mammals, 86–87, 110
Egyptian cats, 23
Elands, 5
Elephants, 37–39
Elephant seals, 104
Elks, 30, 75
Ermines, 116
Europe, mammals of
    badgers, 11
    beavers, 17
    chamois, 45
    elks, 75
    foxes, 41
    hedgehogs, 48
    leopards, 60
    martens, 64
    mongooses, 70
    pikas, 86
    polecats, 40
    rabbits, 93
    red deer, 30
    wild boars, 85

F

Fairy armadillos, 8
Farm pigs, 84–85
Fennec foxes, 42
Ferrets, 40, 88

Field mice, 66
Fin whales, 118
Fishers, 65
Florida Key deer, 30
Flying lemurs, 126
Flying squirrels, 12, 110, 112
Forester (great gray) kangaroos, 57, 58
Foxes, 32, 40–42
Fox squirrels, 111
Fur seals, 101, 102

G

Garden moles, common, 69
Gazelles, 5
Genets, 70
Giant anteaters, 3
Giant armadillos, 8
Giant pandas, 82
Gibbons, 6
Giraffes, 42–43
Gnus, 5
Goats, 44
Golden hamsters, 47
Gophers, 87–88, 112
    See also: Squirrels
Gorillas, 6, 46
Gray foxes, American, 42
Gray squirrels, 111
Gray whales, 118
Gray wolves, 121
Great apes, 6
    See also: Chimpanzees, Gorillas
Great gray kangaroos, 57, 58
Grevy's zebras, 124
Grizzly bears, 15, 16
Ground squirrels, 27, 110, 111–112
Groundhogs, 123
Grunting oxen, 25
Guanacos, 62, 63
Guenons, 72
Guernsey cattle, 25
Guinea pigs, 47

H

Hair seals, 103
Hamsters, 47
Harbor seals, 104
Hares, 92, 93, 94

Hartebeests, 5
Harvest mice, 66
Haymakers, 86
Hedgehogs, 48
Hereford cattle, 25
Hibernating mammals
  bats, 12–14
  bears, 15–17
  hedgehogs, 48
  woodchucks, 123
Himalayan cats, 24
Hinnies, 37
Hippopotamuses, 49
Hogs, See Pigs
Hog-nosed skunks, 108
Holstein cattle, 25
Honey badgers, 11
Hooded skunks, 108
Hooves, See Artiodactyla (127),
  Perissodactyla (127)
Horses, 50–53
House mice, 65
House rats, 66
Howler monkeys, 73
Hyenas, 54
Hyraxes, 55

I
Ibexes, 44

J
Jack rabbits, 92, 93, 94
Jackals, 32, 55–56
Jaguars, 23, 56, 75, 83, 113
Jersey cattle, 25

K
Kaffir cats, 23
Kangaroos, 57–58
Killer whales, 115, 119–120
Kit foxes, 42
Koalas, 59

L
Langurs, 72
Leaf monkeys, 72
Least weasels, 116
Lemmings, 59–60
Lemurs, 74
Leopards, 10, 23, 56, 60, 83
Leopard seals, 103

Lesser pandas, 82
Ligers, 114
Lions, 23, 43, 54, 61, 83, 124
Litter size
  of armadillos, 8
  of badgers, 11
  of beavers, 19
  of black bears, 15
  of cheetahs, 26
  of chipmunks, 28
  of cottontails, 92
  of coyotes, 29
  of deer, 30
  of foxes, 40
  of guinea pigs, 47
  of hamsters, 47
  of hedgehogs, 48
  of hyraxes, 55
  of lemmings, 59
  of leopards, 60
  of lions, 61
  of lynxes, 63
  of martens, 64
  of mice, 65
  of mink, 68
  of moles, 69
  of mountain lions, 76
  of muskrats, 78
  of otters, 80
  of prairie dogs, 90
  of pronghorns, 91
  of raccoons, 95
  of shrews, 106
  of skunks, 107
  of tigers, 114
  of weasels, 116
  of wolves, 121
  of woodchucks, 123
Llamas, 62–63
Long-nosed monkeys, 72
Long-tailed weasels, 116
Lorises, 74
Lynxes, 23, 63–64

M
Macaques, 71–72
Manatees, 100
Mandrills, 10
Manx cats, 24
Marmosets, 72
Marmots, 123

Marsupials (pouched mammals),
  58, 59, 78
  See also: Marsupialia (126)
Martens, 64–65
Meadow mice, 66
Meat-eaters, See Carnivora (127)
Mice, 65–66
Mink, 68
Moles, 68–69
Mongolian wild horses, 53
Mongooses, 70
Monkeys, 6, 9, 10, 71–74
  New World, 71, 72–74
  Old World, 71–72
Moose, 30, 75
Mountain lions, 23, 75–76, 83
Mountain zebras, 124
Mules, 37
Mule deer, 30
Musk-oxen, 76–77
Muskrats, 77–78
Mustache (baleen) whales, 117,
  118–119, 120
Mustangs, 50, 53

N
New World monkeys, 71, 72–74
Nine-banded armadillos, 8
North America, mammals of
  armadillos, 8
  badgers, 11
  bats, 12
  bears, 15–16
  beavers, 17
  black-footed ferrets, 88
  bobcats, 64
  buffaloes, 20
  Canada lynxes, 63
  cats, 22–24
  caribous, 96
  chipmunks, 27
  collared peccaries, 85
  coyotes, 29
  Dall sheep, 105
  deer, 30
  dogs, 32, 34
  elks, 30
  fishers, 65
  foxes, 41, 42
  hares, 93, 94
  horses, 50–53

jack rabbits, 93
lynxes, 63
martens, 64
mice, 65, 66
mink, 68
moles, 69
moose, 75
mountain lions, 75
musk-oxen, 76
muskrats, 77
opossums, 78, 79
otters, 80
pigmy shrews, 106
pikas, 86
pocket gophers, 88
porcupines, 89
prairie dogs, 90
pronghorns, 4, 91
rabbits, 92
raccoons, 95
rats, 66
Rocky Mountain goats, 44
sea cows, 100
seals, 101–104
shrews, 106
skunks, 107, 108
squirrels, 111, 112
weasels, 116
wild sheep, 105
wolverines, 120
wolves, 121
woodchucks, 123
Northern fur seals, 102
Norway rats, 66

O
Okapis, 43
Old World monkeys, 71–72
Opossums, 78–79
Orangutans, 6, 7
Oryxes, 5
Otters, 80–81

P
Pack rats, 67
Pandas, 82
Pangolins, 3, 83
Panthers, 75–76, 83
Peccaries, 85
Persian cats, 24
Pigs, 84–85

Pigmy anteaters, 3
Pigmy hippopotamuses, 49
Pigmy shrews, 106
Pig-tailed macaques, 72
Pikas, 86
Pilot whales, 119
Platypuses, 86–87
Pocket gophers, 87–88
Polar bears, 15, 16–17, 115
Polecats, 40, 88
Ponies, 50
Ponies, Shetland, 50
Porcupines, 48, 65, 89
Porpoises, 36, 119
Possums (opossums), 78–79
Pottos, 74
Prairie dogs, 40, 90
Primates, See Apes, Monkeys
Proboscis monkeys, 72
Pronghorns, 4, 91
Przewalski's horses, 53
Pumas (mountain lions), 23, 75–76

R
Rabbits, 92, 93
Raccoons, 95
Rats, 65, 66–67, 70
Rat kangaroos, 58
Ratels, 11
Razorback hogs, 85
Red deer, 30
Red foxes, 40–41
Red kangaroos, 58
Red squirrels, 64, 111
Red wolves, 121
Reindeer, 30, 60, 96
Rhesus monkeys, 71
Rhinoceroses, 97–98
Right whales, 118
Rock chucks, 123
Rock rabbits, 86
Rocky Mountain goats, 44–45
Rocky Mountain sheep, 105
Rodents (gnawing mammals), 17, 47, 48, 65, 88, 89, 90, 98–99
See also: Beavers, Chipmunks, Guinea pigs, Hamsters, Lemmings, Mice and Rats, Muskrats, Pocket

gophers, Porcupines, Prairie dogs, Squirrels, Woodchucks
Royal antelopes, 5
Russian Blue cats, 24

S
Sables (martens), 64–65
Sable antelopes, 5
Scaly anteaters, 3, 83
Sea cows, 100
Sea lions, 101
Sea otters, 81
Seals, 101–104
eared, 101–102
earless, 103–104
Sheep, 91, 105
Shetland ponies, 50
Short-tailed weasels, 116
Shrews, 106
Siamese cats, 24
Siberian tigers, 114
Silky anteaters, 3
Skunks, 88, 107–108
Sloths, 3, 108–109
Snowshoe hares, 94
South America, mammals of
anteaters, 3
armadillos, 8
cats, small, 23
guinea pigs, 47
jaguars, 56
llamas, 62
long-tailed weasels, 116
mountain lions, 75
opossums, 79
peccaries, 85
porcupines, 89
skunks, 108
sloths, 109
spectacled bears, 15
tapirs, 113
Sows, See Pigs
Spectacled bears, 15
Sperm whales, 119
Spider monkeys, 73
Spiny anteaters, 109–110
Spotted hyenas, 54
Spotted skunks, 107
Springboks, 5
Squirrels, 110–112

flying, 12, 110, 112
   ground, 27, 110, 111–112
   tree, 110–111
Star-nosed moles, American, 69
Stoats, 116
Striped hyenas, 54
Striped skunks, 107
Swift foxes, 42

T

Tamarins, 72
Tapirs, 113
Tarsiers, 74
Thirteen-striped ground squir-
   rels, 112
Three-toed sloths, 109
Tigers, 23, 83, 113, 114
Tigons, 114
Timber wolves, 121
Toothed whales, 36, 117, 119,
   120
Townsend's moles, 69
Trade rats, 67
Tree kangaroos, 58
Tree shrews, 74
Tree squirrels, 110–111
Two-toed sloths, 109

U

Uakaris, 73

V

Vampire bats, 12
Varying hares, 94
Vicuñas, 63
Virginia opossums, 79
Voles, 66

W

Walruses, 115
Wapitis, 30
Warthogs, 85
Water buffaloes, 20
Water-dwelling mammals
   dolphins, 35–36, 119
   fur seals, 101, 102
   sea cows, 100
   sea lions, 101
   sea otters, 81
   seals, 101–104
   walruses, 115
   whales, 117–120
Weasels, 11, 116
Weasel family, *See* Badgers,
   Ferrets, Martens, Mink,
   Otters, Polecats, Skunks,
   Weasels, Wolverines
Whales, 117–120
   baleen (mustache), 117, 118–
   119, 120
   toothed, 36, 117, 119, 120

See also: Dolphins
Whistling hares, 86
White-footed mice, 66
White-tailed deer, 30
White-tailed jack rabbits, 93
Wild asses, 53
Wild boars, 85
Wild cattle, 20, 25, 76–77, 127
Wild cats, 22–23
   See also: Cheetahs, Jaguars,
   Leopards, Lions, Lynxes,
   Mountain lions, Panthers,
   Tigers
Wild dogs, 32, 33
   See also: Coyotes, Dingos,
   Foxes, Jackals, Wolves
Wild pigs, 84, 85
Wild sheep, 105
Wildcats (bobcats), 63, 64
Wildebeests, 5
Wolverines, 120
Wolves, 32, 121–122
Woodchucks, 123
Woodrats, 67

Y

Yaks, 25

Z

Zebras, 53, 61, 124